THE COLUMBIA UNIVERSITY SCHOOL OF PUBLIC HEALTH

COMPLETE GUIDE TO HEALTH AND WELL-BEING AFTER 50

ALSO BY GENELL J. SUBAK-SHARPE

Hormones: The Woman's Answerbook
(with Lois Jovanovic, M.D.)

Frontiers of Medicine series
(with James V. Warren, M.D.)

The Physician's Manual for Patients
(with the Biomedical Information Corporation)

THE COLUMBIA UNIVERSITY SCHOOL OF PUBLIC HEALTH

COMPLETE GUIDE TO HEALTH AND WELL-BEING AFTER 50

Robert J. Weiss, M.D. and Genell J. Subak-Sharpe, Editors

Illustrations by Beth Anne Willert

Times BOOKS

Grateful acknowledgment is made to the following for permission to reprint previously published material:

American Cancer Society: Excerpts from "7-Day Plan to Help You Stop Smoking Cigarettes" published in 1978 by American Cancer Society. Reprinted courtesy of the American Cancer Society.

American Dietetic Association: Adapted from Helen C. Brittin and Cheryl E. Nossaman: "Iron Content of Food Cooked in Iron Utensils." Copyright The American Dietetic Association. Reprinted by permission from the *Journal of the American Dietetic Association,* Vol. 86:897, 1986.

American Heart Association: Excerpts from pages 22–23 of *American Heart Association Cookbook.* Copyright © 1984 by American Heart Association. Excerpts from "Warning Signs of a Heart Attack" from *1986 Heart Facts.* Copyright © 1986 by American Heart Association. Reprinted by permission.

Doubleday & Company, Inc.: Excerpts from *The American Cancer Society Cancer Book.* Copyright © 1986 by American Cancer Society. Reprinted by permission of Doubleday & Company, Inc.

Pergamon Press, Ltd.: Excerpts from "The Social Readjustment Rating Scale" by Thomas H. Holmes and R. H. Rahe. Published in *Journal of Psychosomatic Research,* 11-2. Copyright © 1967 by Pergamon Press, Ltd. Reprinted by permission of the publisher and Thomas H. Holmes.

Library of Congress Cataloging-in-Publication Data

The Columbia University School of Public Health complete guide to health and well-being after 50.

Includes index.
1. Aged—Health and hygiene. 2. Aged—Mental health.
3. Aged—Diseases. I. Weiss, Robert J. II. Subak-Sharpe, Genell J.
III. Columbia University. School of Public Health. IV. Title:
Complete guide to health and well-being after 50. [DNLM:
1. Geriatrics—popular works. 2. Hygiene—in middle age—popular works. 3. Mental Health—in middle age—popular works. WT 120
C726] RA777.6.C65 1987 613′.0438 87-10005
ISBN 0–8129–1325–6

Manufactured in the United States of America
98765432
First Edition

DESIGNED BY BARBARA MARKS

Dedicated
to the
medical
pioneers
who have
made the
second
fifty years
a reality
for an
ever-growing
number of
people.

ACKNOWLEDGMENTS

The creation of any book inevitably involves many people, and this venture is no exception. Scores of dedicated physicians, writers, editors, researchers, illustrators and others have worked closely with us during the last two years to bring this book to fruition. While it is not possible to name all of the people who have lent services and support, there are some whose outstanding contributions cannot be overlooked. Drs. Allan Rosenfield and Stephen Rosenberg have been particularly helpful in reviewing chapters and offering invaluable suggestions. Michael O'Connor has helped keep the project on track by coordinating efforts from the Columbia University School of Public Health. Emily Paulsen and Jane Margaretten-Ohring have lent their considerable editorial and writing skills to help make the text readable. Janet Heath and Judith Wilmott both spent long hours in researching and compiling material. Beth Anne Willert provided the original illustrations. David, Sarah and Hope Subak-Sharpe helped with typing and numerous other details.

Minnie Weiss diligently pulled together masses of resources on educational opportunities for older students; Gerald Subak-Sharpe provided practical insight and suggestions. Jonathan Segal and Sarah Trotta, our editors at Times Books, have done a masterful job in shaping the final manuscript, for which we are particularly grateful. Finally, we are particularly appreciative to the many faculty members at the Columbia University School of Public Health who have contributed their particular insight and expertise; without them, this book could never have been produced.

FOREWORD

Allan G. Rosenfield, M.D.,
DeLamar Professor and Dean,
Columbia University School of Public Health

Since its founding in 1921, the Columbia University School of Public Health has been widely recognized for its global as well as national and community health programs. The protection and improvement of health within specific community and population groups has always been the domain of public health. In our early days, the profession focused on sanitation and the spread of communicable diseases. Widespread immunization and pasteurization programs helped bring these scourges under control, at least in most of the industrialized world.

In recent decades, the domain of public health has broadened to encompass virtually the entire spectrum of health care. Nutrition, environmental concerns, the epidemiology of chronic diseases such as cancer and heart disease, cost-effective use of new technologies, delivery of high-quality health care to rural and urban poor, burgeoning population and disease in third world nations—these are but a few of the vital issues that we deal with every day.

At Columbia, we have developed programs dealing with everything from teenage pregnancy to the myriad problems facing the aged. In looking ahead to the next century, it is obvious that our profession is going to be increasingly involved in the special problems of our "graying population." Today the elderly make up 11 percent of our population, but the Bureau of Census projects that this percentage will nearly double in the next four decades. By the year 2030, about 21 percent of all Americans, 64.5 million people in all, will be 65 or older. In a sobering lecture delivered at a recent meeting of medical educators, Senator Thomas F. Eagleton called upon the health-care profession to face up to planning for the needs of an aging population. All too often, Americans tend to lapse into complacency in dealing with health-care problems, assuming that somehow Washington will rise to meet our needs. But Senator Eagleton noted the folly of this attitude, charging that a pervasive inertia seems to grip Washington when it comes to facing up to long-term social and economic needs. "We politicians tend to be the masters of the quick fix, taking just enough of some sugar-coated pill to avert a crisis until after the election," he said.

It is hard to pick up a newspaper or turn on a television news program without encountering a reference to health-care costs and intimations of impending disaster in caring for our aging population. We tend to take a more optimistic view. Thanks to new technologic advances and increasing attention to preventive health care, an ever growing number of Americans are reaching a healthy old age—in the past 50 was near the end of life expectancy; today, it is the prime of life, with decades more to come.

The Columbia University School of Public Health was one of the first to develop a specific Division of Geriatrics and Gerontology. This book is a reflection of our optimism and concern. We are dedicated to educating both physicians and the general public in sound preventive health-care practices for all ages and walks of life. We know that each individual is his or her own best health-care provider. We firmly believe that knowledge is good medicine, and that a well-informed patient is a physician's best partner in total health care. This book is intended to provide that information, not only about specific diseases but also about the practical aspects of a healthful life-style.

CONTENTS

PART I

HEALTH AND FITNESS

INTRODUCTION

THE NEW PRIME OF LIFE

Fifty is the new prime of life. At the turn of the century, the thirties were looked upon as the key decade during the adult years—the life stage when a person was expected to mark his or her major achievements and enjoy the best of health and wisdom. By the middle of the century, the forties became the prime decade. Today, thanks to the achievements of modern medicine and an unparalleled standard of living, we can expect our second fifty years to be as rich and full as the first. Of course, this does not mean that age does not bring changes, or that we can breeze through our mature years painlessly without any of the stresses and problems associated with aging. Nor does it change the fact that we live in a youth-oriented society. But today people in their sixties, seventies, or even older can—and do—run in the Boston Marathon, earn college degrees, start new businesses, travel throughout the world and experience all of the enthusiasm and excitement of new ventures. In fact, it is now so commonplace for older people to participate in activities once considered the exclusive domain of youth that no one even questions our ability to do so.

Still, advancing years do bring inevitable changes: children grow up, leave home and establish families of their own; retirement from a lifelong career leaves us at loose ends; the body becomes more vulnerable to disease; friends and loved ones move away or die. This book is intended to help you overcome inevitable hurdles and to put life changes in their proper perspective. You will learn how to avoid becoming one of the frail elderly, how to cope with losses, how to recognize medical warning signs and what to do about them. We also suggest resources for everything from adult education to medical insurance and entitlement programs for older Americans.

Throughout this book, you will be repeatedly reminded that an optimistic attitude and positive feelings of self-worth are vital assets in dealing with problems of getting older. It is often said that our middle years represent a time of personal stocktaking—of reevaluating goals, making adjustments, reaching a plateau in our professional lives, and seeking out new interests and activities. At some point in our second fifty years, most of us experience a feeling of coming to a dead end, of being overwhelmed by change and losses. Even the most Pollyannish outlook cannot diminish the very real sense of loss that comes with the death of a loved one, or the feeling of diminished self-worth that comes with retiring from a career that has been a central focus of life for most of our adult years. It is important to realize that grief, anger, sadness and fear are part of the human experience, and that all of us experience these feelings from time to time. How we deal with these negative feelings can be as important to overall health and well-being as daily exercise, proper nutrition and other good health habits. In addition to providing practical health information, then, we also focus on realistic yet positive coping techniques that you can use in dealing with the emotional side of growing older.

❑ It's Never Too Late

We have all heard the old saws: You can't teach an old dog new tricks . . . Time takes its toll and there's nothing you can do about it . . . There's no point in changing a bad habit after 50. . . . Of course, all are patently false, but it is surprising how often we hide behind these lame excuses to avoid making the effort to break a bad habit like smoking. Frequently, we hear people say: "I've smoked (not exercised, been overweight, etc.) for fifty years . . . it's not going to do any good to change at this late date." The fact is, numerous well-documented scientific studies clearly demonstrate that changing a bad habit, no matter what your age, is beneficial. For example, a long-term study by researchers at Harvard Medical School found that within two years of stopping smoking, the risk of a heart attack was about the same as for people who had never smoked. This was true regardless of age or how long a person had smoked. Obviously, it would be better to have never smoked at all, but it is important for the millions of Americans who continue to use cigarettes to recognize that it is never too late to undo at least some of the damage. The same is true of lack of exercise, overweight, poor nutrition, alcohol or drug abuse and other health-impairing habits. Change is difficult at any age, but it is never impossible. Throughout this book, we offer practical guidance on how you can alter old habits and form new, more healthful ones.

In some ways, changing our psychological outlook may be even more difficult than breaking a bad physical habit, but it is not as hard as many people think, and the benefits may be even more rewarding. For example, learning to adopt a slower, less aggressive pace is not easy for the hard-driven Type A professional who is facing retirement, and all too many retired Type A executives live out their life in frustration or turn to alcohol or other destructive outlets. Think how much more could be gained by channeling that drive into community activities, learning a new skill, starting a new career, building stronger personal relationships, or any of a number of other stimulating and worthwhile activities that can help a person retain his or her self-esteem and interest in life.

Even so, it would be a mistake to assume that the basic theses outlined in this book are the exclusive domain of older people. Looking ahead, realistic planning and commonsense approaches to health are important at any age. Nothing mysterious happens when you turn 50, 60, or even 80 or 90. The wise words of an 89-year-old friend, who, incidentally, has just returned from an Elderhostel trip to the Orient, provide an important lesson for all of us: "No matter what the age, we dream the same dreams, have the same hopes and aspirations. My joints may creak a bit, and I know I'm never going to climb Mount Everest or be elected President. But there are thousands of interesting things I can do, and I intend to try as many of them as I can before throwing in the towel." It is hard to imagine that this particular person will ever "throw in the towel." Our goal in creating this book has been to instill a similar outlook in our readers, and to provide a realistic and practical guideline of how to make the second fifty years as full and rewarding as the first.

1

NUTRITION IN THE LATER YEARS

"We are what we eat." The truth of this old adage is obvious, and it is truly amazing that nutrition remains a largely neglected area of modern medicine. Most physicians in this country have little or no training in the effects of nutrition on health, and only now are we beginning to understand the relationship between nutrition and many of our most serious health problems, including heart disease and cancer.

Eating habits are formed early in life and influenced by many factors—cultural heritage, personal likes and dislikes and finances, to name but a few. Because our eating habits are so firmly ingrained, they are perhaps the most difficult of all health practices to change. Still, as we emphasize throughout this book, it is never too late to change unhealthy behavior patterns, and this certainly applies to nutrition. Unfortunately, most people think that adopting more healthful eating habits means a total dietary overhaul, giving up everything they like and existing on a diet that is a boring and expensive mixture of brown rice, seeds, blackstrap molasses, yogurt and other "health-store" specialties. Actually, what is needed in most instances is not a total change, but instead, relatively simple modifications to bring individual dietary patterns and eating habits in line with recommended nutrition guidelines. This may entail a refresher course in the principles of good nutrition and a close look at eating patterns, so let's start with the basics.

❑ Essential Nutrients

All humans require some forty essential nutrients to maintain life and health. Two of these—namely, oxygen and water—are so commonplace that we don't even think of them as nutrients, yet they are the most essential of all. We can survive only a few minutes without oxygen and a few days without water; still, acquiring them requires little conscious effort. We take in oxygen with every breath, and water is readily available in everything we drink and from most foods. The other essential nutrients come from proteins, fats, carbohydrates, vitamins and minerals. These are briefly outlined in Table 1:1, Vitamin and Mineral Facts, and are discussed in more detail below.

Basic Facts about Vitamins for Adults

Nutrient (RDA for adults and children over 4)*	What it does	Sources	Signs of deficiency	Signs of overdose
Fat-Soluble Vitamins				
Vitamin A (1000 retinal equivalent for men: 800 RE for women.)	Helps to form and maintain healthy function of eyes, hair, teeth, gums, various glands and mucous membranes. It is also involved in fat metabolism.	Whole milk, butter, fortified margarine, eggs, green leafy and yellow vegetables and fruit, liver, fish.	Night blindness, growth reduction, impaired resistance, infection, rough skin, drying of the eyes.	Headaches, blurred vision, rashes, extreme fatigue, diarrhea, nausea, loss of appetite, hair loss, menstrual irregularities, liver damage.
Vitamin D (5 to 10 mcg.)	Needed for the body to absorb calcium and phosphorus which build strong bones and teeth.	Vitamin D fortified milk, liver, fish, liver oils, egg yolks, butter. Exposure to the sun's ultraviolet rays enables the body to produce its own.	In children: rickets. In adults: osteomalacia, thinning of the bones leading to spontaneous fractures, may play a role in osteoporosis.	Calcium deposits throughout the body in adults, in kidneys and bloods of infants; nausea, loss of appetite, kidney stones, high blood pressure, high blood cholesterol, fragile bones.
Vitamin E (alpha tocopherol) (10 mg. for men; 8 mg. for women.)	Helps form red blood cells, muscle and other tissues. Prevents fatty acid oxidation.	Wheat germ, vegetable oil, margarine, nuts, seeds, eggs, milk, whole-grain cereals, breads.	Rare except in those with impaired absorption of fat.	Not definitely determined.
Vitamin K* (70 to 140 mcg.)	Needed for normal blood clotting and normal bone metabolism.	Green leafy vegetables, peas, cereals, dairy products, liver, potatoes, cabbage. Also made by intestinal bacteria.	Bleeding problems and liver damage.	Jaundice in infants.
Water-Soluble Vitamins				
Vitamin B_1 (Thiamine) (1.0 to 1.4 mg.)	Helps get energy from food by promoting proper metabolism of sugars and starch; promotes normal appetite and digestion; needed for nerve function.	Pork, poultry, liver, pasta, wheat germ, whole-grain or enriched bread, lima beans, sea food.	Anxiety, hysteria, nausea, depression, muscular cramps, loss of appetite. Extreme: beri-beri, peripheral paralysis and heart failure.	Unknown. However, due to the interdependency of the B-complex vitamins, an excess of one may cause a deficiency of another.

Nutrient (RDA for adults and children over 4)*	What it does	Sources	Signs of deficiency	Signs of overdose
Vitamin B_2 (Riboflavin) (1.2 to 1.7 mg.)	Functions in the body's use of carbohydrates, proteins and fats, particularly to release energy to cells, helps maintain good vision, needed to maintain mucous membranes and certain enzymes that help change food into energy.	Milk, eggs, dark green leafy vegetables, liver, meat, whole-grain or enriched bread and cereal.	Lesions around the nose and eyes, soreness and burning of the lips, mouth and tongue, difficulty eating and swallowing.	See Vitamin B_1.
Vitamin B_6 (Pyridoxine) (2.2 mg. for men; 2.0 mg. for women.)	Has many important roles in protein and fat metabolism. It also aids in the formation of red blood cells and proper functioning of the nervous system, including brain cells.	Green leafy vegetables, meat, fish, poultry, whole-grain cereal, liver, nuts, carrots, herring, bananas, avocados, potatoes.	Depression, confusion, convulsions, inflammation of mucous membrane in the mouth, patches of itchy, scaley skin. Older people and alcoholics are more prone to deficiency.	Overconsumption can lead to dependency and cause deficiency symptoms when reduced to normal levels.
Vitamin B_{12} (Cobalamin) (3 mcg.)	Helps to build vital genetic material (nucleic acids) for cell nuclei, and to form red blood cells. Essential for normal functioning of all body cells, including brain nerve cells as well as tissues that make red cells.	Milk, salt water fish, oysters, meat, liver, kidneys, eggs.	Rare except in strict vegetarians and elderly people. Can produce pernicious anemia. Usually caused by malabsorption.	See Vitamin B_1.
Niacin (B_{39}, Nicotinic acid) (16 to 19 mg. for men; 13 to 14 mg. for women)	Promotes normal appetite and digestion. Necessary for healthy nervous system. Needed in certain enzymes which help change food into energy.	Liver, meat, fish, poultry, green vegetables, nuts, whole grain bread and cereal (except corn) and enriched bread and cereal.	Pellagra, a disease in which the skin forms a reddish rash that turns dark and rough.	Ulcers, liver disorders, high blood sugar, high uric acid.
Biotin* (100 to 200 mcg.)	Involved in the formation of certain fatty acids and the production of energy from the metabolism of glucose. It is essential for the workings of many body chemical systems.	Eggs, green leafy vegetables, kidneys, liver, string beans, milk and meat.	Rare except in infants. Mild skin disorders, depression, insomnia, muscle pain, anemia.	See Vitamin B_1.

Nutrient (RDA for adults and children over 4)*	What it does	Sources	Signs of deficiency	Signs of overdose
Folic Acid (Folacin) (400 mcg.)	Assists in the formation of certain body proteins and genetic materials for the cell nucleus and in the formation of red blood cells.	Green leafy vegetables, liver, wheat germ, legumes, bran, nuts.	Impaired cell division, and altered protein synthesis leading to megaloblastic anemia (abnormal red blood cells) or macrocytic anemia (oversized red blood cells.)	Could mask a B_{12} deficiency.
Pantothenic Acid* (4 to 7 mg.)	A key substance in the body metabolism involved in changing carbohydrates, fats and proteins into molecular forms needed by the body. Also required for formation of certain hormones and nerve-regulating substances.	Found in most animal and plant foods; also manufactured by intestinal bacteria.	Not known in humans except under experimental conditions.	May increase need for thiamine and lead to thiamine deficiency.
Vitamin C (Ascorbic Acid) (60 mg.)	Helps bind cells together and strengthens walls of blood vessels. Needed for healthy gums. Helps body resist infection. Promotes healing of wounds and cuts.	Citrus fruits and juices, green leafy vegetables, tomatoes, melon, cauliflower, strawberries, potatoes.	Scurvy, bleeding gums, loose teeth, hemorrhages under the skin, slow healing, dry rough skin, loss of appetite.	Bladder and kidney stones; urinary tract irritation; diarrhea and blood disorders. Overconsumption can lead to dependency which can cause deficiency symptoms when reduced to normal doses.

Basic Facts about Minerals for Adults

Macrominerals

Nutrient (RDA for adults)	What it does	Sources	Signs of deficiency	Signs of overdose
Calcium (800 to 1200 mg.)**	Helps build strong bones and teeth. Helps blood clot. Helps muscles and nerves function normally. Needed to activate certain enzymes which help change food into energy.	Milk and milk products, green leafy vegetables, citrus fruits, dried peas and beans, sardines (with bones) and shellfish.	Rickets in children; osteoporosis in adults.	Drowsiness, calcium deposits, impaired absorption of iron and other minerals.

Nutrient (RDA for adults and children over 4)*	What it does	Sources	Signs of deficiency	Signs of overdose
Phosphorus (800 to 1200 mg.)	With calcium, helps build strong bones and teeth. Needed by certain enzymes which help change food into energy.	Meat, poultry, fish, eggs, dried peas and beans, milk and milk products, egg yolk, and phosphates in processed foods and soft drinks.	Weakness, bone pain, decreased appetite (rare).	Upset of the calcium-phosphorus ratio, hindering uptake of calcium.
Sodium* (1100 to 3300 mg.)	Helps maintain water balance inside and outside cells.	Table salt, processed foods, ham, meat, fish, poultry, eggs, milk.	Water retention (edema); loss of sodium through extreme perspiration can cause muscle cramps, headache, weakness.	High blood pressure, kidney disease, congestive heart failure.
Chloride* (1700 to 5100 mg.)	Part of hydrochloric acid found in gastric juice and important to normal digestion.	Table salt, same as sodium.	Upsets balance of acids and bases in body fluids (very rare).	Upsets acid-base balance.
Potassium* (1875 to 5625 mg.)	With sodium helps regulate body fluid balance. Needed for transmission of nerve impulses, muscles to contract and for proper metabolism.	Bananas, dried fruits, peanut butter, potatoes, orange juice, other fruits and vegetables.	Muscular weakness, irritability, irregular heart beat (rare but may result from prolonged diarrhea or use of diuretics), kidney and lung failure.	High levels of potassium can cause severe cardiac irregularities and can lead to cardiac arrest.
Magnesium (300 to 350 mg.)	Activator for enzymes that transfer and release energy in the body.	Raw leafy green vegetables, nuts, soy beans, whole grains.	Muscular tremors, twitching and leg cramps, weakness, irregular heart beats. Deficiency is sometimes seen in people with severe kidney disease, prolonged diarrhea, or alcoholism, or people who take diuretics.	Upset of the calcium-magnesium ratio, leading to impaired nervous-system function. Especially dangerous for people with impaired kidney function.
Sulfur (unknown)	Component of several amino acids; used to make hair and nails.	Wheat germ, dried beans, beef, clams, peanuts.	Unknown.	Unknown.
		Trace Minerals		
Iron (10 to 18 mg.)	Combines with protein to make hemoglobin, the red substance in the blood that carries oxygen from lungs to cells, and myoglobin which stores oxygen in muscles.	Liver, meat products, egg yolk, shellfish, green leafy vegetables, peas, beans, dried prunes, raisins, apricots, whole-grain and enriched bread and cereal.	Iron-deficiency anemia; pallor of skin, weakness and fatigue, headache, shortness of breath.	Toxic build-up in liver, pancreas and heart (very rare).

Nutrient (RDA for adults and children over 4)*	What it does	Sources	Signs of deficiency	Signs of overdose
Iodine (150 mcg.)	Necessary for normal function of the thyroid gland.	Iodized salt, seafoods.	Thyroid enlargement (goiter). Causes cretinism in infants.	Could cause poisoning or sensitivity reactions.
Zinc (15 mg.)	Element of the enzymes that work with red blood cells to move carbon dioxide from the tissues to the lungs.	Meats, fish, egg yolks and milk.	Loss of taste and delayed wound healing. Growth retardation and delayed sexual maturation in children.	Gastrointestinal symptoms, such as nausea, vomiting, bleeding and abdominal pain. Premature labor and stillbirth in pregnant women.
Copper (2 to 3 mg.)	Used by several important proteins, including enzymes, involved in respiratory and red blood cell function. Also needed for making red blood cells.	Organ meats, shellfish, nuts, fruit, dried legumes, raisins, mushrooms.	Rarely seen in adult humans. Infants: hypochromic anemia with abnormal development of bone, nervous tissue, lungs and pigmentation of hair.	Liver disease and gastrointestinal symptoms such as vomiting and diarrhea. Overdoses can occur as a result of eating foods cooked in unlined copper pots.
Fluorine* (1.5 to 4 mg.)	Contributes to solid tooth and bone formation, especially in children. May help prevent osteoporosis in older people.	Fluoridated water and food cooked in fluoridated water, fish, meat, tea.	Tooth decay.	Mottling of enamel of teeth.
Chromium* (0.05 to 0.2 mg.)	With insulin, it is required for metabolism of glucose.	Dried brewer's yeast, whole-grain breads, peanuts.	Diabetes-like symptoms.	Unknown.
Selenium* (0.05 to 0.2 mg.)	Interacts with vitamin E; prevents breakdown of fats and body chemicals.	Seafood, egg yolk, chicken, meat, garlic, whole-grain cereals.	Unknown in humans.	Unknown.
Manganese* (2.5 to 5 mg.)	Needed for normal tendon and bone structure; part of some enzymes.	Bran, coffee, tea, nuts, peas, beans.	Unknown in humans.	Unknown.
Molybdenum* (0.15 to 0.5 mg.)	Forms part of the enzyme xantine oxidase.	Legumes, cereals, dark green vegetables, liver, other organ meats.	Unknown in humans.	Loss of copper; joint pain similar to gout.

*RDAs not established; amounts are estimated safe and adequate daily dietary intakes.
**Many experts now recommend women consume 1000 to 1500 mg.

Table 1:1

▪ *Protein*

Protein, made up of chains of building blocks called amino acids, is used for building and maintaining body tissue, maintaining the balance of body fluids and forming antibodies. Twelve percent of total calories should come from protein. As the body ages, its need for protein decreases slightly; although it still has to maintain and repair existing tissue, the body is producing less new tissue. An older person, however, should not reduce the amount of protein in the diet. Since the body's ability to digest and absorb protein decreases with age, we may actually have to consume more protein just to meet the lowered requirement. (See Table 1:2, Sources of Protein.)

Even so, most of us do not have to worry about getting adequate protein; the typical American diet provides more than enough. Protein is found in both animal and plant products. Meat of all kinds, fish, poultry, milk and milk products, and eggs all are high in complete proteins, meaning these products contain all of the essential amino acids. Dried beans, peas and other legumes, grains, nuts and seeds also are good sources of protein, but individually, these items do not contain all of the essential amino acids and must be consumed in the right combination to make complete proteins. (See Table 1:3, on Matching Plant Foods to Make Complete Proteins.)

The typical American diet is high in animal protein and relatively low in plant sources. Since a high-meat diet is likely to also be high in fat and cholesterol, most nutritionists urge a reduction in meat consumption and a corresponding increase in legumes and other plant proteins.

Myths abound concerning the value of protein. For example, many people are convinced that since protein helps build muscles, the more a person consumes, the more muscles they will build.

Sources of Protein

To calculate your protein requirement in terms of grams per day, multiply your ideal body weight by .36. Most healthy adults may reduce this amount by a third without harmful effects.

Food	Portion size	Protein (grams)
ANIMAL SOURCES:		
beef, lean ground	¼ lb. raw	23.4
Cheddar cheese	1 oz.	7.1
chicken, fryer	1 drumstick	12.2
cottage cheese	½ c.	15.0
eggs	2 medium	11.4
flounder	3 oz.	25.5
ham, boiled	3 oz.	16.2
milk, skim	1 c.	8.8
scallops	3 oz.	16.0
tuna, canned	3 oz. drained	24.4
turkey	3 oz.	26.8
yogurt	1 c.	8.3
VEGETABLE SOURCES:		
barley	¼ c. raw	4.1
beans, kidney	½ c. cooked	7.2
beans, lima	½ c. cooked	6.5
bread, whole wheat	1 slice	2.6
lentils	½ c. cooked	7.8
muffin, corn	1 medium	2.8
oatmeal	1 c. cooked	4.8
potato	7 oz. baked	4.0
rice, white	1 c. cooked	4.1
shredded wheat	2 biscuits	5.0
soybean curd (tofu)	1 piece	9.4
spaghetti	1 c. cooked	6.5

Source: Adapted from the U.S. Department of Agriculture handbook, *Nutritive Value of American Foods*, 1975.

Table 1:2

Matching Plant Foods to Make Complete Proteins

Combine	With
legumes*	grains or nuts and seeds
nuts and seeds†	legumes
nuts, seeds, grains or legumes	dairy products

*Legumes include dried peas (black-eyed, chick, cow, field); lentils and dried beans (adzuki, black, cranberry, fava, kidney, limas, marrow, mung, navy, pea, pinto, soy; buckwheat groats and peanuts).

†Nuts and seeds include almonds, beechnuts, Brazil nuts, cashews, filberts, pecans, pine nuts, walnuts, and pumpkin and sunflower seeds.

Table 1:3

This is not true, of course; once muscle tissue has reached its full size, it will not continue to grow, no matter how much protein is consumed. Muscle cells can be strengthened and enlarged by exercise, but consuming extra protein will not increase muscle mass. Instead, excess protein that is not used for repair, energy and other body functions simply will be converted to fatty tissue and stored. There also is some evidence that excessive protein intake may be a factor in Parkinson's disease and prostatic disorders.

▪ *Carbohydrates*

Carbohydrates are the body's major source of energy for all of its tissues and varied functions. There are two major types of carbohydrates: simple (or sugars) and complex (or starches). Simple carbohydrates are quickly converted to glucose or blood sugar, the body's major fuel. This is why a piece of candy, high-sugar soft drink, glass of orange juice or other foods high in sugars or simple carbohydrates give a quick burst of energy. Starches are not as quickly metabolized to glucose, and therefore produce a slower and steadier supply of energy.

Nutritionists recommend that carbohydrates make up about 55 to 58 percent of the daily calories consumed, and that most of these should come from starches, the form of complex carbohydrates. Excellent sources of complex carbohydrates are whole-grain breads and cereals, pastas, potatoes and other vegetables. Simple carbohydrates should come mostly from fruits, which provide important vitamins and minerals in addition to natural sugars, rather than from refined sugar, honey, corn syrups and other sweets, which are essentially empty calories. Milk, which contains lactose (milk sugar), is another good source of simple carbohydrates.

Many people mistakenly assume that pasta, potatoes and other starchy foods are more fattening than high-protein foods. In fact, both proteins and carbohydrates contain the same number of calories—4 per gram. Since meats and other animal proteins usually contain large amounts of fat (and fat contains 9 calories per gram), a high-meat diet actually is much more fattening than one high in starches. In addition, many high-carbohydrate foods also are high in dietary fiber (roughage), which gives a feeling of fullness and is less likely to lead to overeating.

▪ *Fats*

Many people are surprised to learn that a certain amount of fat is essential to maintain health. Since most Americans consume too much fat, we are constantly urged to cut down or eliminate it from our diet. No more than 30 percent of our total calories should come from fats (compared to the 40 percent in the average American diet). For example, a 52-year-old woman of average height and activity level who is not overweight requires 1800 calories a day, of which a maximum of 540, or 60 grams, may be derived from fats. To learn how to reduce your fat intake, see Table 1:4, Cutting Down on Fats.

Most dietary fats are made up of three types of fatty acids: saturated, polyunsaturated or monounsaturated. These fatty acids differ in the number of hydrogen atoms each molecule can carry. Saturated fats, which are found in most meats and in palm and coconut oils, tend to be hard at room temperature and carry the fewest hydrogen atoms, while polyunsaturated fats can carry the most. Monounsaturated fats fall in between. Vegetable fats—olive, peanut, corn and safflower oils, for example—all are high in unsaturated fats of one kind or the other. (See Table 1:5, Kinds of Fats.)

Saturated fats tend to raise the level

of cholesterol in the blood, which increases the risk of heart disease (see Chapter 11, Heart Disease and Circulatory Disorders). In addition, animal fats tend to contain large amounts of cholesterol themselves. In contrast, both mono- and polyunsaturated fats lower blood cholesterol, and, of course, vegetable fats do not contain any cholesterol.

It is important to distinguish between the dietary fat we consume and body fat, which is stored energy and can be made from excess dietary fats, proteins or carbohydrates. We don't need to consume any dietary fat to make body fat, but we do need to consume a certain amount of linoleic acid, an essential fatty acid found in polyunsaturated fats, which the body cannot manufacture. But we can get all of the linoleic acid we need from only about a tablespoon of polyunsaturated fat each day. (See Table 1:6, Cooking Tips to Cut Down on Fats.)

Fats have a number of important functions: They make foods more palatable by adding flavor, aroma and texture. They are needed for growth and to maintain a healthy skin. Fats carry the fat-soluble vitamins (A, D, E and K) and are also essential for the body to absorb these vitamins. Stored fat provides a concentrated source of energy, and it is also essential to make certain hormones and other body chemicals. Body fat also helps prevent heat loss and provides protection for internal organs.

Cutting Down on Fats

If you cut out	Times per day/ week	Approximate reduction in fat consumption (grams)	If you cut out	Times per day/ week	Approximate reduction in fat consumption (grams)
1 oz. light cream in coffee	5/day	200 grams/week	3.5 oz. ground sirloin steak	1/week	34 grams/week
8 oz. ice cream	3/week	48 grams/week	3.5 oz. lamb chop	1/week	26 grams/week
1 slice apple pie	3/week	53 grams/week	8 oz. whole milk	1/day	63 grams/week
1 slice bread and butter	3/week	12 grams/week	2 chocolate chip cookies	3/week	15 grams/week
10 french fries	3/week	20 grams/week	1 oz. Cheddar cheese	3/week	32 grams/week
1 oz. roasted peanuts	4/week	55 grams/week	2 slices bologna	2/week	32 grams/week
10 potato chips	4/week	32 grams/week	1 plain doughnut	3/week	20 grams/week
1 slice cheese pizza	1/week	5 grams/week	2 slices bacon	3/week	20 grams/week
1 tbsp. French dressing	1/day	37 grams/week			

Note: 1 gram of fat contains 9 calories.

Table 1:4

Kinds of Fats

Mostly Polyunsaturated	Mostly Monounsaturated	Mostly Saturated
corn oil	avocado	butter
cottonseed oil	cashew	cheese
fish	olives and olive oil	chocolate
margarine (especially corn, safflower or sunflower oil, or soft)	peanuts and peanut oil	coconut and coconut oil
safflower oil	peanut butter	egg yolk
soybean oil	poultry	lard
sunflower oil		meat
		palm oil
		vegetable shortening

Table 1:5

Cooking Tips to Cut Down on Fats

- Use a broiler, wok, vegetable steamer or non-stick pans instead of frying in fat.
- Switch to a polyunsaturated margarine. Liquid or soft margarines high in corn, safflower or sunflower oil are the best choices.
- Use skim or low-fat milk.
- Buy lean grades of meat and trim away fat. Use smaller amounts of meat by making stir-fried vegetable and meat dishes.
- Increase use of fish, poultry, legumes or pasta for main dishes.
- Use salad dressings made with small amounts of olive or polyunsaturated oil instead of creamed dressings.
- Use low fat cream cheese or yogurt as a substitute for blue cheese and sour cream.
- Bake, broil or roast meats using a rack.
- To reduce cholesterol from eggs, use an egg white plus a teaspoon of polyunsaturated oil instead of whole eggs in cooking; discard every other egg yolk when making an omelette, scrambled eggs or other egg dishes and limit whole eggs to two or three per week.
- Use pan spray instead of fat.

Table 1:6

▪ *Vitamins*

Vitamins are organic substances that the body needs in very small quantities for such essential processes as metabolism, and for the formation of blood cells, hormones, chemicals and genetic materials. The fat-soluble vitamins (A, D, E and K) can be stored in the body and therefore do not have to be consumed daily. Water-soluble vitamins (the B vitamins and C) are not stored and should be consumed every day or so.

The best way to ensure adequate amounts of all the vitamins is to eat a variety of foods from the four food groups. Most people do not need to take extra vitamins; exceptions might be the presence of certain medical conditions that increase the need for certain vitamins.

Despite the rareness of true vitamin deficiencies in this country except in alcoholics or others who do not consume an adequate diet, many people worry that they somehow are not getting enough vitamins and minerals from their foods and resort to taking supplements, frequently in megadoses that are many times the Recommended Dietary Allowances (RDAs) (see Table 1:1, Vitamin and Mineral Facts). This can lead to potentially dangerous overdosing. Most of us do not think of vitamins as being drugs, but when they are consumed in amounts that are greater than the body can handle, they become pharmacologic agents with the same potential for adverse reactions and side effects as any chemical drug.

In fact, many people who shun taking prescribed medications because they are wary of possible side effects think nothing of consuming megadoses of vitamins such as vitamin C. This kind of self-treatment can be as dangerous as taking any drug. For example, taking large amounts of vitamin A or D can cause serious liver damage and even be life-threatening. In general, unsafe dosages start at about three times the RDAs for minerals, five times the RDAs for fat-soluble vitamins and ten times the RDAs for water-soluble vitamins. If supplements are taken, you should consult your doctor first and make sure that the pills do not exceed the RDAs unless he or she specifically prescribes a higher dosage. And contrary to popular belief, it does not make any difference (except in price) whether the vitamin supplement is "natural" or synthetic; both are chemical compounds that are utilized the same by the body.

Since metabolism and body needs change with age, the RDAs for some nutrients do change with age. For example, older people may need additional thiamine (vitamin B_1), but this does not mean that they need to take it in pill form. Simply increasing their intake of pasta, poultry, whole-grain cereals or other thiamine-rich foods will suffice.

Many vitamins can be diminished or destroyed in preparation—for example, by overcooking or boiling vegetables in large amounts of water, which is then drained off. Minimal cooking, such as steaming or stir-frying, conserves vitamins.

Two of the overused vitamins are C and E. Megadoses of vitamin C have been touted as a preventive for everything from the common cold to cancer, but to date, no solid scientific evidence supports this claim. Nevertheless, many people have taken to giving themselves megadoses of vitamin C, just in case. Usually, large amounts of vitamin C are harmless because the excess will be excreted, but evidence has shown that megadoses can cause adverse effects such as nausea, cramps, diarrhea and urinary tract irritation in some people. Megadoses can also interfere with the accuracy of certain laboratory tests, the efficacy of certain drugs and the metabolism of certain other vitamins and minerals.

The claims for megadoses of vitamin E are just as far-reaching as for C and equally unproved. For example, vitamin E has been touted as capable of promoting new hair growth, preventing ulcers and increasing sex drive, among other things. Again, no sound evidence supports these claims. And although low-cholesterol diets may increase the body's need for vitamin E, these diets have built-in sources of extra vitamin E in vegetable-oil margarines, for instance.

▪ *Minerals*

Minerals are inorganic substances that, like vitamins, are needed in very small amounts for a wide array of essential body functions. Seven minerals—calcium, phosphorus, magnesium, potassium, sulfur, sodium and chloride—are referred to as macrominerals because the body needs them in relatively large amounts. The other essential minerals are microminerals, or trace elements, and are needed only in very small amounts. But the amounts are all relative: The difference in dosage is between milligrams and micrograms; and as with vitamins, mineral overdoses can be dangerous.

A well-balanced diet should supply all the body's needs. In fact, the only nutritional deficiencies that occur with any frequency in the United States are of iron, calcium or zinc. In general, unless there are underlying medical conditions, deficiencies can be adequately corrected by varying the diet to include more foods rich in these nutrients, rather than by taking supplements.

Mineral supplements can be particularly dangerous for any older person whose kidneys or liver cannot metabolize the excess. And taking too much of one mineral can upset the balance of others. For instance, excess phosphorus interferes with the body's ability to absorb calcium. Also, excessive minerals can interfere with the action of a number of drugs. A person who is on medication should never take vitamin or mineral supplements without consulting his or her physician. There may be adverse interactions or the nutrient may interfere with the medication's efficacy. Calcium supplements, for example, can interfere with the body's ability to utilize certain antibiotics.

THE SPECIAL CASE OF CALCIUM

In recent years, the public has become increasingly aware of the importance of calcium, and the food and drug industries have been quick to respond. Calcium is now being added to everything from breakfast cereals to soft drinks, and dozens of highly advertised calcium supplements are on the market. Nutritionists, who a few years ago were urging us to increase our calcium intake, now fear that, as with so many nutrition fads, we are getting too much of a good thing. All adults need adequate calcium—800 to 1200 milligrams a day—but today, large numbers of people, especially women, are consuming much more than this. This can increase the risk of kidney stones in susceptible people.

Calcium is the body's most abundant mineral. It is needed to build and maintain bones and teeth; it also helps regulate blood clotting, muscle tone and nerve function, and is necessary for the absorption of B_{12} through the intestines and the release of energy from carbohydrates, fats and proteins. The bones serve as the body's calcium storehouse; about 98 percent is in the bones, one percent is in the teeth and the remaining one percent circulates in the blood. Calcium constantly moves in and out of the bones. When blood calcium levels fall, the bones release enough of the mineral to restore the proper balance. Conversely, when blood levels exceed a certain amount, the calcium is absorbed by the bones or excreted by the kidneys.

Excessive loss of bone calcium can eventually lead to osteoporosis, a condition in which the bones become weak and porous with an increased tendency to fracture. Older women are especially prone to osteoporosis for a number of reasons. After menopause, the ovaries no longer make the female sex hormone, estrogen, which appears to be essential in proper calcium metabolism. Women have less bone mass than men, which makes them more susceptible to osteoporosis.

Many women shun high-calcium foods—milk, cheese and other milk products, sardines with bones—to cut calories. Adequate calcium intake throughout life is important in building and maintaining bones. Waiting until middle-age or after bone-thinning problems appear and then taking calcium supplements is like the proverbial locking of the barn door after the horse has fled. Starting to increase calcium intake at age 50 will not by itself prevent osteoporosis or repair already damaged bones. But adequate calcium is an important component—along with estrogen replacement after menopause, exercise and adequate vitamin D—in the prevention and treatment of osteoporosis.

Aging interferes with the body's ability to absorb calcium. And when people are inactive or are immobile for a period, following injury or illness, for example, their bones do not absorb calcium as efficiently and become further weakened. Other factors that hinder the body's ability to absorb calcium or increase its excretion include a high-protein, high-fat diet; cigarette smoking; and excessive consumption of caffeine, dietary fiber (especially bran), and foods high in phosphorous and oxalic acid (for example, spinach).

Low-fat, preferably skimmed, milk is the ideal source of calcium since lactose, or milk sugar, seems to enhance calcium absorption. Unfortunately, many older people cannot drink milk, often because their digestive system cannot handle the lactose. Calcium is found in tofu, green leafy vegetables and other foods. (See Table 1:7, Dietary Sources of Calcium.)

Many nutritionists urge people past middle age to keep a food diary to see just how much calcium they are getting, and if it is less than the recommended 1000 to 1500 milligrams, that they make up the difference with a calcium supplement. (See Table 1:8, Sample High-Calcium Menu.)

Fluoride, or fluorine, one of the essential trace minerals, is also essential in maintaining strong bones and may be included in the treatment regimen for osteoporosis.

Dietary Sources of Calcium

Food	Serving Size	Calcium (mg.)
Milk and Milk Products:		
milk (skim, whole,† etc.)	8 oz.	300
yogurt, whole milk†	8 oz.	275
yogurt, skim with nonfat milk solids	8 oz.	452
nonfat dry milk	1 tbsp.	57
ice cream, vanilla†	1 c.	208
ice milk, vanilla	1 c.	283
Cheese:		
American†	1 oz.	195
Cheddar†	1 oz.	211
cottage, creamed	1 c.	211
cottage, low-fat dry	1 c.	138
cream cheese†	1 oz.	23
Parmesan, grated	1 tbsp.	69
Swiss†	1 oz.	259
Fish/Seafood:		
mussels (meat only)	3½ oz.	88
oysters	5–8 medium	94
salmon, canned with bones	3½ oz.	198
sardines, canned with bones	3½ oz.	449
shrimp	3½ oz.	63
Fruit:		
figs, dried	5 medium	126
orange	1 medium	65
prunes, dried	10 large	51
Nuts/Seeds:		
almonds or hazelnuts†	12–15	38
sesame seeds†	1 oz.	28
sunflower seeds†	1 oz.	34
Vegetables:		
bean curd (tofu)	3½ oz.	128
beans, garbanzo	½ c.	80
beans, pinto	½ c.	135
beans, red kidney	½ c.	110
broccoli, cooked	⅔ c.	88
chard, cooked*	½ c.	61
collard greens, cooked*	½ c.	152
fennel, raw	3½ oz.	100
kale, cooked*	½ c.	134
lettuce, romaine	3½ oz.	68
mustard greens, cooked*	½ c.	145
rutabaga, cooked	½ c.	59
seaweed, agar, raw	3½ oz.	567
seaweed, kelp, raw	3½ oz.	1093
squash, acorn	½ medium baked	61

*Foods high in oxalic acid, which hinders absorption
† High fat content

Table 1:7

Sample High-Calcium Menu

The following menu illustrates how a person can get adequate calcium, in this example about 1400 mg., from an ordinary diet. If the milk is eliminated, a 600 mg. calcium supplement or other high-calcium foods can be substituted.

Food	Mg. Calcium
Breakfast	
Fresh orange	65
Cereal with ½ c. skim milk	150
8 oz. skim milk	300
Lunch	
Sandwich made with lean ham and 1 oz. low-fat cheese	260
Green salad	40
2 fig bars	100
Beverage	0
Dinner	
Vegetable soup	30
Roast chicken	0
Broccoli	88
Baked potato	0
Green salad	40
½ c. ice cream	100
Before Bed	
1 glass skim milk	300
Total Calcium	1473

Table 1:8

SODIUM

The average American consumes 2 to 4 teaspoons of salt a day—many times what the body actually needs. There is little doubt that to most people, salt is indeed the king of condiments. Once more precious than gold, in ancient times it was so scarce that men went to war for it and explored the earth in its quest. Today, of course, salt is plentiful throughout the industrialized world, and many experts think that our large intake of salt contributes to our great incidence of high blood pressure and heart disease. However, this is still unproved and controversial.

Salt is made up of two essential minerals—sodium and chloride. We have long been taught that salt is an acquired taste, but Dr. Derek Denton, an Austrian scientist whose 650-page book, *The Hun-*

ger for Salt, 2nd edition (New York: Springer-Verlag, 1984), compiles twenty years of research on salt, contends that our appetite for salt is a powerful instinct developed over 30 million years of evolution. He points out that "it is no accident that salt is one of the four primary elements of taste," because without it, life cannot exist. Sodium is one of the essential electrolytes that help cells maintain their delicate fluid balance. Our need for salt is believed to be a holdover from our evolutionary origin in the sea. As multicellular organisms evolved and moved onto land, they carried with them their saltwater origin in their blood. Today our blood plasma is chemically similar to seawater.

Like all essential nutrients, ingesting either too little or too much can be harmful to us. In the case of sodium, the excess is normally excreted in the urine. But if, despite this, the kidneys still cannot handle all of the salt, the body will increase its fluid or blood volume to restore a more normal sodium balance. This may lead to high blood pressure and a buildup of body fluids. People who are genetically predisposed to hypertension, the medical term for high blood pressure, are believed to develop high blood pressure when they consume too much sodium. Excessive sodium also can worsen kidney disease, congestive heart failure and the bloating that many women experience during their premenstrual phase.

Sodium is found naturally in a variety of foods, including cheeses, eggs, meat and fish. The average person can usually satisfy the RDA of 1100 to 1300 milligrams without any added salt. The 1986 American Heart Association's dietary guidelines recommend consuming no more than 1 gram of sodium per 1000 calories, not to exceed 3 grams a day. (One gram of sodium is equal to slightly less than 1/2 teaspoon of salt.)

Removing the saltshaker from the table and not adding salt during food preparation are two good ways to cut down on sodium intake. But for people who should markedly reduce sodium consumption, these steps may not be enough. Studies have found that most of the sodium we consume is actually hidden in processed foods—in everything from breakfast cereals to canned goods, including many that don't taste at all salty. (Table 1:9 lists the sodium content of common foods; Table 1:10 lists common "hidden" sources of sodium.) Sometimes salt can be reduced in convenience foods by draining or rinsing. For example, high-salt canned foods such as tuna can be drained and rinsed in water for one minute to lower sodium content.

A diet designed to cut down on sodium should emphasize fresh fish and poultry, fresh vegetables, fruits and grains. Alternative seasonings are highly recommended and readily available. Remember, seasoned or flavored salts, such as garlic or onion salt, are just as high in sodium as regular salt. Soy sauce is especially high, although there are now low-salt varieties. Check the labels for the sodium content of processed foods. Many foods are labeled "lite," but this does not necessarily mean that they are truly low salt; it simply means that the product contains less than what would normally be found in it. Table 1:11, Interpreting Food Labels, outlines the Food and Drug Administration's criteria for sodium labeling. Not all sodium is listed as such on the label: baking soda and monosodium glutamate (MSG) are examples of high-sodium ingredients not so listed.

Remember, too, that food is not the only source of sodium: It is also found in many beverages, such as soft drinks and beer, as well as in a wide variety of medications.

Common Foods High in Sodium

Food	Portion	Mg. of Sodium
MEATS:		
bacon (cured, broiled or fried crisp)	1 strip	76
bologna	1 slice	364
Canadian bacon	1 oz. slice	384
corned beef, cooked	3½ oz.	1740
frankfurter, cooked	1 average	542
ham, chopped	1 oz. slice	387
salami, beef	1 oz. slice	356
sausage, links	1 link	740
FISH AND SHELLFISH:		
clams, hard or round, meat only	5 large or 10 small	205
crab, canned	½ c.	850
herring, smoked	3 oz.	5234
mussels, meat only	3½ oz.	289
CANNED SOUPS AND VEGETABLES:		
canned soups, condensed e.g., beef or chicken noodle, minestrone, tomato	1 can	1937–2459
asparagus, canned, green or white	6 spears	271
beans, green, canned	½ c.	270
corn, canned, kernels	1 c.	590
mixed vegetables, canned	1 c.	504
peas, canned	¾ c.	236
potatoes au gratin, with cheese	1 c.	1095
tomatoes, canned	½ c.	130
BREADS:		
crackers (saltines)	2 crackers	66
graham crackers	2 crackers	94
raisin	1 slice	84
Ritz crackers	3 crackers	97
rye, American	1 slice	128
soda crackers	2 crackers	154
white	1 slice	117
whole wheat	1 slice	121
CEREALS:		
All-Bran, Kellogg's	1 c.	567
Bran Buds, Kellogg's	1 c.	774
Corn Flakes, Kellogg's	1 c.	216
Grape-Nuts, Post	1 oz.	174
Raisin Bran, Kellogg's	1 c.	293
Raisin Bran, Post	1 c.	443
MILK, CHEESE AND OTHER DAIRY PRODUCTS:		
American	1 oz.	318
Cheddar	1 oz.	197
cottage (1 or 2% fat)	1 c.	918
cottage, creamed	1 c.	516
cream	1 oz. (2 tbsp.)	84
Muenster	1 oz.	178
Parmesan, grated	1 tbsp.	93
Swiss, American	1 oz.	199
Swiss, Switzerland	1 oz.	74
butter, regular	1 tbsp.	124
butter, whipped	1 tbsp.	93
buttermilk (from skim milk)	1 c.	318
buttermilk (from whole milk)	1 c.	212
margarine	1 tbsp.	148
milk, fresh	1 c.	122
milk, canned, condensed	⅓ c.	112
milk, evaporated, canned	½ c.	118
yogurt, plain, low-fat	1 c.	159
CONDIMENTS:		
A-1 sauce	1 tsp.	82
ketchup	1 tbsp.	156
mayonnaise	1 tbsp.	84
mustard, yellow	1 tsp.	63
soy sauce	1 tbsp.	858
teriyaki sauce	1 oz.	1150
Worcestershire sauce	1 tsp.	49
COOKING AIDS:		
baking powder	1 tsp.	339
baking soda	1 tsp.	821
bouillon cubes	1 cube	7714
garlic salt	1 tbsp.	1850
meat tenderizer	1 tsp.	1745
salt	1 tsp.	1955
SNACKS:		
peanut butter, regular	1 tbsp.	97
peanuts, dry-roasted, salted	1 c.	602
pickles, dill	1	928
CARBONATED BEVERAGES:		
cola, low-calorie	12 oz.	58
grape soda	12 oz.	38
DESSERTS:		
chocolate chip cookies	2	88
chocolate pudding, prepared	½ c.	148–222
ice cream	1 c.	75–82
DIGESTIVE AIDS:		
Alka-Seltzer	1 tablet	521
Bromo Seltzer	1 tablet	717

Source: Bowes and Church's *Food Values of Portions Commonly Used,* revised by Jean A.T. Pennington, Ph.D., R.D.; and Helen Nichols Church, B.S. (New York: Harper & Row, 1980).

Table 1:9

"Hidden" Sources of Sodium

The following are ingredients in many processed foods. Their listing on a food label indicates an added source of sodium.

- Baking powder (baking soda plus acid): used to leaven quick breads, muffins and cakes.
- Baking soda (sodium bicarbonate or bicarbonate of soda): used to leaven breads and cakes; sometimes added to vegetables in cooking to keep them bright green.
- Brine: table salt and water used to flavor corned beef, pickles and sauerkraut, as well as to preserve vegetables and condiments.
- Disodium phosphate: used in some quick-cooking cereals and processed cheese and in meat to retain liquids.
- Dry skim milk: used in a number of products including baked goods.
- Hydrolyzed vegetable protein: used as a filler.
- Monosodium glutamate (MSG): a tenderizer and seasoning used in cooking and preserving foods.
- Sodium alginate: used in many chocolate milks and ice creams for smooth texture.
- Sodium ascorbate: used as a preservative.
- Sodium benzoate: used a a preservative in many condiments, such as relishes, sauces and salad dressings.
- Sodium citrate: used as a flavoring.
- Sodium cyclamate and sodium saccharin: used in some low-calorie soft drinks and desserts.
- Sodium hydroxide: used in food processing to soften and loosen skins of ripe olives, hominy and certain fruits and vegetables.
- Sodium nitrate and sodium nitrite: used to cure meats and sausages.
- Sodium propionate: used in pasteurized cheeses and in some breads and cakes to inhibit growth of mold.
- Sodium sulfite: used to bleach certain fruits in which an artificial color is desired; also used as a preservative in some dried fruit.
- Soy sauce and soy isolates: used as flavoring.
- Whey solids: the liquid drained off from yogurt, used as filler.

Table 1:10

Interpreting Food Labels

The Food and Drug Administration has established the following criteria for labeling regarding sodium content.

When the label says:	It means:
Lite	Processed with less than the usual amount of salt
Low sodium	140 mg. or less per serving
Reduced sodium	Processed to reduce the usual level of sodium by 75%
Sodium free	Less than 5 mg. per serving
Unsalted	Processed without the normally added salt
Very low sodium	35 mg. or less per serving

Table 1:11

POTASSIUM

Reducing salt is only half the story. Recent studies suggest that a low-potassium intake may also contribute to high blood pressure. Like sodium, potassium is an essential electrolyte needed to maintain fluid balance. Potassium is also vital for proper nerve and muscle function. It is abundant in a number of fruits and vegetables—the staples of our prehistoric ancestors' diets. Because potassium was plentiful and sodium rare, our bodies evolved to conserve sodium and excrete potassium. Today the situation is reversed: Our typical diet—high in fats, meat, sugar and sodium—is relatively low in potassium. But our bodies have not changed in keeping with the modern diet, as our kidneys still are designed to conserve sodium and excrete potassium. Societies that consume a largely vegetarian (high-potassium), low-salt diet have very little high blood pressure and associated problems. Recent studies by Dr. Louis Tobian and his associates at the University of Minnesota have found that a low-salt, high-potassium diet protects animals, including strains of mice that are genetically susceptible to hypertension, from developing high blood pressure, strokes and kidney damage, all of which are common in litter mates fed high-salt, low-potassium diets.

Potassium can be added to the diet simply by increasing one's intake of fruits and vegetables. Table 1:12 lists high-potassium, low-salt foods. People taking diuretics popularly known as "water pills" should be particularly careful to increase potassium intake as they will excrete large amounts of potassium. But a word of caution: Too much potassium can cause serious problems. Some salt substitutes contain large amounts of potassium. There have been cases of potassium toxicity among people who use these in addition to potassium supplements prescribed along with their antihypertensive medication.

IRON

Although normally a person on a well-balanced diet should not be at risk for iron deficiency, this is the most common nutritional deficiency seen in the United States. Iron is essential to make hemoglobin, the part of the red blood cell that carries oxygen to all of the body's cells. Prolonged iron deficiency can lead to anemia; signs include fatigue, pallor, shortness of breath and general malaise.

Organ meats and red meat are among our best sources of iron, although it is found in small amounts in a variety of foods (see Table 1:13, Sources of Iron). Since many elderly people tend to subsist on a low-calorie diet, they are at risk of developing iron-deficiency anemia. Iron deficiency may also be caused by internal bleeding from stomach ulcers, the intestinal tract or other organs. Frequent use of aspirin or other anti-inflammatory drugs used to treat arthritis, for example, also can cause intestinal bleeding, resulting in an iron deficiency.

Although only a small amount of iron is needed daily by the body (10 to 18

High-Potassium, Low-Salt Foods

Food	Serving Size	Potassium (mg.)	Sodium (mg.)
apricots	3 medium	281	1
asparagus	6 spears	278	2
avocado	½ medium	604	4
banana	1 medium	559	1
beans, green	1 c.	189	5
beans, white cooked	½ c.	416	7
broccoli	1 stalk	267	10
cantaloupe	¼ medium	251	12
carrots	2 small	341	47
dates	10 medium	648	1
grapefruit	½ medium	135	1
mushrooms	4 large	414	15
orange	1 medium	311	2
orange juice	1 c.	496	3
peach	1 medium	202	1
peanuts (plain)	2½ oz.	740	2
potato	1 medium	504	4
prunes (dried)	8 large	940	11
spinach	½ c.	291	451
sunflower seeds	3½ oz.	920	30
tomato	1 small	244	3
watermelon	1 slice	600	6

Table 1:12

Sources of Iron

Food	Serving Size	Iron (mg.)
apricots (dried)	8 halves	2.5
avocado (Calif.)	½ medium	1.3
beef, roast	3 oz.	6.1
beet greens	1 c. (cooked)	2.8
blood sausage	2 oz.	1.0
calves liver	3½ oz.	14.2
chicken	3 oz.	1.5
chicken livers	3 oz.	7.0
clams or oysters	3 oz.	5.0
collard greens	1 c. (cooked)	1.7
corn grits	¼ c. (cooked)	1.4
egg	1 medium	1.1
farina	1 c. (cooked)	2.0
kidney beans	½ c. (cooked)	2.8
lima beans	½ c. (cooked)	3.5
liverwurst	3 oz.	4.5
molasses (blackstrap)	1 tbsp.	3.2
mustard greens	1 c. (cooked)	2.5
oatmeal	1 c. (cooked)	1.7
orange (Valencia)	1 medium	1.0
pork chop	3½ oz.	4.5
pumpkin seeds	3 oz.	7.1
raisins	½ c.	2.5
rice (enriched)	1 c. (cooked)	1.6
sardines	3½ oz.	5.2
shrimp	3 oz.	2.5
soybean curds (tofu)	3½ oz.	1.9
spinach	1 c. (cooked)	0.8
sunflower seeds	3 oz.	7.1
veal cutlet	3½ oz.	3.0
walnuts	¼ c.	1.1

Table 1:13

Sample High-Iron Menu

The following day's meal provides about 20 mg. of iron, with a good source of vitamin C at each meal to increase absorption.

BREAKFAST
4 oz. grapefruit juice
8 dried prunes
½ c. wheat farina
¼ c. skim milk
Coffee or tea with lemon

MIDMORNING SNACK
Dried fruit mix of apricots, raisins and walnuts
6 oz. low-calorie cranberry juice

LUNCH
Sardine sandwich
Carrot/raisin salad
Orange

AFTERNOON SNACK
Fruit juice
4 whole wheat crackers

DINNER
½ chicken breast
1 c. mustard greens
Tofu/buckwheat kasha
Coleslaw
Gingerbread (made with dark molasses)

Table 1:14

Increasing Food's Iron Content by Cooking with Iron Utensils

	Iron Content (mg./100 g.)		
Food	**Raw**	**Non-iron utensil**	**Iron utensil**
baked cornbread	0.67	0.83	0.86
beef liver with onions	3.10	3.82	3.87
beef-vegetable stew	0.66	0.81	3.40
chili with meat and beans	0.98	1.28	6.27
fried chicken	0.88	1.37	1.89
fried corn tortillas	0.86	1.14	1.23
fried egg	1.92	1.84	3.48
pan broiled hamburger	1.49	2.00	2.29
pancakes	0.63	0.81	1.31
poached egg	1.87	1.71	2.32
scrambled egg	1.49	1.79	4.76
spaghetti sauce	0.61	0.69	5.77
spaghetti sauce with meat	0.71	0.94	3.58
Spanish rice	0.87	0.83	2.25
stir-fried green beans	0.64	0.69	1.18
unsweetened apple-sauce	0.35	0.28	7.38
white rice	0.67	0.86	1.97

Source: *Journal of the American Dietetic Association*, vol. 86, no. 7, July 1986, pp. 897–901.

Table 1:15

milligrams), the body does not absorb all the iron we consume, and with age, iron absorption tends to decrease even more. Thus, it is possible to eat foods with iron without supplying the body with an adequate amount (see Table 1:14). Liver, red meat and eggs are the richest and most easily absorbed sources of iron but are also high in cholesterol.

Only about 5 percent of the iron from plant sources is absorbed. Consuming iron-rich foods, particularly the less-absorbed plant sources, at a meal with citrus or other foods high in vitamin C appears to increase iron absorption. Including a small amount of meat, fish or poultry also boosts iron absorption. Iron content of foods also can be increased by cooking in uncoated iron utensils. The greatest increase in iron comes from acidic foods with a high moisture content that require a long cooking time. (See Table 1:15.)

Iron deficiency can be treated with iron supplements, but these should be taken only on the advice of a physician after true anemia has been documented and, if it is due to internal bleeding, its source found and treated.

▪ *Water*

About 65 percent of body tissue is actually water. Aside from oxygen, it is our most essential nutrient. It regulates body temperature, circulation and excretion, holds substances in solution and aids digestion. Water comes both from the liquids we drink as well as from foods, such as fruits, vegetables and even meat. All adults should consume six to eight glasses of liquid a day. Coffee and tea, probably our most common sources of water, should not be exclusively so because they have a diuretic effect and also contain caffeine and other potentially harmful substances. Soft drinks and juices are other common sources of water, but remember, these contain calories (or in the case of low-calorie drinks, artifical sweeteners). If you dislike plain tap water, try keeping a pitcher of water with added lemon slices in the refrigerator. This makes a low-cost refreshing drink. Seltzer, either plain or fruit-flavored, is another noncaloric alternative to regular soft drinks.

❑ Other Dietary Factors

▪ *Fiber*

Fiber is the fashion today. And like most other fads, it has its pluses and

Foods High in Fiber

Food	Portion	Fiber (g.)
CEREALS:		
bran	½ c.	2.3
bran flakes	1 c.	1.3
bran flakes with raisins	1 c.	1.5
oatmeal, cooked	1 c.	0.6
wheat, cracked (bulgar), dry	2 tbsp.	0.2
wheat, shredded	2 biscuits	1.1
BREADS AND CRACKERS:		
Bread		
cracked wheat	1 slice	0.1
pumpernickel	1 slice	0.4
raisin	1 slice	0.2
rye	1 slice	0.1
whole wheat	1 slice	0.4
Crackers		
graham, plain	4 crackers	0.3
whole wheat	4 crackers	0.4
FRUITS:		
apples, unpared	1 small	1.0
apples, pared	1 small	0.6
apricots	2–3 medium	0.6
bananas	1 small (6″)	0.5
blueberries	½ c.	1.2
grapes	22 medium	0.6
oranges	1 small (2½″)	0.5
papaya	½ c. pulp	1.1
peaches	1 medium	0.6
pears, with skin	1 medium (3 x 2½″)	2.8
prunes, dehydrated, uncooked	8 large	2.2
raisins, dried, seedless	½ c.	0.7
raspberries, black	½ c.	3.7
raspberries, red	½ c.	2.0
strawberries	10 large (⅔ c.)	1.3
VEGETABLES:		
asparagus	5–6 spears raw or ⅔ c. cooked	0.7
avocados, California	½ med.	1.9
avocados, Florida	½ med.	2.8
beans, green or yellow	1 c., cut	1.0
beets	2 medium (2″ diam)	0.8
broccoli, cooked	⅔ c., cut	1.5
Brussels sprouts, cooked	6–7 (⅔ c.)	1.6
cabbage, raw	1 cup shredded	0.8

minuses. Moderate dietary fiber (approximately 20 to 30 grams a day) can benefit the body in several ways:

- It may reduce the risk of cancer of the colon and rectum.
- It may help reduce the incidence of diverticulosis and other intestinal disorders.
- It helps prevent constipation.
- It may help control blood sugar levels.
- It may help lower cholesterol.

Many people mistakenly assume that increasing fiber intake means adding bran to a variety of foods or consuming large amounts of bran cereals. There is increasing evidence that too much bran

Foods High in Fiber (cont.)

Food	Portion	Fiber (g.)
carrots	1 large or 2 small raw or ⅔ c. cooked	1.0
cauliflower	½ c. cooked or 1 cup flowers raw	0.6
celery, raw	1 c. diced	0.6
corn, cooked	1 medium ear	0.7
cucumbers, unpared	½ medium	0.3
cucumbers, pared	½ medium	0.15
eggplant, cooked	½ c. diced	0.9
Jerusalem artichoke, raw	4 small (1½" diam.)	0.8
lettuce, raw	3½ oz.	0.6
mushrooms, raw	10 small or 4 large	0.8
okra, cooked	8–9 pods	1.0
onions, cooked	½ c.	0.6
peas, green, cooked	⅔ c.	2.0
potatoes, cooked with skin	1–2 ½" diam.	0.5
spinach, raw or cooked	3½ oz.	0.6
squash, summer, cooked	½ c.	0.6
squash, winter, cooked	½ c.	1.4
tomatoes, ripe, raw	1 small	0.5
turnips, cooked	⅔ c. diced	0.9
watercress, raw	3½ oz. or 100 sprigs	0.7
LEGUMES, GRAINS AND NUTS:		
almonds	⅔ c.	2.6
barley, pot or Scotch, raw	½ c.	0.9
beans, lima, cooked	½ c.	1.6
beans, mung, sprouted, raw	1 c.	0.5
beans, red, cooked	½ c.	1.7
beans, white, cooked	½ c.	1.5
Brazil nuts	25 medium or ⅓ c.	3.1
cowpeas, mature seeds, cooked	½ c.	1.8
lentils, cooked	⅔ c.	1.2
macadamia nuts	6 whole nuts	0.4
peanut butter	1 tbsp.	0.3
peanuts, roasted, with skins	2.5 oz.	2.7
pecans	12 halves	0.3
pistachio nuts	30 nuts	0.3
popcorn, plain	1 c. popped	0.3
rice, brown, cooked	1 c.	0.5
soybeans, cooked	½ c.	1.6
soybeans, sprouts, raw	1 c.	0.8

Source: Values derived from Agriculture Handbook No. 8: *Composition of Foods* by Bernice K. Watt and Annabel L. Merrill, Consumer and Food Economics Institute, Agricultural Research Service, United States Department of Agriculture, 1963.

Table 1:16

fiber can actually increase the risk of colon cancer as well as irritate the intestinal tract and reduce the body's absorption of calcium, zinc and other essential minerals.

Dietary fiber, or roughage, are the parts of plant food that we cannot digest because our intestinal tract lacks the needed enzymes to break it down. There are several types of fiber in our diet, the most common of which are cellulose, pectin, hemicellulose, lignin and the gums and mucilages used as thickening agents or to improve the texture of processed foods. A diet that provides a variety of whole-grain cereals and breads, vegetables and fruits will contain ample amounts of different fibers. (See Table 1:16 on high-fiber foods.)

It is not necessary, and may even be harmful, to sprinkle bran on whole-grain cereal or add bran to a variety of foods, as has been advocated in the past. Nutritionists agree that no more than 10 to 15 grams of bran fiber should be consumed per day. Any more than that can upset intestinal function and actually create some of the problems it is intended to prevent or solve, such as intestinal gas, constipation or even intestinal blockage. The accompanying Table 1:17, Conserving Dietary Fiber, outlines food preparation steps that sensibly describe a balanced fiber intake.

Conserving Dietary Fiber

- Avoid peeling potatoes, apples and other fruits and vegetables with edible skins
- Stir-fry or steam vegetables to minimize breakdown of fiber
- Use brown rice instead of white
- Substitute whole wheat flour where possible
- Use the dark green outer leaves of lettuce, cabbage and other vegetables; they contain more fiber and nutrients than the softer inner leaves
- Use pectin instead of cornstarch to thicken fruit pies or stewed fruits
- Avoid removing the strings from celery, beans and other such vegetables
- Avoid overcooking vegetables and fruits; many can be served raw or cooked only until just tender

Table 1:17

Caffeine

In moderate amounts, caffeine is generally considered harmless. Moderation, however, is the key, especially since a person's tolerance to caffeine declines with age. A cup of coffee contains about 150 milligrams of caffeine, more than the average over-the-counter stimulants. Although coffee is perhaps our most common source of caffeine, it is by no means the only one. Chocolate, colas and other soft drinks, tea, some aspirin compounds and other medications also contain caffeine. If you are trying to cut

Sources of Caffeine

Source (amount)	Mg. of caffeine
Coffee (5 oz. cup):	
drip	146
percolated	110
regular instant	53
coffee/grain blends	35
decaffeinated instant	2
Tea (5 oz. cup):	
1-minute brew	9–23
3-minute brew	20–46
5-minute brew	20–50
instant	12–28
canned iced tea (12 oz.)	22–36
Cocoa and Chocolate:	
cocoa from mix (6 oz.)	10
milk chocolate (1 oz.)	6
baking chocolate (1 oz.)	35
Soft Drinks (12 oz. cans):	
Dr. Pepper	60
regular colas	30–45
diet colas	50
Mountain Dew	50
Tab	45
Nonprescription Drugs:	
Prolamine	280
NoDoz, Caffedrin, Vivarin	200
Aqua-ban	200
Dietac, Dexatrim	200
Excedrin	130
Midol	65
Anacin	65
Dristan, other cold remedies	20–35

Table 1:18

down on caffeine, check labels on medications and other items for sources of hidden caffeine. (See Table 1:18, Sources of Caffeine.)

The effects of too much caffeine range from anxiety and irritability to insomnia, migraine headaches, diarrhea, indigestion and irregular heartbeat. The possible link between coffee and heart attacks is disputed. The long-term Framingham Heart Study has failed to find a connection, but a recent long-term study carried out at Johns Hopkins found that a high consumption of coffee—more than five cups a day—more than doubled the risk of a heart attack. Earlier studies have found that caffeine may increase the risk of a heart attack in those with abnormal heart rhythms. Excessive caffeine may also lead to palpitations and irregular heart rhythms in susceptible individuals, for example, those with valvular heart disease. Switching to a decaffeinated brand (water- rather than chemically processed) is recommended in such cases.

▪ *Nitrites*

Nitrites are added to food to prevent the growth of botulism and add color and flavor. Although there is no concrete evidence that nitrites are linked to cancer, when they combine with the muscle fat of meats they form carcinogenic nitrosamines. Since the evidence became known, the U.S. government has been instituting regulations regarding nitrite use. Avoiding cured meats such as bacon and frankfurters, unless the label specifically states that they are nitrite-free, cuts down on exposure to nitrites.

▪ *The Question of Food Additives*

Anyone who regularly reads the lists of ingredients on processed foods (something everyone should do) frequently comes across terms like BHA, BHT, ascorbyl palmitate, potassium bisulfite and dozens of other equally mysterious terms. Obviously, they are chemical additives, but beyond that, most people have no idea what they are doing in our food.

Food purists have long decried the presence of chemicals in food. Actually, all food, both natural and concocted, is made up of chemicals. Indeed, as human beings we are a complex arrangement of chemicals. Some chemicals are essential to sustain life, others are beneficial and still others are highly toxic.

A wide array of chemicals are used in the processing of food. Some improve nutritional content, others make it more attractive or flavorful. Perhaps the most important are the large number of preservatives that are added to keep food from spoiling. Some preservatives, such as salt, sugar and certain acids, have been used for centuries. In recent decades, these have been joined by scores of other formulations that make it possible for us to enjoy a wide variety of foods from all over the world in every season. But many people worry that these additives may be harmful or alter the nutritional quality of food. Since the early 1970's, the Food and Drug Administration has been studying the safety of various preservatives, including more than two dozen that have been used for many years, but never scientifically tested. This summary discusses the pros and cons of the major classes of preservatives and their current GRAS (generally recognized as safe) status.

TWO BASIC TYPES

Modern preservatives fall into two categories: the antimicrobials, which inhibit the growth of molds, yeasts and bacteria, the microorganisms that spoil food; and the antioxidants, chemicals that keep food from becoming rancid or developing off-flavors, odors and discolorations.

Ascorbates and erythorbates. These are basically antioxidants and include ascorbic acid (vitamin C, which also has some antimicrobial properties), ascorbyl palmitate, calcium ascorbate, erythorbic acid, sodium ascorbate and sodium erythorbate. They are used in small amounts to prevent some foods, such as pears or potatoes, from turning brown. They also are used in baked goods, candies, fats and oils, cereals, pickling brine and processed meats. The FDA recognizes all as safe, with the exception of calcium ascorbate, and data is still being collected on this substance. It is a derivative of vitamin C and has a rather limited use in foods.

Benzoic acid and sodium benzoate. These are used to retard the growth of yeasts, bacteria and some molds in many foods, especially in acidic foods. Benzoic acid occurs naturally in raspberries and other berries, prunes, tea, cinnamon and cloves. It is used mostly in soft drinks and alcoholic beverages, soft candies, chewing gum, fats and oils, baked goods, condiments, nondairy creamers, gelatins, puddings, frozen dairy products and cheese. Sodium benzoate appears in these foods plus baked goods, processed vegetables, margarine, meat products, instant coffee, cereals and meat products.

BHA (butylated hydroxyanisole) and BHT (butylated hydroxytoluene). These are chemically similar compounds that are widely used as antioxidants to keep foods from turning rancid, especially those with fat and oils. They have been used in foods for more than forty years, but their safety is still under study by the FDA, which has ruled that BHA and BHT, either alone or in combination, cannot make up more than 0.02 percent of the fat and oil content of a food.

Parabens. These are antimicrobial agents chemically similar to benzoic acid and include methylparaben and propylparaben. Their safety has been reaffirmed by the FDA, and they are used to inhibit the growth of molds and yeasts in acidic foods. They also may be added to jams, jellies, pickles, syrups, grain products, cheese, soft drinks, baked goods, processed vegetables and frozen dairy products.

Propionic acid and its salts. These are antimicrobial agents and include calcium propionate, sodium propionate, dilauryl thiodipropionate and thiodipropionic acid. They are most effective against fungi and are widely used in baked goods and cheese products. The FDA has reaffirmed the safety of dilauryl thiodipropionate and thiodipropionic acid; the other two are under study and can be used only in very small quantities.

Propyl gallate. This is an antioxidant that has been reaffirmed as safe. It is often combined with BHA and/or BHT and is widely used in fats, oils, meat products, nuts, grain products, snack foods, baked goods, soft candy, gum and soft drinks.

Sorbates. These include sorbic acid and calcium, potassium and sodium sorbate. Their safety has been affirmed, and they can be used in small quantities in a variety of processed foods.

Stannous chloride. This is an antioxidate, sometimes referred to as tin chloride. It prevents food from changing color or developing offensive odors. It has been reaffirmed as safe, but can be used only in very minute quantities because it is derived from metallic tin.

Sulfiting agents. These are antioxidants that prevent discoloration of foods, especially vegetables, potatoes and fruits. Sulfiting agents include potassium and sodium bisulfite, potassium and sodium metabisulfite and sulfur dioxide. There have been numerous reports of serious, even fatal allergic reactions to these agents, especially when consumed by asthmatics. The FDA is studying their safety, but has advised food processors and restaurants that consumers should be informed if sulfiting agents are used. However, this is not always done; anyone with serious allergies or asthma should specifically ask if sulfiting agents have been added to vegetables, fruits and other foods. If in doubt, it is a good idea to avoid foods that may have been treated with them.

Tocopherols. These are chemically related substances that contain vitamin E and are used as antioxidants. Many occur naturally in meat, vegetable oils, cereal grains, nuts and leafy vegetables. They are used in baked products, cereals, dairy products, infant formulas and other foods to prevent them from turning rancid. They are generally considered safe.

Cholesterol

No doubt about it, Americans have become increasingly cholesterol-conscious in recent years. We are eating less red meat and butter, fewer eggs and more fish and poultry. Even so, misinformation and confusion abound, and many people who think they are making low-cholesterol substitutes actually end up consuming more cholesterol and saturated fats than before. For example, many people eating in a fast-food restaurant will order a fish sandwich or fried chicken instead of a hamburger, thinking that they will be cutting down on cholesterol and calories. Actually, if the hamburger is reasonably lean and broiled, it is likely to contain less fat and cholesterol than breaded fish or chicken that is deep-fried in lard. Or a person may shun beef in favor of Cheddar or some other hard cheese. Unless the beef is very fat, the cheese is likely, ounce for ounce, to have more cholesterol and fat than the meat. Remember, too, that many fast-food restaurants cook fried potatoes in lard, adding a hefty amount of fat and cholesterol to a naturally low-fat vegetable that normally would be cholesterol free.

Cholesterol is a waxy alcohol that is essential in forming all animal cell membranes. It also is needed for proper nerve function, reproduction and a number of other vital processes. Without it, we cannot survive. But it is not necessary to consume any cholesterol in the diet; our bodies are capable of manufacturing all that we need. Essential fatty acids are converted to cholesterol in the liver. Each day we require about 100 milligrams of cholesterol, and under normal circumstances, the body manufactures 500 to 1000 milligrams, depending upon need. The American Heart Association advises that we limit cholesterol consumption to about 300 milligrams per day—about the amount in one egg yolk. If the diet provides too much cholesterol, the amount circulating in the blood rises. In time, this can lead to atherosclerosis, or hardening of the arteries. The deposits of fatty plaque that clog the coronary arteries and are responsible for most heart attacks are made up mostly of cholesterol.

Americans tend to have high levels of total cholesterol: Readings of 250 to 300 milligrams/deciliters or even higher are very common, and the average cholesterol level for adult Americans is now about 220. In the past, doctors have tended to consider cholesterol readings of 250 or less in the normal range, but this has changed in recent years. The American Heart Association now recommends that adults should have cholesterol levels below 200 milligrams/deciliters, and the lower the better. It should be noted, however, that cholesterol rises somewhat with age, so a level of up to 240 milligrams/deciliters in a person over 40 constitutes only a moderate risk instead of the high risk for a younger person.

But total cholesterol is not the whole story. Since cholesterol is a fatlike substance and fat and water do not mix, in order for cholesterol to travel through the blood (which is mostly water), it must be attached to a water-soluble substance. Three proteins, called lipoproteins, have this function. Two—low-density and very low-density or LDLs and VLDLs—carry cholesterol to the blood vessel linings and are instrumental in the development of atherosclerosis. The other, high-density lipoprotein, or HDL, carries cholesterol away from the vessel walls and is referred to as "good" cholesterol because it seems to protect against atherosclerosis. When blood cholesterol is measured, the test results should include a breakdown of HDL and LDL cholesterol, and also state the ratio of total cholesterol to HDL. A person can have a relatively low total cholesterol and still develop atherosclerosis if the HDLs are very low. In general, if the ratio of total cholesterol to HDL is greater than 4.5:1, efforts should be made to improve the balance by raising HDL. Of course total cholesterol should also be reduced, especially if it is about 220 to 240 (see Table 1:19).

Cholesterol and Cardiovascular Risk

The following table, developed by the National Cholesterol Education Program, shows cholesterol levels for corresponding risk of a heart attack.

Cholesterol (mg/dl)	Risk	Recommended action
200 or less	Normal	Recheck within 5 years
200–239		
No heart disease or risk factors	Borderline	Recheck annually Dietary counseling
With heart disease or two risk factors	High	Measure HDL/LDL levels Dietary therapy plus drugs if needed
Over 240	High	

Table 1:19

Factors that appear to raise HDLs include exercise, a vegetarian diet, estrogen replacement in menopausal women, pectin, and high-dose niacin.

Many people are still confused about the sources of cholesterol, and much of this confusion is fueled by food advertising. *Cholesterol is found only in animal products,* not in any vegetable oils or other plant products. Thus advertising claims that products such as a certain brand of margarine or peanut butter contain no cholesterol are superfluous. Unless animal fats have been added, they obviously do not contain cholesterol. They may, however, be high in palm, coconut or hardened oils. These are high in saturated fats and therefore capable of raising our own cholesterol levels. In fact, these fats are thought to raise blood cholesterol more than eating cholesterol-rich foods.

Cholesterol is usually, but not always, found in association with fat. Egg yolks, fatty meats, whole milk, butter, liver, and other organ meats and hard cheese all are high in cholesterol (see Table 1:20, Cholesterol/Fat Content of Foods). Contrary to popular belief, fish, chicken and other poultry also contain cholesterol, and in about the same amounts as beef and other meats. In fact, some fish and seafoods contain more cholesterol than beef. But the fish still would be a better overall meal choice because its fat tends to be unsaturated, which helps lower total cholesterol and increase protective HDL cholesterol. In contrast, saturated fats raise cholesterol. Ideally, no more than 30 percent of our total calories should come from fats, and these should be about evenly distributed among saturated, monounsaturated and polyunsaturated fats.

Virtually everyone with even moderately elevated cholesterol can benefit from a low-fat, low-cholesterol, high-carbohydrate diet. The American Heart

Cholesterol/Fat Content of Foods

Food	Chol. (mg.)	Fats (g.) Sat.	Mono.	Poly.
MEAT, POULTRY AND FISH:				
1 oz. lean beef	26	0.9	0.8	0.1
1 oz. fatty beef	27	2.2	2.0	0.2
1 oz. veal	28	0.9	0.8	0.1
1 oz. chicken (dark meat)	26	0.8	1.0	0.6
1 oz. chicken/ turkey (white meat)	22	0.3	0.3	0.2
1 oz. pork	28	0.9	0.8	0.1
1 oz. beef liver	83	0.1	0	0
1 oz. lean fish	28	0	0.1	0.1
1 oz. fatty fish	25	0.9	1.1	1.1
1 oz. water-packed tuna	11	0	0	0
1 oz. lean lamb	17	0.1	0.2	0.2
FATS AND OILS:				
1 tsp. margarine (1.6/1.9 poly/sat)	0	1.4	3.3	2.4
1 tsp. corn oil	0	0.6	1.1	2.6
1 tsp. safflower oil	0	0.4	0.6	3.3
1 tsp. veg. oil	0	0.7	1.0	2.6
2 tsp. avocado	0	0.8	2.1	1.3
EGGS AND DAIRY PRODUCTS:				
1 egg	274	1.7	2.2	0.7
1 tsp. butter	12	1.9	1.4	0.2
2 oz. 5% fat cheese	20	1.6	1.0	0.1
2 oz. Cheddar	56	12.0	6.0	0.5
1 c. whole milk	34	4.8	2.4	0.1
1 c. 2% milk	22	2.4	2.0	0.1
1 c. skim milk	4	0.3	0.1	0
1 c. 1% yogurt	14	2.3	1.0	0.1
1 c. ice cream	56	16.8	9.6	0.3

Table 1:20

Association's guidelines for a heart-healthy diet are outlined in Table 1:21; Table 1:22 lists suggested portions and Table 1:23 gives sample menus.

The way food is prepared can make a major difference in whether it will raise or lower your cholesterol level. Fat content of meat and poultry can be lowered considerably simply by buying lean cuts and then trimming off as much visible fat and/or skin as possible. Many people who have given up meat in favor of cheese, nuts or peanut butter may be surprised to learn that they are now consuming more calories and fat, ounce for ounce, than before. Table 1:20, already referred to above, lets you see at a glance the best choices as far as cholesterol, fats and calories are concerned.

TIPS FOR LOWERING CHOLESTEROL

Experts agree that diet and exercise are the best places to start when it comes to lowering cholesterol. Studies have found that increasing exercise and shedding excess weight will lower total cholesterol and improve the HDL/LDL ratio.

People who have very high cholesterol or signs of atherosclerotic heart disease may need to take additional steps. A number of cholesterol-lowering drugs may be prescribed, and other highly promising agents are awaiting final FDA approval. These drugs should be used only under the close supervision of a doctor, however, since their potential adverse effects include liver problems.

Large doses of niacin, one of the B vitamins, also have been found to lower LDL and raise HDL cholesterol, but this should not be taken without consulting a doctor. Recent studies at Beth Israel Hospital in Boston have found that 1000 to 3000 milligrams of niacin a day can lower cholesterol by up to 30 percent. This dosage is lower than the 7000 to 8000 that has been recommended in the past and is not as likely to cause side effects. In the 7000 to 8000 milligram range, most people will experience hot flashes and other unpleasant effects, as well as possible liver damage. By starting with 250 milligrams of niacin a day and working up gradually to 1000 to 3000 milligrams over a period of several weeks, the Boston researchers found that most patients could tolerate the drug and still gain the cholesterol-lowering benefits.

Niacin offers another important advantage over other cholesterol-lowering drugs—namely, it is not as expensive.

American Heart Association's Guidelines for a Heart-Healthy Diet

Fruits and Nonstarchy Vegetables:
- All are acceptable choices (except coconut, avocado and olives, which are listed under fats).
- Allow 3 servings of each per day. A serving equals 1/2 cup cooked or canned; 1 cup raw vegetables; 1 medium-sized piece of fruit; 6 ounces juice.
- To cut calories, use unsweetened or juice pack; avoid cream, butter or margarine sauces; use herbs, spices, lemon juice, etc. for flavorings.

Bread, Cereals and Starchy Foods:
- Use any plain breads, rolls, cereals, rice, pasta, starchy vegetables and low-fat crackers.
- Avoid commercial cookies, cakes, pies and other such baked goods, croissants, eggs, butter or cheese breads and rolls, granola-type cereals with coconut or coconut oil, chow mein noodles, french fried potatoes and other fried vegetables, other baked goods high in fats.
- Reduce serving sizes to 75 to 100 calorie portions (for example, 1 slice bread, 2/3 to 3/4 cup prepared cereal, 1/2 cup potato, lima beans, green peas).

Crackers and Snack Foods:
- Use low-fat crackers, bread sticks, Melba toast, matzo, rusks, zwieback, unbuttered air-popped popcorn, etc.
- Avoid sweets and other high-calorie foods.
- Use fruits and vegetables as snacks.

Milk:
- Use only skim or low-fat (1 percent butterfat or less) milk, either dry or fluid.
- Use low-fat (2 grams or less per ounce) cheese.
- Use dry curd, low-fat cottage cheese.
- Use skim or low-fat plain yogurt.
- Avoid all other dairy and nondairy substitutes that contain butterfat or saturated fats.
- Use sherbet, frozen yogurt or ice milk in place of ice cream.

Meat, Poultry, Seafood and Eggs:
- Reduce consumption of red meat in favor of veal, poultry, fish, seafood and meat substitutes. Increase use of meatless main dishes to three or more per week.
- Reduce total cholesterol intake to 300 milligrams or less per day.
- Reduce total fat consumption to 30 percent or less of total calories.
- Avoid prime or marbled meats, sausages, spare ribs, all cured meats, duck, goose, poultry skin, any other fatty poultry, fatty organ meats (for example, brains), pork and beans, gravy and any commercial fried meats, poultry or seafood.
- Increase use of legumes and other meat substitutes.
- Reduce egg consumption to no more than two egg yolks per week (egg whites can be used in any quantity).
- Consume 6 ounces or less of meat per day.

Fats and Oils:
- Increase use of polyunsaturated fats (for example, safflower, sunflower, corn, soybean and cottonseed oils) in preference to saturated fats, especially butter, lard or other animal fats.
- Avoid use of coconut, coconut oil, palm or palm kernel oils; other hardened oils; and shortening, cheese dressings, chocolate, meat drippings, cashew, macadamia and pistachio nuts.
- Use margarine or polyunsaturated oil in place of butter or shortening.
- Prepare homemade salad dressing using safflower, corn or sunflower oil.
- Use fat-free desserts.

Note: For more information, contact your local American Heart Association chapter for a copy of the booklet "Eating for a Healthy Heart," or write to the American Heart Association, National Center, 7320 Greenville Avenue, Dallas, TX 75231.

Table 1:21

For example, cholesterol-lowering therapy with cholestyramine (Questran) costs $217 a month, compared to $5 a month with niacin.

❑ Age-Related Changes

As we grow older, our metabolism slows. We also tend to lose some of our muscle mass while the percentage of body fat increases. Typically, our physical activity also decreases. Taken altogether, these factors mean that as we grow older we do not need to eat as much; as a rule of thumb, a person's caloric requirement falls by approximately 2 to 10 percent for each decade past 20. Thus, a middle-aged person who continues to eat as he or she did when 20 will gain weight. But attention to diet and sound nutrition, plus maintaining a high level of physical activity, will help keep the pounds from creeping up. Acceptable weight is what is comfortable and healthy, not what may be fashionable. Generally, a gain of 20 to 25 pounds after age 30 is not considered harmful to health, but it may be upsetting to find you can no longer fit into a certain size. If this is so, then there is no harm in observing a moderate reduction in calories, coupled with increased physical activity, to provide for a gradual weight loss until you once again achieve the weight comfortable for you.

Insurance companies have devised standard height and weight tables that give "ideal" weights according to sex and body type. (See Table 1:24 on Desirable Weight for Height.) Total weight, however, is not the only indicator of being overweight: The ratio of muscle to fat is just as important. The skin-fold test can serve as a guide: If a person can pinch more than one inch in a place like the abdomen over the hipbone or the loose skin fold on the underside of the upper arm—places where fat usually accumulates—he or she is overweight.

Maintaining acceptable weight can bring numerous health benefits. Extra weight puts extra stress on bones and joints, and may worsen arthritis or osteoporosis. Obesity has been associated with hypertension, adult-onset diabetes, certain forms of cancer and heart disease. In addition, excess pounds can complicate other health problems and restrict a person's mobility, which in itself can lead to health problems.

The keys to successful weight loss are moderation, balance and maintenance.

Suggested Daily Food Portions for a Low-Fat, Low-Cholesterol Diet

Food Group	Portion Size
Fruits and Vegetables	Four or more servings of ½ cup fruit or vegetable juice, ½ cup cooked fruit or vegetable or one medium (3-inch) fruit or vegetable
Breads, Cereals and Starchy Foods	Four or more servings of one slice bread, one cup dry cereal, ½ cup cooked cereal, pasta, rice or noodles, one tortilla, one cup popcorn or two graham crackers
Milk and Cheese	Two or more servings of one 8-oz. glass of low-fat or nonfat milk or buttermilk, one 8-oz. carton low-fat yogurt, 1 oz. low-fat cheese or ⅓ cup low-fat cottage cheese
Fish, Poultry, Meat, Dried Beans, Peas, Nuts, Egg Yolks	Maximum of two servings daily of 2-3 oz. meat, fish or poultry. Unlimited egg whites
Polyunsaturated Fats, Oils	Two tablespoons per day

Table 1:22

Sample Menus

The new AHA diet allows almost unlimited variety in menu planning. Following are a few sample dinner menus that are economical, easy to prepare, low in calories and fats, and good tasting.

Manicotti shells stuffed with chicken, spinach and mushrooms
Tossed green salad
Fresh fruit ice
Fortune cookies
Beverage

Poached fish fillets served with lemon or horseradish sauce
Broccoli
Baked potato
Ginger ale sherbet
Beverage

Homemade vegetable soup
Linguini with mushroom sauce
Tomato, onion and basil salad
Yogurt with fresh or frozen (unsweetened) strawberry topping
Beverage

For recipes and additional menu planning, consult *The American Heart Assocation Cookbook,* fourth edition (New York: McKay, 1984).

Table 1:23

Desirable Weight for Height

MEN

Height (in shoes)	Weight (when dressed) Small Frame	Medium Frame	Large Frame
5′2″	112–120	118–129	126–141
5′3″	115–123	121–133	129–144
5′5″	118–126	124–136	132–148
5′6″	121–129	127–139	135–152
5′7″	124–133	130–143	138–156
5′8″	128–137	134–147	142–161
5′9″	132–141	138–152	147–166
5′10″	136–145	142–156	151–170
5′11″	140–150	146–160	155–174
6′	148–158	154–170	159–179
6′1″	152–162	158–175	164–184
6′2″	156–167	162–180	168–189
6′3″	160–171	167–185	173–194
6′4″	164–175	172–190	182–204

WOMEN

Height (in shoes)	Weight (when dressed) Small Frame	Medium Frame	Large Frame
4′10″	92–98	96–101	104–119
4′11″	94–101	98–110	106–122
5′	96–104	101–113	100–125
5′1″	99–107	104–116	112–128
5′2″	102–110	107–119	115–131
5′3″	105–113	110–122	118–134
5′4″	108–116	113–126	121–138
5′5″	111–119	116–130	125–142
5′6″	114–123	120–135	129–146
5′7″	118–127	124–139	133–150
5′8″	122–131	128–143	137–154
5′9″	126–135	132–147	141–158
5′10″	130–140	136–151	145–163
5′11″	134–144	140–155	149–168
6′	138–148	144–159	153–173

Table 1:24

All too often, however, we resort to crash or fad diets. Most of these diets have little regard for proper nutrition or good eating habits. They all have one common denominator—a reduced intake of calories, which is why all of them, when followed for any period of time, result in weight loss. But studies have found that more than 95 percent of the people who lose weight on a crash diet regain it within a few months. Typically, a person will "go on a diet," lose the desired 10 or 15 pounds, and then go off the diet and resume the same old eating habits that produced the original weight problem. The secret to long-term weight control is to forget about dieting, and instead, modify eating habits to prevent taking in more calories than are burned up.

While this may sound simple, in practice it can be quite difficult. Eating habits are firmly ingrained from an early age, and most people find them difficult to change, especially if they try to tackle everything all at once. If is far better to concentrate on one or two of the most important areas at a time and gradually adopt a more healthful eating pattern. For example, if you determine that reducing your intake of fats and cholesterol should take priority, then concentrate on these first, and leave things like cutting down on sugar and salt for later, after you have succeeded with your initial goals.

Although most overweight problems can be traced to consuming more calories than are expended, with the excess being stored as body fat, there are instances in which the overweight is related to hormonal problems or other diseases. Certain drugs, such as cortisone or other steroid hormones, also promote weight gain. And some people have a genetic tendency to gain weight: They simply metabolize food more efficiently than others and do not need as many calories. Even people who do have a genetic predisposition to gain weight can alter their metabolism through crash dieting to produce the same effect. When the body is deprived of calories, it will naturally slow down its metabolism to conserve energy, burning calories at a lower rate. After all, the body's centers of metabolism and appetite control do not differentiate between deliberate dieting and involuntary starvation. They know only that the body is running short of fuel and will reset the metabolism rate at a lower level to conserve it. When the dieting ends, the body does not necessarily reset the metabolic rate at its previous level. As a result, a person may gain weight more rapidly than ever.

Always check with your doctor before making any major dietary change, especially if you are more than 20 percent overweight. Successful weight loss requires a balanced, flexible eating plan that will produce a gradual weight loss and a permanent change in eating habits. Many people find that joining a group, such as Weight Watchers or Overeaters Anonymous, makes this easier to achieve than solo dieting.

Exercise is an essential part of any weight-reduction program. In addition to burning up calories (see Table 1:25), exercise improves muscle tone and provides a trimmer look. Exercise will also help maintain the body's normal metabolic set point, in addition to helping control appetite.

Calorie Expenditures for Physical Activities

Activity	Calories Used Per Hour
strolling at 1mph	150
walking at 2 mph	200
walking at 4 mph	350
racewalking	500
jogging	600
running	800–1000
cycling at 5 mph	250
cycling at 10 mph	450
tennis (doubles)	350–450
tennis (singles)	400–500
swimming (breast or backstroke)	300–600
swimming (crawl)	700–900
acrobic dancing	600–800
ballet exercises/ calisthenics	300
handball	650–800
cross-country skiing	700–1000

Table 1:25

▪ *Determining Your Caloric Needs*

All of us need a certain number of calories each day simply to carry on essential body processes, such as circulation, maintaining body temperature, digestion, breathing, etc. This is called the basal metabolic rate (BMR), the body's minimum daily need for calories. To calculate your approximate BMR, multiply your weight (in pounds) by 10. Men should add twice their weight to this, and women their weight. For example, the calculation for an 180-pound man would be:

$$180 \times 10 = 1800 + 360 = 2160$$
calories per day

or for a 125-pound woman:

$$125 \times 10 = 1250 + 125 = 1375$$
calories per day

Now add to this the number of calories you burn up in your various daily activities—working, sitting, watching TV, walking the dog, etc. (See Chapter 2, Exercise—The Key to Lifelong Fitness, for tables on the calorie expenditure of various activities.) As a rule of thumb, you can use the formula in Table 1:26, Average Caloric Needs, to calculate how many calories you need to sustain your BMR and normal activities.

A reasonable goal for a weight-loss program is a loss of one or two pounds a week. One pound equals 3500 calories, so consuming 500 calories less than is burned up each day should produce the desired weight loss. The 500 calories can come from a combination of decreased food intake and increased physical activity. For example, if you cut your food intake by 300 calories a day—a very modest reduction that can be accomplished by simply eating smaller portions of most foods or making substitutions (for example, a 90-calorie apple instead of a 350-calorie piece of apple pie; a 90-calorie glass of skim milk instead of a 150-calorie glass of whole milk)—and increase exercise by 200 calories (for example, a 45-minute brisk walk), you will accomplish your goal of one pound a week. You can double the weight loss by cutting your food intake by 600 calories (but don't go below 1000 to 1200 calories a day) and doubling your exercise—swim for 45 minutes in addition to a 45-minute walk or an equivalent activity.

Average Caloric Needs

Divide your weight by 2.2 to arrive at kilograms.

Weight Status	Activity Level: Sedentary	Moderately Active	Very Active
overweight	15–20	25	35
normal	25	30	40
underweight	30	35	45

Examples: If you are a sedentary housewife weighing 160 pounds (about 73 kilograms) who should lose 25 pounds, you would calculate your daily calorie needs using column one for overweight individuals. If you aim to consume 18 calories per day per kilogram, your total intake should be about 1314, and your weight will come down.

If you are a moderately active and normal weight woman weighing 132 pounds (60 kilograms), your daily caloric intake should be 30 calories per kilogram, or about 1800.

If you are very active, weighing 120 pounds (about 54.5 kilograms) but should weigh about 132, you should consume about 45 calories per kilogram, or about 2450 calories per day.

Table 1:26

▪ *Keeping a Food Diary*

Almost any weight-loss program is doomed unless it is accompanied by a conscious effort to adopt more healthful food habits. And to alter food habits, it is essential to know where you are going wrong. Most people actually have no idea how much they eat and under what circumstances. Many overweight people insist that they eat very little and still gain weight. When they keep careful food diaries, they are surprised to learn just how much they do eat. Keeping a food diary before starting on a diet is a good way to analyze current eating habits to find out what triggers eating—for instance, social situations, boredom, stress—and at what times during the day one's temptation to eat is greatest.

Use the sample daily food record (Table 1:27) to get started. Table 1:28, which shows how to analyze a food diary and revise one's menus accordingly, gives an example of putting a food diary to use.

The Columbia University Institute of Human Nutrition has developed a model weight-loss plan, which appears in Table 1:29. This plan includes food choices from all the basic groups (Table 1:30). Total calories can be divided into five or six meals, if preferred, instead of three, which may keep hunger from tempting a person to overeat when mealtime finally arrives. (See Table 1:31 for sample weight-loss menus.) A supply of nutritious, low-calorie snacks such as fresh vegetables or whole-grain crackers will stave off hunger and prevent overeating if they are incorporated into the day's eating plan and caloric allowance. Eating slowly will allow the body to register the feeling of fullness, and serving smaller portions on luncheon (instead of dinner) plates will reduce the temptation to overfill one's plate and prevent feelings of deprivation.

The diet plan developed by Columbia University's Institute of Human Nutrition is designed to bring about gradual weight loss with a nutritionally balanced, varied and flexible eating plan. But remember, any weight-loss plan, no matter how balanced and sensible, will fail if you view it as a temporary measure to achieve a short-term goal, after which you can slip back into your former eating habits and forget all you have learned.

SAMPLE DAILY FOOD RECORD

Date ____________

Check Type of Day: Workday Non-Workday

Place:				
H*	**A†**	**Time**	**Food eaten**	**Amount**

*H = Home
†A = Away

Table 1:27

Analysis

Mr. Greene, who is 40 pounds overweight and has high blood pressure, insists he's a light eater, and for most of the day that's true. Up until 6 p.m. he had only consumed 705 calories, less than a third of what his nutritionist determined was his total daily requirement. But from 6 p.m. until he went to bed he consumed a whopping 4545 calories. He joined a couple of friends at a local pub for a beer and ended up munching on a cup of salted peanuts—bad for both his diet and hypertension. His wife, thinking that chicken is healthier than Mr. Greene's favorite steak, served a frozen fast-food variety, loaded with extra fat, for dinner. The same amount of skinless roast chicken would have had a third the calories. Similarly, a baked potato would have had less than half the calories of his french fries. By adding 3 tablespoons of blue cheese dressing to his salad, he turned a 15-calorie dish into one with 235. For dessert, a piece of fruit or frozen ice would have had fewer calories than the ice cream. Popcorn and a low-calorie beer or seltzer would have saved more than 1000 calories while he watched TV. A before-bed snack of a glass of skim milk and one cookie again would have saved 245 calories.

His diet, typical of what millions of Americans eat every day in varying quantities, is high in fat and sugar, low in complex carbohydrates and fiber. By increasing the last two and distributing the food more evenly through the day to prevent extreme late-day hunger, Mr. Greene could stay on his recommended 1500-calorie reducing diet and in the course of a year, lose his excess weight. In the process, he also may be able to bring his high blood pressure under control. What's more, he would acquire eating habits that would help maintain his proper weight for life.

A Sample Food Diary

Name: Alan Greene **Date: 7/20/86**

Food Eaten	Time/Circumstance	Calories
coffee (cr. & sug.)	7:15 a.m. Bkfst.	40
orange juice		110
donut		130
coffee (cr. & sug.)	10:30 a.m. Break	40
yogurt (fruit)		200
coffee (cr. & sug.)	12:30 p.m. Lunch	40
Coke	4 p.m. Break	145
1 beer	6 p.m. Relaxing after work	150
peanuts (1 c.)		1200
Ky. fried chicken (3 pieces)	7:30 p.m. Dinner/family	500
french fries (1 g.)		220
lettuce salad		15
blue cheese dressing		220
ice cream (1 c.)		300
coffee (cr. & sug.)		40
2 beers	8:30–10 p.m. Watching TV ballgame	300
potato chips (8 oz.)		1170
ice cream (½ c.)	10:30 p.m. Hungry/before bed	150
3 cookies		280
Total calories		5250

Mr. Greene's Revised Menu

Food Eaten	Time/Circumstance	Calories
½ grapefruit	7:15 a.m. Bkfst.	40
shredded wheat		90
skim milk (1 c.)		90
1 slice whole wheat toast		55
1 tsp. low-calorie margarine		15
coffee (sk. mk./½ tsp. sugar)		15
skim milk	10:30 a.m. Break	90
bran muffin		100
sliced turkey sandwich on rye bread	12:30 p.m. Lunch	250
apple, medium		90
coffee (sk. mk./sugar)		15
seltzer	4 p.m. Break	0
2 RyKrisp crackers		45
roast chicken breast	7:30 p.m. Dinner/family	180
baked potato/1 tsp. margarine		100
green salad/lite dressing		40
broccoli/with lemon		35
pear		60
coffee (sk. mk./sugar)		15
popcorn (1 c. unbuttered)	8:30–10:30 p.m. Watching TV ballgame	10
seltzer		0
skim milk	10:30 p.m. Before bed	90
1 low-calorie cookie		15
Total calories		1440

Table 1:28

Basics for Menu Planning

List	Total Calories 1000	1200	1500	1800
1. Free foods	Unlimited	Unlimited	Unlimited	Unlimited
2. Vegetables	2	2	2	2
3. Fruits	3	3	3	3
4. Starches	3	5	7	9
5. Proteins	6	6	7	7
6. Milk	2	2	2	3
7. Fats	2	2	6	7

Source: *Nutrition and Health*, vol. 1, no. 2 (1979), Columbia University Institute of Human Nutrition.
Note: See Table 1:30, Food Choices.

Table 1:29

Food Choices

List 1: Free Foods
(no specific amounts)
bouillon
chicory
Chinese cabbage
clear broth
coffee
endive
escarole
gelatin, unsweetened
lemon
lettuce (all kinds)
lime
mustard
parsley
pickle, sour or unsweetened dill
radishes
soy sauce
tea
vinegar
watercress

List 2: Vegetables
(½ c. cooked or 1 c. raw, except as indicated)
all leafy greens, except those in List 1
asparagus
bean sprouts
beans, green or wax
beets
broccoli
Brussels sprouts
cabbage (all kinds)
carrots
cauliflower
celery
cucumbers
eggplant
ketchup (2 tbsp.)
mushrooms
okra
onions
peppers, red or green
rutabaga
sauerkraut
summer squash
tomato or vegetable juice (6 oz.)
tomatoes

List 3: Fruits
apple, ½ medium
applesauce, ½ c.
apricots, dried, 4 halves
apricots, fresh, 2 medium
bananas, ½ small
blueberries, ½ c.
cantaloupe, ¼ medium
cherries, 10 large
dates, 2
figs, dried, 1 small
fruit cocktail, canned, ½ c.
grapefruit, ½ small
grapes, 12
honeydew, ⅓ medium
mango, ½ small
nectarine, 1 small
orange, 1 small
papaya, ⅓ medium
peach, 1 medium
pear, 1 small
pineapple, ½ c.
prunes, dried, 2
raisins, 2 tbsp.
strawberries, ¾ c.
tangerine, 1 large
watermelon, 1 c. cubed
JUICES:
apple, pineapple, ⅓ c.
grape, prune, ¼ c.
grapefruit, orange, ½ c.

List 4: Starches
BREADS:
any loaf, 1 slice
bagel, ½
bun (hamburger or hot dog), ½
cornbread, 1½″ cube
dinner roll, 1, 2″
English muffin, ½
tortilla, 1, 6″ diam.
CEREALS:
bran, 5 tbsp.
dry flakes, ⅔ c.
dry puffed, 1½ c.
hot cereal, ½ c.
pasta, ½ c.
rice, ½ c.
wheatgerm, 2 tbsp.
DESSERTS:
angel food cake, 1½″ square
fat-free sherbet, ½ c.
VEGETABLES:
beans or peas (dried), ½ c. cooked
corn, ⅓ c. (½ ear)
parsnips, ⅔ c.
potato, white, 1 small or ½ c.
pumpkin, ¾ c.
winter squash, ½ c.
CRACKERS:
graham, 2, 2½″
matzo, 4 x 6″
Melba toast, 4
oyster, 20
pretzels, 8 rings
RyKrisps, 3
saltines, 5
ALCOHOL:
beer, 5 oz.
whiskey, 1 oz.
wine, dry, 2½ oz.
wine, sweet, 1½ oz.

List 5: Proteins
beef, dried, chipped, 1 oz.
beef, lamb, pork, veal, lean only, 1 oz.
cottage cheese, uncreamed, ¼ c.
egg, 1 medium
fish, 1 oz.
hard cheese, ½ oz.
lobster, 1 small tail
oysters, clams, shrimp, 5 medium
peanut butter, 2 tsp.
poultry, no skin, 1 oz.
salmon, pink, canned, ¼ c.
tuna (in water), ¼ c.

List 6: Milk
buttermilk, fat-free, 1 c.
1%-fat milk, 7 oz.
skim milk, 1 c.
yogurt, plain, made with nonfat milk, ¾ c.

List 7: Fats
avocado, ⅛ of 4″ diam.
bacon, crisp, 1 slice
butter, margarine, 1 tsp.
French dressing, 1 tbsp.
mayonnaise, 1 tsp.
oil, 1 tsp.
olives, 5 small
peanuts, 10
Roquefort dressing, 2 tsp.
Thousand Island dressing, 2 tsp.
walnuts, 6 small

Table 1:30

Sample Weight-Loss Menus

The following menus show how you can space food through the day to prevent excessive hunger, stay within calorie limits and still consume an interesting, healthful diet.

1200 Calories

BREAKFAST
¼ cantaloupe
1½ c. puffed wheat
1 c. skim milk
Tea/coffee

MIDMORNING SNACK
½ bagel/1 tsp. margarine
¼ c. herbed cottage cheese

LUNCH
¼ c. tuna with 1 tsp. mayonnaise and lettuce on a bun
Sliced tomatoes
Apple
Tea/coffee

MIDAFTERNOON SNACK
RyKrisp crackers/1 oz. Swiss cheese
Skim milk

DINNER
Clear broth soup with pasta or rice
2 oz. roast chicken
Broccoli
Lettuce and endive salad with lemon juice
Yogurt with fresh berry topping

1500 Calories

BREAKFAST
Orange
½ c. Wheatena/½ c. skim milk
½ English muffin/1 tsp. margarine
Tea/coffee

MIDMORNING SNACK
¼ c. herbed cottage cheese
RyKrisp crackers
Tea/coffee

LUNCH
Tomato/rice soup
2 oz. turkey breast/1 tsp. mayonnaise/lettuce/rye bread
Tea/coffee

MIDAFTERNOON SNACK
Crackers
2 tsp. peanut butter

DINNER
Fruit cup
Chili/rice
Green salad with oil and vinegar dressing
Sherbet

BEFORE BED
1 c. skim milk
Pear

1800 calories

BREAKFAST
½ grapefruit
Shredded wheat/½ banana/skim milk
Boiled egg
1 slice whole wheat toast/margarine
Tea/coffee

MIDMORNING SNACK
Small corn muffin
1 c. skim milk

LUNCH
Spaghetti/tomato and meat sauce
Green salad/oil and vinegar dressing
Angel food cake
Tea/coffee

MIDAFTERNOON SNACK
½ c. raw vegetables with ¼ c. herbed cottage cheese

DINNER
Clear soup
Chinese stir-fry dinner (sprouts, tofu, Chinese cabbage, strips of lean beef, soy sauce, peanut oil)
Rice
Green salad with dressing
Stewed pear
Tea/coffee

BEFORE BED
¾ c. yogurt flavored with cinnamon

Source: Menus adapted from *Health & Nutrition* newsletter, Columbia University School of Public Health, vol. 1, no. 7.

Table 1:31

❑ VEGETARIAN DIETS

Many of us associate vegetarian diets with rebellious young people, offbeat religious sects, or boring regimens of seeds, nuts and beans. Actually, there are many different kinds of vegetarian diets, and when approached with common sense and sound nutritional principles, they can be varied, interesting and healthful—naturally low in cholesterol and saturated fats, high in the complex carbohydrates, vitamins and minerals.

Not all vegetarian diets are the same

Types of Vegetarians

- Strict vegetarians or vegans: Diet provides no animal foods, not even milk, cheese or eggs.
- Lactovegetarians: Diet does not include meat, fish or eggs, but milk, cheese and other dairy products are allowed.
- Ovolacto vegetarians: Eggs are added to the lacto-vegetarian diet.
- Part-time vegetarians: Diet is mostly ovolacto vegetarian, with occasional additions of fish or poultry.

Table 1:32

(see Table 1:32, Types of Vegetarians). Those who eat milk, eggs and other dairy products, or those who will occasionally have fish, have no trouble getting enough complete proteins. Others who eat only plant foods will need to match vegetable proteins to ensure that they consume all of the needed amino acids—the building blocks that make complete proteins. (See Table 1:3 back on page 12.)

▪ *Potential Problems with Vegetarian Diets*

Aside from the potential problem of inadequate or incomplete protein, many vegetarian regimens may fall short of providing enough iron and vitamin B_{12}. Iron is added to many foods, including fortified cereals and enriched bread and pasta; it is also found in raisins and other dried fruits, nuts, dried beans and peas, blackstrap molasses and green leafy vegetables. Cooking acidic foods in cast iron pots also can increase dietary iron.

Vitamin B_{12} occurs naturally only in meat and other animal products and some types of seaweed, but it is added to fortified breakfast cereals and brewer's yeast. Eventually, some strict vegetarians may need supplements, although deficiency symptoms or pernicious anemia are rare except in alcoholics or others who are malnourished. Getting adequate calcium may be a problem for strict vegetarians who shun milk and milk products—the best sources of this mineral. Those who do not eat dairy products should emphasize dried peas and beans, green leafy vegetables, citrus fruits and nuts, all of which contain calcium. Women, in particular, should be sure they are getting enough calcium; those who are strict vegetarians and do not drink milk may want to discuss the possible need for a supplement with their physician. With proper planning and balance, however, most vegetarians do not need extra supplements.

❑ Special Problems of the Elderly

As a whole, our elderly population is probably the most poorly nourished. Social and economic reasons account for much of this malnourishment. People living alone, sometimes without adequate cooking or refrigeration facilities, subsist on tea, toast, canned soups, candy and snack foods. Many have difficulty shopping and still others have little incentive to prepare themselves nutritious and appetizing meals.

Economics may often be the primary cause of poor nutrition in the elderly. Developing thrifty shopping habits with an eye to sound nutrition can solve some of the problems in the food/money equation (see Table 1:33). A pound of pasta and fresh tomatoes and squash can be the ingredients of a healthy meal and are less expensive than many convenience foods. (See Table 1:34 for menu-planning guide and sample menus.) Often, an older person on a fixed income is forced to choose between missing the rent payment or medical bills and cutting back on food. Many older people are unaware that they may be eligible for food stamps; others are too proud to apply. A phone call to the local food stamp office or the Department of Aging will clarify the requirements.

Cutbacks in government-supported

meal programs, such as Meals on Wheels or meals served at senior citizen centers, have been especially hard for the elderly poor. Many older people are unable to get to senior citizen centers, community centers, churches or other sites of meal programs for the elderly. And, of course, availability and programs vary widely from area to area. What may be readily available in an urban area may be totally lacking in a rural or suburban community. Still, there are many resources and very often, people simply do not know what is available. The local Department of Aging, the Health Department, Visiting Nurse Association, senior citizen centers or the individual's own physician, minister or

Food Tips for Older People

When shopping:

- Plan menus for several days or a week. Don't forget to include leftovers in your planning.
- Buy items in quantities that you are sure you will use—for example, a half carton of eggs or a pint of milk. Don't be afraid to ask a grocer to open packages of produce so you can buy the quantity you need.
- When buying fruit, select only one or two pieces that are ripe for immediate eating, and others that are less ripe for later use.
- If access to a supermarket is a problem, check with your local agency on aging or social service department to see if there is a bus service or other transportation program for people in your situation. Consider working out an exchange with a neighbor, for example, baby-sitting in exchange for transportation to a shopping center.

If you are on a limited budget:

- Check whether you are eligible for food stamps, Meals on Wheels and other food programs.
- Check with your local community center or senior citizens' program for other assistance programs that may apply to you.
- Check newspaper ads or store circulars for specials.
- Use coupons, but only for items you use and need.
- Read nutrition labels.
- Look for unbranded or store-brand items.
- Buy fresh fruits and vegetables in season.
- Look for less expensive sources of protein (peanut butter, legumes, liver, chicken, canned fish, eggs).
- Avoid "health" or "organic" foods, which are more expensive and no more healthful than regular foods.
- If you have freezer space, use it for extras and leftovers.

If you lack a refrigerator, try stocking the following items:

- Nonfat dried milk
- Peanut butter
- Enriched or whole-grain cereals and breads (small loaf)
- Canned fish, stew, chunky soups, hash, pork and beans
- Dried fruits and nuts
- Dried peas and beans

If chewing is a problem:

- Use fish, ground meat, baked beans, cottage cheese and other "soft" protein foods.
- Cook stews, soups and casseroles (freeze leftovers for future use).
- Chop or puree vegetables and fruits.

If your appetite is poor or you eat alone:

- Plan regular meals and try to occasionally exchange cooking with a friend.
- Resist eating out of a pan; treat yourself to an attractive table and eating from real dishes.
- A glass of wine may help perk up appetite (but don't substitute alcohol for food).
- A pet may provide needed companionship.
- Try to get some exercise each day, even if it's only a walk to the corner and back.
- Turn on some music or a favorite radio or TV program while you eat.

If you are trying to lose weight:

- Eat smaller portions.
- Use low-fat milk, diet margarine and other low-calorie foods.
- Eat more often; don't let yourself get too hungry. Five small meals consumed throughout the day will prevent you from getting so hungry that you end up overeating at night.
- Avoid fad or crash diets.
- Eat pasta, fruits, vegetables and sources of vegetable protein (dried peas, beans, rice, etc.) instead of meat. If you eat meat, buy low-fat cuts and trim off all visible fat. A gram of fat contains 9 calories, compared to 4 calories in a gram of carbohydrate or protein foods. Roughage or high-fiber foods contain fewer calories because the fiber is not digested.

If you are trying to gain weight:

- Use whole milk and fortify drinks with an egg, ice cream or dried milk.
- Eat more often; include snacks of cheese, peanut butter or nuts in your diet.
- Add cheese or cream cheese to soups, casseroles and other dishes.

Table 1:33

All-Purpose Menu Planning

Following are basic menus designed to meet the nutritional needs of older adults. Serving sizes should be adjusted according to weight needs. Eat small portions if you are trying to lose weight; moderate if you are maintaining your present weight. If you need to gain weight, eat more frequently.

BREAKFAST
1 serving of citrus or other fruit high in vitamin C
1–2 servings of grain food
1 serving of meat or protein food
1 serving of milk or milk product

LUNCH
1 serving of meat or protein food
1 serving of fruit or vegetable
1 serving of grain food
1 serving of milk or milk product

DINNER
1 serving of meat or protein food
2 servings of vegetables or fruit
1–2 servings of grain food
1 serving of milk or milk product

Sample Menus on a Moderate to Low Budget

BREAKFAST
Orange juice or half of grapefruit
Whole wheat toast with peanut butter
Glass of milk
or
Orange juice or fresh berries
Poached egg
Bagel or whole wheat toast
Milk

LUNCH
Tuna sandwich (made with rye or pumpernickel bread)
Canned tomato soup (made with milk)
or
Macaroni and cheese
Lettuce and tomato salad

DINNER
Fish fillet
Broccoli
Rice or potato
Yogurt with fresh fruit topping (e.g., banana or sliced strawberries in season)
or
Beef stew (with carrots and potatoes)
Tossed salad
Rolls
Rice pudding

Table 1:34

rabbi are good sources of information.

Very often, older people complain that they simply do not feel like eating. Taste and smell tend to decrease with age, which is another reason some elderly people may eat less. Some try to compensate for this by adding extra salt. A better alternative is to use different spices and pungent herbs like thyme, sage or basil. Serving foods that have always been favorites in a way that is visually pleasing can also be an incentive to eating.

Most of us dislike eating alone, and the elderly are no exception. Try to organize a group of people who are in similar circumstances, and arrange group meals where each person brings one dish and everyone has company for dinner. Or a different person can host the dinner for the group each day of the week.

▪ *Other Special Problems*

Chewing. If chewing is a problem, a blender or food grinder will be helpful. The diet should emphasize soft but nutrient-rich foods like fish and chicken, yogurt and eggs. In many cases, proper-fitting dentures will eliminate chewing problems, so a dental checkup is important.

Medications. More than 85 percent of all people 65 and older take at least one prescription drug, and large numbers take several. The more drugs consumed, the greater the chance of drug-drug and drug-food interactions. Many medications alter the nutritional status of, or the way the body uses, food. For example, large numbers of older people take diuretics for high blood pressure, edema or congestive heart failure. These drugs can lead to excessive loss of potassium, calcium and other important minerals. The problem may be compounded by a diet that is inadequate in these nutrients.

Many drugs cause a loss of appetite; others may produce nausea, constipation, diarrhea and other side effects. One should be aware of possible adverse reactions and side effects associated with various medications, and report these to one's doctor if they occur. Sometimes the problem can be remedied by the timing of medications: Some should be taken with meals, others before or after eating. Remember, too, that alcohol is a drug and can produce adverse reactions when combined with other drugs. It also affects metabolism, and excessive alcohol consumption can cause serious nutritional deficiencies.

Constipation. Many older people complain of being constipated and frequently resort to overuse of laxatives. Not uncommonly, the constipation is a result of laxative abuse. Older people who have difficulty chewing may shun high-fiber foods in favor of soft, easy-to-eat items. Lack of exercise and inadequate fluid intake also can promote constipation. Some laxatives, such as mineral oil, decrease absorption of fat-soluble vitamins A, D, E and K. Others interfere with absorption of minerals and other important nutrients. Increasing the intake of foods that are high in fiber or roughage, yet still easy to chew, will help. Examples include whole-grain hot cereals like oatmeal or farina; whole-grain cold cereals like bran or wheat flakes; stewed or canned fruits; cooked dried beans, lentils or vegetables that are steamed until tender; brown rice; and salads made with lettuce, tomatoes and other "soft" greens or vegetables.

Indigestion. The production of gastric juices may decrease with age, resulting in increased susceptibility to digestive problems. A hiatal hernia, resulting in heartburn from a backflow of gastric juices from the stomach into the esophagus, also becomes more common with age. Eating small, frequent meals, avoiding foods that seem to promote stomach upsets, judicious use of antacids (some are also good sources of extra calcium), and avoiding lying down for an hour or two after eating usually will minimize the problem.

▪ *Nutrition Quackery*

Older people are particularly vulnerable to food faddism and nutrition quackery. Unfortunately, nutrition charlatans do not hesitate to prey upon older people, many of whom suffer from chronic diseases like arthritis, heart disease, cancer or diabetes, among others. Nutrition charlatans do not hesitate to promise that their particular diet, supplement or potion will help a person recapture lost youth, overcome infirmities, live longer and so on and on. Their products tend to be expensive and even harmful, or at least worthless. It is far better to spend the money on wholesome nutritious foods than on an assortment of supplements, expensive "organic" foods and other unproven nutritional remedies.

One of the most common of the questionable nutrition practices involves promoting megadoses of vitamins and minerals. Many people who shun taking needed medications because they fear side effects think nothing of taking pharmacologic doses of vitamin C, A, E, B complex and other nutrients. Whenever a nutrient is taken in amounts that exceed what the body can utilize, it takes on the property of a drug and carries a risk of side effects and adverse reactions. Before taking any vitamin or mineral in excess of the RDA, a person should check with his or her doctor.

Similarly, people should avoid potions such as Herbalife that are marketed as nutritional products, but in reality have little or no nutritional value and may even be harmful. There are no licensing requirements or educational standards for "nutritionists." While many may be well-qualified and dispense legitimate advice, many others have little or no qualifications and trade in nutritional nonsense.

The problem is distressingly common. At hearings before the Senate Committee on Aging in 1983, those testifying repeatedly noted that nutrition and medical quackery was the most frequent and lucrative fraud perpetrated on the elderly. In 1984, Representative Claude Pepper held a congressional hearing into "Quackery: A 10-Billion-Dollar Scandal," at which it was again stressed that the elderly and ill are the prime victims of nutrition charlatans. Many call themselves "doctor," but investigation discloses that their degrees are from mail-order Ph.D. mills. Dr. Victor Herbert, a leading nutrition educator and foe of nutrition fraud, demonstrated how easy it is to get a "nutrition degree, complete with impressive-looking certificate" when he enrolled his dog Sassafras and cat Charlie as professional members of the American Association of Nutrition and Dietary Consultants. All he had to do was fill out forms and send in $50 for each certificate. "At least 10,000 people have obtained similar certificates," he says, "and it is safe to assume that many, if not most, are now practicing nutrition 'therapists.' "

There are numerous legitimate sources of sound nutritional advice and information. Anyone who claims to be a nutrition therapist should have a degree from an institution accredited by the Council of Postsecondary Accreditation in Washington, D.C. Be particularly wary of strange-sounding degrees like Doctor of Naturopathy (N.D.), Doctor of Metaphysics (Ms.D.) or Doctor of Holistic Medicine (DHM). A qualified registered dietitian (RD) or physician who has taken extra courses in nutrition is your best source of nutritional counseling.

2

EXERCISE —THE KEY TO LIFELONG FITNESS

Increasingly, exercise is emerging as one of the best ways to avoid many of the infirmities associated with growing older. In fact, recent studies show that many problems thought to be chronic diseases of aging are really symptoms of disuse. A regular program of exercise may help retain joint movement as well as strengthen muscles and thereby counter the effects of age-related arthritis. It also is vital in maintaining healthy bones and is part of prevention and the treatment regimen for osteoporosis. People who exercise have an enhanced feeling of well-being and are not as vulnerable to depression. Active people have fewer problems in controlling their weight. They sleep better and feel better about themselves. And, of course, the benefits of regular exercise in improving cardiovascular and lung functioning are now an accepted tenet of modern medicine.

❑ Getting Started

Many over-50 people, especially those who have led relatively sedentary lives, often feel that it is too late for them to take up an exercise program, that the damage of their inactivity is too advanced to overcome. The good news is, it is never too late to start exercising. Every day people of all ages and physical conditions are discovering that even moderate exercise can make a huge difference in the way they feel and look. Granted, there are dozens of excuses to avoid exercise: "I don't have the time," "I don't have the right shoes (equipment, clothes, etc.)," "It's boring" . . . and on and on. But none of these are really valid. As little as 20 to 30 minutes a day, four times a week—time all of us waste watching TV, gossiping on the telephone or performing any number of other nonessential tasks—is all it takes to get started on an exercise regimen. As for fancy clothing and equipment, all that is really needed are a pair of comfortable shoes and a loose-fitting pair of sweatpants and T-shirt for most activities.

When embarking on an exercise program, many of us make the mistake of trying to overcome the effects of years of sedentary living overnight. We often equate exercise with jogging, aerobic dancing or some other very intense activity when, in fact, walking at a moderately brisk pace, combined with stretching exercises to keep joints flexible and prevent muscle strain, is preferable to the jarring motions of jogging or dancing. Especially when dancing, an exercise which appears deceptively light and easy, remember not to get carried away. The tortoise approach—slow and steady wins the race—is much more effective than trying to do too much too fast and winding up sidelined with an avoidable orthopedic injury or some other physical problem.

❑ Designing Your Own Exercise Program

A number of factors should be considered in developing your exercise program. After appropriate medical tests (see Table 2:1, The Pre-Exercise Checkup), your doctor will be able to suggest appropriate activities that take into consideration any medical problems you may have. In addition, an exercise physiologist or sports medicine specialist may be consulted regarding flexibility, muscle strength, percentage of body fat and other factors that affect exercise ability. When beginning a new program of exercise, remember that different types of physical activity require different sets of muscles. Proficiency at one form of activity does not mean a person can perform other exercises at the same level of intensity.

In developing an exercise program, many people overlook one of the most important factors, namely, personal likes and dislikes. If you feel uncomfortable in water, swimming obviously is not a good exercise choice for you, even though it may be one of the most physically beneficial. People who enjoy companionship and have a good sense of rhythm may enjoy aerobic dancing, while others, who feel awkward and dislike dance music, may find this activity more of a chore than pleasure. Competitive individuals may do better if they select tennis, handball or some other sport; more solitary types may prefer walking or a stationary bicycle. Table 2:2, Matching Exercise to Your Lifestyle, provides guidance in picking activities that are particularly suited to your personality and preferences.

There are things to do to make the exercise period more interesting. Riding a stationary bicycle can be timed with an interesting television program or the morning or evening news. Walking to the store to get the newspaper can be substituted for having it delivered.

Your overall level of fitness also is a factor in developing your own exercise program. Even without a medical checkup, you can get a good idea of your level of fitness by timing yourself on a brisk walk. If you can walk a mile in less than 15 minutes, chances are you are reasonably fit.

The Pre-Exercise Checkup

Before embarking on an exercise conditioning program, all people over the age of 50 should have the following medical examinations:

- An exercise tolerance (or stress) test. This entails exercising on a treadmill or exercise bicycle while undergoing continuous electrocardiogram (EKG) monitoring of the heart. The test will determine safe levels of activity and also may help detect undiagnosed heart abnormalities.
- Blood pressure measurement. People with high blood pressure have a higher-than-average risk of a heart attack and may require a special exercise prescription.
- Evaluation of blood cholesterol.

In addition, people with specific health problems may require additional examinations. Depending upon the problem, these may include:

- *Diabetes.* Measurement of blood glucose before and after exercise.
- *Arthritis.* Evaluation of joints to design exercises to increase mobility without damage to structures.
- *Emphysema, asthma and other lung disorders.* Pulmonary function tests.
- *Obesity.* Evaluation of heart and joint function.
- *Circulatory problems.* Evaluation of heart function.

Table 2:1

Matching Exercise to Your Lifestyle

	Walking	Jogging	Competitive Running	Aerobic Dancing	Tennis (singles)	Tennis (doubles)	Cycling (indoors)	Cycling (outdoors)	Handball/Racquetball	Rope Jumping	Rowing (machine)	Rowing (outdoors)	Skating	Basketball	Mini-trampoline	Ballet	Cross-Country Skiing	Swimming	Exercise Class/Health Club	Mountain Climbing	Racewalking
You're competitive			•		•	•			•					•							•
You have joint problems*	•						•								•			•			•
You want to go it alone	•	•		•			•	•		•	•		•		•	•	•	•			•
You want companionship	•	•	•	•	•	•		•	•			•	•	•		•	•	•	•		•
You like a set routine	•	•		•			•	•		•	•		•		•	•		•	•		•
You want adventure								•				•					•			•	
You don't have much time							•			•	•				•						
You have loads of time	•	•		•	•	•		•	•			•	•	•		•	•	•	•	•	•
You're out of shape	•			•		•	•			•	•						•				
You have loads of endurance																					•
You have a heart problem*	•	•				•	•				•							•	•		
You are easily bored			•	•	•	•			•			•	•	•			•		•	•	
You want to be outdoors	•	•	•		•	•		•				•	•				•	•		•	•
You want to be indoors				•			•		•	•	•		•		•	•		•	•		
You're on a budget	•	•		•						•											
You are goal oriented			•		•	•			•					•						•	•

*Check with your doctor first.

Table 2:2

▪ *Types of Exercises*

There are three basic kinds of exercise:

Flexibility and stretching. Stretching and flexibility training acts as a holding action against loss of joint mobility. It loosens muscles, enabling them to relax, and prepares them for further exercise stress. Gently bending, extending or rotating the neck, shoulders, elbows, back, hips, knees and ankles increases the flexibility of tissues and protects against injury. (Figures 2:1 through 2:5 show basic stretching exercises.)

Aerobic and Endurance Activity. Rhythmic, repeated movement, done rapidly and long enough that breathing and heart rate become faster than usual, leads to improved efficiency of heart, lungs and muscles, as well as to an increase in their capacity to do work and withstand stress. The most basic and safest aerobic exercise is walking. Cycling, swimming and dancing are also enjoyable aerobic activities for older people. To be effective, aerobic conditioning should take place at least three times a week and be continued for at least half an hour. (People not in shape should work up to this level.) Stationary bicycles can be used indoors very effectively in inclement weather.

Strength building. Strength building such as weight lifting and other isometric activities increases muscle mass and also promotes improved muscle tone. Moderation should be the key to

Stretching Exercises

These exercises are designed to keep the body limber. They also can be used as warm-up exercises before more vigorous workouts.

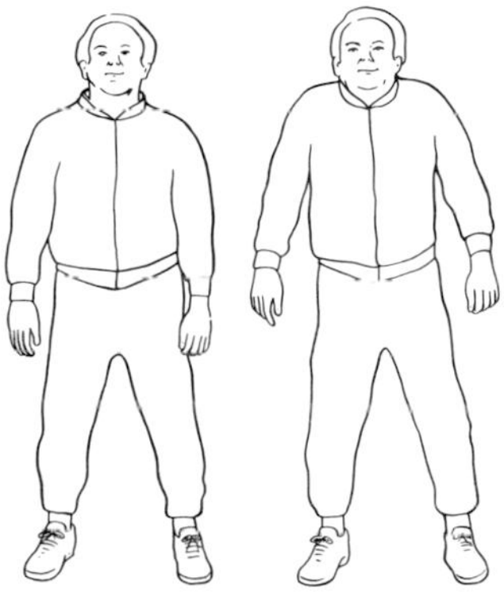

Figure 2:1.
Neck and shoulder stretch. Stand in a comfortable position. Tense and lift both shoulders while inhaling a deep breath. Hold for a count of 3, exhale and drop shoulders to resting position. Repeat 5 times.

Figure 2:2.
Arm and shoulder stretch. Stand in a comfortable position with arms straight out at a 45-degree angle. Slowly raise arms as high over your head as you can. Take a deep breath, hold for a count of 3, exhale and slowly lower arms. Repeat 10 times.

Figure 2:3.
Whole body stretch. Start from a standing position with arms raised to shoulder height. Extend one leg and slide arm down that side toward ankle while raising opposite arm above head. Do to a count of 5, repeat 10 times.

Figure 2:4.
Back stretch. Start from a standing position with feet about 18 inches apart and arms extended at shoulder height. To a count of 7, bring arms forward until hands touch and slowly bend forward and try to touch toes of one foot. Keep knees as straight as possible. Using alternate sides, repeat 10 times.

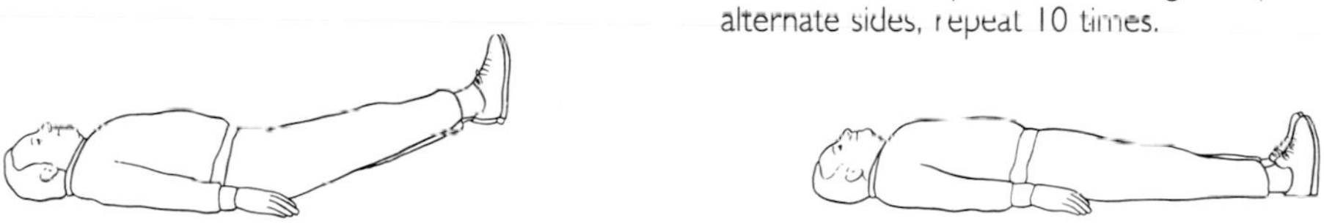

Figure 2:5.
Lower back and leg stretch. Start by lying flat on floor with arms at side and toes pointed upward. Keeping upper body flat on floor, slowly raise both legs 4 to 6 inches off floor. Hold for a count of 3 and slowly lower. Repeat 5 to 10 times.

strength building, especially for older people. Age entails the loss of a certain amount of muscle mass, which can be minimized or even reversed to a degree by strength building. These exercises also protect bones and soft tissues from injury.

An ideal exercise regimen will provide a balance of these basic types of exercise. Remember, the benefit of any exercise is really the product of two factors: the intrinsic value of the activity and the ability to do it regularly. The highest gain is likely to come from activity that can be begun with a minimum of fuss, bother and travel time. It shouldn't feel like punishment (or you won't keep doing it), but it does have to feel like exertion. Listen to the body signals. Soreness in unused muscles is common after beginning exercise, but pain is a signal to rest the body.

▪ *When to Expect Results*

Most people begin to see the benefits of regular conditioning exercise within a few weeks. True physical fitness is the ability to exercise at or near your body's maximum potential, and that may take up to three months of gradual buildup to reach. Studies have found that a year of regular conditioning exercise can bring the body back to the level that it was ten years previously. Unfortunately, there are no shortcuts to achieving your full potential, but getting in shape is not as difficult as many people assume. And despite what you hear, it should not be painful. Pain is a warning sign that should not be ignored; it means that you are trying to do too much too fast or that you have injured a muscle, tendon or other structure. Minor soreness that comes from using long dormant muscles may be relieved by a heating pad or warm bath; a little massage at the point of soreness also may help. The sore muscles should be rested for a day or two, although gentle stretching and moderate walking usually will not provoke further pain. If the pain worsens or the soreness persists for more than a couple of days, consult your doctor.

Frequency, intensity and duration all are important in a conditioning exercise program. Most conditioning programs require a minimum of three or four 20- to 30-minute sessions a week, preferably on alternating days; and some exercise physiologists recommend four or five sessions. Most exercise physiologists caution against daily workouts because the body needs a day off now and then to allow for muscle growth and repair, and to heal the minor injuries that may occur. As we grow older, the repair process may be slower. In short, heed your body's warning signs: Slow down if it tells you you are doing too much too fast. The level of intensity depends upon physical condition, but for most people, the pulse rate is the best indicator of whether or not the exercise is sufficiently vigorous to produce a conditioning effect. (See Table 2:3, Target Pulse Ranges.)

▪ *How to Determine Your Exercise Potential*

Your pulse rate, or number of heartbeats per minute, is a key indication of whether you are exercising in your conditioning zone. During exercise the pulse rate should rise. Cardiovascular conditioning takes place when the heart beats at 70 to 85 percent of its maximum safe rate. Your maximum heart rate is approximately 220 minus your age.

You should take your pulse before starting to exercise, again after exercising for 10 or 15 minutes and immediately after stopping. In the beginning, your doctor may also ask you to take your pulse 15 minutes after stopping to see how long it takes your heart to return to its normal rate.

The heart rate can be measured at any place where you can feel your pulse. The inside wrist, over the carotid artery in the neck or over the artery in the temple are all easy to find. Using a stopwatch, count your pulse for 10 seconds, then multiply by 6 to get the beats per minute. An adult resting pulse rate is about 70 to 80 beats per minute, although this varies from person to person. People who are in good physical condition often have a slower resting pulse because their heart is working more efficiently than that of more sedentary persons. During exercise a pulse that is under your target range indicates you should speed up, while one that is higher means you should slow down. Table 2:3 lists average pulse ranges; check with your doctor to make sure your range is appropriate for you.

There is no right or wrong time to exercise. For some people, a workout first thing in the morning gets them going for the day; some prefer a midday exercise break, and still others find an evening session helps them relax and makes sleep easier. It's all a matter of personal preference. The important thing is to make exercise a part of your regular routine, just like brushing your teeth.

Wear loose-fitting clothing that breathes to allow for air circulation. Wearing a hat outdoors is a good idea in cold weather because it prevents losing too much body heat and reduces the chance of sunburn on sunny days. Rubberized, vinyl and plastic warm-up clothing should be avoided; they don't allow for proper air circulation and evaporation of perspiration, which is necessary in regulating body temperature. Comfortable, well-fitting shoes appropriate to the exercise are important. Joggers and runners should always carry identification, as well as change for emergency phone calls.

Don't eat right before exercising. Take only light snacks like crackers and juice. Replacing loss of liquids is very important, especially in hot, humid weather. During hot weather, exercise in the cooler morning or evening hours and reduce intensity. Dehydration is dangerous, and in times of heavy sweat drinking enough cool liquids, especially water, is vital. Avoid ice-cold drinks, which may cause cramps. At first, regular exercise may seem like more bother than it is worth. But within a couple of weeks, most people begin to see the results—firmer muscles, an enhanced feeling of well-being, increased endurance, better appetite control and more energy for day-to-day tasks. After a month or so, most exercisers admit they are "hooked," that they somehow don't feel right if they go more than a day or two without exercising. (For activities that build endurance, see Table 2:4.)

Target Pulse Ranges

Age	Maximum Heart Rate	Target Range
50	170	119–145
55	165	115–140
60	160	112–136
65	155	109–132
70	150	105–128
75	145	102–123
80	140	90–112
85	135	95–115
90	130	91–110

Table 2:3

▪ *Exercises for Heart Patients*

Over the last thirty years exercise has increasingly become an important part of treatment for heart patients. At one time, heart patients were cautioned to avoid exercise in the mistaken fear that activity might increase the chances of a heart attack. The late Dr. Paul Dudley White, the physician to President Dwight D. Eisenhower, demonstrated to the world that a person could resume an active life, even after a severe heart at-

Activities That Build Endurance

In addition to increased heart rate, the conditioning value of a specific physical activity is assessed according to the number of calories consumed during a certain time period. The following table lists a variety of activities and the number of calories consumed per minute:

Activity	Calories Used per Minute	Activity	Calories Used per Minute
Walking		Swimming (backstroke)	
1 mile per hour	2–2.5	1.6 miles per hour	10–11
2 miles per hour	2.5–4	Jogging	
3 miles per hour	4–5	5.5 miles per hour	10–11
3.5 miles per hour	5–6	Running	
5 miles per hour	7–8	8 miles per hour	11–12
Cycling		Tennis	
6 miles per hour	4–5	doubles	5–6
10 miles per hour	5–6	singles	7–8
11 miles per hour	7–8	Vigorous dancing	5–6
12 miles per hour	8–10	Aerobic dancing	7–8
13 miles per hour	10–11	Skating (ice or roller)	6–7
Swimming (breaststroke)		Squash or handball	10–11
1 mile per hour	6–7	Rowing	11–12
1.6 miles per hour	7–8	Cross-country skiing	11–12
Swimming (sidestroke)		Competitive handball or squash	11–12
1 mile per hour	8–10		

Table 2:4

tack. Within weeks after Eisenhower suffered his heart attack, Dr. White not only had him back in one of the world's most demanding jobs, but also out on the golf course and again leading an active, vigorous life. Since then, many thousands of other heart attack patients have learned that exercise is an essential key to recovery.

Exercise also has become an important part of preventive medicine, especially for people who already have signs of coronary disease or who have a high risk of developing it. Numerous studies during the last few decades have confirmed that regular conditioning exercise lowers many of the major cardiovascular risk factors. For example, exercise can bring about a gradual reduction in moderate high blood pressure; it also can lower total cholesterol as well as increase the ratio of beneficial HDL cholesterol to harmful LDL cholesterol. Exercise is important in overall weight control, thereby reducing obesity, still another factor that raises heart attack risks.

Exercise benefits the heart in several ways. Since the heart is made up mostly of muscle (myocardium), any sustained physicial activity will strengthen it, enabling it to pump more blood with each beat. Indeed, exercise conditioning enables the entire body to function more efficiently. For example, well-trained muscles are capable of taking more oxygen from the blood. The lungs also function more efficiently, and this combination of factors improves endurance. Most people notice that after only a few weeks of exercise conditioning, they do not tire as rapidly when exercising. Tasks such as climbing a flight of stairs that once produced breathlessness or perhaps even anginal pains no longer have these effects.

AFTER A HEART ATTACK

Getting a heart attack patient out of bed is now an early treatment goal. As soon as a patient has stabilized and the immediate danger has passed, usually within a couple of days depending upon the severity of the heart attack and other circumstances, a doctor will have him or her sitting up and taking a few steps around the room. This early activity prevents the muscle wasting and weakness that comes with prolonged bed rest; it also is an encouraging sign to the patient. Before leaving the hospital, the patient may be given a modified exercise test to determine a safe level of physical activity. Many heart attack patients now leave the hospital with an exercise prescription in hand. Others may be enrolled in a cardiac rehabilitation program that includes exercise as well as other lifestyle changes, such as smoking cessation or diet and behavior modification.

Whatever the approach, postcoronary treatment almost always includes a gradual program of progressive exercise to improve heart function, increase tolerance, and overcome the fear and depression that is so common after a heart attack. Even persons with serious heart disease can benefit from a supervised conditioning program. In general, moderation is advised in beginning a post–heart attack exercise program, and it is sometimes a good idea to exercise in a group setting under the guidance of a person trained in handling medical emergencies. But very few people with heart disease encounter exercise-related problems. Studies have found a higher cardiovascular death rate among sedentary persons than among those who undertake a commonsense exercise regimen. Symptoms that indicate you should stop exercising and see a doctor are listed in Table 2:5, Exercise-Related Warning Signs.

Exercise-Related Warning Signs

Any of the following are signs to stop exercising and see your doctor:

- excessive fatigue
- any unusual joint, muscle, ligament problem
- chest pain
- pain in the teeth, jaws or ear
- light-headedness, dizziness or fainting
- nausea and/or vomiting
- headache
- shortness of breath
- sustained increase in heart rate after slowing down or resting
- irregularity of pulse

Table 2:5

DESIGNING AN EXERCISE PROGRAM FOR HEART PATIENTS

Moderate aerobic exercise, coupled with stretching warm-up and cool-down routines, forms the basis of any exercise prescription for heart patients. Walking is considered the ideal exercise; stationary bicycles, water walking or swimming also may be recommended, especially for people who have orthopedic problems that make walking difficult.

In general, heart patients should avoid strenuous weight lifting, especially if it entails downward straining, which can result in a buildup of lung pressure when trying to exhale against a closed glottis. Lactic acid, which is created as a waste product by muscles during isometric or static exercise, can increase the possibility of cardiac arrhythmia.

Cool-down routines are particularly important for heart patients. Clinical studies show that the period just after exercise is when a person is most vulnerable to rhythm disturbances. Thus patients should avoid abruptly stopping exercise; instead, they should gradually allow the heart to return to its resting rate.

Each exercise session should include a 10- to 15-minute warm-up period, then the aerobic phase, followed by the cool-down. Keep a record of your exercise, and remember to check your pulse count frequently, especially in hot/humid weather when the body is under greater stress. Drink plenty of water before, during and after exercise. Be flexible. A physically exerting day at the office or home can make you feel fatigued prior to exercise, so adjust your exercise accordingly. Your heart rate may increase to your target with a lower level of exercise; there is no need to match a previous session's level.

If for some reason you miss a week or so of exercise, don't attempt to pick up where you left off when you resume your sessions. Instead, again work up gradually, just as you did when you originally started exercising. Although it may take several weeks or even longer to reach your exercise potential, it takes only a few days off to begin to lose the conditioning effect.

▪ *Exercise and Arthritis*

Almost everyone who lives long enough will develop some degree of arthritis, a term that is used to describe a whole group of disorders characterized by joint inflammation and pain. Most people with arthritis learn to live with their joint problems without serious handicap. Some forms of the disease, however, are more disabling than others; this is especially true of rheumatoid arthritis, a progressive, systemic disease that can produce marked joint destruction and deformities.

Exercise is an important component in the treatment of most forms of arthritis because it helps maintain flexibility and joint mobility. But unlike the strenuous workouts of aerobic conditioning exercises, the regimens prescribed for arthritis should emphasize gentle, range-of-motion movements. Maintaining a full range of motion is especially important to prevent a stiffening or even immobility of the joints. These exercises are designed to maintain muscle strength and proper joint alignment without placing too much stress on inflamed joints. Arthritis causes pain with movement, and the amount of pain a person feels is an important guide to safe exercising. Pain should not last longer than two hours after exercising. Any joint that is inflamed or feels "hot" to the touch should be rested, although the rest of the body should be put through its full range of movement.

The joint cartilage is lubricated and nourished by synovial fluid. Movement increases the amount of this fluid, thus increasing the lubrication to the joints and connecting tissues.

It is important to remember that if a loss of function has occurred, it will not be recovered immediately. Still, in most cases a daily program of individually prescribed exercises can help most arthritis sufferers regain at least some lost function and, in most instances, again perform the day-to-day tasks that are so important to maintaining independence.

To begin an exercise program, the first step is to select a place for exercising that allows for full movement on all four sides. Timing also is important; some arthritis patients have less pain and more mobility at the beginning of the day, while others may find the opposite is true: They are stiff in the morning, but gradually loosen up as the day goes on. Remember, pain is a signal that something is wrong; if you have a tendency to overexercise when using painkillers, it may be a good idea to time your sessions before, instead of after, taking your medication. However, before embarking on an exercise regimen, you should check with your physician or physical therapist to make sure that the exercises are right for you.

▪ *Exercise and Lung Function*

Most of us give very little thought to the way we breathe, which is natural since breathing is an automatic function. As we grow older, our lung's vital capacity—the maximum amount of air that can be expelled in a single, forceful breath—declines steadily, but most researchers now believe that this is due more to the way we breathe than to physical factors related to aging.

There are two ways in which we can improve maximal oxygen uptake (the greatest amount of oxygen the heart-lung system can deliver in a given span of time): aerobic exercise conditioning and improved patterns of breathing. Most adults breathe too shallowly; when inhaling, you should expand your chest and use the diaphragm—the muscle that lies just below the rib cage. The ribs should expand outward and the abdomen tighten.

A number of exercises, including yoga, improve breathing techniques. Deep breathing should not be confused with hyperventilation, the tendency to take shallow, rapid breaths of air. People who suffer from anxiety sometimes feel that they are not receiving enough air and, panicking, they begin to breathe rapidly. This changes the balance of oxygen and carbon monoxide in their blood and can result in alarming symptoms, such as rapid heartbeat, lightheadedness and increasing panic. Breathing into a paper bag can ease the symptoms and restore the normal oxygen balance.

Practice breathing correctly as part of your exercise warm-up. Or you may want to schedule 5 to 10 minutes of breathing exercises daily as part of a relaxation routine. People with specific respiratory problems, such as emphysema or asthma, also can benefit from breathing exercises to control their shortness of breath. (Table 2:6 on breathing exercises describes these in greater detail.)

▪ *Exercise Equipment*

Many people make the mistake of assuming that in order to exercise you need to join an exercise club or buy a lot of expensive equipment. While exercise clubs and a well-equipped home gym may be nice, they certainly are not essential. Indeed, many people invest large sums of money in club memberships or exercise equipment only to have them go unused. The only essential "equipment" is your own motivation; all the rest is like icing on the cake. All you really need for a good exercise program are a pair of comfortable walking shoes and a place to walk. In recent years, shopping mall parking lots have become favored places for informal exercise groups that meet regularly and walk briskly on "walking courses" laid out at the malls. A park, high school track, untrafficked road or quiet side street are other ideal walking places.

Still, many people find the companionship and motivation that come from

Breathing Exercises

Basic Deep Breathing

1. Relax. Let your neck and shoulders droop.
2. Rest both hands on your abdomen.
3. Breathe in through your nose and let your abdomen come out as far as it will. Keep your upper chest relaxed.
4. Breathe out slowly through pursed lips. If you feel dizzy, wait a few breaths before trying it again.

IMPORTANT: To be sure your diaphragm is moving properly, ask your doctor, nurse or physical therapist to check your technique.

Chest Muscle Exercise

Deep breathing is easier when all the breathing muscles are used. The following exercise helps loosen tight chest muscles and increases your ability to expand the lower lungs.

1. Place your hands on the side of your lower chest.
2. Breathe in slowly through your nose. Your lower chest should move your hands out. Keep your shoulders and upper chest relaxed.
3. Breathe out slowly through pursed lips. Your hands should move in.

Practice this exercise several times a day for a few minutes at a time. Rest if you feel dizzy.

NOTE: EXERCISE IS HELPFUL IN SOME TYPES OF LUNG DISEASE AND NOT IN OTHERS. BE SURE TO CHECK WITH YOUR DOCTOR BEFORE MAKING IT A PART OF YOUR DAILY PROGRAM.

Table 2:6

exercising with a group important in helping them stick to a regimen. For them, an exercise club or group may be an ideal solution. Many YMCAs and YWCAs have special exercise programs. Community organizations, church groups, senior citizen centers, adult education programs and work-site fitness centers are among the many groups offering exercise classes and programs. But before joining a club or program, you should follow some guidelines to make sure your choice is appropriate for your needs. Specific questions you should ask before joining an exercise club include:

1. Does the club welcome visits by prospective members at various times of the day or only at a prearranged time? Although many clubs will not permit nonmembers to actually try out their facilities (for insurance reasons), you should be able to visit at the times of day that you are most likely to use the club to observe how crowded it is and whether the activities are appropriate for you.

2. Are the instructors qualified? Is someone trained in emergency medical procedures available at all times when the club is in use?

3. Does the club require medical clearance before enrolling? This is important for over-40 members who are embarking on exercise conditioning.

4. Are you likely to fit in with the other members? A group composed mostly of young, competitive handball enthusiasts probably will not have much in common with a middle-aged woman who wants to tighten sagging abdominal muscles.

5. Is the equipment in good repair and adequate for the number of users? No one wants to spend a large portion of his or her workout time waiting in line for equipment.

6. Do the exercisers have adequate space? Overcrowding promotes injury and discourages a good workout.

7. Does each workout include a warm-up and cool-down segment?

8. Are the locker and changing rooms adequate and clean? Ask other members if theft has been a problem.

9. Are you being pressured into signing a long-term contract before you have a chance to carefully read what is involved? Can you clearly determine what is included and what are extras? Can you get a refund if you move away or have to give up your membership for some unforeseen reason?

10. Does the facility offer classes in other areas that may be of interest to you, such as nutrition, weight control, and smoking cessation?

BEFORE BUYING HOME EXERCISE EQUIPMENT

Selecting appropriate home exercise equipment entails the same sort of research and questioning as picking an exercise club. There is no single piece of equipment that will exercise every part of the body, but several types come close. Table 2:7, A Buyer's Guide to Fitness Machines, lists major types of exercise machines, selected models and 1985 retail prices.

Before buying a piece of home exercise equipment, make sure that you try it out first to ensure that it is appropriate for you. There is little point in paying several hundred dollars for a stationary bicycle or ski machine only to use it as a clothes rack. The stationary bicycle is one of the most popular pieces of home equipment, and one that is recommended generally for everyone except people who suffer from bad knees and need to limit stress on these joints. Whether the stationary bicycle is an exercycle or an ergometer (which comes with built-in gauges for instant feedback on how far you've gone and how fast you're going), it should have a heavy flywheel weighing at least 30 pounds, a comfortable seat that lets you fully extend your legs to the pedals and easily adjustable wheel tension. Make sure that you try out several models, and then pick the one that feels best for you.

Rowing machines also rate very high aerobically. They're great for building strength in the back, lower body and upper arms, and provide a more strenuous workout than a stationary bike. A new addition to the home gym is the stationary cross-country skiing machine. Other more elaborate weight training and Nautilus machines are available for home use but are very expensive and may not be recommended for people with chronic heart disease.

Less expensive but still useful are the ankle and wrist weights. These are based on the principle that more energy is expended when doing exercise while wearing the weights (usually weighing about 2 pounds each), and they can build up strength. They do not build up muscle bulk as such, but they can improve tone, endurance and power. The weights should not be too heavy, and they should be placed on the body evenly to avoid feeling off balance.

Skipping rope and other impact-causing exercise equipment and exercises should be avoided to lessen the chance of joint injury. There are many exercise programs on television as well as a growing number of exercise videos for home use. Proceed cautiously with these. Most are designed for the in-shape, vigorous exerciser, and even they can overextend themselves trying to keep pace with a professional physical exercise leader. Little attention is paid to the beginning, over-50 group in these types of programs. Becoming overly enthusiastic while exercising to a film program, especially one that is done to fast, catchy music without a proper warm-up,

A Buyer's Guide to Fitness Machines

For those of you who would like to get some exercise but never seem to get yourself to the gym or health club, the home gym may be the answer. The cost of equipment ranges from less than $200 on up.

Exercise machines come in many different models designed to strengthen and tone the different muscles of the body. In his book *The Home Gym: A Guide to Fitness Equipment* (New York: Avon, 1984), Michael Lafavore offers some practical advice on how to buy just one all-purpose machine.

The listing below shows the types of fitness machines available for home use.

Model Name/ Manufacturer or Distributor	Suggested Retail Price*
STATIONARY BICYCLES (REGULAR TYPES)	
Slendercycle, Model RC-PX26 Vitamaster Industries Brooklyn, NY (212) 858-0505	$190.00
Tunturi Home Cycle, Model ATHC Amerec Corp., Bellevue, WA (800) 426-0858	$275.00– $360.00
Schwinn Air-Dyne Excelsior Fitness Equipment Co. Northbrook, IL (312) 291-9100	$595.00
ERGOMETERS	
Tunturi Ergometer, Model ATEE Amerec Corp., Bellevue, WA (800) 426-0858	$510.00
Exercycle Ergometer Exercycle Corp., Woonsocket, RI	$639.00
ROWING MACHINES	
Deluxe Rower, Model RM-907 Vitamaster Industries Brooklyn, NY (212) 858-0505	$170.00
Avita 950 M&R Industries, Redmond, WA (206) 885-1010	$350.00
Proform 935, Model PPF935 The Sharper Image San Francisco, CA (800) 344-4444	$365.50
CROSS-COUNTRY SKI MACHINES	
Nordictrack, Model 505 PSI, Chaska, MN (800) 328-5888	$470.00
Fitness Master, Model XC-1 Fitness Master Inc. Chanhassen, MN (800) 328-8995	$579.00

*The prices listed here are those suggested by manufacturers; many are available at discounts, so shop around.

Table 2:7

can cause injury, or at least serious soreness that will inhibit further exercising.

Any exercise program or equipment should be discussed with your physician. As in all types of exercise, moderation, especially in the beginning, is most important.

▪ *Exercises for a Bad Back*

At one time or another, almost everyone suffers from backaches, and with a distressingly large number of people, the problem becomes chronic. However, the majority of back problems can be alleviated and/or prevented with exercises designed to strengthen the supporting muscles.

Typically, a person will suffer a back injury, such as a strained muscle or even a ruptured disk. This can cause inflammation and pressure on nerves, resulting in pain and muscle spasms. Increased pain leads to more muscle spasm and inflammation—in effect, a vicious cycle. Depending upon the nature of the injury, rest may be prescribed during the initial period. Muscle-relaxing drugs may be prescribed to ease the muscle spasms. Long-term preventive therapy invariably entails a program of exercises. The exercises illustrated in Figures 2:6 to 2:10 are typical of those recommended for a bad back. Before attempting them, however, you should check with your doctor. An added caution: If a back exercise provokes pain, stop and consult your doctor or physical therapist.

▪ *Water Workouts*

For many people, especially those with orthopedic or weight problems, exercising in water is an ideal alternative to brisk walking, jogging and other types of land exercise. Swimming, for example, works the cardiovascular system as effectively as running and provides a powerful workout for the upper body and legs without the joint-jarring, injury-causing drawbacks of running, aerobic dance and other land sports.

Water aerobics—dancing exercises done to music while standing in waist-deep water—is now offered by a number of exercise programs geared to older people. These exercises are particularly suitable for older women who may be experiencing early signs of osteoporosis. Water aerobics or swimming provides the benefits of activity without placing undue strain on an already weakened skeleton. Figures 2:11 to 2:14 on water exercises illustrate some of the movements that can be done under water to exercise specific body parts without straining joints or bones.

▪ *Fitness Walking*

At times, it may seem that jogging is the national pastime, but an increasing number of people, especially those 50 and over, are exchanging their running shoes for walking. Fitness walking does not carry the risk of joint and muscle injury that is inherent to jogging or running. And, when done at a brisk pace, it can provide the heart with an equally good workout. In fact, racewalking is a recognized Olympic sport. For those who can no longer take the constant pounding and jarring of jogging but need the psychological benefits of competition and the same physical benefits of running, this revved-up version of normal walking may be the answer.

For most of us, simply walking at a brisk pace is sufficient. With proper shoes, just about everyone can walk for fitness. Challenge yourself but don't overdo. A brisk walk of 30 to 60 minutes three or four times a week is enough to provide cardiovascular conditioning. A walk to the corner and back or getting off the bus and walking the last mile to

Exercises for a Healthy Back

These are gentle exercises, designed specifically to strengthen abdominal and back muscles.

Figure 2:6.
Pelvic tilt. Lie flat on the floor, with arms at your side, the knees slightly bent. Pull in your stomach so that the small of the back lies flat on the floor. Squeeze buttocks and slowly raise hips off the floor. Hold for a count of 10. Work up to 5 to 10 per session.

Figure 2:7.
Lower back stretch. Start from basic position lying flat on the floor with legs straight and toes pointed upward. Gently bring one knee as close to the chest as possible, then return it slowly to the starting position and relax. Repeat up to 10 times for each leg.

Figure 2:8.
Leg raises. Start from basic position of lying flat on the floor with legs straight and toes pointed upward. With one leg flat on the floor, slowly raise the other as high as you can without producing pain. Return leg to starting position and repeat with opposite leg. Using alternate legs, repeat up to 10 times.

Figure 2:9.
Knee to forehead. Start from basic position of lying flat on the floor with legs straight and toes pointed upward. Bend one knee and bring it up to the chest. Grasp the knee with both hands and raise shoulders off the floor and bring knee as close to forehead as you can without producing pain. Return slowly to the starting position. Repeat, alternating legs, 5 to 10 times.

Figure 2:10.
Modified sit-ups. Start from basic position. Bend knees and with arms extended and raised off floor, raise upper part of your body 6 to 8 inches off floor. Return to original position, relax and repeat up to 10 times.

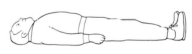

Exercising in Water

People who find it difficult to exercise on land because of arthritis or other joint problems usually can work out in water, which makes the body buoyant and also absorbs the impact an exerciser would normally encounter when the foot strikes the ground while walking or jogging. These exercises are designed to maintain joint flexibility.

Swimming, water walking or jogging also will provide an excellent aerobic workout. If a person has trouble keeping his or her balance in the water, there are special flotation vests available such as the Wet Vests athletic trainers use to train competitive athletes without the danger of muscle injuries.

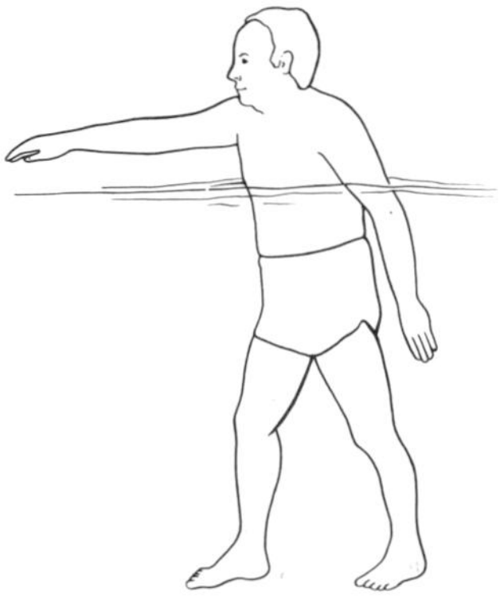

Figure 2:11.
Water walking. Stand in water that is chest high (or deeper if upper body joints are affected) with one arm extended for balance and the other in the water. Rotate the arms as if you were swimming and walk from one end of the pool to the other. This exercise is good for people with hip or knee problems.

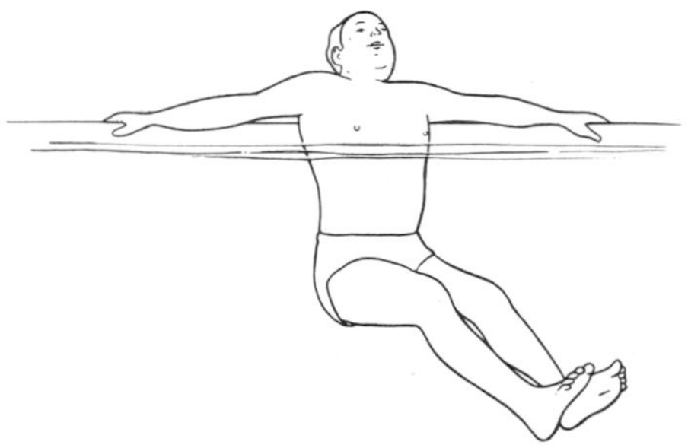

Figure 2:12.
Leg and abdominal muscle stretches. Stand at the edge of the pool, with arms extended and hands grasping the sides. Lift lower body off pool bottom and extend legs outward. Repeat 10 to 20 times.

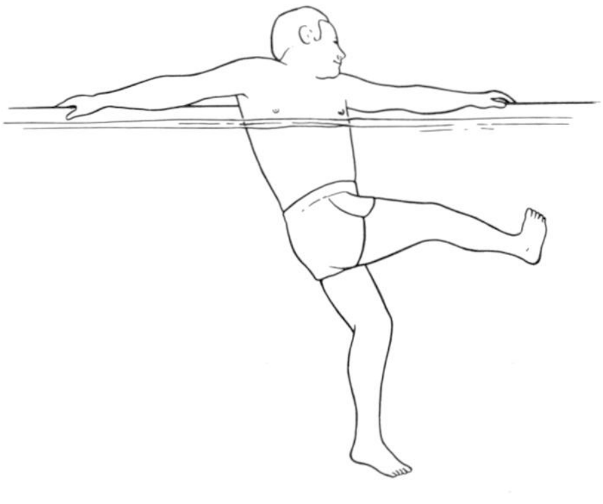

Figure 2:13.
Lower-body stretch. Stand with back to the side of the pool, arms extended and hands grasping the edge. Lift one leg and try to touch side of the pool. Using alternating legs, repeat 10 times.

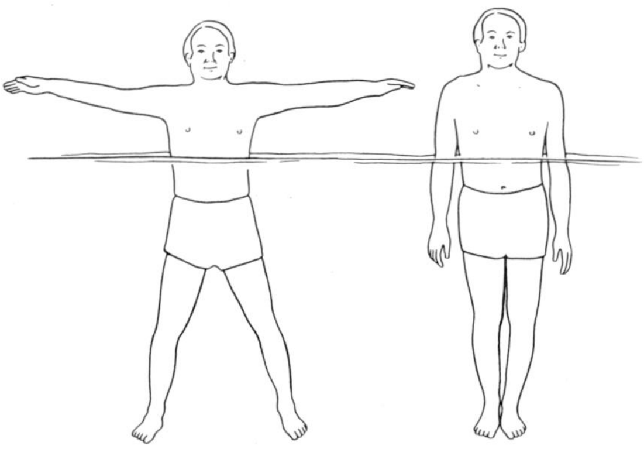

Figure 2:14.
Water jumping jacks. Stand in water chest deep with arms extended at sides. Using arms for balance and with legs extended, bounce up, landing with them together. This provides an aerobic workout similar to jumping rope, but without the impact on knees, ankles and other weight-bearing joints.

or from work may be the way to begin.

Racewalking, which entails a rhythmic form of brisk walking and a pumping arm movement, provides a more vigorous workout and may not be recommended for people with certain forms of heart disease or a chronic pulmonary disorder. For those suited to racewalking, the sport provides a good workout for virtually every major muscle group—buttocks, thighs, calves, arms, chest, back and abdominals, and in less time per session than is needed with regular walking.

❏ Overcoming Problems

People find many aspects of aging unpleasant and would like to avoid them. These include the tendency to huff and puff after minor exertion, diminished muscle strength, a general stiffening of the joints and loss of bone mass (osteoporosis). Fortunately, all of these conditions can be helped by exercise. Just learning to improve your posture (see box, "Stand Tall") can help minimize joint and back problems. Physical inactivity can make the body age prematurely. Muscles atrophy quickly and bones begin to lose calcium soon after a person becomes inactive.

People who exercise are less prone to chronic fatigue and are able to sleep more easily. Tiredness is often the result of poor circulation, which in turn arises from a lack of physical activity. Exercise improves circulation. Another often overlooked benefit of exercise is improved balance and agility. People who wear bi- or trifocal lenses are especially prone to lose their sense of balance. A well-maintained sense of balance can compensate for dizziness caused by changes from one optical to another. Agility is useful in reducing the chance of injury by lessening the chance of falling and also allows one to move more quickly in an emergency.

The joints of older persons often go through a vicious cycle of increasing stiffness and limitation. An episode of arthritis or bursitis, causing pain in movement, may make it impossible to swing a joint through its full range of motion. Activities are then restricted to accommodate the stiff joint. This inactivity, however, causes more stiffness. But unless there is significant damage inside the joint itself, mobility can be regained with training. Disuse of a joint takes a toll in two ways: The lubricant that keeps the joints working (synovial fluid) dries up, and the connective tissue surrounding the joint begins to shorten and lose its resilience. Also the increased strength of the muscle helps to take some of the strain off arthritic joints.

The increasing fragility of bones (osteoporosis) in aging is a particularly common problem for certain groups of postmenopausal women. As bones age, they lose some of their mineral content, becoming light and more prone to breakage. The action of muscle working against bone helps strengthen the bones by increasing calcium absorption. (Estrogen replacement after menopause is also needed to help maintain bones.) Thus it is particularly important for older people to maintain joint flexibility so they can engage in the types of exercise that will promote bone strength. The range-of-motion exercises in Figures 2:15 to 2:19 are designed with this in mind.

Flexibility and range-of-motion exercises are best done daily. The fingers, arms, shoulders, knees, ankles, hips, back and neck all should be rotated slowly and carefully to their full range of movement. Many people who have started flexibility exercises in their later years, even seventies and eighties, have made remarkable progress toward self-rejuvenation. In beginning a program,

Range-of-Motion Exercises

These exercises are designed to maintain joint flexibility and are particularly good for people with arthritis. Try doing them in the morning after you have had a shower and a chance to limber up a bit.

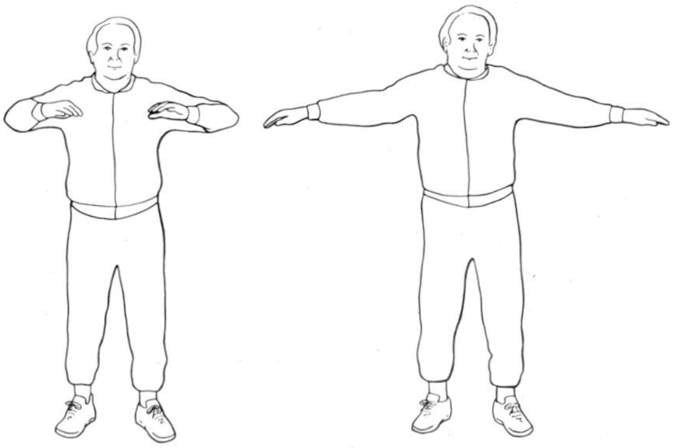

Figure 2:15.
Arms and elbows. Stand in a comfortable position. With elbows bent, bring hands chest high and slowly straighten arms. Repeat 10 times to a count of 7.

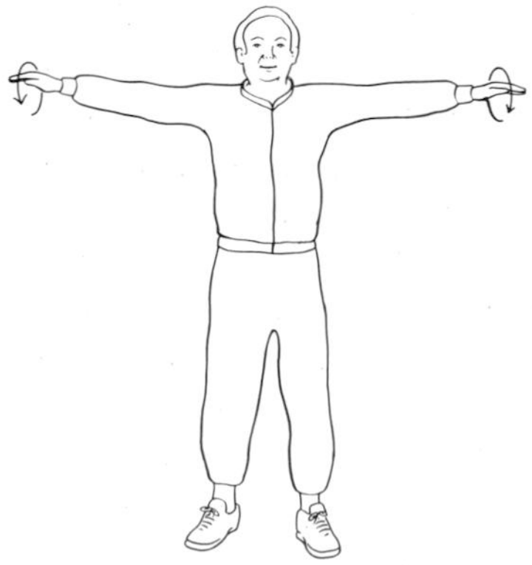

Figure 2:16.
Arms and upper back. Stand in a comfortable position with arms extended straight from shoulders. Make small circles, using entire arm. Repeat 20 times.

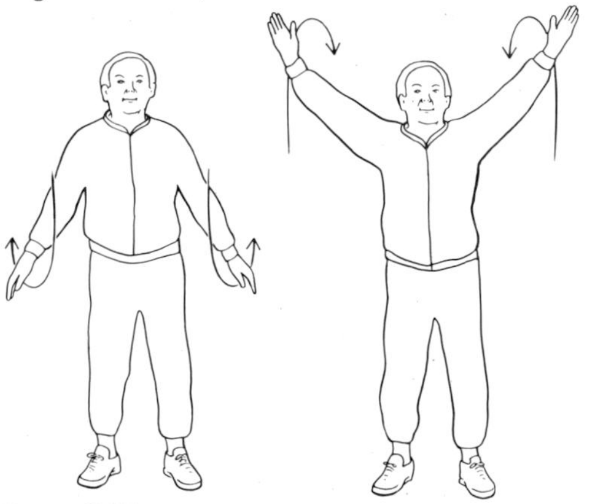

Figure 2:17.
Arms and shoulders. Stand in a comfortable position, and to a count of 7, slowly make large circles with arms, raising hands as high over head as you can. Repeat 10 times.

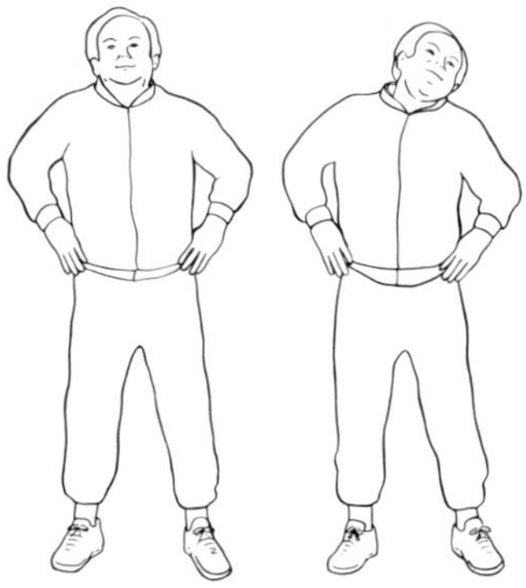

Figure 2:18.
Neck. Stand in a comfortable position, with hands relaxed on hips. To a count of 5, slowly rotate neck and head. Repeat 10 times.

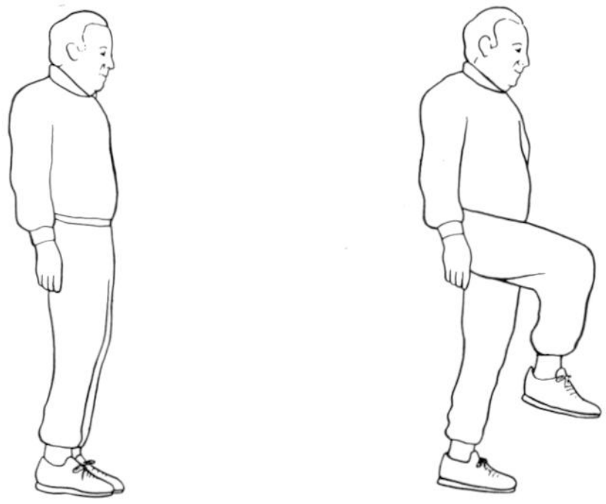

Figure 2:19.
Lower back, legs and knees. Stand in a comfortable position with arms at the side. With knee bent, slowly raise one leg and lower it to a count of 5. (If this is too difficult, stand using the back of a chair for support.) Using alternate legs, repeat up to 10 times.

start with relatively easy, short-term goals. For example, if it is difficult for you to bend over to put on stockings or tie your shoes, make performing these tasks with greater ease an initial goal. Then move on to more difficult goals. (See Table 2:8 concerning some important precautions to take when embarking on a new exercise regimen.)

Remember, too, that progress in exercising is never made in a straight upward line. There will be days when less is accomplished than on other days. Avoid trying to be overly competitive with yourself or others. After all, your goal is increased independence and peace of mind, not winning a self-styled competition.

Stand Tall

Good posture not only gives a more youthful appearance, it also tells the world you are self-confident and proud of who you are. Of course, certain diseases like osteoporosis or arthritis can produce bad posture, but for most of us, slouching is more of a habit than a result of physical causes. To improve your posture, do the following routine at least three times a day.

1. Wearing low-heeled shoes (or no shoes at all), stand with your back against a wall. The feet should be pointing straight forward or slightly outward. Knees should be straight but not locked. The heels should be about 3 inches from the wall.
2. Shoulders should be relaxed but straight. Press back of head, shoulders and buttocks against the wall; tilt hips forward so that spine also touches the wall. The space between the wall and the small of your back should be no wider than an inch. Practice walking away from the wall with your head, shoulders and hips aligned in this position.

Once you have felt correct posture, practice doing daily activities while maintaining correct alignment. It will take time and effort at first, but it will become easier and will actually give you more energy and make you less prone to backaches and other joint problems. (See also Exercises for a Healthy Back, page 59.)

Exercise Precautions and Tips

1. Do not do too much too soon. Injuries slow down progress and take a longer time to heal as the body ages.
2. Wear loose clothing that does not restrict movement, and of a material that breathes.
3. Do not take hot baths or go into a sauna immediately after exercising, especially if you have high blood pressure, varicose veins or other circulatory problems.
4. Always do warm-up exercises to avoid injuries. Cool-down exercises are also important, especially for heart patients.
5. Don't exercise while taking pain relievers.
6. Overstretching is possible in older persons. Move slowly and methodically. All movements should flow.
7. Avoid vigorous jogging, rope jumping, aerobic dancing, and all jumping and pounding motions that will cause joint injury.
8. Never exercise in water alone.
9. Keep your heart rate within your conditioning target range.
10. Three to five workouts a week, lasting 20 to 30 minutes, is optimum.

Table 2:8

3

BREAKING BAD HABITS—IT'S NEVER TOO LATE

Whoever coined the phrase "you can't teach an old dog new tricks" obviously did not know much about older people. Statistics show that older people are more likely to be successful in making lifestyle changes, especially breaking bad health habits, than younger people. On the other hand, some older people continue their smoking or excessive drinking habits on the assumption that "the damage is done—why stop now?" In reality, it is never too late to change and never too late to reap the benefits from adopting a more healthful lifestyle.

❑ Smoking

A few years ago physicians often did not urge older smokers to quit because they assumed that a few more years of smoking was not going to significantly increase the risk of cancer or heart disease. New statistics show, however, that great benefits can be obtained by quitting smoking at any age.

Tobacco companies would have us believe that smoking makes you more sophisticated, relaxed, independent or successful. Of course, smoking does none of these things; in fact, it does just the opposite in many cases. By now, we all know that smoking is bad for you. The latest Surgeon General's report on the effects of smoking claims that tobacco use is directly linked to 350,000 deaths a year. It is by far the leading cause of lung cancer, emphysema and other chronic lung diseases, and also a major factor in heart attacks. Of course, the statistics are well known; less well known is what is actually happening each time you take a puff.

There are more than 4,000 components in tobacco smoke, many of which are known toxins and carcinogens. If these substances were in our food, we would be appalled and eat something else. We fight to reduce and control the amount of toxic substances in the air in our cities. We would not leave our car running in a closed garage for fear of carbon monoxide poisoning. Yet millions of people continue to smoke, ignoring the realities of the toxins they breathe in with every puff.

Smokers contend that they enjoy smoking: It relaxes them; it increases their productivity; it wakes them up. They say they know it is bad for them but they are willing to take their chances. But usually all of these claims are only excuses, empty explanations to hide their addiction to nicotine.

Nicotine is a powerful stimulant. It prompts the adrenal glands to secrete catecholamines such as adrenaline (epinephrine). This causes a rise in the heart rate and in blood pressure, and constriction of the capillaries. The smoke decreases the amount of oxygen available to the heart and brain. In essence, it simulates stress and keeps the body in a state of heightened tension. When that tension wanes, the smoker reaches for another cigarette to start the process all over again.

Nicotine is detoxified in the liver. Just as chronic drinking can cause liver damage, smoking may also impair liver function. This can lead to deficient activation of vitamin D, which is necessary for the absorption of dietary calcium into the bones. Scientists now believe that this process may lead to an increased incidence of osteoporosis (thinning of the bones) among women who smoke. The statistics bear this out. Women who smoke have reduced levels of estrogen, which appears to be important in proper calcium and bone metabolism. Reduced levels of estrogen, in turn, can lead to an early menopause, which further decreases levels of estrogen and increases again the chances of developing osteoporosis.

Combine the effects of nicotine with the toxins in cigarette smoke, such as carbon monoxide, and the result can be lethal. Because the smoker is breathing in many other gases in addition to oxygen with each puff, the blood receives less oxygen. Moreover, carbon monoxide causes the oxygen to bind more tightly to the red blood cells (carboxyhemoglobin), rendering it less available to the heart and other tissues. The heart has to work harder just to keep the smoker going, one reason smokers run out of breath more often and faster than nonsmokers.

Chronic exposure to carbon monoxide in smoke raises the concentrations of carboxyhemoglobin in the blood to 3 to 8 percent, far above the concentrations for normal nonsmokers (.5 to .8 percent) and within the danger zone of 5 to 10 percent that can result in impaired central nervous system function—that is, reduced vision and learning ability. For older people worried about failing eyesight and memory, quitting smoking has special benefits.

Because the heart has to work harder all the time, it is more susceptible to coronary heart disease. In fact, heart and blood vessel diseases are the major causes of death for smokers, and 40 percent of deaths from heart attack are linked to cigarette smoking. People who smoke are more likely to have a heart attack and more likely to die from that attack. To quote the 1983 Surgeon General's report, "Cigarette smoking should be considered the most important of the known modifiable risk factors for coronary heart disease in the United States." Since being over 50 also increases your risk for heart attack, quitting smoking is especially important for older people.

Stroke is another health concern of older people. Cigarette smoking, by contributing to the artery-clogging arteriosclerotic process, is definitely a major factor in this often life-threatening breakdown of the central nervous system.

In addition to impeding the circulation of blood to the brain, cigarette smoking can also reduce the amount of oxygen-carrying blood getting to the skin. This can result in increased susceptibility to wrinkles and age lines.

Larger doses of the cyanide in cigarette smoke can cause optic nerve damage, especially when combined with a vitamin B_{12} deficiency (which is more common among older people). Cyanide in some instances can cause hearing loss and impaired judgment.

In addition to the poisonous gases in cigarette smoke, the smoker also inhales small particles called tar. Even filtered cigarettes cannot strain out all of the particulate matter in the smoke. Basically, the smoker is breathing in small pieces of dirt, which break down the tiny hairs (cilia) that clean the lungs. This leads to the accumulation of mucus, creating a hospitable environment for the development of infections. People who smoke have greater incidences of bronchitis, influenza, sinusitis and emphysema than nonsmokers. Smokers report more sick days, more days in bed and higher medical costs—averaging about $1,000 a year—than nonsmokers.

Reasons for Quitting Smoking

1. Add years to your life
2. Help avoid lung cancer, emphysema, bronchitis and heart attacks
3. Give heart and circulatory system a break
4. Get rid of smoker's hack
5. Feel more vigorous in sports
6. Improve stamina
7. Stop smoke-related head- and stomachaches
8. Regain sense of smell and taste
9. Have smoke-free rooms and closets
10. End cigarette breath
11. Save money
12. Eliminate stained yellow teeth and fingers
13. Stop burning holes in clothes or furniture
14. Get rid of messy ashtrays, ashes on carpets
15. Set a good example for others
16. Prove self-control
17. ____________________
18. ____________________
19. ____________________
20. ____________________

Table 3:1

Some of the particulate substances in cigarette smoke are known carcinogens. Although it has not been determined which substances are instrumental in the development of cancer in smokers, the eight different nitrosamines identified in cigarette smoke are known animal carcinogens and are the most likely culprits. Researchers have been unable to induce cancer in laboratory rats exposed to cigarette smoke, but the statistics on smoking and cancer are overwhelming proof of the connection. Eighty-five percent of lung cancer patients are longtime smokers (twenty years or more). Smokers, especially those who also are heavy drinkers, run an increased risk of oral and esophageal cancers—some of the more incurable types of cancer. Cancers of the bladder and pancreas are also much more common among smokers than nonsmokers.

The facts are there: Cigarette smoking is taking years off your life and reducing the quality of the time you have left. Experts have estimated that for every cigarette smoked, 5½ minutes of expected longevity are lost. And those minutes can add up to years.

So, is the damage done? To be truthful, yes, some of the harmful effects of longtime cigarette smoking are irreparable. However, there are many benefits to quitting, many of which are realized within months, even days of quitting. Stopping smoking is no easy task but it's well worth the effort. (See Table 3:1.)

▪ *What Smoking Is Doing to Those Around You*

Smokers are not the only ones adversely affected by their habit. Spouses, children, grandchildren and friends—in short, everyone coming in contact with you and your cigarette—run the risk of compromised health.

There are actually two sources of cigarette smoke: mainstream and sidestream. Mainstream is that inhaled and exhaled by the smoker. Sidestream smoke is that emitted by the burning end of the cigarette between puffs—for example, when it is sitting in an ashtray.

Chemical studies show that sidestream smoke, because it does not go through the dual filtering system of the cigarette tip and the smoker's lungs, actually contains higher concentrations of many of the poisonous elements. These include carbon monoxide, formaldehyde and nicotine. Eighty-five percent of the smoke in a smoke-filled room is from the sidestream source.

The effects of cigarette smoke on nonsmokers include increased risks of angina, pulmonary disorders and lung cancer. People, especially young children, exposed to great amounts of passive cigarette smoke have higher incidences of bronchitis, pneumonia and middle ear infections. Exposure to cigarette smoke can induce an asthma attack in asthma sufferers. In addition, many people exposed to passive smoking report allergy symptoms such as watery eyes, coughing, nasal congestion, headaches, wheezing and sneezing. For some, exposure to cigarette smoke can provoke serious, even life-threatening attacks of asthma.

Exposure to cigarette smoke may hasten the onset of angina in those with heart disease. Emphysema sufferers will have even more trouble getting sufficient oxygen in the presence of cigarette smoke. Clearly the benefits of quitting extend to everyone around the smoker, as well as to the smoker.

▪ *Health Benefits of Quitting*

And now the good news. Many of the adverse effects of cigarette smoking can be reduced or, in some cases, eliminated by quitting.

Almost immediately after your last cigarette, your body begins to repair itself. The release of stress hormones, such as epinephrine (adrenaline) recedes to normal levels. Your circulation will improve as you breathe in more oxygen, and your capillaries expand to allow easier passage of the blood to the extremities, heart and brain. This is especially important to older people. Studies have shown that within a few months of quitting, the amount of blood getting to the brain increases significantly, thus reducing the risk of stroke and improving cerebral functions.

No longer barraged by the particulate matter in cigarette smoke, the cilia in the lungs start to function again, cleaning out the lungs of mucus and dirt. At first, it may seem as if your smoker's cough has gotten worse, but actually this is part of the cleansing process as you cough up the mucus caught in your lungs. Researchers estimate that in smokers with no permanent lung damage, lung clearance is back to normal within three months of quitting.

Of more concern to most people are risks of cancer and heart disease. After one year of not smoking, the risk of coronary heart disease drops significantly. After ten years the risk is comparable to one who never smoked.

Immediately upon quitting, breathing rates improve and deterioration of the lungs is slowed. After ten to fifteen years risks of cancer of the lung, larynx and mouth approach that of nonsmokers. Life expectancy is also prolonged to a near-normal length, although it is always somewhat lower than that of people who never smoke.

Ex-smokers often report that they feel stronger, more alert and healthier than when they were smoking. Taste buds, which can be dulled by smoking, regain sensitivity. Your sense of smell may also improve. Smoking-induced head- and stomachaches, which you may have attributed to stress, may disappear or become less frequent. Digestion becomes easier. Teeth or dentures can be cleaned and stay white longer. Your breath will be sweet, not sour. Clothes will smell clean and fresh, not smoky.

In short, the quality, as well as the length of your life, may improve dramatically. But the key is to focus on these benefits of quitting, rather than on how much you miss your old habit. Sooner than you think, you'll find you hardly miss it at all.

▪ *Quitting Smoking*

Cigarette smoking is addictive, both physically and psychologically. Quitting is no easy task, but 30 million ex-smokers in America can attest it *is* possible. The large majority, 95 percent, quit on their own, usually cold turkey. The others (5 percent) seek outside help from stop-smoking clinics, behavior modification therapy or hypnosis. Although those who quit cold turkey report a somewhat higher success rate, use whatever technique will be effective for you. Every smoker is different, so different methods will be better suited to each one. And, remember, if at first you don't succeed . . . try again and again and *again*. Each time you try to quit, your chances of succeeding improve.

GETTING READY TO QUIT

Putting yourself in the right frame of mind for quitting is an important step toward becoming an ex-smoker. Table 3:2, Tips for Quitting Smoking, lists suggestions on how to get started. It is also helpful to determine what motivates you to smoke, since some quitting techniques work better for certain types of smokers than others. (See Table 3:3 on keeping a daily cigarette log.) Dr. Daniel Horn at the National Clearinghouse for Smoking and Health has developed a questionnaire to determine the reasons behind your habit. (See Table 3:4, Why Do You Smoke?)

SOURCES OF HELP

There are many organizations devoted to helping people quit smoking (see Table 3:5). Nonprofit groups such as the American Cancer Society, American Heart Association and Seventh-Day Adventist Church give out free information or hold stop-smoking clinics. SmokEnders, Smoke Watchers and other commercial programs also have a high success rate and the money you spend to join may act as an extra incentive. Many employers also offer smoking cessation clinics; check with your company's medical director. Even if your company does not offer such programs, the situation may change if there is sufficient employee interest. Employers have a special interest in inducing people to stop smoking. Studies have shown that a smoker costs an employer at least $1000 a year more in increased insurance and health costs than is paid for nonsmokers.

Self-hypnosis is still another method that works well for large numbers of people. Dr. Herbert Spiegel, a psychiatrist affliated with Columbia University and a widely acclaimed leader in clinical hypnosis, has treated some 10,000 smokers with self-hypnosis, with long-term success rates of up to 70 to 80 percent. The technique seems to work best for smokers who are readily hypnotizable and who have a spouse or partner who cares about their well-being.

❑ Alcohol Abuse

Alcohol abuse among older people has only recently begun to receive the attention the problem warrants. It is estimated that 10 percent of men and 2 percent of women over age 65 are alcohol abusers. While this percentage is

Tips for Quitting Smoking

- *List your reasons for quitting.* Include your own individual motivations as well as the health and cosmetic reasons. Place this list where you will see it several times a day to remind yourself of your goals.
- *Think positively.* If you expect to succeed, chances are good that you will. Slipping back in the past does not indicate inevitable failure again. Even if you break down and have one cigarette, it does not mean you have failed to become an ex-smoker. Just start again, and with even greater resolve.
- *Keep a record of your smoking habits.* Record each cigarette you smoke for a couple of days. (See Table 3:3.) Note the time and situation and how much you feel you wanted each cigarette. This record will help you prepare for or avoid situations in which you will most likely crave a cigarette.
- *Set the date for quitting and stick to it.* Pick a date that will not coincide with other periods of stress. Vacation time or other low-stress periods may be the best time to try to quit smoking. The first day of the month, the first day of spring, your birthday, New Year's Day are all dates that signify new beginnings; use one to begin your new life without cigarettes.
- *Involve other people.* Some smokers are hesitant to make known their intentions to quit for fear of public failure. However, most people, even nonsmokers, know that quitting is difficult. They will have some idea what you are going through and are likely to be encouraging, not judgmental. Their support and encouragement may be just what you need to keep you away from cigarettes.
- *Start to get in shape physically.* Aerobic exercise, such as running, swimming, aerobic dancing or cycling, is a great way to strengthen your heart and your resolve to be an ex-smoker. While you're exercising, you can't be smoking, and the more you exercise, the more you will realize how much smoking holds you back. Building your endurance is yet another reason to quit.
- *Change brands of cigarettes.* While there is no "safe" cigarette, low-tar and low-nicotine cigarettes may reduce your pleasure in smoking and therefore make it easier to quit. Buying one pack at a time will make smoking a little less convenient.
- *Talk with your doctor.* Research indicates that even a short conversation with a physician will increase your chances of success. Your doctor may have some special advice or tips that may help you. In some cases, physicians will prescribe nicotine chewing gum to ease the craving for that addictive cigarette ingredient. Although nicotine itself is a stimulant that raises blood pressure, it is preferable to smoking. It is also less enjoyable than smoking for most people and is easily given up once the craving for cigarettes subside. Still, nicotine gum should not be chewed for more than two weeks, since it, too, is habit forming.

The First Few Days:

- *Throw away all of your cigarettes.* Hide all the ashtrays, matches and other objects associated with smoking at home and at the office.
- *Know what to expect.* Physical withdrawal symptoms from smoking may last about one to two weeks, but the worst is usually over in three days. Forty to 50 percent of smokers report no withdrawal symptoms at all.
- *Increase fluid intake.* Drinking fruit juice and plenty of water will help speed up the process of flushing the nicotine out of your bloodstream.
- *Distract your attention from cravings.* After the first few days of quitting, the process of withdrawal is mostly psychological. Intense craving is to be expected, but you can effectively distract your attention from it by taking two or three deep breaths, talking to someone or taking a brisk walk.
- *Join the nonsmokers.* Seek out places where smoking is prohibited and avoid situations in which you would usually smoke (refer to your record of cigarette smoking). Plan to go to a museum, theater or health club instead of a cocktail party. If you must attend a function where there are many smokers, prepare yourself in advance and make a conscious effort not to smoke. Find nonsmokers or ex-smokers to talk to. Once you get through the event, plan something special to celebrate.
- *Keep alcohol consumption to a minimum.* Cigarettes and alcohol often go hand in hand, so it may be wise to forgo drinking completely after you first quit (also, alcohol affects your willpower adversely). The same is true of coffee. If you always have a cigarette with your coffee, try going for a walk or drinking something else until you can divorce the two in your mind.
- *Watch what you eat.* Although experts have estimated that it would take gaining over 75 pounds to offset the benefits of quitting smoking, many people worry that they will gain weight. Indeed, many people do gain a few pounds, both because of improved metabolism and a perked-up appetite. But even those few can be avoided. Your appetite will improve after quitting, so have carrot and celery sticks handy. Try not to increase the size of your meals, or, if you must, fill up on nonfattening items such as salad with low-fat dressing. However, protein is important for the body's mending process, so be sure you're eating enough. Exercise will not only burn off calories but help release the tension caused by nicotine withdrawal as well. (Note that although quitting smoking causes tension, it is actually less than the tension caused by smoking itself.)

Table 3:2

Daily Cigarette Count

Instructions: Cut out this table and attach it to your pack of cigarettes with rubber bands. Complete the information each time you smoke a cigarette (those from your own pack or those offered by someone else). Note the time and evaluate how much each cigarette means to you (1 is for a cigarette you feel you can't do without; 2 is less necessary; 3 is one you could really go without). Make any other additional comments about your feelings or the situation. This record helps you understand why and when you smoke.

Time	Need	Feelings/Situation
6 A.M.		
6:30		
7		
7:30		
8		
8:30		
9		
9:30		
10		
10:30		
11		
11:30		
12 P.M.		
12:30		

Time	Need	Feelings/Situation
1		
1:30		
2		
2:30		
3		
3:30		
4		
4:30		
5		
5:30		
6		
6:30		
7		
7:30		
8		
8:30		
9		
9:30		
10		
10:30		
11		
11:30		
12 A.M.		
12:30		
1		
1:30		

Table 3:3

Stop-Smoking Groups

The following organizations can provide information on stop-smoking groups. Check your telephone white pages for listings of local chapters.

American Cancer Society
National Office
4 West 34th Street
New York, NY 10001
Ask for information about their Fresh Start quit-smoking program and their "7-Day Plan to Help You Stop Smoking Cigarettes."

American Heart Association
National Center
7320 Greenville Avenue
Dallas, TX 75231
Distributes stop-smoking literature, including "Calling It Quits."

American Lung Association
1740 Broadway
New York, NY 10019
Write for their "Freedom from Smoking in 20 Days" and "A Lifetime of Freedom from Smoking" brochures.

Office of Cancer Communications
National Cancer Institute
Bethesda, MD 20205
Write for their "Helping Smokers Quit Kit" and "Clearing the Air: A Guide to Quitting Smoking."

Table 3:5

Why Do You Smoke? A Self-Assessment Test

Here are some statements made by people to describe what they get out of smoking cigarettes. How often do you feel this way when smoking? Select one number for each statement.

5 = always	2 = seldom
4 = frequently	1 = never
3 = occasionally	

A. I smoke cigarettes in order to keep myself from slowing down. __
B. Handling a cigarette is part of the enjoyment of smoking it. __
C. Smoking cigarettes is pleasant and relaxing. __
D. I light up a cigarette when I feel angry about something. __
E. When I have run out of cigarettes I find it almost unbearable until I can get them. __
F. I smoke cigarettes automatically without even being aware of it. __
G. I smoke cigarettes to stimulate me, to perk myself up. __
H. Part of the enjoyment of smoking a cigarette comes from the steps I take to light up. __
I. I find cigarettes pleasurable. __
J. When I feel uncomfortable or upset about something, I light up a cigarette. __
K. I am very much aware of the fact when I am not smoking a cigarette. __
L. I light up a cigarette without realizing I still have one burning in the ashtray. __
M. I smoke cigarettes to give me a "lift." __
N. When I smoke a cigarette, part of the enjoyment is watching the smoke as I exhale it. __
O. I want a cigarette most when I am comfortable and relaxed. __
P. When I feel "blue" or want to take my mind off cares and worries, I smoke cigarettes. __
Q. I get a real gnawing for a cigarette when I haven't smoked for a while. __
R. I've found a cigarette in my mouth and didn't remember putting it there. __

How to Score:

1. Enter the numbers you have selected for the test questions in the spaces below, putting the number you have selected for question A over line A, for question B over line B, etc.
2. Add the three scores on each line to get your totals. For example, the sum of scores over lines A, G, and M gives you your score on Stimulation, etc. Scores of 11 or above indicate that this factor is an important source of satisfaction for the smoker. Scores of 7 or less are low and probably indicate that this factor does not apply to you. Scores in between are marginal.

____ + ____ + ____ = ______________
(A) (G) (M) Stimulation

____ + ____ + ____ = ______________
(B) (H) (N) Handling

____ + ____ + ____ = ______________
(C) (I) (O) Pleasurable Relaxation

____ + ____ + ____ = ______________
(D) (J) (P) Crutch: Tension Reduction

____ + ____ + ____ = ______________
(E) (K) (Q) Craving: Psychological Addiction

____ + ____ + ____ = ______________
(F) (L) (R) Habit

Source: Adapted from "Smoker's Self Test" by Daniel Horn, Ph.D., director of the National Clearinghouse for Smoking and Health, Public Health Service.

Interpreting Your Score

Stimulation: You smoke because you're stimulated by the cigarette. It gives you a lift, peps you up when you're tired. When you try to give up smoking, substitute a brisk walk to wake you up or a few simple exercises whenever you feel the urge to smoke.
Handling: You like the ritual and trappings of smoking, tapping the cigarette on the back of your hand, striking matches or waving your cigarette to emphasize a point. You can find other ways to keep your hands busy. Pick a new object to use, like a coin, piece of jewelry, pen or pencil.
Relaxation: You get a real sense of pleasure out of smoking; it's the time when you feel good about yourself. An honest consideration of the harmful effects of this habit may take some of the "pleasure" away from the smoking and help you quit.
Crutch (for negative feelings): If you mostly light up when you're angry or depressed, you're using smoking as a tranquilizer. You've got to prove to yourself that smoking isn't helping you deal with problems effectively. In a tough situation, take a deep breath to relax, call a friend and talk over your feelings. If you've coped with stress a few times without smoking, you're on your way to quitting.
Craving: Quitting smoking is difficult for you if you feel you're psychologically dependent. It means you start craving your next smoke as soon as you've put out a cigarette. Try to crave quitting. Tell everyone you're going to quit. Once you've stopped, it will be possible to resist the temptation to smoke because the withdrawal effort is too tough to face again.
Habit: If you usually smoke without even realizing you're doing it, you should find it easy to break the habit pattern. Cutting down gradually may be effective for you, particularly if you make a point of becoming aware of each cigarette you smoke. Start by asking "Do I really want this cigarette?" You may be surprised at how many you *don't* want. Help yourself by changing smoking patterns: Put your cigarettes in a locked drawer, or stop carrying matches.

Source: Adapted from "7-Day Plan to Help You Stop Smoking Cigarettes," The American Cancer Society, 1978.

Table 3:4

comparable to statistics on other age groups, older drinkers are more likely to be adversely affected by excessive drinking and less likely to be detected and treated for their problem.

▪ *What Happens When You Drink*

Because alcohol is so readily available, we often forget that it is, in fact, a drug. And, as with most drugs, alcohol can be both beneficial or toxic, depending on its use and its user. (See Table 3:6, Tips on Safe Drinking.)

In small doses, alcohol relaxes the body, stimulates the appetite and produces a feeling of well-being. (Even so, there may be some adverse effects for people who have high blood pressure or for pregnant women.) In large doses, it is a powerful poison that accounts for 10 percent of all deaths, either directly (due to physical damage to the body caused by the alcohol itself) or indirectly (by accidents caused by alcohol abusers).

Alcohol contains calories (see Table 3:7), but no other useful nutrients. In fact, it can even deplete the body's source of vitamins and minerals or make them difficult to absorb.

When alcohol is ingested, 95 percent is absorbed by the stomach and small intestine or duodenum directly into the bloodstream. Within minutes, the alcohol has permeated every part of the body that contains water: the lungs, kidneys, heart and brain. The presence of small amounts of alcohol in the brain initially acts as a stimulant. The drinker at this point feels more sociable and active. However, as more alcohol is absorbed, it begins to act as a sedative or depressant with a calming or tranquilizing effect. If enough alcohol is ingested, it will start to act as a hypnotic, inducing sleep.

Reaction time, physical coordination, eyesight and depth perception are all compromised by the presence of alcohol

Tips on Safe Drinking

- *Never drink on an empty stomach.* Always serve snacks (preferably cheese and crackers, rather than salty potato chips, which increase thirst) when offering alcoholic beverages.
- *Dilute liquor with ice and water.* Drink slowly, in a relaxed and comfortable setting. Do not drink if you are depressed, nervous or tired.
- *Alternate nonalcoholic drinks with alcoholic ones.* Always have plenty of soda and fruit juice on hand at parties for those who choose not to drink.
- *Never drink and drive.* If you go to a party with a friend, decide beforehand who will drive home. That person should not drink. Even walking home when intoxicated increases the danger of being a victim of a crime or car accident. Call a cab, stay overnight or have a nondrinking friend drive you home.
- *Do not mix alcohol and drugs.* This applies to over-the-counter, prescription and illicit drugs. Alcohol depresses the central nervous system. If you are taking a drug with the same side effect, the combination may have serious depressive effects.

Table 3:6

Caloric Content of Alcoholic Beverages

Drink	Amount	Calories
WINES:		
champagne	4 oz.	85
dessert (18.8% alcohol)	4 oz.	155
port	4 oz.	180
red, white or sherry	4 oz.	100
dry vermouth	4 oz.	120
sweet vermouth	4 oz.	190
BEER AND OTHER MALT LIQUORS:		
beer	12 oz.	150–160
lite beer	12 oz.	100
ale	12 oz.	150
DISTILLED LIQUORS:		
gin, rum, whiskey or vodka		
80-proof	1 oz.	70
86-proof	1 oz.	75
90-proof	1 oz.	80
94-proof	1 oz.	83
100-proof	1 oz.	90
fermented cider	6 oz.	70
cognac or brandy	1 oz.	70

Table 3:7

in the blood. Driving, or any other activity involving complex and rapid decision-making or calling for physical action, should be avoided completely while drinking and for a period of time afterward.

Alcohol affects body functions by slowing down metabolism, breathing and circulation. In fact, alcohol has the potential to paralyze breathing altogether, leading to death. This is a relatively rare occurrence, since the body at some point starts to rid itself of the toxin by vomiting or the drinker passes out before consuming a fatal amount of alcohol. However, many older people may be more sensitive to the toxic effects of alcohol and may therefore reach the fatal dose at a lower level.

Alcohol in the bloodstream is broken down by enzymes in the liver, producing carbon dioxide and water which are then excreted. The liver can only process the alcohol at a certain rate—about an ounce of pure ethanol (less than an ounce of hard liquor) in an hour. The only antidote for drinking too much is to wait until the liver can convert the alcohol into a nontoxic substance. Black coffee, cold showers and other popular "remedies" are not effective.

Later, as the body recoils and repairs itself from the onslaught of too much alcohol, a hangover occurs. Blood vessels in the brain that became dilated (opened up) by the presence of alcohol now return to their normal state, producing headache. The gastric juices altered by the harsh alcohol produce stomach upset. The kidneys, stimulated by the alcohol, excrete too much water, resulting in dehydration. There is some evidence that older people become more susceptible to these unpleasant side effects, even at lower dosages.

The cure for a hangover? Sleep, aspirin, bland food, plenty of liquids and time.

▪ *The Effects of Long-Term Alcohol Abuse on the Body*

For most people without health problems, the hangover is the only physical consequence of an occasional drinking binge. However, long-term alcohol abuse and heavy drinking will take a toll on the body. Vision, sexual function, circulation and nutrition are all impaired by alcohol abuse. In fact, alcohol abuse is cited by many experts as the number-one cause of vitamin and nutritional deficiencies (especially vitamin B_{12} and folic acid) in older people.

Because of its role in metabolizing alcohol, the liver is a prime candidate for the detrimental effects of alcohol abuse. In the presence of alcohol, the liver will choose to process it as fuel rather than as the usual fatty acids. The resultant buildup of unprocessed fatty acids in the liver causes it to enlarge, a reversible condition referred to as fatty liver. This condition, which can be induced even by steady social drinking (four or five drinks daily for several weeks), does not usually cause any symptoms. The liver will return to normal size when excessive drinking is curtailed.

Heavy drinking may also lead to inflammation of liver cells, or alcoholic hepatitis. Fever, pain and jaundice are common symptoms of this condition. If alcohol consumption is curtailed, alcoholic hepatitis may be reversible. However, if drinking continues, the next stage of liver deterioration—cirrhosis—is irreversible and often fatal.

In cirrhosis of the liver, fibrous scar tissue obstructs the flow of blood through the organ. As a result, the liver cannot perform its various functions: it cannot convert glycogen into usable glucose for energy, so blood sugar drops and hypoglycemia ensues. It can no longer effectively detoxify the blood nor eliminate dead red blood cells, leading to a buildup of waste products in the blood. The cirrhotic liver cannot manufacture bile to digest fat, prothrombin to clot blood and prevent bruising, globulin to fight infection, nor albumin to maintain cell function. Liver malfunction can also lead to malabsorption of several important vitamins, including A, D, E and K.

The heart is another area adversely affected by alcohol abuse. Heart patients should be especially careful in monitoring consumption since even a one-time binge may cause irregular heartbeats in some people. Heavy drinkers have greater incidences of high blood pressure, heart attack and other cardiac conditions. Since these conditions are more common among people over age 50 anyway, older people should be especially wary of the exacerbating consequences of alcohol abuse. Cardiomyopathy, a disease of the heart muscle that is quite rare in the general population, is more common among longtime drinkers. Strokes are also more common among people who use even moderate amounts of alcohol than among nondrinkers. A recent study found that people who regularly consumed the equivalent of one or two glasses of wine, a beer or a mixed drink had a much higher incidence of stroke than abstainers. In addition, alcohol affects the central nervous system, slowing down the brain activity, imparing reaction time, mental awareness, judgment and coordination. Studies show that as one grows older, the brain becomes more susceptible to these effects of alcohol. The increased risk of taking falls when drinking, combined with the increased injury due to a fall, makes alcohol abuse hazardous for older people. Choking on food, another kind of accident that can be fatal, is also much more common among people—especially those with false teeth—when they drink heavily during a meal. Alcohol also has a detrimental effect on other parts of the nervous system, and can cause visual problems, tremors and other signs of nerve damage. Impotence, for example, is very common among alcoholic men.

The older person's digestive tract is also more susceptible to the detrimental effects of alcohol. As one gets older, the intestine's ability to move food through the digestive tract is reduced. Ulcers are also more common among older people. Large amounts of alcohol cause intestinal membranes to swell, further inhibiting digestion. Alcohol also increases secretion of digestive juices which erode the stomach lining, exacerbating or causing ulcers.

Heavy drinking may also lead to malabsorption of certain vitamins, specifically vitamin B_{12} and folic acid. Deficiencies of these nutrients may cause fatigue and increased susceptibility to infection.

Finally, a recent study by Harvard University researchers found that women who regularly consume alcohol—even one drink a day—have an increased risk of breast cancer. Although more research is needed to confirm this, women who are at risk for breast cancer

Drugs That Should Not Be Taken with Alcohol

- *"Minor" tranquilizers*: Valium (diazepam), Librium (chlordiazepoxide), Miltown (meprobamate) and others.
- *"Major" tranquilizers*: Thorazine (chlorpromazine), Mellaril (thioridazine) and others.
- *Barbiturates*: Luminal (phenobarbital) and others.
- *Painkillers*: Darvon (propoxyphene), Demerol (meperidine) and others. (Note: Mixing alcohol and high-dose aspirin can increase bleeding problems.)
- *Antihistamines* (both prescription and over-the-counter forms found in cold remedies).

In addition, alcohol should not be taken with anticonvulsants, anticoagulants or certain antidiabetes drugs because it alters the drugs' actions. ALWAYS ASK YOUR DOCTOR IF IT IS SAFE TO DRINK WHILE TAKING A MEDICATION.

Table 3:8

(e.g., those with a strong family history of the disease) might well be advised to curtail alcohol consumption.

Although people over 65 constitute only 11 percent of the population in the United States, they consume 25 percent of all medications prescribed in this country. Therefore, among older people who drink, the chances of an adverse drug interaction with alcohol are greatly increased. (See Table 3:8.) Always let your doctor know what other drugs, both prescription and over-the-counter, you are taking and what your drinking habits are whenever a new medication is advised.

What Are the Signs of Alcoholism?

This test may be used to learn if you or someone you know has some of the symptoms of alcoholism.

	Yes	No
1. Do you occasionally drink heavily after a disappointment or quarrel, or when the boss gives you a hard time?	☐	☐
2. When you have trouble or feel under pressure, do you always drink more heavily than usual?	☐	☐
3. Have you noticed that you are able to handle more liquor than you did when you were first drinking?	☐	☐
4. Did you ever wake up on the "morning after" and discover that you could not remember part of the evening before, even though your friends tell you that you did not "pass out"?	☐	☐
5. When drinking with other people, do you try to have a few extra drinks when others will not know it?	☐	☐
6. Are there certain occasions when you feel uncomfortable if alcohol is not available?	☐	☐
7. Have you recently noticed that when you begin drinking you are in more of a hurry to get the first drink than you used to be?	☐	☐
8. Do you sometimes feel a little guilty about your drinking?	☐	☐
9. Are you secretly irritated when your family or friends discuss your drinking?	☐	☐
10. Have you recently noticed an increase in the frequency of your memory "black-outs"?	☐	☐
11. Do you often find that you wish to continue drinking after your friends say they have had enough?	☐	☐
12. Do you usually have a reason for the occasions when you drink heavily?	☐	☐
13. When you are sober, do you often regret things you have done or said while drinking?	☐	☐
14. Have you tried switching brands or following different plans for controlling your drinking?	☐	☐
15. Have you often failed to keep the promises you have made to yourself about controlling or cutting down on your drinking?	☐	☐
16. Have you ever tried to control your drinking by making a change in jobs or moving to a new location?	☐	☐
17. Do you try to avoid family or close friends while you are drinking?	☐	☐
18. Are you having an increasing number of financial and work problems?	☐	☐
19. Do more people seem to be treating you unfairly without good reason?	☐	☐
20. Do you eat very little or irregularly when you are drinking?	☐	☐
21. Do you sometimes have the "shakes" in the morning and find that it helps to have a little drink?	☐	☐
22. Have you recently noticed that you cannot drink as much as you once did?	☐	☐
23. Do you sometimes stay drunk for several days at a time?	☐	☐
24. Do you sometimes feel very depressed and wonder whether life is worth living?	☐	☐
25. Sometimes after periods of drinking, do you see or hear things that aren't there?	☐	☐
26. Do you get terribly frightened after you have been drinking heavily?	☐	☐

How to Interpret

If you answered "yes" to any of the questions, you have some of the symptoms that may indicate alcoholism.

Several "yes" answers to questions in the following sections indicate the following stages of alcoholism:

Questions 1 to 8: Early Stage of mild dependence.

Questions 9 to 21: Middle Stage of moderate dependence.

Questions 22 to 26: The beginning of Final Stage of dependence with physical and mental deterioration.

Source: Reproduced with permission from the National Council on Alcoholism, 12 West 21st Street, New York, NY 10010.

Table 3:9

▪ *Helping the Older Problem Drinker*

There are two general types of older problem drinkers: chronic, longtime abusers and situational abusers. Chronic abusers—lifetime drinkers who have not received effective help for their problem—make up approximately two thirds of older alcoholics. Although many chronic abusers succumb to the physical damage of longtime abuse before age 65, a number survive to old age.

Situational abusers are older people who have turned to alcohol in response to the increased stresses associated with growing older: retirement, fixed income, health problems and the deaths of friends and family members.

In fact, social pressures and age-related problems play a key role for both types of alcoholics. (See Table 3:9.) The longtime alcoholic is likely to have alienated family and nondrinking friends. His or her drinking friends may have already died from the consequences of alcohol abuse. The situational alcoholic may also lack a close family unit due to the loss of friends and family members. In his or her case, however, the loss spurred the drinking, rather than vice versa.

Both types of older alcoholics are likely to be unemployed or retired. Again, for the longtime alcoholic, unemployment is probably a consequence of alcohol abuse. For the late-onset alcoholic, retirement or loss of job precipitated the drinking problem.

No matter which came first, the drinking or the social problems, group socialization and counseling are essential for effective treatment of the older alcoholic. Involvement in volunteer activities in the community, recreational activities and special-interest groups will increase the older person's sense of self-worth and confidence. Counseling aimed at sharpening social skills needed to make friends and to open up to old friends and family members is also especially helpful for the older problem drinker. The better a person feels about him- or herself, the less likely he or she is to reach for solace from a bottle.

In longtime alcoholics, however, there is a greater need for medical treatment and longer detoxification programs. Longtime drinkers are more susceptible to alcohol-related illnesses, and older alcoholics may need more time to rid their bodies of the toxins. (See Table 3:10, Steps in Detoxification.)

Steps in Detoxification

Stopping Alcohol

- Initial phase should be done under a physician's supervision.
- Patient should stay home or be in a hospital or clinic for at least five days.
- Home detoxification requires that the patient have someone who can help him or her through withdrawal phase.
- Benzodiazepines (Valium) may be given in declining dosages for the first week to reduce withdrawal symptoms. Should not be given on a long-term basis because of the danger of substituting one addiction for another.
- Vitamin injections may be needed for the first week or longer if there is serious nutritional deficiency or evidence of brain damage.

Long-Term Abstinence

- Consider joining Alcoholics Anonymous or some other support group.
- Disulfiram (Antabuse) or citrated calcium carbimide (Abstem) may be taken as extra motivation not to drink. These drugs sensitize the body to alcohol. If a patient who takes these drugs then drinks, he or she will experience very unpleasant side effects, such as flushing, palpitations, nausea, fainting or headache. The drugs should not be used by people with heart disease or who are impulsive or suicidal. Caution must be taken to avoid hidden alcohol in foods, mouthwashes, medications and other sources.
- Don't be fooled into thinking you can take one or two drinks and then stop. Some recovered alcoholics may be able eventually to engage in social drinking, but they are rare. Alcoholism is a disease that lasts for life. It cannot be cured, but can be controlled by not drinking.

Table 3:10

How to Spot a Drinking Problem

Not everyone who drinks regularly is an alcoholic. The National Institute on Aging has compiled the following list of symptoms that indicate a drinking problem:

- Drinking to calm nerves, forget worries or reduce depression
- Loss of interest in food
- Gulping drinks and drinking too fast
- Lying about drinking habits
- Drinking alone with increasing frequency
- Injuring oneself, or someone else, while intoxicated
- Getting drunk often (more than three or four times in the past year)
- Needing to drink more alcohol to get the same effect
- Frequently acting irritable, resentful or unreasonable during nondrinking periods
- Experiencing medical, social or financial problems due to drinking

Table 3:11

Sources of Help for Alcoholism

Al-Anon Family Group Headquarters
Alateen
P.O. Box 182
Madison Square Station
New York, NY 10159
(212) 683-1771

Alcoholics Anonymous
General Service Office
P.O. Box 459
Grand Central Station
New York, NY 10163
(212) 686-1100

American Council on Alcohol Problems, Inc.
2980 Patricia Drive
Des Moines, IA 50322
(515) 276-7752

Association of Halfway House Alcoholism Programs of North America
786 East 7th Street
St. Paul, MN 55106
(612) 771-0933

Citizen's Council on Women, Alcohol and Drugs
8293 Main Street
Ellicott City, MD 21043

Hazelden Foundation
Box 11
Center City, MN 55012
(800) 328-9000

Mothers Against Drunk Driving
669 Airport Freeway, Suite 310
Hurst, TX 76053
(817) 268-6233

National Association of Alcoholism Treatment Programs, Inc.
2082 Michelson Drive
Irvine, CA 92715
(714) 975-0104

National Association of Children of Alcoholics, Inc.
P.O. Box 421691
San Francisco, CA 94142
(415) 431-1366

National Clearinghouse for Alcohol Information
P.O. Box 2345
Rockville, MD 20852
(301) 468-2600

National Council on Alcoholism, Inc.
12 West 21st Street, 7th floor
New York, NY 10010
(212) 206-6770

National Institute on Alcohol Abuse and Alcoholism
Parklawn Building
5600 Fishers Lane
Rockville, MD 20852
(301) 443-3885

The Christopher D. Smithers Foundation
P.O. Box 67
Mill Neck, NY 11765
(516) 676-0067

Table 3:12

Counseling specifically about alcohol abuse is usually most effective when older alcoholics and recovering alcoholics are involved in group discussions. Problems with alcohol are just one issue among many concerning older drinkers, and every opportunity should be given to discuss these issues with peers.

Studies show all of these programs are most effective in a nonthreatening environment, such as a senior citizen center. These centers often offer a variety of activities, including community meals and other social programs. Transportation is less likely to be a problem and escort services are often available to older people concerned about traveling alone.

Since older people are more likely to live alone and to be retired or unemployed, they are not as visible to the community at large. Drinking problems may go undetected. Family members, neighbors and friends should keep a lookout for older people, especially those who have suffered a series of losses or disabilities. (See Table 3:11, How to Spot a Drinking Problem.)

Older alcoholics are very likely to deny the existence of a problem. They may be ashamed of their drinking or afraid that treatment programs would be ineffective, unnecessary or too late for them. Families of older problem drinkers may also deny the problem or attribute it to the normal effects of aging. However, studies show that older alcoholics have a high rate of success in overcoming drinking problems, given the appropriate services. Recovering alcoholics report greater mental clarity and self-esteem. Many of the symptoms they previously attributed to aging are relieved by abstinence from drinking.

The bottom line is that help is available to the older alcohol abuser, and seeking it out may be a step toward improving the quality of life for that person and the people around him or her. (See Table 3:12, Sources of Help for Alcoholism.)

❑ Drug Abuse

We tend to associate drug abuse with younger people, but this can be a mistake. Although the use of cocaine, marijuana and other so-called recreational drugs may be more common among the young, there are middle-aged and older users. More common, however, is the abuse of prescription or other legal drugs. Abuse of legal drugs has long been overlooked, although there are numerous examples, both from recent and past history, in which legal drugs have been a major source of dependency or addiction.

Historically, morphine addiction has been particularly notorious. Typically, a patient would be given morphine to control pain and end up becoming addicted. Alcoholics often turned to the more respectable alcohol-based tonics, which were legal during Prohibition. Today a wide assortment of drugs, especially prescription painkillers, tranquilizers such as Valium, and diet pills, are abused by people of all ages (see Table 3:13 for a list of commonly abused legal drugs). Betty Ford's public disclosure of

Commonly Abused Legal Drugs

Painkillers:
- Codeine preparations
- Darvon
- Demerol
- Percodan
- Other painkillers with propoxyphene, morphine, oxycodone and other narcotic ingredients

Tranquilizers:
- Benzodiazepines (Librium, Valium and others)

Sedatives/Sleeping Pills:
- Seconal, Phenobarbital, Nembutal and other barbiturates
- Dalmane, Doriden, Halcion and other nonbarbiturates

Table 3:13

her problems with both alcohol and painkillers helped bring abuse of legal drugs into the open.

The problem of drug dependency should be approached in much the same manner as alcoholism. Stopping the drugs will often produce uncomfortable withdrawal symptoms, and a doctor's help is needed during the acute phase. Care must be taken at this time not to substitute one addiction for another.

❑ A Final Word

Almost from the beginning of time, humans have sought pleasure from mind- or sensation-altering substances. Virtually every culture and society has its high-producing drugs. Some are used for religious purposes; others simply for pleasure. Sadly, all too often there is another side to using these substances. It is very easy to become addicted to many, if not most, of them, and once "hooked," it can be very hard to stop their use.

An occasional drink, cigarette or even marijuana may not produce any long-term harm. But once started, it is very hard, if not impossible, to limit their use. After smoking only a few cigarettes, most people become habitual smokers. Alcohol may be easier to control, except for genetically predisposed people who can very quickly become alcoholics. And once addicted to any of these substances, a person begins to suffer the physical and psychological consequences.

People who have been down the road of trying to stop smoking, to quit drinking or to get off illicit or legal drugs invariably agree that it is far better not to start than to go through the struggle of detoxification and withdrawal.

Of course, hindsight is always wise, and knowing that you should never have started a bad habit is of little comfort to one who is trying to break it. Difficult as it may be to stop smoking, quit drinking or break a drug dependency, the benefits to be gained in terms of better health, enhanced self-esteem and a renewed outlook on life are worth the difficulty.

4

COPING WITH STRESS

We have a tendency to think that stress is an "invention" of our fast-paced twentieth-century world. The fact is, stress is an inevitable part of living, no matter what the culture or the age. Although we talk a good deal about stress, many people do not have a clear idea of what it means. In simple terms, stress is any condition or situation that requires adjustment on the part of a person. Thus stress can be physical or psychological, or a combination of the two.

Although we usually think of stress as involving a negative event or situation—facing a big examination, losing a job, coming face to face with danger—joyous occasions also carry a degree of stress. Winning a long-sought promotion, going on a vacation, buying a new home all produce stress. We often complain, "I can't take the stress anymore" or "the stress is killing me," but a certain amount of stress adds spice to life and is even desirable in helping us reach our goals.

Just as there are different kinds of stress, so are there different levels or degrees within the kinds. Some stress is mild and brief—missing a bus, misplacing keys or glasses, coming close to hitting a car or animal while driving are common examples. Moderate stress lasts longer and is more difficult to deal with—examples might include getting ready for a wedding or holiday, overwork, the temporary absence of a spouse or child. Severe stress is more prolonged and difficult to deal with—chronic illness or death of a spouse, threatened loss of a job, impending retirement.

It is the severe, chronic stress—the kind we often feel we cannot escape from, coupled with poor techniques for dealing with it—that is the most likely to cause problems. For example, stress has been linked with a variety of disorders, both mental and physical. There is still much we do not understand about how the mind and body work together, but recent research indicates that stress may depress the body's immune system and make us more vulnerable to illness.

It is well-known that people are more likely to fall ill during high-stress periods. Increasingly, physicians are emphasizing effective stress management as an important part of health promotion and preventive medicine. (See Table 4:1, Steps to Help You Achieve Emotional Well-Being.)

❑ How Stress Affects the Body

Our response to stress is firmly ingrained in our evolution. Whenever we are faced with danger or other stress, the body reacts with a fight-or-flight response. The late Dr. Hans Selye, a world authority on stress and its effects, observed the body has a three-phase response to stress: alarm, resistance and exhaustion.

In the first phase, at almost the instant the body senses the stress, the pituitary gland sounds an internal alarm and stimulates the adrenal glands to secrete increased amounts of stress hormones—adrenaline, or epinephrine, and corticosteroid hormones that ready the body to take immediate action. Heart rate and blood pressure increase, the pupils dilate, muscles become tense and we feel a heightened alertness. The body is thus prepared to fight or flee. When appropriate action is taken and the source of stress is relieved, hormone levels drop to normal. If the source of stress is not removed, however, the body stays on the alert, or the resistance stage. Eventually, this leads to a state of exhaustion, and unless relieved, a person is likely to develop a stress-related disorder: a stress headache or simply an inability to concentrate and function.

In our modern society, we are not likely to encounter the kinds of stress in which a full-blown fight or flight is appropriate. But the body will still react in much the same manner when it receives stress signals from the brain. Thus, when a boss asks us to redo a report or we are running late for an appointment, the body reacts in much the same manner as if it were placed in a dangerous situation.

Over a longer period of time, repeated

Steps to Help You Achieve Emotional Well-Being

- Learn to recognize your own symptoms of stress. These may include irritability, sleeplessness, social and/or sexual withdrawal, loss of interest in activities, lack of appetite.
- Talk about stressful events to a friend or spouse before you reach a breaking point. If you can, let go and cry. Like talking, crying externalizes pent-up feelings and may reduce the risk of stress-related illness. If you need extra help, seek counseling from a mental health professional.
- Recognize that some things cannot be changed and put your energy toward those that can.
- Cultivate an optimistic attitude. Don't talk yourself into believing that you can't cope.
- Reduce your exposure to pet peeves. Go to the bank at an off-hour to avoid maddening lines. Mask outside noise by turning on relaxing music.
- Learn to express anger in a constructive way. Keeping anger pent up adds to feelings of stress; blowing up in a rage is almost as bad. Simply being able to say "that makes me very angry" and working out ways of avoiding anger-provoking situations are positive steps in dealing with anger.
- Focus on others rather than your own problems. If time permits, do a few hours of volunteer work each week.
- Exercise every day, even if you have time for only a brisk, 20-minute walk.
- Pay attention to such signs of stress as a tension headache and stop what you are doing for a rest break. If possible, take a warm bath or treat yourself to a massage during periods of stress. If this is not possible, practice deep abdominal breathing whenever you feel muscular tension setting in.
- Don't neglect your diet. Start off with a breakfast containing protein and carbohydrates for sustained energy and don't let the demands of your day get in the way of lunch.

Table 4:1

inappropriate responses to stress, with the accompanying bodily changes in blood pressure, increased flow of gastric acid and other hormone-related changes, can take their toll. Many experts believe that excessive stress, or perhaps more accurately, inappropriate responses to stress, can play a role in developing heart disease, asthma, ulcers, diabetes and other diseases. In addition, many people seek to relieve stress by turning to cigarette or alcohol use or overeating, which further compromises health.

The Social Readjustment Rating Scale

Life Event	Mean Value
1. Death of spouse	100
2. Divorce	73
3. Marital separation from mate	65
4. Detention in jail or other institution	63
5. Death of a close family member	63
6. Major personal injury or illness	53
7. Marriage	50
8. Being fired at work	47
9. Marital reconcilation with mate	45
10. Retirement from work	45
11. Major change in the health or behavior of a family member	44
12. Pregnancy	40
13. Sexual difficulties	39
14. Gaining a new family member (e.g., through birth, adoption, oldster moving in)	39
15. Major business readjustment (e.g., merger, reorganization, bankruptcy)	39
16. Major change in financial state (e.g., a lot worse off or a lot better off than usual)	38
17. Death of a close friend	37
18. Changing to a different line of work	36
19. Major change in the number of arguments with spouse (e.g., either a lot more or a lot less than usual regarding child-rearing, personal habits)	35
20. Taking out a mortgage or loan for a major purchase (e.g., for a home, business)	31
21. Foreclosure on a mortgage or loan	30
22. Major change in responsibilities at work (e.g., promotion, demotion, lateral transfer)	29
23. Son or daughter leaving home (e.g., marriage, attending college)	29
24. Trouble with in-laws	29
25. Outstanding personal achievement	28
26. Wife beginning or ceasing work outside the home	26
27. Beginning or ceasing formal schooling	26
28. Major change in living conditions (e.g., building a new home, remodeling, deterioration of home or neighborhood)	25
29. Revision of personal habits (dress, manners, associations)	24
30. Trouble with the boss	23
31. Major change in working hours or conditions	20
32. Change in residence	20
33. Changing to a new school	20
34. Major change in usual type and/or amount of recreation	19
35. Major change in church activities (e.g., a lot more or a lot less than usual)	19
36. Major change in social activities (e.g., clubs, dancing, movies, visiting)	18
37. Taking out a mortgage or loan for a lesser purchase (e.g., for a car, TV, freezer)	17
38. Major change in sleeping habits (a lot more or a lot less sleep, or change in part of day when asleep)	16
39. Major change in number of family get-togethers (e.g., a lot more or a lot less than usual)	15
40. Major change in eating habits (a lot more or a lot less food intake, or very different meal hours or surroundings)	15
41. Vacation	13
42. Christmas	12
43. Minor violations of the law (e.g., traffic tickets, jaywalking, disturbing the peace, etc.)	11

Source: T. H. Holmes and R. H. Rahe, "The Social Readjustment Rating Scale," *Journal of Psychosomatic Research II* (1967): 213–18. Reprinted with permission of publisher.

Table 4:2

▪ *Sources of Stress*

As people age, sources of stress change. Common stressful events for those over 50 include illness of spouse or self, death of spouse, parent, family member or friend, or a grown child leaving home. Chronic pain, such as that sometimes associated with rheumatoid arthritis, produces stress. Retirement is a major stressor, but changing to a different line of work or even getting a promotion also produce stress. The greater the number of stressful events in a given period, the more likely a person is to experience stress-related illness. (See Table 4:2.)

▪ *Individual Reactions to Stress*

Both on a hormonal and a personal level, individuals react differently to stress. Some people secrete higher levels of hormones and for longer periods of time than others, even when responding to similar situations. And everyone knows people who thrive when working under pressure and actually put off tasks to create this pressure when none exists. The Type A personality, first described in 1959 by two San Francisco cardiologists, Drs. Meyer Friedman and Ray Rosenman, is an example of chronic overresponse to stress. Type As are characterized by aggressive behavior, competitive drive and a preoccupation with time and deadlines. Type As tend to overrespond to almost any situation, whether closing a business deal or mowing the lawn, playing a friendly game of tennis, standing in line at the bank. Almost any situation can provoke a stress-related response. As might be expected, studies have linked Type A behavior with a higher incidence of heart attacks and other stress-related illness. A Type A personality alone probably does not lead to a heart attack, but when it is combined with other risk factors, the likelihood is increased.

❑ DEVELOPING COPING STRATEGIES

Beyond differences in the nervous system affecting hormone release and personality structure, much of how we cope with stress stems from our childhood. Those who were overprotected as children find it more difficult to cope with the normal stresses of adult life than those who were exposed in small doses that allowed the development of coping mechanisms. Social and economic status, ethnic background and, of course, the amount of significance that is attached to a particular event also determine how well stress is handled. People who deal with stress by escaping to a fantasy world, diverting their energy to concerns about imaginary illness (hypochondriac behavior), projecting their own reactions onto others or handling different problems with a single inflexible style are at risk for stress-related illness.

At certain times, though, it is beneficial not to face a stressful situation, at least not immediately. A person who denies that he or she has a serious illness shortly after learning the diagnosis may actually be "buying time" in order to gather coping strengths.

In general, the feeling of being in control of a particular situation reduces the physiological effects of stress. Predictable but stressful events also give the individual time to think about how he or she will cope. Simply learning how to organize time to avoid feeling pressured can go a long way to relieving stress. (See Table 4:3, Tips on How to Organize Time.)

Psychologists use the term "adaptive behavior" to describe healthy stress management. This entails developing alternatives to the usual fight-or-flight response and starts with mobilizing inner personal resources to overcome stress. Each of us possesses different types of

Tips on How to Organize Time

- Plan your day to include work breaks which physically or mentally take you away from the office. Try not to bring office work home.
- When you have an overwhelming number of things to accomplish, set priorities and postpone less important tasks. Learn to delegate matters that cannot be put off. Deal with concerns on a day-at-a-time basis.
- Make a realistic list of what you need to accomplish in a given day, with the most important things at the top. Tackle them one at a time, and don't start a second until you have finished the first.
- Look at your *modus operandi*. Are you a perfectionist? If so, try to decide which tasks truly require meticulous attention to detail and which can be done casually. For example, if you have a high-powered job and a relative in the hospital, don't put a lot of energy into keeping your household spotless.
- Control the timing of stressful events. For example, if you have recently become widowed, defer moving to a different residence until you have had some time to make an emotional adjustment. Similarly, try not to make major decisions when you are overtired or anxious.

Table 4:3

adaptive behavior. Dr. David Hamberg, when he was at Stanford University Medical Center, classified adaptive behaviors as follows:

Information seeking. This enables a person to keep his or her options open and to approach the stressful situation with a basis for sound problem-solving and decision-making.

Organizing feelings and information. By sorting out conflicting feelings and information, a person can avoid disorganization and emotions that may preclude sound decision-making. Making a list of pros and cons helps focus priorities and make wise decisions.

Maintaining flexibility. Freedom of action must be retained in order to make sound decisions. This may entail making alternative plans and shifting priorities as the need arises. Flexibility in timing is also important. Today's crisis may not be a crisis tomorrow if a decision can be delayed until more information is obtained.

Ability to compromise. Rigidity can make coping with stress very difficult, if not impossible. Being able to realistically assess a situation and arrive at a solution that maintains self-esteem are keys to any successful coping technique.

▪ *Special Techniques to Reduce Stress*

All of us possess the basics of coping skills needed to deal with stress. Humans have survived largely because we are able to adapt to our environment and different situations. If you can learn how to handle stress while retaining self-esteem and a measure of control, you will have mastered dealing with stress. Of course, this is often easier said than done. But just remember, everyone has the potential to cope effectively. A baby, although totally helpless and dependent upon others, quickly learns how to get what he or she needs. Insistent crying will bring food, dry diapers or cuddling; a smile will produce delighted praise, and so forth. As we grow older, we become more self-sufficient and at the same time, more skilled in altering our environment to meet our needs. In the final analysis, dealing with stress is not unlike coping with any other problem.

Medical researchers have found that practicing daily systematic relaxation techniques reduces stress and in some cases produces symptom relief in current disease. These methods have been shown to reduce blood sugar in people with diabetes and blood pressure in hypertensives, and to relieve pain in patients with rheumatoid arthritis. How relaxation works is not clearly understood, but researchers speculate that it somehow may make receptors in body tissue less sensitive to high hormone levels produced as part of the stress response.

Some people have a natural ability to concentrate deeply and put themselves into a relaxed state. Most others need some sort of training either by reading a book or attending a class. In general, the individual should practice the technique in a quiet spot, wearing comfortable clothing and not on a full stomach. Although the techniques are typically practiced 20 minutes a day, the effects last far beyond this period.

▪ Special Methods to Reduce Stress

Focusing. With eyes closed, concentrate on any pleasing mental image as an aid to blocking out distracting thoughts.

Alternatively, continuously repeat a word or sound to achieve the same results. Still another method is to let thoughts wander in and out of consciousness while concentrating on the image or sound.

Progressive muscle relaxation. With eyes closed, first tense, perhaps for a 10-second period, then relax small groups of muscles, starting with hands and fingers and working down to the feet and toes. The act of tensing followed by release makes you more aware of what tension feels like and increases the subsequent feeling of relaxation.

Biofeedback. Using a special machine and sensors to record muscle contractions and skin temperature, you can learn to control normally involuntary processes such as heart rate and blood pressure that increase under stress. The machine "feeds back" the efforts and eventually you can recognize and control facets of the stress response by yourself. Once viewed with skepticism, the control of "involuntary" responses is now seen to be effective in the treatment of migraine headaches, asthma and other disorders in certain individuals.

Self-hypnosis. Hypnosis involves entering an altered state of consciousness in which all concentration is focused on a single objective or image, with all other stimuli blocked out. Many people think that hypnosis is something that a hypnotist imposes on his or her subject, or they confuse it with a sleeplike state. Others think they cannot be hypnotized. Anyone who can lose him- or herself totally in an engrossing book or movie or become so absorbed in a task that they are oblivious to their surroundings is actually practicing a form of self-hypnosis. Once a person learns self-hypnosis, he or she can use it to relieve tension and feelings of stress or anxiety. (Table 4:4 lists sources of additional information.)

More Information for Reducing Stress

Books

Benson, Herbert, M.D. *The Relaxation Response*. New York: Avon Books, 1976.

Locke, Steven, M.D., and Douglas Colligan. *The Healer Within: The New Medicine of Mind and Body*. New York: E. P. Dutton, 1986.

McQuade, Walter, and Ann Aikman. *Stress: What It Is, What It Can Do to Your Health, How to Fight Back*. New York: Bantam, 1975.

Organization

Biofeedback Society of America
10200 West 44th Avenue
Wheatridge, CO 80033
(303) 422-8436
Provides information on the credentials of biofeedback practitioners.

Table 4:4

5

LOOKING YOUR BEST

We have been conditioned to equate beauty with youth, and as we grow older, many of us become increasingly wary of the changes we see in the mirror. No matter what our age, it is natural to want to look our best. There is no way that a man or woman of 50 or 60 can recapture the wrinkle-free skin and youthful appearance of a 20-year-old, but this does not mean that all is lost. Every age has its pluses and minuses, and while it may sound trite, there is considerable truth to the old saying that true beauty comes from within.

The actress Helen Hayes proudly proclaims that she has never had a face-lift or any other cosmetic operation, and her serene beauty is every bit as attractive as the glamour of much younger actresses who concede that they have "something done" to their face or body every year of two. Obviously, no single course is right for everyone. Betty Ford, another much admired public figure, proudly showed off her face-lift, and her example has inspired many others—both men and women—to follow suit. What we do about keeping our looks is largely a matter of personal preference. Simply maintaining good health and a sense of well-being—exercising to keep muscles firm and the body trim, controlling weight, avoiding cigarette smoking and excessive alcohol use—contribute to personal attractiveness. For those who want to do more, a variety of surgical procedures can, to varying degrees, erase some of the marks of time. In this chapter, some of the more popular of these procedures will be discussed.

❑ How the Skin Ages

Many factors contribute to the wrinkling, spotting and sagging of aging skin. Some skin types have a genetic tendency to wrinkle more than others; white skin, for example, tends to wrinkle at an earlier age than the skin of

Asians and blacks. But with age, wrinkles, the permanent infolding of the outer layers of the skin, are inevitable. Smoking, which decreases blood flow to the skin, and exposure to the sun, which causes premature wrinkling and drying, as well as skin cancer, augment whatever genetic predispositions a person may carry for wrinkling. Although skin-saving measures should ideally start early in life, the benefits of quitting smoking and avoiding prolonged sun exposure will be apparent at any age.

Age-related changes may be more easily accepted if you understand, by looking at the skin's structure, why they happen. Below the epidermis or outer skin layer lies the dermis, which contains water, elastic fibers and the protein collagen, as well as blood vessels, nerve fibers, sweat and sebaceous glands and muscle tissue. Below the dermis is the fatty subcutaneous layer. As skin ages, it loses moisture, sweat glands and elasticity, which results in dryness and a loss of resilience. The natural loss of subcutaneous fat that comes with aging may exaggerate bony areas of the face. Loss of pigment-producing melanocytes drains color from the skin. (Conversely, accumulation of the pigment lipofuscin may produce "age" or "liver" spots on heavily exposed areas such as the face and hands.) The skin becomes altogether thinner, making blood vessels and uneven areas of color more prominent. Decades of the pull of gravity combined with the thinner, less elastic skin cause the face, breasts, abdomen and other structures to begin to sag. Extreme weight fluctuations over the years can also contribute to looser skin and increased facial wrinkling.

As a person ages, the rate at which cells from the base of the epidermis are pushed to the surface to form new skin decreases. The surface skin in an older man or woman, therefore, really *is* older and for that reason may lack a youthful glow.

Beyond these small-scale events, the repeated pulling and pushing of facial skin into characteristic expressions—smiles as well as frowns—result in crow's-feet around the eyes, furrows between the brows and creases running from the sides of the nose to the corners of the mouth.

Not all skin ages at the same rate or to the same extent. Men's oilier skin ages less rapidly than women's. Shaving stimulates a faster turnover of the epidermal layer, making the skin look fresher. Different complexions age at varying rates, depending on their sensitivity to the sun. Albinos, who lack the pigment melanin, are most sensitive, those with fair skins are next, followed by medium, and then those with olive complexions. Black people have thicker skin layers and greater amounts of melanin, which affords the skin more protection from the sun's ultraviolet rays. Any skin protected by clothing, of course, ages more slowly than areas exposed to the sun.

❑ What Can Help

Regular exercise improves blood flow to the skin, nourishing the collagen fibers. Adequate amounts of fluid and vitamins A and C prevent skin-related deficiencies. Eliminating smoking is vitally important for the health of the whole body as well as that of the skin, especially in women. Not only does smoking decrease blood flow to the skin, it also lowers a woman's estrogen levels, and this is believed to speed up the skin's aging.

Avoiding the sun will not reverse damage to the collagen fibers or make surface blood vessels less visible, but wearing a sun-blocking agent during any prolonged exposure prevents further wrinkling and protects against skin cancer.

A balanced diet that provides adequate amounts of vitamins A and C, both important in maintaining the skin, is important. Researchers have achieved some success in reversing wrinkling by the topical application of a vitamin A derivative called retinoic acid. A word of caution, however: Excessive vitamin A is highly toxic, and self-treatment with megadoses of it or its derivatives should be avoided. More research is required to determine whether there is a safe dosage or method of using vitamin A for cosmetic purposes.

Scores of cosmetic products claim to restore the skin by "feeding" it. Skin grows from below and is nourished by a network of tiny blood vessels. The outer visible layers are actually dead tissue, and nothing applied to them can provide "food" for the underlying living layers. Drying of the skin hastens wrinkling; moisturizing creams, lotions and oils that help the skin retain its natural oils and lubricants may help. But contrary to cosmetic claims, none of these products can "feed" the skin or erase wrinkles. Even the highly promoted and very expensive collagen creams will not restore the skin's natural collagen, simply because the molecules are too large to be absorbed through the skin. The same is true of claims made for creams that contain hormones; some hormones are absorbed through the skin, but their topical application will not restore the skin. In short, the purpose of moisturizing creams or lotions is to provide an oily film that prevents water from the skin from evaporating. An inexpensive oil, such as petroleum jelly, will do this just as effectively as an expensive, elaborately packaged and heavily advertised product. Indeed, the basic ingredients may even be the same; the difference is in the scent and presentation.

▪ *The Skin*

WRINKLING

A number of procedures can make facial wrinkles less prominent. For example, dermabrasion, chemical peeling and collagen injections are used to remove fine wrinkles and superficial changes in texture and pigmentation. They are considerably less expensive than a face-lift, but will not remedy sagging skin.

Dermabrasion makes use of a skin planing tool that literally sands the skin to remove fine wrinkles around the brow, eyes and mouth, and smooth out old scars, including acne marks. Dermabrasion is also effective in removing actinic keratoses, the flat, pink, scaly spots that result from overexposure to the sun and can become malignant. The process takes about half an hour and is done under local anesthesia. After dermabrasion, the newly surfaced skin will be raw and pink, gradually returning to normal in about two weeks.

Some specialists note that the process does not always produce the desired results. The skin may grow back unnaturally shiny, too pink in tone or lacking in pigmentation. Some cosmetic surgeons feel the procedure is not effective on large areas of the face but can be used successfully on smaller sections. The use of computers to guide the dermabrasion tool may make future operations more finely tuned with results that are more predictable.

Chemical peeling, also known as chemosurgery, uses a mild acid to "burn off" the surface layer of skin. It is effective in removing the leathery wrinkles that result from excess sun exposure. A smoother, and sometimes paler, layer grows in to take its place. The type of acid used depends on the depth of the wrinkles to be removed; trichloracetic acid (TCA) is used for superficial wrinkles, phenol for deeper ones.

Chemical peeling is a more aggressive and uncomfortable procedure than dermabrasion, taking weeks, and sometimes months, for the skin to return to normal. The burned layer forms a scab that comes off in about ten days, exposing a dark or red new layer which gradually lightens. The patient should avoid prolonged sun exposure for the next six months. If this is not possible, a sun-blocking agent should be applied before going out into the sun.

The process works best on fair skinned individuals, with results lasting up to five years. Asians, blacks and dark-skinned people risk areas of irregular pigmentation when the new skin grows in.

▪ *Collagen Injections*

Collagen injected into the dermis replaces the soft tissue lost as the skin ages or suffers trauma from injury, surgery or disease. Frown lines, pronounced smile lines at the corners of the lips and eyes, and creases running from the sides of the nose to the mouth respond to this treatment. The injections will not erase fine lines around the mouth or eyes, or hide hard scars or lines with well-defined edges.

Collagen injection

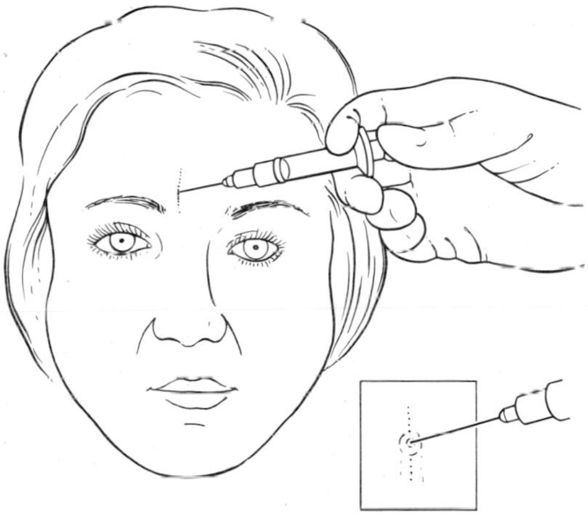

Figure 5:1
Collagen being injected to fill out forehead wrinkle.

Treatment consists of at least two injections given at two-week intervals. One month after preliminary testing for allergic reactions, the physician injects a mixture of collagen and lidocaine, a local anesthetic, into the depression of the wrinkle or scar. (See Figure 5:1.) The patient may have some soreness and swelling afterward. The effects last from six months to two years, after which shots may need to be repeated.

Much of the collagen used today is taken from cattle skin and then purified. Allergic reactions are rare. Some patients may have slight swelling after drinking alcohol, sunbathing for long periods or during hay fever attacks. Cold sores (herpes simplex) may reappear over the treated area.

People with autoimmune diseases, such as lupus, are not advised to have collagen treatments. They should also be avoided by anyone with past hypersensitivity reactions or allergy to lidocaine. A tendency to develop skin infections also may be a contraindication.

AGE SPOTS

Many age-related skin changes do not require cosmetic surgery. "Age" or "liver" spots, for example, will fade with the use of bleaching creams; however, the treated areas may turn blotchy if exposed to sunlight. Seborrheic keratoses, the raised black or brown wartlike growths appearing on the trunk, arms, neck or face, although not malignant, may be removed for cosmetic reasons, or if they rub against clothing. These growths are usually frozen or burned off under local anesthesia in a dermatologist's office.

Moles should not be confused with age spots. A mole, known medically as a nevus pigmentosus, is a pigmented skin lesion that is often slightly elevated. It may range in color from light pink to dark brown or nearly black (although there are some rare white moles). Some moles are warty in appearance, others are smooth. Most moles are harmless, but some give rise to melanoma, a highly lethal form of cancer. There has been a marked increase in melanoma in recent years, especially among people who spend a good deal of time in the sun. It is a good idea to have moles inspected by a physician at some point in adulthood, and then check them regularly yourself for any changes. Warning signs to watch for include any change in size, shape or color; itching; bleeding or "weeping" discharge; and a blurring or invasion of borders into surrounding skin.

❏ Cosmetic Surgery

At one time, cosmetic surgery was primarily for actors, actresses and others whose livelihood depended upon their face. Today this has changed; people of all ages and of both sexes are having cosmetic surgery. The number of cosmetic operations performed in the United States rose 61 percent between 1981 and 1984, according to the American Society of Plastic and Reconstructive Surgeons. Although the majority of operations are still sought by middle-aged women, this also is changing. Some women in their seventies or eighties seek surgery to correct breast sagging or a deformed nose; and men, who once considered surgery for aesthetic reasons unmasculine, accounted for 25 percent of nose surgery and 10 percent of face-lifts done in 1984.

Of course, not all plastic surgery is done for aesthetic reasons. Some people have a genetic tendency to develop sagging eyelids, which can eventually interfere with vision or irritate the cornea. A deviated septum in the nose not only causes a bump, it also can interfere with breathing.

Like any operation, cosmetic procedures are not without risks and a person contemplating plastic surgery should first determine whether his or her expectations are realistic. Results are not always predictable or what the individual expected. A face-lift will not save an unhappy marriage or help close a business deal. But for those men and women who have a healthy sense of themselves and a positive attitude about growing older, cosmetic surgery is a way to bring the outer self more in line with an inward sense of achievement and satisfaction.

More than 75 percent of cosmetic surgery today is done on an out-patient basis, often in a doctor's office or free-standing ambulatory surgical clinic. If the procedure is to be done in an out-patient setting, the facility should be equipped to handle any medical or surgical emergency. The would-be consumer should choose a physician who is board-certified in plastic and reconstructive surgery, or who is board-certified in the specific system affected (for example, ophthalmology for eye surgery), plus having the qualifications to do a cosmetic operation. Physicians who make unrealistic claims for the operation—for example, those who promise that you will look twenty years younger—should be avoided. Names of member physicians who are board-certified and information on specific procedures can be obtained from:

American Society of Plastic and
Reconstructive Surgeons
233 North Michigan Avenue,
Suite 1900
Chicago, IL 60601
312-856-1834

Although people from all economic backgrounds are having plastic surgery, it should be noted that it can be expensive and many procedures are not covered by insurance. The cost will depend on the geographical area, the physician, the specific procedure and whether it will be done on an in- or outpatient basis.

▪ *Face-lifts*

Face-lifts, although more expensive and riskier than less drastic cosmetic procedures, remain the preferred remedy for sagging skin. Contrary to popular belief, there is no age limit for having a face-lift; people in their seventies and eighties have them. But anyone considering this surgery should remember that the greater the loss in skin elasticity initially, the less pronounced the effects of the operation will be.

Anyone with heart disease or other conditions that increase the risk of surgery should discuss the potential hazards with a doctor beforehand. Ideally, before a face-lift or any other cosmetic surgery, the plastic surgeon should meet with the patient's internist to discuss his or her general health. People with uncontrolled hypertension, glaucoma, coronary artery disease or certain other disorders may have to delay surgery until these conditions stabilize. A complete physical examination, including an electrocardiogram, chest X-ray and laboratory tests, is recommended. Depending on the patient and the surgeon, a face-lift may be done in the hospital or on an outpatient basis, using either general anesthesia or a local preceded by a sedative.

In the conventional operation, the surgeon makes an incision running from ear to ear and under the hairline, pulls down the skin flap and cuts away excess fatty tissue underneath. (See Figure 5:2.) Loose neck and facial skin is then pulled back tightly, the excess trimmed away and the skin flap sutured back into place. A chemical peel, eyelid surgery or chin augmentation may be done at the same time.

Results vary from person to person. As a rule of thumb, however, a face-lift can restore a person's face to the way it looked ten years earlier, and the results last five to ten years, after which another face-lift may be done if the patient so desires. Recently, a more extensive and longer-lasting type of operation called SMAS (superficial muscular aponeurotic system) has been developed. It involves cutting away the smooth connective tissue, as well as the fat, lying next to the

Face-lift

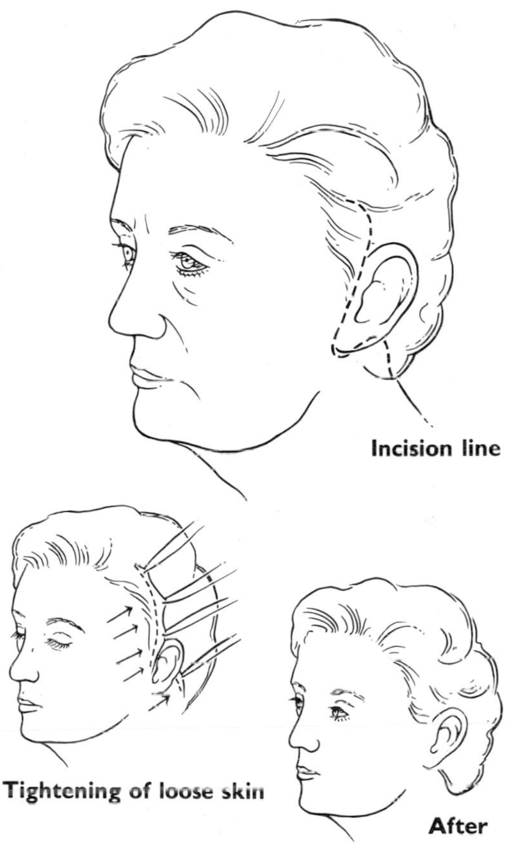

Figure 5:2
Top drawing shows incision line and type of sagging chin line and facial wrinkles that can be corrected with a face-lift. At the lower left, skin is pulled tight and excess is removed. Lower right drawing shows finished results, with firmer jawline and smoother facial contour.

muscle. This creates a firm look, but one that is softer than the sometimes tight appearance of the typical face-lift. The newer operation results in less stress on the skin and a more evenly distributed tension on the face, with results lasting even nine years or longer. Because the deeper-cutting surgery involves a greater risk of facial nerve damage, however, plastic surgeons are divided regarding its safety.

After either operation, the face will be swathed in bandages during the initial recovery period. It may take two or three weeks for the puffiness to disappear and the scars to heal. A woman should wait one week before applying any makeup and three weeks before using hair coloring.

Face-lifts are relatively safe operations, but some people do exerience complications, such as injury to facial nerves, hair loss around the incisions, misplacement of the earlobe, skin tears or damage, and hematomas (blood-filled swellings caused by injury to blood vessels). In rare instances, there may be eye damage caused by bleeding behind the eyes and death or deterioration of the skin flap that was lifted. The resulting scar tissue from these complications usually improves without treatment; however, some people, especially blacks, Asians or dark-skinned whites, develop keloid scars, smooth, shiny raised areas which are hard to treat.

Certain factors increase the risk of complications during or after the operation. Owing to higher pressure within the blood vessels, patients with hypertension may have increased bleeding during surgery, as may those who take large amounts of aspirin, which acts as an anticoagulant. Because smoking impairs blood circulation and robs the tissues of oxygen, the skin of a smoker may scale or heal poorly following surgery.

Other conditions which make face-lifts and other cosmetic operations inadvisable are burns which have left scarring, previous radiation therapy which can damage blood vessels, psoriasis and other skin diseases, and any disorders that affect blood circulation. People with skin that has healed poorly in the past should approach surgery with caution, if at all.

▪ *The Eyes*

Like skin on other parts of the body, the eyelids lose elasticity with age. Changes around the eyes may be even more pronounced. The skin here is somewhat thinner than on other parts of the face. Repeated actions such as blinking and squinting contribute to sagging lids. Smoking and overexposure to the sun age skin here as elsewhere on the body. Aging, an inherited tendency or certain diseases may cause puffiness or "bags" under the eyes. The bags develop when ligaments around the eyes weaken, allowing fat to bulge outward.

Eyelid surgery, or blepharoplasty, removes these defects and, following breast enlargement, is the second most common cosmetic operation. The procedure is performed under local anesthesia, takes one hour to complete and is often done on an outpatient basis, although a 24-hour postoperative hospital stay is preferable to observe for signs of bleeding. The loose tissue is cut away through incisions made in the fold of the upper lid and immediately below the lower lash line. (See Figure 5:3.) Dark glasses may be worn to hide any swelling or discoloration during the approximately two weeks it takes for looks to return to normal.

Complications, if any, are rare and usually temporary. One of the most serious is a sudden rise in blood pressure after surgery, which can lead to a hematoma. If the blood-filled swelling presses against the skin, cutting off the blood supply, the skin can slough off. Other complications include increased tearing and double vision due to swelling of the membranes lining the eyeball and lid (the conjunctiva) or to disturbances in the underlying muscle. Patients may find that they cannot close their eyes completely for several days after the operation. If this problem persists, the patient will have to use eye drops to help distribute tears over the eyeball, a function normally performed by the lid. The most troublesome complication of blepharoplasty is ectropion, where the lid is turned out and away from the eye when too much skin has been removed. Skin grafts must then be used to rebuild the lid.

Eyelid Surgery

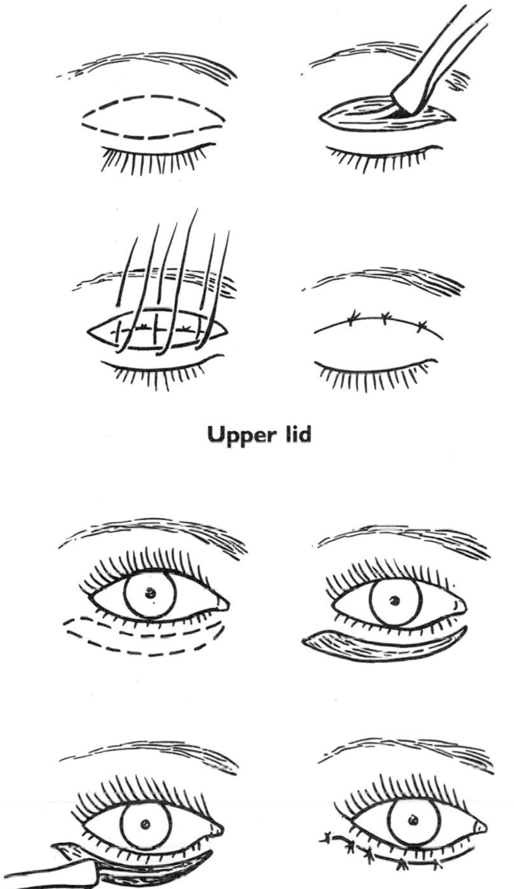

Figure 5:3
Drawings show typical procedures to remove fat pads and excessive skin from both upper and lower eyelids.

A new procedure, developed by Dr. Michael E. Sachs, director of plastic surgery research at New York Eye and Ear Infirmary, shows promise in removing eye bags without undergoing surgery. Dr. Sachs's procedure uses an electric needle to, in effect, vaporize the fat. The procedure takes about 30 minutes and is done using a local anesthetic. A tiny incision is made to identify the fat pockets; the needle is then inserted into the fat. Since fat is about 90 percent water, it can be vaporized with the needle's electric current. The heating actually strengthens the supporting ligaments, so there is less likelihood of recurrence of sagging. This new operation also carries less risk of bleeding or other complications than traditional eyelid surgery. Complete healing takes about a week. Other surgeons across the country are now being trained in this new operation, which is expected to become more common in coming years.

▪ *The Nose*

Rhinoplasty, or nose jobs, remain the most popular of all cosmetic operations. The shape of the nose has a profound effect on the appearance of the entire face. At one time, most people who underwent rhinoplasties ended up with pretty much the same-looking upturned nose. Today, however, plastic surgeons are more skilled in reshaping a nose to fit an individual face.

In the past, most nose operations were sought by younger people, but today it is not uncommon for men and women in their sixties and seventies to undergo rhinoplasty. In a typical operation, the surgeon makes an incision through the nostril, separates the skin from cartilage and bone lying underneath, and reshapes the bone for the desired result. (See Figure 5:4.) The nostrils are then packed and the nose is splinted to hold the new shape. For the first 24 hours after surgery, the patient will be on a liquid diet and must rest in bed, whether at home or in the hospital. The splint is removed after five to seven days. It may take two or three weeks for the discoloration around the nose and eyes to disappear, but the patient can usually resume light but normal activity within a week or two.

Complications associated with rhinoplasty are rare. The most serious is bleeding, which can show up as late as two weeks after surgery. This is usually treated by inserting a medicated packing into the nostril. Severe hemorrhage, although rare, may require hospitalization. Other side effects are usually minor—a diminished sense of smell for several weeks, nasal congestion or skin irritations from the bandages.

▪ *The Chin*

Chin remodeling is still another popular operation that is often done at the same time as a rhinoplasty or face-lift. A prominent chin can be made smaller simply by removing some of the bone. Receding chins can be remedied by inserting a silicone implant, or alternatively, bone transplanted from elsewhere in the body. In one of the more common procedures (illustrated in Figure 5:5), the surgeon makes an incision inside the lower lip or under the chin, slips in the prosthesis and bandages the area to limit movement during the initial healing period. The main risk is that the implant will protrude from the chin. If this occurs, or in the unlikely case in which the implant shifts, it can be replaced.

Sometimes the problem is related to malalignment of the teeth. In such instances, the chin surgery may be preceded by orthodontic work to correct the dental problem.

Rhinoplasty

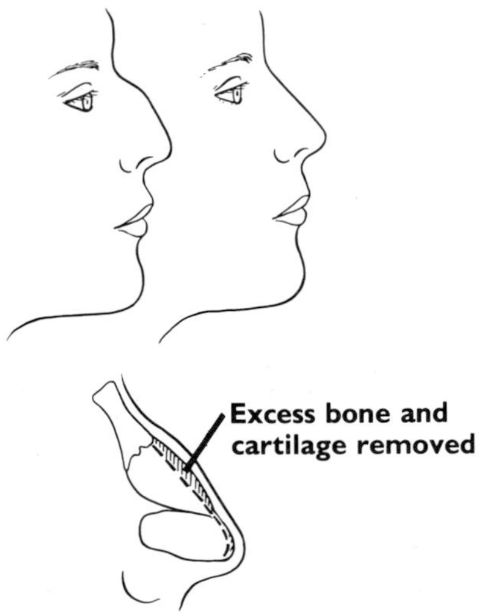

Figure 5:4
Upper drawing shows before and after nose contour; the lower drawing shows how nose is reshaped from inside nostril.

Chin Implant

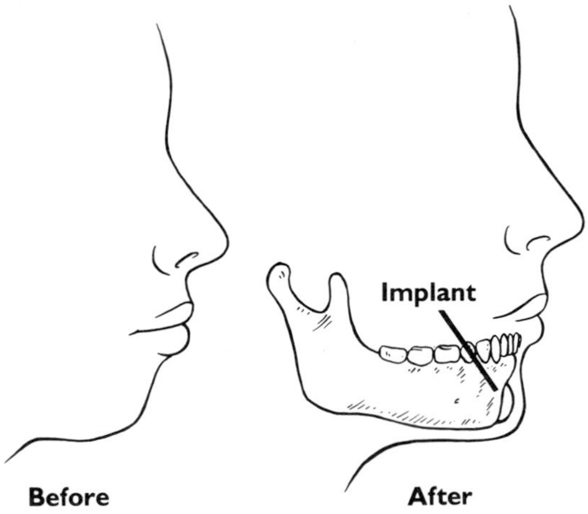

Figure 5:5
Drawing shows insertion of implant to correct receding chin.

▪ *Beyond the Face*

Of course, today's cosmetic surgery is by no means limited to the face; there also are a number of body-contouring operations aimed at improving bustlines, sagging abdomens, fatty thighs and other perceived imperfections. It should be noted that for many older people, these operations may be riskier and less successful than facial plastic surgery. Body skin in general is thicker than facial skin, and may heal unevenly, with prominent scar tissue. Most cosmetic operations on the body require general anesthesia, which carries a greater risk than local anesthetics. Obviously, people with chronic illnesses should consult their regular physicians before considering any elective surgery.

There is no age limit on most cosmetic procedures, with the exception of a new surgical technique called liposuction, or suction lipectomy. This operation usually is not recommended for anyone over 45 or 50. As its name implies, liposuction entails sucking fat through a thin tube inserted between skin and muscle. If liposuction is done on an older adult, the decreased skin elasticity may result in a sagging, mottled appearance when the underlying fat is removed. Anyone over 50 who is considering this procedure should have his or her surgeon thoroughly explain this drawback.

BREAST AUGMENTATION AND REDUCTION

In recent years breast surgery has become increasingly common. The majority of operations are performed in conjunction with a mastectomy for breast cancer and entail reconstructing the missing breast and, if needed, altering the remaining breast to match the reconstructed one. (See section on breast cancer in Chapter 12.)

Other breast operations may be performed to improve the contour of the natural breast. In breast enlargement, or augmentation, a silicone implant is inserted under the glandular tissue to "fill out" the breast. The surgeon makes the incision in the fold under the breast, creates a pocket to snugly hold the implant and slips in the prosthesis. (See Figure 5:6.) Some implants have an adhesive backing which adheres to tendons in the chest for extra protection against unwanted movement. Liquid silicone injections are no longer used because of the tendency of the liquid to "migrate" from its original location in the breast.

Because the implant is under natural tissue, there is usually no decrease in sensation in the breast. A newer implant, made from polyurethane foam, may offer a solution to the hardening of the implant or the surrounding tissues that 20 percent of the women who had the surgery experienced. However, long-term use statistics on this are not yet available.

Breast reduction can produce firmer breasts with a greater lift in the older woman with large sagging breasts. Cutting into the fold under the breasts, the surgeon removes excess fat and skin and sutures the skin flap back into place. (See Figure 5:7.) In both operations, scar tissue is largely hidden by the fold.

Augmentation and reduction surgeries are done under general anesthesia and require three to five days in the hospital. It takes about three weeks for tissues to heal well enough for the woman to resume normal activity. During this recovery period, the patient should not lift even moderately heavy objects or move her arms excessively.

Complications include postoperative infection, skin abscesses, failure of the wound to close properly and fluid buildup under the skin flaps. Less common risks include excessive bleeding or impairment of blood circulation.

Breast Enlargement Surgery

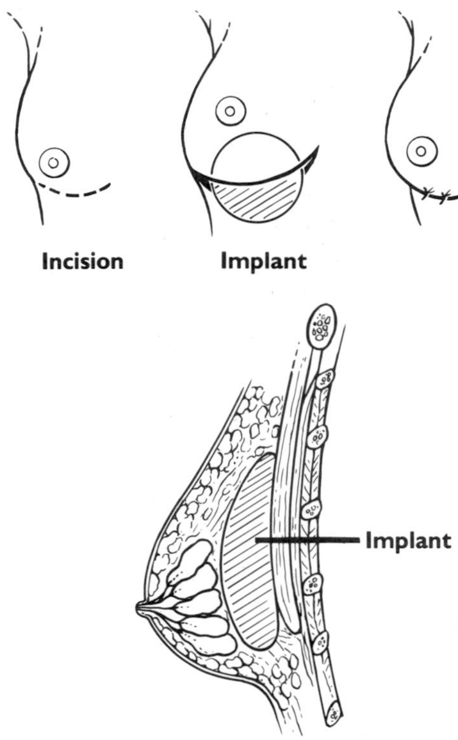

Figure 5:6
Implant is inserted under normal tissue to augment breast.

Breast Reduction Surgery

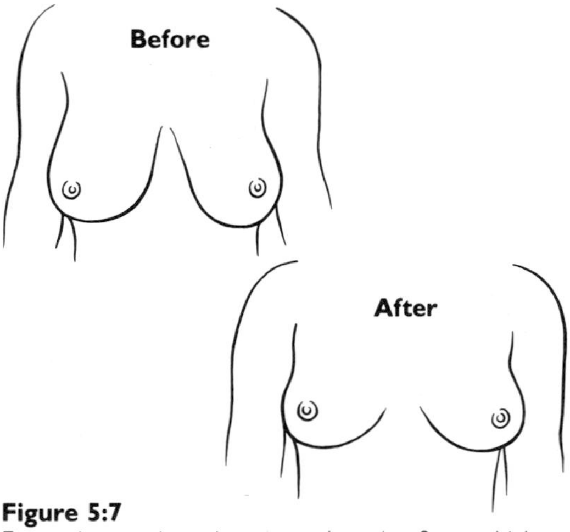

Figure 5:7
Excess breast tissue is removed to give firmer, higher contour.

THE ABDOMEN

Abdominal plastic surgery, often referred to as "tummy tucks," is intended to correct the sagging that occurs most often in older women who have had several children. Weight loss and exercises to strengthen abdominal muscles may be just as effective as the surgery, and much safer. Although the term "tummy tuck" may sound benign, or even frivolous, this is a serious operation with a relatively high risk of complications.

In a typical operation, the surgeon makes an incision through a fold, usually above the pubic area, and removes excess fat and skin, and sutures back the skin flap. The procedure is done under general anesthesia and requires two weeks in the hospital, followed by another two to three weeks of convalescence when a limited amount of activity is possible. During the initial recovery period, the patient will usually feel discomfort when sitting or walking. Support hose and an abdominal girdle must be worn for several months to support the tissue and prevent phlebitis. Possible complications include infection, bleeding and circulatory problems. The enforced bed rest also carries a risk of thrombophlebitis.

❑ Hair

As we age, sex differences regarding hair distribution become apparent. Women may grow more body and facial hair while men may become bald.

At menopause, estrogen production drops sharply, leaving the male hormones androgen and testosterone to make up a larger proportion of total sex hormones. One of the consequences is increased body and facial hair. Shaving, tweezing, bleaching and depilatory creams will temporarily remove or lighten hair. Because they can irritate sensitive skin, bleaching or depilatory preparations should be tested on a small sample of skin before each application. Another method is hair waxing, a relatively long-lasting process which strips both surface hair and part of the shaft below the skin.

The only permanent way to remove hair is by electrolysis. This expensive, somewhat uncomfortable process kills the hair at its root through the use of a weak electric current. Because this method is not without risk of infection, it should be done only by a licensed operator.

▪ *Baldness Treatments*

Although some men make it into their later years with a full head of hair, the majority will experience at least some balding by the time they reach 60. Aging, heredity and a not completely understood interaction between the androgen hormones and hair follicles are responsible. Artificial hairpieces or hair weaving can hide a balding head. But the only permanent way to restore hair is to transplant it. In this form of cosmetic surgery, small plugs of flesh containing hair and hair follicles are transplanted, under local anesthesia, from a hairy to a bald section of the scalp. (See Figure 5:8.) From ten to sixty plugs are done per session, with the entire procedure taking two to three months.

Hair Transplants

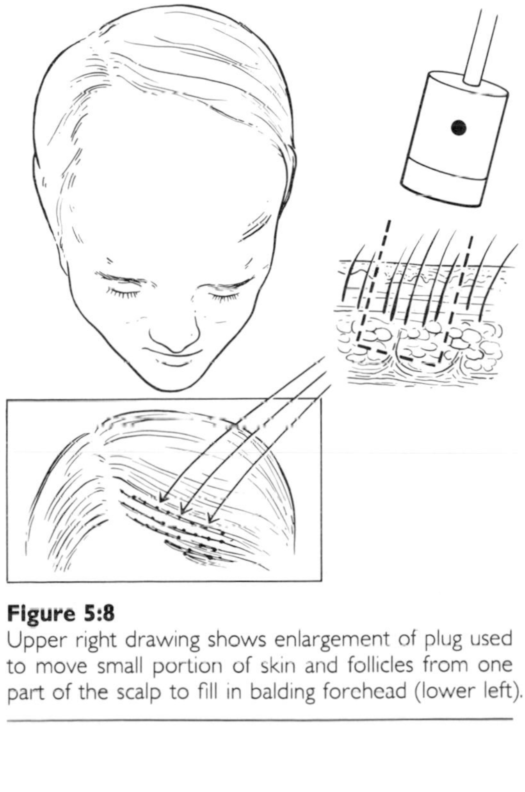

Figure 5:8
Upper right drawing shows enlargement of plug used to move small portion of skin and follicles from one part of the scalp to fill in balding forehead (lower left).

Although the transplanted hairs usually fall out, new ones begin to grow in the transplanted follicles after about three months. Hair transplant is usually painless, and complications or rejection of the plugs is rare when done by a qualified physician.

The newest development in the treatment of baldness is the topical application of the drug minoxidil, used to treat high blood pressure when given orally. When applied to the skin, this prescription medication causes the fuzz on a bald head to thicken and darken. In about a third of the men, new hair growth appears. Minoxidil does not cure baldness; once applications are stopped, the fuzz returns to its former appearance and any new hair falls out.

❑ The Eye of the Beholder

As stressed at the beginning of this chapter, physical attractiveness is largely a matter of personal style and outlook. The actress Helen Hayes proudly proclaims she has earned her wrinkles and has never had a face-lift. Betty Ford, on the other hand, talks openly about the psychological boost she got from her face-lift. A good lesson in how to apply makeup may be just as effective, and a lot less costly and risky, as a face-lift or eye job. And even the most wrinkled face is beautiful to an adoring grandchild, loving spouse or a public that admires qualities that are more than skin deep.

PART II

EMOTIONAL WELL-BEING AND RELATIONSHIPS

6

MIDLIFE CRISIS: THE MAN'S SIDE

Most of us, up to a certain age, harbor a secret conviction that somehow we'll be the ones to find the Fountain of Youth and beat the aging process. Then there comes a day when we realize that the Fountain of Youth just doesn't exist to find, and we are growing older like everyone else. This realization usually hits hardest just as a man enters his second 50 years, and it can lead to major shifts in attitudes and emotional upheaval—in short, midlife crisis.

During middle age many men go through what is often described as a "second adolescence," or "middlescence." Like adolescence, this midlife transitional period is characterized as a time of risk taking, appraisal (or reappraisal) of life's situation and direction.

Although often touted as a negative period of restlessness and irrational change, the midlife transition can be a positive opportunity, one from which to achieve a greater sense of satisfaction and self-awareness in one's life. It is a time when a man's personality may take a major developmental step forward. For example, many men find they are more self-confident and less intolerant of shortcomings in others. Ultimately, the type of midlife experience a man has is totally dependent on his ability to determine his goals and to adapt to change; basically, it can be whatever you expect it to be.

❑ Threats from Without and Within

As a man approaches middle age, changes become more frequent, and perhaps more frightening. These changes may be physical, exhibited as the graying or thinning of hair or the need to wear eyeglasses; or they may be external, indicated socially in ways such as in increased competition with younger people. If a man has measured his masculinity by the traditional yardsticks of sexual performance, acquisition of money and success on the job, he may be more susceptible to a negative midlife experience and likely to perceive these changes as a threat.

A balding man may worry about his attractiveness to women and his sexual capacity (although baldness has nothing to do with either of these things). As a result, he may pursue younger women in the hope of rebuilding his ego through sexual conquest. Infidelity during the midlife transition often has its basis in this attempt to prove attractiveness and strength. However, this attempt may fail miserably when the younger woman feels a need to be with her peers, thus confirming the man's belief that he is no longer attractive.

The man who on the job feels increased competition from younger associates moving up in the firm may start to doubt his own capacity to be useful. New ideas may become threatening to him and the office may become a source of anxiety. To soothe this tension and enable him to face the competition, a man may turn to alcohol or drugs. For a while, he may experience the "as if" phenomenon of substance abuse—he feels "as if" he has achieved, "as if" he can compete confidently.

But actually, prolonged abuse of alcohol and drugs diminishes a man's capacity to be successful and useful on the job, and his fears become a self-fulfilling prophecy. His decreased performance may lead to demotion or unemployment.

However, these two painful and negative scenarios can be avoided by a positive attitude toward the changes encountered in midlife. Concentrating on the positive aspects of growing older can lead to acceptance and even enjoyment of the changes a man experiences.

For example, there is no evidence that intelligence diminishes as one grows older. In fact, years of experience increase one's capacity to bring together stored knowledge and provide valuable advice to less experienced colleagues. Instead of fearing new ideas, a man in middle age can use what he has learned through the years to judge the viability of his juniors' suggestions. He is actually at the peak of his usefulness within the company. In his role as adviser, he can take pleasure in his unique ability to guide younger employees toward innovative ideas that can work.

One's flexibility is the key in dealing with the midlife transition effectively. Those who are set in their ways and rigid become defeated by an ever-changing world that won't stand still for them. Unless a man actively adapts to his new roles and new abilities, he *will* become antiquated and less useful. Again, an unfounded fear can become a self-fulfilling prophecy.

❑ The Road Not Taken

The midlife transition is also a time of reassessment of one's life achievements and directions. A man may begin to dwell on "the road not taken" and on "what might have been" and vow to "change all that" in his remaining time. He may seek a totally new and different lover or profession in order to explore the possibilities he opted against earlier in life.

However, starting a new family or career later in life may present some unique problems. Young children demand a great deal of time, energy and patience, and a man in his fifties may not have adequate supplies of any of these to meet this demand. Stepchildren may also present a whole new set of problems, either stemming from the family situation or from the children's own personalities. Gaining acceptance from a reluctant stepchild is difficult at any time, but later in life it can be more trying.

This is not to say that there are no

valid reasons for divorce in middle age or that a man (or woman) should accept the status quo of a bad marriage. But very often people are too willing to throw in the towel before attempting to make the changes that might make their present situation more rewarding.

Flexibility and adaptability are also necessary in order to start a new job. Of course, these qualities are needed in order to be successful anytime one switches jobs, but it may be more difficult for the older person to put into practice without some extra effort. Although it is certainly unhealthy to remain in an unsatisfying and unpleasant job just for the sake of avoiding change, it may be easier for a man to restructure his job within his present company or to take a comparable position in a similar company than to start again from scratch.

At a time of personal reevaluation, a man has the unique opportunity to confront the contradictions in himself and so come to know himself more clearly. Daniel J. Levinson, in his book *The Seasons of a Man's Life* (New York: Knopf, 1978), summarizes these attitudinal contradictions as: young versus old; destruction versus creation; masculine versus feminine; attachment versus separateness. Throughout life these opposite qualities and capacities within each human are encountered but, during the explorative midlife transition, Levinson says, a man is afforded a special chance to come closer to integrating and resolving them within himself. As a result, a man may emerge from the midlife crisis as a more sensitive, loving partner and a wiser, more cooperative colleague—more willing to reveal and explore both sides of his nature.

❑ Empty Nest Syndrome

Although depression after the children leave home is more often associated with women than men, the empty nest does affect fathers. Suddenly, without the diversion of children and their activities, the husband and wife must deal directly with each other. This mutual rediscovery may be negative, but it is most often experienced as the positive reawakening of a time-tested and valued friendship.

❑ Single in Middle Age

Owing to divorce or death of a spouse, many men may find themselves again living the single life in middle age. Indeed, this may be the first time ever that some men have lived alone, without a mother or wife to cook, clean and keep track of social engagements. The newly single man in middle age will have much to learn about taking care of himself and his home.

Maintaining friendships with married people may be difficult, particularly after divorce. A single friend in a group of couples may make hosts feel uncomfortable, as if they must provide a date for the man. In a divorce situation, friends of the couple may not want to appear to be "taking sides" by inviting the husband and not the wife, or vice versa. Therefore, the single person may have to make a special effort to stay in touch, even when he may feel that others should be reaching out to him.

The single man must embark on a new search for identity, make new friends and sometimes restructure old friendships to meet his needs as a single individual. Friendship skills that may have had little use during married years must be rediscovered. Dating, romance, companionship and sex all become issues again. Seeking out people in similar situations (such as church or synagogue groups for single people or organizations like Parents Without Partners) may provide a supportive network of friends.

❑ Preparing for Retirement

Many men look forward to a retirement life of no plans and no responsibilities, only to find themselves bored and wishing they were back at work after a mere month or two of leisure. Retirement may come at different ages for different men—indeed, some men never retire but continue to work into their eighties and nineties. Retirement may be the man's choice, but it can also be forced upon him by company policies or illness. In any case, it is an important part of middle age to prepare mentally for retirement and plan the activities that will make this period as rewarding as it was meant to be.

One way to keep active during retirement is to become involved in volunteer activities in the community. But rather than waiting until you have stopped working to find areas that interest you, start getting involved before retirement. Volunteer work, especially on issues in which you have a personal stake, will help maintain that feeling of purposefulness and usefulness that you may formerly have derived from work.

Also, the people you meet through volunteer work can provide a valuable social network that may reduce the stress of changing your lifestyle and it can improve your sense of well-being. In fact, current research indicates that people who are involved in churches or other active organizations are less likely to suffer illnesses. This may be due to the social interaction the network provides and by the feeling of responsibility the work supplies. (See Chapter 10, Planning for Retirement.)

❑ Physical Changes

Middle age is a time when many of the chronic diseases of later life make themselves evident. At this time, many men become preoccupied with their health, fearing that every twinge or symptom means an impending heart attack, cancer, or some other dreaded disease. Others take an opposite tack, ignoring serious warning signs and pretending that nothing can possibly strike them down. The heart attack death of author and runner Jim Fixx, who had a history of heart trouble, is an oft-cited example of the latter.

Obviously, the best approach lies in between—careful attention to common-sense preventive measures and a lifestyle that promotes good health without making it a major preoccupation. Keeping your weight under control, eating a prudent, low-fat diet, learning how to cope with stress, staying physically active but knowing your limits—these are but a few of the positive health measures everyone, male or female, can and should pay attention to.

In the past, men were urged to have a complete physical every year. This is no longer considered necessary, but all men should undergo certain tests periodically (see Table 6:1, Medical Tests for Men).

▪ *Prostatic Disorders*

During their fifties, most men for the first time become aware of the prostate gland because this is the decade when it is most likely to start causing problems.

The prostate is a small gland that can cause big trouble for some men. Surrounding the male urethra (the 8-to-10-inch-long tube through which urine and ejaculate pass on their way out of the body), the gland starts to grow during puberty in response to the release of the male hormone testosterone. In a healthy adult, the gland is about the size of a walnut.

The function of the prostate gland is limited but important. As the ejaculate passes from the seminal vesicle to the urethra in preparation for orgasm, the

Medical Tests for Men

All 50-plus men should have the following medical tests on a periodic basis. Other tests may be required under special circumstances or as dictated by symptoms.

Test	Frequency
Blood pressure measurement	Annually; more often if under treatment for hypertension
Blood tests (i.e., diabetes, anemia)	Biannually after age 45
Cholesterol	Every 5 years; more often if under treatment for atherosclerosis or coronary disease or if level is greater than 200 mg/dl
Dental examination	Every 6 to 12 months
Dental X-rays	Every 2 to 3 years
Electrocardiogram	Every 3 years after age 50; more often if under treatment for heart disease
Eye examination	Biannually
Test for occult blood in stool	Annually
Prostatic examination	Annually
Rectal examination (digital)	Annually
Sigmoidoscopy	Every 5 years after 2 consecutive negative examinations at 50 and 51
Testicular examination	Annually
Complete physical	Every 5 years to age 60; biannually to 65 and annually thereafter

Table 6:1

prostate gland secretes the enzyme-containing portion (about one-third) of the seminal fluid that activates the sperm. Although the prostatic fluid is not necessary for sexual performance, the lack of it causes infertility.

In most men, the prostate gland goes through another growth spurt around age 50. Indeed, the gland shows some signs of enlargement in most men by age 45; by age 65, virtually all men are affected to some degree. (See Figure 6:1.) The growth, in most cases, is benign and, depending on the location of the enlargement, causes few if any minor symptoms and requires no special treatment. Researchers are not certain what causes the prostate gland to enlarge as a man grows older. A hormonal imbalance may be the cause, or it may just be a normal part of the aging process. The prostate may double in size without causing severe symptoms in some men, while in others, even a small enlargement in the wrong place may cause symptoms distressing enough to warrant surgery. If urinary flow is obstructed by the enlarged prostate, surgery is indicated.

SYMPTOMS OF PROSTATIC ENLARGEMENT

The gland's location is at the root of the problem. When enlarged, the gland can press on the urethra, leading to pain and difficulty upon urination. The blockage of the urethra may cause a small amount of urine to become trapped in the bladder, leading to bladder or kidney infections. Sleep may be disturbed by the frequent need to urinate (nocturia). The enlarged prostate may also affect sexual function by causing pain on erection or ejaculation.

Symptoms of difficulty in starting to urinate or emptying the bladder fully lead to a sense of urgency and at times to painful urination. These symptoms may be caused by an enlarged prostate gland, infection and other diseases. They may also be precipitated by certain drugs, especially antihistamines. Thus cold pills, allergy medications and other drugs containing antihistamines should be used with caution by older men.

Currently, the usual treatment is surgical removal of a portion of the gland, a procedure known as prostatectomy. The most common procedure for treating a benign prostatic growth is known as transurethral resection of the prostate, or TURP. A fiber-optic instrument called a resectoscope is inserted through the urethra into the urinary bladder. The surgeon uses the electrified loop at the end of the instrument to shave away the excess tissue within the gland, leaving a hollow shell and thus removing the obstruction. A catheter to facilitate the flow of urine from the bladder is left in place for three to five days. Within five to seven days the patient may return home, where he may be told to rest for several weeks following the operation. With recent advances in anesthetic techniques, this operation is now safe for men even in their nineties.

However, there is always some risk involved in general anesthesia, and it is important to note that unless the symptoms are seriously affecting the quality of the man's life, surgery may not be the answer. If increased bladder and kidney infections and frequent urination are the only symptoms, symptomatic treatment with antibiotics or sulfa drugs may be sufficient.

In a Veterans Administration study of men aged 55 to 64 who underwent prostatectomy, many had serious difficulties such as impotence and continued urinary problems following surgery, and 50 percent obtained no relief at all from the procedure. Cases are also known in which the operation has had to be repeated.

In patients with complete urinary obstruction, however, there is no alternative to surgery, usually a partial prostatectomy. This procedure should return normal urinary function without adversely affecting sexual potency and orgasm. In some cases (about 50 percent), however, the semen is passed to the bladder, rather than through the penis, rendering the man infertile. The impotence that may follow partial prostatectomy is often temporary; it may be due to postoperative swelling or to psychological factors.

Another clear indication for surgery is a suspicious nodule on the prostate discovered during a rectal examination, regardless of the presence of other symptoms of prostatic enlargement. The nodule should be removed and biopsied for cancerous cells. In addition to a rectal exam, screening by ultrasound offers reportedly good results in the detection of prostatic lesions 2 millimeters in size. The technique is still considered experi-

Enlarged Prostate

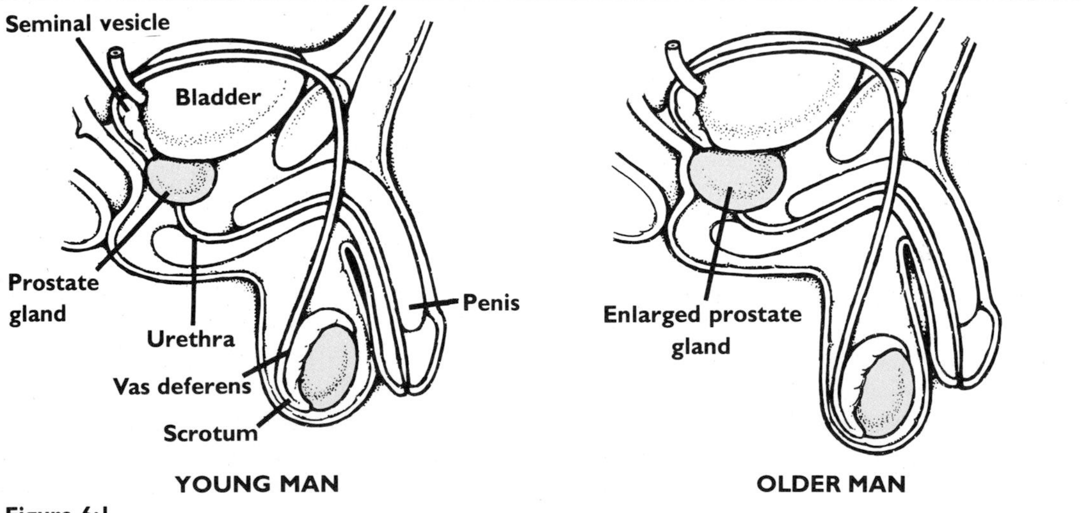

Figure 6:1
The drawing at the left shows a normal-sized prostate gland in a young man; at the right, the enlargement that typically occurs after age 50.

mental. The experimental injection of radioactive iodine to destroy the tumor without surgery has also been reported by some institutions. If prostatic cancer is discovered early enough, only the affected portion of the gland may have to be removed to obtain good results. There has been some association between this treatment and an increased incidence of the development of metastatic cancer; however, the data to determine long-range results is not yet in. This disease is considered to be virtually ubiquitous among men who live to an advanced age.

Experiments with laser surgery offer new hopes of more precise and effective surgery. By using the laser—a concentrated beam of light—in effect to vaporize a portion of the prostate, rather than surgically removing it, relief can be provided without the danger of postsurgery bleeding problems. Although the procedure is too new for adequate follow-up statistics, laser surgery may well improve results of prostatectomy.

More serious side effects are encountered when the whole prostate must be removed, such as in cases of advanced prostatic cancer (the second most common form of cancer among men; 86,000 cases are reported each year, resulting in 25,000 deaths). Ninety percent of men undergoing the standard procedure for radical prostatectomy are impotent as a result. The reason is that the nerves that trigger erection and ejaculation are located along the back of the prostate gland. Although the gland itself is not necessary for sexual function, these nerves, which are often damaged or severed during the operation, are.

For these reasons, and because prostatic cancer is often slow-growing and may never prove fatal, many urologists and their patients opt for hormonal therapy or partial prostatectomy to treat the disease. Radiation therapy is another alternative treatment for prostatic cancer. Fifty to 60 percent of men undergoing radiation treatments remain sexually functional.

However, a new technique developed at Johns Hopkins University may offer a cure without such a high risk of impotence. The modified surgery avoids the essential nerves, leaving them intact. Preliminary results show that 70 percent of men undergoing this procedure retain potency—a vast improvement over the standard operation. Surgeons at other institutions are beginning to adopt this procedure, which may become more common in the next few years.

Early detection and treatment of prostate cancer is important, especially now that a treatment with fewer side effects has been developed. Almost three quarters of prostatic cancers go undetected until they are in an advanced stage in which cure is more difficult. The most common and effective method of detection is the annual rectal examination that is recommended for all men over the age of 45. Normally, the prostate gland is smooth and soft. A hard, irregular gland with a nodular surface may indicate prostatic cancer and a biopsy of the gland should be performed.

▪ *The Special Problem of Impotence*

Impotence affects about 10 million American males. Until recently many physicians thought that 90 percent of cases were due to psychological causes. However, sleep studies of spontaneous erections in most men now lead researchers to believe that 50 to 60 percent of impotence has a physical cause.

Most men have had short periods when they cannot achieve an erection, perhaps related to work or family problems. But true impotence is the persistent inability to have an erection. A man whose impotence stems from emotional factors will have erections during periods of REM sleep, characterized by dreaming and rapid eye movements, the studies showed. Lack of erections during REM sleep strongly suggests a physical basis. Resolution of the problem may be as simple as changing a blood pressure medication which causes impotence as a side effect. The most common causes of impotence are given in Table 6:2; Table 6:3 lists drugs that may cause impotence.

FINDING THE CAUSE

Comprehensive testing at a sleep laboratory is desirable to establish whether impotence falls into the psychological or physical category. But for those who cannot afford this or who live far from such a facility, there are several simple ways a couple can check for nightly erections at home. One is for the woman to simply stay awake and observe her sleeping partner. A second is to paste a strip of stamps around the flaccid penis at bedtime. If the strip is torn in the morning, erection has probably occurred. This test should be repeated several times for reliability.

If erections occur, the couple should seek counseling from a sex therapist affiliated with a local university or teaching hospital or a qualified psychotherapist with experience in sex counseling. If there are no erections, see your physician or urologist.

Once a physical cause is suspected, the physician will try to pinpoint it by doing a complete history and physical exam, including blood tests for hormone levels, measurements of blood flow to the penis and nerve conduction studies as necessary.

FORMS OF TREATMENT

Treatment may be as simple as changing the type, dose or time when a medication is given to avoid this side effect. Endocrine-related impotence may be treated with hormone supplements. Drug or alcohol detoxification may help the substance abuser, provided liver or nerve damage is not widespread. Surgery to unblock blood vessels and increase blood flow to the penis has recently been introduced, but is still in the early stages and not always successful.

For those with damage due to diabetes, spinal cord injury or other irreversible causes, penile prostheses offer a way for men to resume sexual intercourse. These are inserted into the corpora cavernosa under local anesthesia to simulate natural erections. The simplest of three types available consists of a pair of semi-rigid silicone rods which keep the penis constantly erect. Close-fitting

Possible Causes of Impotence

- *Circulatory disorders.* Blocked blood vessels or other conditions which decrease blood flow to the penis.
- *Congenital or other structural defects of the penis.* In Peyronie's disease scar tissue builds up near the corpora cavernosa, causing contorted erections that make intercourse difficult or impossible.
- *Diabetes.* As many as half of all diabetic men are impotent. The disease causes damage to the nerves that allow the opening of valves leading to the corpora cavernosa, the spongy blood vessels in the penis which fill with blood resulting in erection.
- *Hormonal causes.* Disorders of the hypothalamus, pituitary or thyroid gland resulting in decreased sex hormones or increased prolactin, a hormone that stimulates the production of breast milk.
- *Medications.* Besides blood pressure medications, drugs used in the treatment of depression and other conditions may cause impotence through their actions on the nervous or endocrine system.
- *Neurological disorders.* Injuries or diseases affecting the spinal cord, such as multiple sclerosis and syphilis.
- *Substance abuse.* Cocaine and even moderate use of alcohol may cause temporary impotence. Alcoholism causes damage to the liver, which metabolizes sex hormones. Narcotics can cause nerve damage.
- *Surgery.* Repair of aneurysms in the abdominal aorta, extensive surgery on the bladder, colon or prostate gland can sever nerves involved in erection. However, new techniques using laser beams in prostate surgery reduce the risk of impotence.
- *Toxic chemicals.* Ingredients used in pesticide manufacture and other toxic substances can cause impotence.

Table 6:2

underwear can be worn to push the penis against the lower abdomen or thigh, thus avoiding an embarrassing bulge.

Another type consists of a flexible metal wire sheathed in plastic or rubber. As with the first type, the penis will be constantly erect, but can be bent up or down to be concealed. The most complicated prosthesis uses a miniature hydraulic pump and small inflatable tubes to simulate erections. The surgeon inserts the tubes into the corpora cavernosa, places a small water-filled reservoir behind muscles in the lower abdomen and implants a pump into the scrotum. By alternately squeezing the scrotum or activating a release valve, the tubes fill up with water, causing an erection, or empty back into the reservoir, leaving the penis flaccid.

Cost of the implants and surgery varies from $2,500 to $10,000, depending on the type of prosthesis. Your doctor will discuss the specific advantages and drawbacks of each type with you. Table 6:4 lists sources of help and information regarding impotence.

Drugs That May Cause Impotence

Here is a list of some of the more common medications which may cause impotence as a side effect. Not everyone on a particular medication will have the same side effects. Report impotence to your doctor, but do not stop taking any drug on your own.

Blood Pressure Medications (partial list)
chlorothiazide sodium (Diuril)
chlorthalidone (Hygroton)
hydrochlorothiazide (Esidrix, Hydrodiuril)
furosemide (Lasix)
spironolactone (Aldactone)
atenolol (Tenormin)
metoprolol (Lopressor)
nadolol (Corgard)
propranolol HCL (Inderal); also used in heart disease
clonidine HCL (Catapres)
methyldopa (Aldomet)
prazosin (Minipress)

Antidepressants
imipramine HCL (Tofranil)
desipramine HCL (Norpramin)
amitriptyline HCL (Elavil)
nortriptyline HCL (Aventyl)
protriptyline HCL (Vivactil)
doxepin HCL (Sinequan)

Stimulants
amphetamine sulfate (Benzedrine)
dextroamphetamine sulfate (Dexedrine)

Antipsychotics (also used to control nausea and vomiting)
chlorpromazine (Thorazine)
prochlorperazine (Compazine)
thioridazine HCL (Mellaril)
trifluoperazine HCL (Stelazine)

Tranquilizers
diazepam (Valium)
chlordiazepoxide (Librium)

Table 6:3

Sources of Help for Impotence

Impotence Anonymous
National Headquarters
5119 Bradley Boulevard
Chevy Chase, MD 20815

Information and support group for impotent men and their partners.

Organizations of Accredited Sex Therapists

The American Association of Sex Educators, Counselors and Therapists
1 East Wacker Drive, Suite 2700
Chicago, IL 60601

Membership list available for $5.

American Society for Sex Therapy and Research
℅ Dr. Robert Dickes
Department of Psychiatry, Box 1203
Downstate Medical Center
450 Clarkson Avenue
Brooklyn, NY 11203

Membership list available for $3.

Table 6:4

7

MIDLIFE CRISIS: THE WOMAN'S SIDE

Just as different cultures affect what defines an age-related crisis, so do different times. Financial need and the women's movement that influenced more women to join the work force, the growing number of over-50 glamorous actresses like Joan Collins and Elizabeth Taylor, the tendency to postpone childbearing until a later age, and advances in medicine and awareness of preventive measures all are changing our definition of the midlife crisis for future generations. Still, for today's woman, the fifties represent a decade that may be one of significant stress. The departure of children and the onset of menopause remain major turning points in any woman's life that must be recognized and dealt with.

Midlife crisis may be defined as the reaction both to increasing physical signs of aging and to major life events, such as a reduction in income due to retirement, divorce or death of a longtime partner. One may feel less attractive suddenly or fear the straying of one's spouse during *his* midlife crisis; these fears can be exaggerated by our society's emphasis on youthful beauty, although fortunately this is changing. For the woman whose identity and major preoccupation have been tied to the mothering role, the "empty nest" may bring on both loneliness and a sense of loss of purpose in life. Furthermore, the loss of reproductive function at menopause may trigger both psychological and physical stresses.

But there is a plus side. Midlife brings the freedom to pursue interests that were subordinated to the parental role and the cost of raising a family. While it may be painful to see children leave home to establish their own lives, most women at this time also experience a deep sense of accomplishment and pride at having launched children successfully into adulthood. This sense of accomplishment should be a valuable source of self-esteem that can be transferred to other pursuits. The departure of children may also provide an opportunity to renew a relationship with one's spouse or to end an unhappy marriage that was endured "for the sake of the children."

Rather than being viewed as the beginning of the end, this period in a woman's life can and should be perceived as a new beginning—it is all a matter of attitude. With age, people tend to see the positive side of negative events as well as the negative side of positive ones. But this optimistic viewpoint is one that does not necessarily come naturally; it must be actively cultivated. And women, as well as men, should concentrate on their abilities rather than on the physical limits of growing older.

Being open to new experiences, rather than giving in to rigid behavior and attitudes, can help retain intellectual vitality and can expand one's horizons in exciting ways. More than ever, common-sense health practices should be a part of daily routines; in large measure, health maintenance during these middle years will determine whether or not a person enjoys a healthy, vital old age or joins the ranks of the frail elderly. And there are other benefits. Maintaining appropriate weight through good nutrition and regular exercise can forestall certain health problems and maximize physical attractiveness. Exercise has the added benefit of being a natural mood elevator, or "upper." Practicing sound preventive medicine, which includes periodic medical checkups and tests (see Table 7:1) should also be a priority.

Medical Tests for Women

Test	Frequency
Blood pressure measurement	Annually; more often if under treatment for hypertension
Blood tests (i.e., diabetes, anemia)	Biannually after age 45
Breast examination	Annually
Cholesterol	Every 5 years; more often if under treatment for atherosclerosis or coronary disease or if cholesterol exceeds 240 mg/dl
Dental examination	Every 6 to 12 months
Dental X-rays	Every 2 to 3 years
Electrocardiogram	Every 3 years after age 50; more often if under treatment for heart disease
Eye examination	Biannually
Mammography	Biannually between ages 40 and 49; annually age 50 and above
Test for occult blood in stool	Annually
Pelvic examination (including rectal and Pap smear)	Every 1 to 2 years
Sigmoidoscopy	Every 5 years after 2 consecutive negative examinations at 50 and 51
Complete physical	Every 5 years to age 60; biannually thereafter

Table 7:1

❏ Menopause

In our society, many women anticipate menopause with dread. Traditionally, menopause has been looked upon not only as the end of a woman's reproductive years, but also as an end to her sexual attractiveness and as the beginning of old age. Fortunately, this is changing. Today American women enter menopause at a later age—the average is about 52 years—and live longer than their counterparts at the turn of the century, when the average age of menopause was about 46 and the life expectancy was 51 years. Now the average life expectancy has been increased to 78 years, so a woman can expect to live 25 or 30 years, or even longer, following menopause. For a growing number of women, these years are even more productive and rewarding than what came before. Today women in their fifties and sixties are entering public life, forging new careers, going back to school to earn degrees ranging from high school diplomas to Ph.D.s—all after menopause. No longer is menopause the beginning of the end, but instead, for increasing numbers of women, often a new beginning.

▪ *The Physical Side of Menopause*

Actually, reproductive capacity begins to decline long before a woman has her last menstrual period. Production of estrogen, the hormone controlling ovulation, may start to drop in the late twenties or early thirties. At the same time, the number of egg-containing follicles in the ovaries continues their decline from the nearly half a million present at birth. By the time a women reaches her fifties, the ovaries cannot produce enough estrogen to stimulate egg maturation and ovulation. Progesterone, the hormone that promotes the shedding of the uterine lining, thus producing the menstrual flow, depends upon ovulation. Thus, when ovulation stops, menstrual periods will taper off and gradually cease. This does not happen overnight; menopause is a process that may take two to five years to complete.

The age of menopause is largely determined by genetic makeup; daughters of women who entered menopause in their forties are likely to follow suit, while those whose mothers menstruated until their mid-fifties are likely to experience a late menopause. However, removal of the ovaries, which is frequently done as part of a hysterectomy, will result in an abrupt menopause, if done in a woman who is still menstruating. In these cases, the symptoms are more severe than those occurring with a natural tapering off. Heavy smoking, tubal ligation or removal of the uterus but not the ovaries may bring on menopause somewhat earlier than normal.

MENOPAUSAL SYMPTOMS

The vast majority of menopausal American women—at least 75 percent—experience symptoms related to decreased estrogen. These may be severe enough to cause one to seek medical attention or barely noticeable. (Some of the more common symptoms are listed in Table 7:2, Symptoms Associated with Menopause.)

Surveys of menopausal women have found that hot flashes are among their most common and troubling symptoms. These sensations of intense heat travel up the body from the waist to the neck. The drop in estrogen is believed to somehow affect the body's temperature control center in the brain, resulting in periodic dilation or opening of the surface blood vessels. This causes the sensation of heat and accompanying reddening of the skin, especially on the neck and face. In response, the body tries to regulate the temperature by sweating, which is sometimes drenching. Hot flashes range from mild to severe and can occur infrequently or, in severe cases, forty to fifty times a day. They are usually more intense at night and may even wake a woman up. Although hot flashes can be unnerving, they are harmless and often disappear

Symptoms Associated with Menopause

Not all women experience all of the following, but these are among the more common signs and symptoms related to menopause:

- Tapering off and then cessation of menstruation
- Hot flashes
- Sweats, including night sweats
- Depression, mood swings
- Insomnia
- Feelings of anxiety
- Irritability
- Palpitations
- Generalized itching
- Vaginal dryness, itching, increased susceptibility to infection
- Shrinking and sagging of breasts
- Thinning of scalp and pubic hair
- Increased facial hair
- Increased thinning of bones
- Drying and wrinkling of skin
- Weight gain, bloating
- Increased brittleness of nails; grooving and slower growth
- Joint pain
- Headaches
- Rise in LDL cholesterol

Table 7:2

by themselves within two and a half years. Taking replacement estrogen suppresses the abnormal activity of the brain's temperature center and eliminates hot flashes. Women who do not take estrogen should avoid wearing excess clothing, use of alcohol, caffeine, hot beverages and spicy foods, all of which may bring on hot flashes. Stress and emotional upsets also can provoke them.

The sharp reduction in estrogen also produces atrophy or thinning of vaginal tissue, causing it to lose its natural lubrication. Although regular sexual stimulation helps postpone the atrophy, women will usually experience pain during intercourse within five to ten years after the onset of menopause. In addition to discomfort, changes in the vagina also lead to increased irritation, inflammation and the risk of infection. Good personal hygiene and the use of replacement estrogen, which can be in the form of vaginal cream, are the most effective preventive measures. Even if vaginal atrophy has existed for many years, taking estrogen will reverse the symptoms.

A similar tissue-thinning process takes place in the urethra and bladder, making the urinary tract more vulnerable to irritation and infection. Estrogen replacement combined with good personal hygiene and drinking plenty of liquids help reduce the risk of urinary infection. After menopause, many women also experience increased problems of stress incontinence, the involuntary loss of urine when sneezing, reaching or during exercise. The Kegel exercises to strengthen muscles controlling the flow of urine often can help. (See Table 7:3.)

Perhaps the most serious consequences of estrogen deficiency is osteoporosis, the thinning of bone. At some point or another, approximately a quarter of the postmenopausal women in this country suffer osteoporosis-related bone fractures; complications from these fractures account for 30,000 deaths each year. As the bones become increasingly thin, even a very minor fall or injury will result in a fracture, and sometimes a bone will simply break spontaneously. Deaths typically occur in cases in which an older woman will break a hip and then succumb to complications, such as a pulmonary embolism or pneumonia.

In recent years we have become increasingly aware of osteoporosis as a major health problem. (See Figure 7:1.) Much of this attention has focused on the body's need for calcium to maintain bone strength. While it is important to get adequate dietary calcium throughout life, calcium supplements alone will not solve the problem of postmenopausal osteoporosis among women predisposed to develop it. (See Table 7:4, Factors That Increase the Risk of Osteoporosis.) The body needs estrogen in order for the calcium to be absorbed into the bones. Exercise and vitamin D also are essential to maintain strength.

Women who are at high risk to develop osteoporosis should be particu-

Kegel Exercises

In the 1950's, Dr. Arnold Kegel, a surgeon at UCLA, devised a series of exercises to strengthen the pubococcygeal (PC) muscles between the vagina and the anus. This area, known as the pelvic floor, slackens during pregnancy and childbirth. Many women are unaware of their weakened PC muscles until menopause, which brings a thinning of tissue in this area.

1. As a first step, learn to identify the PC muscles. You can do this by attempting to stop the flow of urine in midstream, or alternatively, by inserting a finger into the vagina and tightening the muscles until you feel your finger being squeezed.
2. Tighten these muscles in a front to back motion, starting first with the muscles that control urination and ending by tightening the anus. Hold for a count of 5 and repeat 15 to 20 times at each session.

These exercises can be performed anywhere at any time. For maximum effect, they should be repeated 50 to 100 times a day.

Table 7:3

Height Loss Due to Osteoporosis

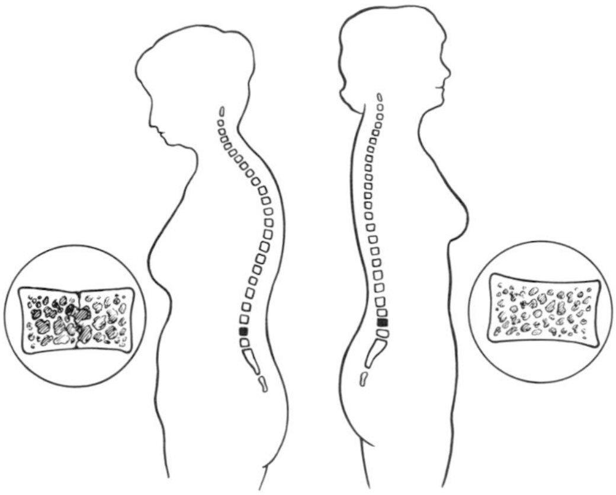

Figure 7:1
A height loss of 3 to 8 inches is not unusual in advanced osteoporosis.

Factors That Increase the Risk of Osteoporosis

- Sex. Women are more likely than men to develop osteoporosis.
- Ethnic background. Caucasians of northern European descent, especially women with light eyes and fair skin, have the highest incidence, as do Japanese and certain other Asians.
- Physical build. Women with a small bone structure have less bone mass to start with, and are at a higher risk than larger boned women and men. A slender build also increases risk; fatty tissue converts adrenal hormones to estrogen, so very thin women have lower levels of estrogen.
- Early menopause. Women who have an early, abrupt menopause because of a hysterectomy or ovarian failure develop osteoporosis at an earlier age, with more pronounced bone loss than women who undergo a later natural menopause.
- Sedentary lifestyle. Physical activity and stress on the bones is essential for proper bone metabolism.
- Cigarette smoking. Smoking lowers estrogen levels and also hinders calcium metabolism.
- Heredity. Women with a family history of osteoporosis are more likely to develop the disease.
- Calcium deficiency. Many women, especially those who shun milk, cheese, and other dairy products, may have a chronic calcium deficiency without knowing it. The problem may be compounded among women who have had several children and breastfed their babies without taking adequate dietary calcium.

Table 7:4

larly diligent about preventive measures. Adequate calcium (1000 to 1500 milligrams a day; see Chapter 1, Nutrition in the Later Years, for listings of calcium-rich foods), vitamin D and exercise all are important in maintaining bone strength. Fluoride, which is now added to drinking water in most parts of the country to prevent dental cavities, is also needed to maintain bone strength and may be prescribed as part of the treatment regimen for osteoporosis. But without estrogen, it is doubtful that any of these measures will be highly effective in preventing and halting the progression of osteoporosis. For maximum benefit, estrogen replacement should be started soon after menopause, although it has been shown effective in preventing further bone thinning when started by women in their seventies and eighties. (See Pros and Cons of Estrogen Therapy later in this chapter.)

After menopause, women also become more vulnerable to heart disease, although their risk of a heart attack is still less than that of men. It is thought that estrogen has a beneficial effect on the heart, presumably by raising HDL cholesterol, which is protective against the buildup of fatty deposits in the coronary arteries and lowering the harmful LDL cholesterol. Estrogen does increase the tendency for blood to clot, so women who already have clotting problems, high blood pressure, or atherosclerosis may be advised not to take it or to compensate by adding low-dose aspirin to suppress the blood platelets and prevent excessive clotting. A doctor should be consulted before self-treatment with aspirin, however, since it can promote bleeding problems.

Many women notice that they begin to gain weight at about the time of menopause, and that the extra pounds seem to be centered around the waist and abdomen—the dreaded middle-aged spread. Metabolism slows down as we grow older, so we do not need as many calories. Increased exercise and a lowered intake of food can help prevent weight gain. But this is not the whole story. Changing hormone levels help redistribute fat: Breasts and buttocks may lose fatty tissue while the abdomen gains fat. This is believed to be due to the lowered estrogen and high levels of androgens, which result in women acquiring the midsection fat padding that is common in men. Poor tone of the abdominal muscles also can cause sagging; toning exercises such as leg lifts and partial sit-ups will help prevent this and keep the midsection flat.

Sexuality becomes a major concern for many women going through menopause. They worry that with the loss of their reproductive function, they will no longer be attractive to their sexual partners. Some women experience diminished sexual desire with menopause, but this is by no means universal. Many women, no longer fearing an unwanted pregnancy, find they are more sexually responsive. Sexuality is a fragile combination of physical and psychological factors, and something that requires considerable nurturing to keep fresh and alive. If a couple experiences sexual problems, and are unable to discuss them, they should seek the help of a qualified therapist.

A word of warning regarding contraception during menopause: Many women assume that once they stop menstruating, they no longer have to worry about birth control. This may be true in many instances, but there are enough unplanned pregnancies among women going through menopause to dispel this notion. Experts recommend that birth control be practiced until periods have stopped completely for a full year and a doctor has verified that the woman is no longer ovulating, even sporadically. Finding an appropriate means of birth control is often a problem for older women. In general, the pill is not recommended for women over the age of 40, although the progesterone-only, or mini-pill, is safe and an acceptable alternative for older women. Because ovulation is erratic, the rhythm or natural family planning methods are even more unreliable than in younger women. Barrier methods—the diaphragm and spermicide for women, condoms for men—are reliable if used properly and consistently, carry no side effects and in the case of condoms, help prevent transmission of the AIDS virus. If a woman experiences pain or irritation during intercourse in which the man is wearing a condom, it should be lubricated. Problems due to sensitivity to latex can be remedied by using the more hypoallergenic condoms made from lamb intestines.

Heretofore, the IUD has been a favored contraceptive for older women; however, all but one type of IUD has been taken off the market in the United States because of lawsuits over complications brought against manufacturers of the devices. Many doctors still think the IUD is suitable for older monogamous women and will recommend having one inserted in Canada, where they are still widely available. This is not recommended for a woman with multiple sex partners or a history of pelvic infections. And, of course, sterilization is an increasingly popular method of birth control for couples whose families are complete. Many women in their early forties think that there is little point of undergoing sterilization at their age, but considering that they may have ten or more years of contraception ahead of them, it is still a viable alternative to other methods.

Of course, not all problems associated with menopause are physical; mood swings, depression, insomnia, irritability and other largely psychological disturbances also are very common during this time. While many of these problems may be related to all of the other life changes taking place during the late forties and early fifties, they also have organic causes related to shifting hormone levels.

Psychological changes accompanying menopause can be very disturbing, especially since many doctors and spouses tend to dismiss them as trivial or imaginary. Any woman who has regularly experienced symptoms associated with premenstrual syndrome knows that they are not "all in the head," and that the mood swings, crying spells, irritability and other psychological symptoms are related to their cyclic hormonal changes. During menopause hormonal levels also are shifting and can produce many of the same symptoms, only on a more constant basis. The symptoms also may be exacerbated by a woman's attitude toward aging and other circumstances, such as the stress of having children leave home or the prospect of losing a mate. Hormone therapy may help relieve some of the symptoms, but it should be accompanied by psychological therapy. This may take the form of individual counseling, group therapy or simply sharing your experiences with other women with similar problems. Coming to terms with the physical changes of menopause and developing a positive attitude about the future can go a long way toward easing the psychological stresses and symptoms.

▪ *Pros and Cons of Estrogen Therapy*

Doctors still are not in full agreement as to whether lifelong estrogen replacement should be recommended for all or most postmenopausal women. Proponents of estrogen replacement note that today's increased life expectancy means that women are living longer in a menopausal (estrogen-deficient) state, and that hormone replacement is vital in preventing osteoporosis as well as relieving the distressing symptoms of menopause. On the other side are physicians who fear that long-term hormone therapy may increase the risk of cancer or other problems. They point to studies published in the 1970's reporting a marked increase in endometrial cancer among women on long-term estrogen therapy. Following these reports, there was a marked swing away from long-term estrogen replacement, which is thought to be a factor in the current increase in osteoporosis among older women.

Today the pendulum is swinging back in favor of estrogen replacement, only with a number of modifications since the 1950's and 1960's. The dosage of estrogen is lower than in the early days of homone therapy; the current regimen also incorporates progesterone, another female sex hormone. Typically, a woman will take .625 milligrams of estrogen (e.g., Premarin) for 25 days, then take 10 milligrams of progesterone (e.g., Provera) for 7 to 13 days, and nothing for the next 5 days. (See Table 7:5.) This combination of hormones mimics the body's normal levels of the two hormones and prevents a buildup of the uterine lining, which lowers the risk of endometrial cancer. Women who have had their uterus removed do not have to take progesterone.

After stopping the progesterone, a woman will have about three days of light bleeding, similar to what happens during menstruation. The bleeding is usually lighter than a regular period, and after a couple of years of hormone therapy, it tapers off and eventually stops. Recent studies indicate that this regimen may actually lower the risk of

Hormone Replacement Therapy Medications

Estrogen doses vary according to reason for treatment. In general, atrophic vaginal changes usually require the lowest dose; osteoporosis, an intermediate dose; and hot flashes, the highest dose. The initial dose may be adjusted up or down as determined during the individual course of treatment. Your physician may prescribe the hormone on a continuous or cyclic basis.

Brand Name	Generic Name	Route	Dose (per day)
ESTROGENS			
Estinyl	ethinyl estradiol	oral	.02–.05 mg.
Estrace	estradiol	oral	1–2 mg.
		vaginal cream	2–4 grams as marked on applicator
Estraderm	estradiol	skin patch	.05 mg. Change patch twice a week
Estrovis	quinestrol	oral	100 mcg.
Ogen	estropipate	oral	Ogen625 (.75 mg. estropipate) to Ogen5 (6 mg.)
		vaginal cream	2–4 grams as marked on applicator
Premarin	conjugated estrogens	oral	.3–1.25 mg.
		vaginal cream	½–1 applicatorful
PROGESTOGENS			
Amen	medroxyprogesterone acetate	oral	10 mg. for 10 days of each cycle
Provera	medroxyprogesterone acetate	oral	10 mg. for 10 days of each cycle

Table 7:5

cancer. What's more, the recent introduction of the estrogen skin patch eliminates some of the side effects associated with oral estrogen by providing a more constant level in the blood.

Depending on the reason for taking hormones, the estrogen may be given in pill form, transdermal (skin) patch or vaginal cream. Some indications, such as risk for osteoporosis and vaginal atrophy, require lifelong treatment; others, such as most cases of hot flashes, may be short-term and at a higher dosage than long-term replacement therapy. (Estrogen may also be given as a long-lasting injection, but this is not recommended because there is no way to eliminate it quickly from the body in case of serious side effects.)

Possible contraindications for estrogen therapy include cancer of the uterus, estrogen-dependent breast cancer or a family history of either. A past medical history of phlebitis (a blood clot in a vein, usually in the leg) may also be a contraindication, although replacement estrogen doses and the risk of clotting are significantly lower than for oral contraceptives. Women with gallbladder disease, once a contraindication, may now safely use transdermal estrogen, which, unlike the oral form, bypasses the liver.

Routine estrogen replacement therapy should not be started until a woman has gone for twelve consecutive months without a period, although larger doses of estrogen may be prescribed earlier to relieve symptoms such as hot flashes. Before starting estrogen replacement therapy, a woman should have a complete physical examination, including a breast examination and mammogram, pelvic exam and Pap smear, and blood tests for cholesterol, glucose, thyroid and liver function. A biopsy to check for abnormal cells in the endometrium is also recommended. At this time, there is no widely available, reliable and inexpensive way to screen for risk of osteoporosis. Presence of risk factors and/or loss of height can be used to determine the need for estrogen replacement.

POSSIBLE SIDE EFFECTS

Side effects from estrogen replacement are usually temporary and include breast tenderness, fluid retention, nausea and slight weight gain. More serious side effects include persistent severe headaches, swelling, redness, warmth or tenderness in the extremities, any of which might mean formation of a blood clot. If any of these side effects occur, they should be reported to a doctor immediately and may be an indication to stop hormones.

Many women will experience vaginal bleeding due to the addition of progesterone. This occurs after the progesterone is stopped at the end of the cycle and is light, lasting for only two or three days. Any heavy bleeding or blood clots, bleeding lasting more than three to five days or bleeding at any other time in the cycle is abnormal and should be checked as soon as possible by a doctor.

Women on hormone replacement therapy should see their doctors every six months for follow-up breast and pelvic exams, Pap smear and other pertinent tests—for example, blood sugar and blood pressure measurements for those with diabetes or hypertension.

▪ If Hormone Therapy Is Not For You

Some women cannot take estrogen replacement for medical reasons. Others may feel that their symptoms are not troublesome enough to warrant hormone therapy. Here are some of the alternative means of coping with menopausal symptoms:

Diet. To keep supplementary estrogen production at a maximum, be sure to take in sufficient protein and calories. A minimum of 1200 calories a day is necessary for adequate nutrition, although lower calorie diets may be permissible for a week at a time for people who are overweight. Vegetarians should know how to combine foods to obtain complete protein. Remember, however, that too much protein interferes with calcium absorption, increasing the risk of osteoporosis. (For a more complete discussion, see Chapter 1, Nutrition in the Later Years.)

Temperature regulation. To help moderate hot flashes, drink cool beverages, have a cool shower or turn on the air conditioner if a room is warm. Wear layers of clothes that can be removed in the event of a hot flash.

Sleep inducers. In case of insomnia, either due to hot flashes or as a separate symptom, try a small glass of wine, warm milk or a warm bath before bedtime. Learn relaxation techniques or make up your own; worrying about falling asleep is the worst way to fight insomnia. Exercise earlier in the evening (but not immediately before going to bed) also helps induce sleep. Self-hypnosis is also an effective way to overcome insomnia.

Coping techniques. Biofeedback training, meditation, relaxation exercises and self-hypnosis all have been shown effective in helping some women control hot flashes, mood swings and other symptoms. Self-help discussion groups in which women with similar problems discuss their difficulties and solutions also are helpful.

Women need to recognize that menopause does entail change, but it is a natural milestone that can be passed with a minimum of difficulty with the right attitude, plus medical and personal support. A woman often hesitates to discuss her fears of growing older with her spouse and children; simply being able to talk about what is happening, both physically and psychologically, can make a big difference.

❑ Coping with the Empty Nest Syndrome

Preventive medicine and advances in treatment of many diseases mean that today's couples live longer in an empty nest than those fifty years ago. For a woman who has not had a job outside the home since her children were born, the departure of children can be particularly unsettling. In effect, she suddenly finds herself "out of work," with no recent experience that qualifies her to compete in the job market. Of course, holding a job is not the only alternative, but it is important that a woman develop new interests if she is to lead a satisfying life.

For those who do not want or need a paying job, taking on volunteer work or finding a consuming interest will not only provide mental stimulation but also enlarge the circle of friends and ease emotional dependence on a spouse. Local hospitals, community agencies, churches or synagogues may have a wide variety of volunteer opportunities to suggest. For anyone who has ever felt the desire to remedy any of society's ills, working with the homeless or pregnant teenagers might be satisfying. Or perhaps you have a hankering for public life. There are scores of political organizations that constantly need volunteers for everything from stuffing envelopes to handing out campaign literature and manning polls during elections. Schools and day-care centers are still other possibilities that offer a woman an opportunity to use her mothering skills to help youngsters of all ages.

In caring for a family, many women have not had the time or energy to focus on their own development. Now is the time to do so. Some women might consider parlaying handicraft or cooking skills into a business. Teaming up with others to form a catering service can be fun and profitable, as well as time-consuming and demanding. Other women might satisfy creative leanings by joining a local theater group, learning to play a musical instrument or learning how to make pottery, quilts or other handicrafts. The possibilities are endless; the task is to focus on an activity that will be a pleasurable and rewarding one, rather than merely time-filling.

▪ *The Changing Marital Relationship*

Once the children leave home, both an empty house and the need that many women feel to redefine their identity may put a strain on the marriage. Physical signs of aging plus the loss of reproductive function can be devastating to a woman whose feeling of femininity is closely tied to appearance and the ability to bear children. At the same time, her husband may be struggling with his own feelings about aging. Unrealized career hopes and the awareness that he has limited time left to make his mark may leave him feeling that he is in a rut, producing a restlessness that may spill over into other areas of his life, such as the marriage.

The high divorce rate among couples who are suddenly faced with an empty nest and the need to reestablish their own relationship attests to the difficulty involved. Still, if a couple can resist focusing on problems alone, this can be a time of joyous rediscovery and strengthening of a marriage. There are dozens of examples—Ronald and Nancy Reagan immediately come to mind—of older couples who are as much in love as newlyweds. Finding shared interests is an important key to revitalizing a marriage. Reading aloud to each other, listening to music and sharing a mutual hobby provide an opportunity for rediscovery and growth.

Communication is vitally important in keeping marriage healthy. A good sense of humor, an open attitude toward developing new interests, seeing new sides of a mate and a lot of patience are important in getting through this often-difficult transition period. Of course, in some instances, despite the desire and efforts of partners to stay together, the marriage may break up. Or the early death of a spouse may leave a woman alone. According to the 1980 U.S. Bureau of the Census report, only 41 percent of married women 65 and older had a living spouse, compared to 80 percent of married men in the same age group.

The abundance of women, plus the tendency of men to marry substantially younger partners, makes remarriage far less likely for older women compared to older men—all the more reason for a woman to develop independent interests and a network of supportive friends. Very few of us enjoy the extended family situation of past generations and other societies, which can ease the strain of adjusting to the newly single or widowed state, but all of us have access to friends or other people in similar circumstances. To tap these resources, it may be necessary to make the first move—something many people find difficult—in reestablishing a social life. But the rewards of building a supportive network are worth the effort. Table 7:6 lists suggested starting points for reestablishing a social life on one's own.

❑ Going Back to Work

Returning to work or taking a job for the first time can be a matter of necessity, choice or a combination of both. In ever-growing numbers, women of all ages are reentering the work force. According to the 1980 U.S. Bureau of the Census report, 60 percent of women age 45 to 54 and 42 percent of those between 55 and 64 are employed outside the home.

Now is the time to explore career op-

Reestablishing a Social Life

- *Keep active.* The more time you have to brood, the worse your outlook will be. Even if you initially engage in an activity just to keep busy, chances are it will soon become enjoyable in and of itself.
- *Become a joiner.* Find a group that fits in with your interests. Church or synagogue groups, health clubs, gardening clubs or a local Y or library are only a few of those available.
- *Take in a roommate.* If you live alone and have extra space, why not share it? Large urban areas often have roommate referral services that do preliminary screening. In smaller communities, check public bulletin boards and classified ads or ask friends or coworkers. A local college also may need housing for students or staff. Be sure to interview any prospects carefully. Honesty, financial responsibility, consideration for others and similar attitudes toward household chores are as important as compatibility.
- *Speak up.* We grow up being warned against talking to strangers; still, conversations started in a museum, laundry room, bookstore, library, etc. can lead to friendships. Of course, discretion and common sense are important, but it is also important to realize that most people are not out to cause misery or harm.
- *Tap local resources.* Think twice before moving to another community. Although this may be an ideal time to relocate, a totally new environment may be very lonely and unsettling.
- *Look your best.* Wearing makeup and flattering clothing can lift spirits, even though you may have to push yourself to do so at first.
- *Get back in circulation.* If you are ready to date, consider some of the newer methods of meeting men, as well as the tried-and-true friendship or work contacts. Urban communities may have video dating services that enable you to see and be seen before actually meeting a date. Special interest or metropolitan magazines often run personal ads placed by people seriously interested in establishing relationships. (Publications that charge more for placing an ad—rates may be as high as $80 to $100—may attract more reputable, professional men compared to those that charge less.)
- *Go back to school.* Young people have long known that class is an ideal place to meet others with similar interests. Almost every community offers some sort of adult education at the local high school, college, community center, etc.

Table 7:6

Choosing a Career

- Make an inventory of your interests. Do you like to work with figures or with people, with children or the elderly? Do you like to be left on your own or do you like to work under close supervision in a highly structured environment?
- Make an inventory of your skills. Do you speak a second language? Can you type? Cook? Sew? Keep books? Use a computer? Ride a horse? Tell the difference between an antique and a reproduction? Remember, almost any skill can be marketed.
- Are you willing to relocate? To travel for a certain percentage of time?
- Make an inventory of what you need for a given job. Do you need a refresher course? A special certificate? License? Special training?
- Do you work best alone or with other people? Are you a candidate to start your own business?
- What is your minimum salary requirement? Can you afford to do volunteer work or take a part-time job to get the necessary background? Are you willing to accept temporary employment that might turn into full-time work?

Table 7:7

tions. Even if pressing financial needs dictate that a woman return to work, she should make every effort to fully investigate available opportunities to find truly satisfying employment. Too many of us spend our lives working at jobs that really do not excite or interest us, but we simply do not know how to change our situations. Table 7:7, Choosing a Career, outlines possible steps in finding a rewarding midlife career.

Once you have analyzed your skills and interests, check the *Dictionary of Occupational Titles* and the *Occupational Outlook Handbook*, available in most library reference departments, for actual job descriptions and growth opportunities in various fields. If possible, try to spend a day observing someone who works in your area of interest to see what the job actually entails.

▪ *Job Search Tactics*

If you have good clerical skills but haven't decided on a particular field of interest, consider registering with a temporary employment agency. Working for different companies will give you an idea of which ones have desirable environments and may also lead to a permanent job.

For those seeking work in a specific area, it is important to regularly read the classified ads and register with an employment agency. Attend any career days your community sponsors and talk to relatives, friends or anyone in your community who might have contacts in your field of interest. Read trade publications, available at any good library, for possible leads. Employment agencies may be helpful, but caution is needed in selecting one that is right for you. (See Table 7:8, Using an Employment Agency.)

Many jobs never appear in the classified ads. A company may promote from within; the person who chooses the candidate may have a stack of unsolicited résumés; or the employer simply may not have seen a particular need that could be filled by an applicant with the right combination of talents. To find a job in this "hidden" market, check with the reference section of a good library for a wealth of directories that list businesses, hospitals, miscellaneous associations and other categories. Select promising possibilities and note the names of those heading the relevant departments. Always write to an area head rather than to the personnel department, which may not hear of an opening that the employer can easily fill. If there are thirty interesting companies, send your résumé to all of them. (See Table 7:9 for tips on writing a résumé.) Only a small percentage may be interested in you, and "blanketing the market" is the best way to find those few.

Using an Employment Agency

- Match the agency to your skills. If you have a specialized skill, going to a general agency may result in its counselors trying to place you in a job for which you are overqualified.
- Register with more than one agency. This increases your job prospects, but let each one know that you are registered elsewhere, as employers may list the same job with more than one service.
- Ask questions. Make sure the counselor is both giving you a true picture of what a job entails and honestly representing your qualifications to the potential employer.
- Double-check agency listings. Read the classified ads to see if the job is already advertised. Agencies sometimes solicit business by calling firms that place ads and collecting a fee for a job you could get without any charge.
- Who pays the fee? Sometimes employers pay the fee; other times it's the job seeker.
- Read the fine print. Employment agencies are regulated by state law. Make sure you have a copy of the contract and understand the fee schedule. You may be entitled to a full or partial refund under certain circumstances.

Table 7:8

Writing Your Résumé

- Make it look professional. A résumé should be typed on plain paper, single-spaced, and run no more than two pages.
- Find an appropriate format. Check sample résumés and pick a format that is appropriate for you. List all previous jobs, dates and a brief description of duties.
- Emphasize experience and skills. If work experience is limited, mention high school or college courses that you excelled in, significant extracurricular activities, scholarships and academic honors.
- Emphasize accomplishments. If you performed beyond the specific job description or accomplished special tasks—for example, increasing production, exceeding fundraising goals—list these.
- Analyze your relevant life skills. If you are seeking a job in health care and cared for a seriously ill relative, you may have performed various nursing functions and become familiar with social service agency resources.
- Be concise. Employers are not impressed by inflated descriptions.
- Include a cover letter addressed to a specific person. Briefly state how you would be a valuable employee and say that you will call the following week to discuss job opportunities.
- Follow up. Don't wait for a prospective employer to call you; instead, call him or her to arrange for an interview.

Table 7:9

❑ Sorting Out Priorities

In this chapter, we have covered a wide range of areas that are ripe for creating midlife crises. But it would be a mistake to assume that the middle years always bring major life crises. Many women move through their fifties with enviable equanimity; they seem to have their priorities in order and are able to sort out what really matters. For all of us, these middle years are a period of setting priorities. What seemed terribly important at 20 or 30 may be trivial today, and vice versa. The midpoint is a good time to look both back and ahead—to readjust goals and make realistic assessments. Ask yourself: "Is it realistic to think I'm going to win a Nobel prize, write a best-selling novel, climb Mount Everest? If so, what is it going to take to achieve my goal? Is it worth the effort?" The questions may be hard and the answer hard to accept, but now is the time to do the asking. And then, as the line in a popular commercial goes: Master the possibilities.

8

CHANGING RELATIONSHIPS

As we grow older, our relationships with family, friends, colleagues and even casual neighborhood acquaintances inevitably change. Children grow up and leave home. Divorce, death, retirement, moving to a new community all alter long-established social and professional networks. Growing old alone is a fear that haunts all of us, and for many, it is a prospect that we have to work at to avoid.

At the turn of the century, it was assumed that an elderly parent, grandparent, aunt or uncle would always have a home—and a place in life—with members of the younger generation. This is no longer the case. Today's society is much more mobile than any in the past. Grandparents may live on one coast, their children on the other and grandchildren somewhere in between. The increased financial independence of older people means that more can live on their own, and do not need to depend upon children or other relatives. This can be a blessing for both the elderly and their family, though financial independence does not necessarily resolve the emotional need for close human contact.

Families today not only are more scattered than in the past, they also are smaller. At the turn of the century, it was not unusual for a person to have seven or more siblings; today one or two is more likely the norm. (Or, in the sociologist's terms, each family has approximately 1.8 children.) And a host of other demographic changes are at work which mean it is not just that the total size of the family is smaller but that the nature of the relationships is different now, too. People today live much longer. It is not uncommon for four generations of a family to be alive at the same time; even five is not that unusual.

The common practice of divorce and remarriage is also changing our traditional approach to family relationships. Today's children may have two sets of living grandparents, and an equal number, or even more, step-grandparents. Not uncommonly, grandparents lose contact with grandchildren when custody is granted to the daughter- or son-in-law.

❑ Importance of Networks

Throughout life all of us establish various networks that we can draw upon for friendship, emotional support and other needs. In general, women fare somewhat better than men in establishing and maintaining networks of both friends and relatives. This is particularly important in cases of divorce or death, because it is usually the woman who winds up alone. Married couples generally have wider friendship systems than widowed or divorced people, except in the case of elderly widows.

Friendships are particularly important during times of transition such as retirement. Retirees, however, sometimes find it difficult to make friends to replace the former co-workers and friends from the workplace. Since the older person may not have a built-in social network like the workplace, it is particularly important for him or her to have other friendships. Making an effort to join in new activities, to attend events at the community center and to renew old friendships that may have faded during the working years are all useful strategies.

Siblings can become important sources of support and friendship in the later years. Many people report that they grow closer to siblings as they get older, seeing or speaking to them more frequently, sharing memories and offering moral support during times of stress or transition. Any rivalries or competition that may have existed has usually dissipated by the later years and the siblings can enjoy their shared histories and keep track of events in each other's present lives. Although adult children are the primary source of support when an elderly person needs help, siblings are considered reliable sources of assistance and will usually offer to do what they can.

As the family grows older, the nature of relationships is bound to change gradually; in fact, it is often the function of the family to promote changes in those relationships. The "middle generation" adults in the family configuration may face several transitions in relationships all at the same time—for example, coping with the departure of the last child at a time when one of their own parents is dying. Understandably, both can be major sources of stress. Increasingly, physicians recognize that people are more likely to fall ill during times of stress. Coming to grips with the major comings and goings within a family's structure is never easy; still, planning for inevitable changes and being prepared for their consequences can make them less stressful.

❑ Departure of Children

When the children first leave home, they create a huge gap in the lives of the parents: The house may seem empty, too big and devoid of activity. For women who have not worked outside the home or who worked only part-time, this period is equivalent to the stage of losing a job or retirement for the husband. The woman whose main role came from her function as a mother may feel a loss of identity and have more difficulty coping with this period than other women who have maintained a career or other interests over the years.

After an initial period of adjustment, however, this time of life can become a satisfying and fulfilling one. In surveys, many people at this stage of life report that they are happy to be free of household and financial responsibilities and that they enjoy the increased freedom to do things by themselves and for themselves. (See Chapter 7, Midlife Crisis: The Woman's Side.) The parents' relationship with the children is now a more mutual, voluntary one based on enjoyment rather than obligation and involves a more evenhanded give-and-take quality.

Obviously, the departure of children prompts a major change in a couple's own relationship. Unfortunately, divorce at this stage of life is all too common. A couple may be faced with the fact that they had little in common aside from their role as parents; when this ends, so does the marriage. For those couples who stayed together "for the children" or whose marriage has fundamental problems that were not dealt with while the children were in the home, it would be illogical to expect some magical transformation to the kind of relationship they had as newlyweds before their children were born. Marriage counseling can be a helpful option for some couples who may need objective professional help to deal with long-term problems as well as to cope with the ways in which each person may have changed over the years. For some, divorce may be the best solution; for others, rebuilding the marriage.

Of course, not all couples find this a difficult time. Many look forward to moving on and anticipate this stage of life as a time to renew their relationship, to get to know each other again. Many couples say that their marriage improves during this period since they can concentrate on each other, free of the pressures and presence of children. There is also less personal uncertainty at this stage. As a rule, the couple will be financially secure, with no major changes expected in the near future. By now, most people are established in their chosen careers and retirement is likely to be a decade or so in the future.

This is a time to develop new interests and activities that can be shared by both spouses, not only providing a focus for this period of life but a good preparation for retirement. Remember, however, that too much togetherness can be just as detrimental to a relationship as too little; there is considerable truth in the old saw: "I married you for life, but I never counted on having you around for lunch every day." Individual activities and private times also are important.

Many women who did not work earlier see this as an opportunity to enter the labor force or to begin an educational program. Women generally direct their attention to outside interests during this time, concentrating on nondomestic achievements. At the same time, men become somewhat less achievement-oriented and are more likely to seek to satisfy domestic and inner needs. Or, somewhat freed from the financial pressures of rearing and educating children, a man or woman may find that this is the ideal time to start a new career. Simply look around; chances are you will find dozens of examples of unlikely midlife career changes: the actor who went into politics and became President of the United States; a publishing executive who earned his law degree at 65 and landed a job with a top New York law firm; a physician who retired to New Hampshire to run an inn.

Whatever the orientation, this is a period during which people concentrate on achieving personal satisfaction, whether that comes from finally finishing a degree, getting a job or cutting down on working hours. This is a time when people need to expand their network of friends, and a natural way to do so is to get involved in new activities. The way people deal with changes during this period of life has important consequences for the future, a point stressed by Shirley Campbell in an article entitled "The 50-

Year-Old Woman and Midlife Stress" (*International Journal of Aging and Human Development*, vol. 18, no. 4, p. 300). She suggests that a person who can cope successfully with the transitions of his or her fifties is likely to do equally well with adjusting to future aging.

❑ Aging Parents

One of the effects of the changing longevity pattern is that more and more people are surviving into what is considered "old" old age. Therefore middle-aged people may be called on to support their aging parents, with financial aid or varying degrees of care.

The majority of people enter old age with better health and a more stable financial situation than in the past. Elderly people, while they may want to live near their children and to see them often, express a desire to maintain their own residence and independence whenever possible. However, eventually inflation, illness or physical handicaps may create conditions that erode the independence of the elderly and make it necessary for their adult children to help in some way. Generally, an elderly man who becomes ill or deteriorates physically will have a wife to care for him, since women live longer and men tend to marry younger women. Women are not so fortunate; all too often an elderly woman who is left on her own may find she needs some sort of assistance, and this usually comes from adult children.

Studies have shown that most adult children will voluntarily help their parents and that most say that they have a good relationship with their parents. However, the parents' need for help often comes at a time when the middle-aged children are dealing with many other demands on their resources: helping young married children or still supporting younger children at home, planning for their own retirement and anticipating a reduced retirement income, or coping with the changes produced by aging or health problems themselves. The resulting situation is sometimes referred to as the "middle-generation squeeze," when middle-aged adults have to try to balance the demands of younger children, aging parents and their own personal and financial needs.

Traditionally the daughter is the caregiver in families. This may have worked well in the past, but in today's world, where the daughter is more likely to work outside the home, caring for an elderly parent can be a source of major stress, something neither the adult child nor the parent wants. There are no pat solutions, but many problems can be avoided by realistic planning and early preventive action. Obviously, health is a major determinant: It is the frail elderly who are most likely to wind up dependent upon others. It cannot be overemphasized that sound preventive health measures—good nutrition, appropriate exercise, varied interests that will help retain psychological well-being, and supportive formal and informal networks—are major keys to avoiding joining the ranks of the frail elderly. There are numerous examples of independent people in their nineties or even hundreds who still care for themselves and lead vital, interesting lives. (If you doubt this, simply tune in to NBC's *Today* show and listen to the daily birthday greetings to people who have passed the 100-year mark, and note how many proudly proclaim they still keep house, garden and perform myriad other activities.)

Even if an elderly person moves in with an adult child, it is important for all concerned that the parent retain a feeling of independence. Of course, this may not be possible in the face of serious, disabling illness, but this is the exception rather than the rule; most older people do not end up severely disabled. Ideally, there should be adequate space to ensure privacy for all. Converting a basement playroom into a small apartment, or declaring Grandma or Grandpa's room off-limits to other family members except upon invitation, are possibilities that should be considered if at all possible. (For more concerns, see Table 8:1, Before Having a Parent Move In.)

All too often, parent and child feel that their natural roles have been reversed, and that the offspring has, in effect, assumed the parenting role. Understandably, this can be emotionally and physically trying, unless approached with considerable give-and-take on all sides. An elderly parent who fears becoming a burden and wants to retain as much independence as possible may challenge the adult child's control of the situation, resulting in power conflicts within the family. Economic dependency may make the older person feel that he or she is losing control in all areas of life, and the resulting anxiety may cause the person to behave aggressively, manipulatively or in other inappropriate ways. In addition, the elderly person may have different expectations of what kind of help is needed than does the adult child, leading to feelings of frustration and dissatisfaction on both sides.

There is a tendency to infantilize elderly parents, making them more dependent and childlike. This provokes hostility on the part of the parent and resentment from the rest of the family. In recent years, we have heard a good deal about elder abuse, but the emphasis has been on physical mishandling; abuse does not have to be physical; psychological abuse can be even more devastating than the physical.

As more people survive into old age it is important for everyone to make an effort to understand the aging process. One of the reasons that middle-aged adults may resent caring for their parents is that they fear that they will be in the same position in a number of years. If people know what to expect, what the potentials and limitations are, they will be able to plan better for the future and will be able to meet the needs of the elderly more effectively. Many of the problems that come up are the result of a mismatch of expectations. The child may be providing a lot of assistance—in money or time—but it may not be the kind of help that the parent feels he or she needs. Open communication between parents and children about what is needed and what is feasible can prevent situations that will lead to conflict from developing.

Often, the way the decision to have a parent move into the home is made influences the way the situation progresses. Permanent decisions should not be made hastily at a moment of crisis; otherwise they can turn out to be serious mistakes, leading to unpleasantness for all concerned. For example, after an elderly mother falls and breaks a hip or suffers other serious illness, there may

Before Having a Parent Move In

Following are questions that should be asked before setting up a multigenerational household:

- Will the adult child's marriage suffer adverse effects?
- Will there be constant conflicts and clashes?
- Is there enough space to assure privacy for everyone?
- Is someone available to provide care if needed?
- Will the elderly person feel comfortable in new surroundings and with new people?
- Are finances adequate?
- Have all other alternatives been weighed and is this really the best solution?
- Are there community services or other resources that can be tapped?
- Will the parent have a useful role in the household?

Table 8:1

be a great temptation to sell the house and have her move in with one of the children. By the time everyone realizes that a mistake has been made and that everyone would have been happier with some other arrangement, such as a part-time homemaker or live-in help, it may be too late to go back. Any arrangement should be made with the expectation that it will be examined and reviewed as a step toward more permanent solutions. Today many frail elderly are able to remain at home with assistance from home care services. (See Table 8:2, Role of the Home Care Worker.)

Everyone likes to feel in control of his or her life, and this does not change with age. Most elderly people prefer to remain in their own home with assistance from their children when needed. Sometimes the adult children, out of a sense of guilt, genuine concern or a vague feeling that they should do "what is right," intervene too drastically in the elderly parents' life, in effect making them more dependent than they really are. If the parents are making an effort to stay active and are enjoying their lifestyle, then children should not force them to make a change simply to relieve their own guilt or anxiety. The older person's needs and wishes must be taken into consideration. If adult children are worried about their elderly mother living in an urban area, perhaps they can offer to arrange to have a visiting service check in on her periodically, rather than trying to persuade her to leave her independent life to live, dependently, with them.

In many cases, what is needed is psychological and moral support. The knowledge that help is there if wanted and needed can relieve an older person's anxiety. And if it becomes necessary for the parent to move into the home, support services are available that can help reduce stress on everyone. (See Table 8:3, Resources for Care-Givers.) Day-care centers, visiting nurses, geriatric aides and respite programs can be of invaluable assistance, depending on the care needs of the elderly parent. Senior centers that can offer the elderly person some means of social contact outside the family are also helpful to both parties. Surveys show that older people who have relationships with peers are more satisfied than those whose lives are completely tied up with their own family. And the social activities that the elderly parent participates in will give the adult children the time and opportunity to pursue *their* own interests.

It is important to discuss the issue of what to do about aging parents openly with all interested parties present. If an elderly parent can no longer live alone, what is the best solution? A nursing home or senior citizen community? Living with one child or alternating between the children's homes? None of these options can be chosen unless everyone who will be affected is invited into the decision-making process and all of the issues—financial, psychological,

Role of the Home Care Worker

Although duties of home care workers (variously known as homemakers, home health aides and other titles) vary with training, amount of time spent in the home and the particular state agency certification requirements, the basic job description usually includes:

- Grocery shopping and meal preparation
- Personal care, including bed baths or assisting with tub baths, shampooing, brushing and combing hair, shaving (men) with an electric razor, brushing teeth, cleaning and cutting fingernails and toenails (except for diabetics)
- Changing bed linens and making bed, even for an individual who is bed-bound
- Helping person transfer from bed to chair, walker or wheelchair
- Helping person take medications, for example, opening a pill bottle. Does not include actually giving the medication, unless properly trained and licensed

Source: Adapted from *In-home Personal Care and Homemaker Chore Service Standards*, published by the Missouri Department of Social Services, Division of Aging, Jefferson City, Missouri.

Table 8:2

practical—are discussed honestly. Once the situation is realistically appraised, it should be possible to work out a solution that will be acceptable to everyone involved.

Too often, middle-aged children of aging parents assume that it is somehow up to them to take over. Sometimes this may be required, but very often they take an initiative when it really should be the parent(s) who do the help-seeking. It is important for people of all ages to recognize that there are numerous sources of help: A clergyman, physician or social worker at a local governmental agency for the aged may be better qualified to assess the situation and refer the parent to the appropriate resources. Simply being old does not mean that a person cannot make decisions or seek help.

Frequently an older person may not want to assume this responsibility and may prefer to let things slide. In such instances, a child may suggest that the parent consult a physician or other adviser, but if at all possible, the older person should be encouraged to seek help when needed and look after his or her own needs. Support from peer groups and networks, both formal and informal, is very important in establishing independence and retaining control. Sometimes this may mean taking an initiative or breaking out of old habits. For example, if you have always driven yourself to the shopping center but can no longer drive, try to make arrangements for yourself, even if it means taking a taxi or public transportation, instead of waiting for a family member to drive you. When you give up trying to solve your own problems, you may have no choice than to do what you are told instead of acting on your own. Making such concessions may not be easy, but they are better than the alternative of losing independence.

The importance of such planning cannot be overemphasized. Before the need ever arises, parents and children should discuss personal preferences about the later years. Plans may have to be changed, but at least the lines of communication will be open. Talking about such matters as where you want to live (and with whom), financial planning

Resources for Care-Givers

Book:
MacLean, Helene. *Caring for Your Parents: A Source of Options and Solutions for Both Generations.* New York: Doubleday, 1987.

Organizations:
Concern for Dying
250 West 57th Street
New York, NY 10107
212-246-6962

Information about Living Wills and state legislation covering their use.

Children of Aging Parents
2761 Trenton Road
Levittown, PA 19056
215-946-4012

The National Support Center
for Children of the Aging
Box 245
Swarthmore, PA 19081
215-544-3605

Help establish local self-help groups, maintain a referral service, etc.

The National Association for Home Care
519 C Street NE
Stanton Park
Washington, DC 20002

The National Home-Caring Council
235 Park Avenue South
New York, NY 10003

The National Self-Help Clearing House
City University of New York Graduate Center
33 West 42nd Street, Room 1222
New York, NY 10036

Information and resources for home care.

Table 8:3

and the mutual exploration of options well before changes have to be made is the best prevention against having to accept unsatisfying arrangements when the time comes.

❑ Grandparenthood

Grandparents, who have always enjoyed a unique position in society, are finding that their role today is much different from what they may have expected. The increased tendency for couples to divorce and remarry has blurred the generational lines. Many men in their fifties and sixties are establishing new families, and find that they have children and grandchildren of the same ages.

Today's fifty-year-old is likely to be physically younger than in the past, so our traditional image of the grandparent as a wise elder is changing. Indeed, some people who are trying to hang on to their youth may react with mixed feelings to their entry into the grandparent role. Even though they may have been anticipating grandchildren for some time, when it becomes a reality they may feel that they are really "too young to be grandparents." Even while delighting in the child, they may feel that they are being pushed into a role that they are not ready to accept. With more and more people becoming grandparents in their forties and fifties, of course, this perspective on "premature" grandparenthood is bound to change.

Although many grandparents see grandchildren as a source of renewal of interest in life, or a symbol of its pleasing continuity, giving them a connection with the present as well as the future, few seem to regard grandparenthood as somehow a renewal of parenting. Indeed, as a rule, grandparents see the grandchildren as a source of pleasure without the constraints and demands of responsibility. The older grandparents who have already retired have the time to do things with the grandchildren that they may not have had the time or money to do with their own children. Even younger grandparents usually have more money than they did when raising their own children, and they often enjoy being able to indulge their grandchildren with luxuries that they may not have been able to give their own daughters or sons. Becoming a grandparent also gives people the opportunity to succeed in a new role. Any regrets or failures they felt about parenting need not carry over into this new stage.

▪ *Defining the Relationship*

Unlike the parenting role, grandparenthood is vaguely defined. The shape the relationship between grandparents and grandchild will take may depend on the grandparents' current lifestyle, their view of their role within the whole family system, the children's living situation—whether, for instance, the adult children need financial assistance or some other kind of support—and the grandparents' relationship with the adult children. The attitude of the adult children toward their parents can determine the amount of contact or the nature of contact that grandparents have with their grandchildren. A parent-child relationship characterized by persistent conflicts, for example, may produce clashes over issues that concern the grandchildren, which may have an effect on how frequently grandparents see their grandchildren.

Despite the deep affection that most grandparents express for their grandchildren, they do not necessarily want to see them more frequently, or perhaps more pertinent, to be pressed into a frequent baby-sitting role. Maintaining ties with peers and remaining active in various undertakings are essential to achieving a satisfying life. The grandchildren may be an important part of that life, but they should not become the only focus. Grandparents who have to help care for grandchildren because of a a divorce or financial problems inevitably must sacrifice some of their independence and personal life in this "surrogate parenting" role. Although most grandparents will offer help when it is needed, just as adult children offer help to parents when the occasion arises, doing so may be a considerable sacrifice for them. Some grandparents who live close to their children have found it helpful to put certain limitations on "nonemergency" help—such as offering to baby-sit once a week, but no more often—in order to preserve their own lifestyles. This should not be considered an unloving attitude on their part, but a way of maintaining the autonomy of both family units.

A long-distance relationship does not seem to affect the closeness of ties between most grandchildren and their grandparents. Although those who live in the same town may see the grandchildren more often, those who live at a distance usually maintain contact by phone calls and letters and tend to have extended visits when they do come to town.

Problems may arise when there is a disruption of the adult children's family. Typically, the husband's parents are the ones who lose touch with the children if there is a divorce. The wife's parents may have a closer bond because they are the ones who will more likely be turned to for help. With the steady increase in divorce and remarriage, many grandparents find themselves with step-grandchildren. Their reaction to the divorce, their feelings about the first spouse and about the new spouse, and their relationship with the adult child can all affect the quality of their relationship with the new grandchildren.

▪ *The Family Connection*

The older generation in a family, particularly the older woman, is often responsible for keeping family ties intact, maintaining acquaintances, arranging for the family to get together, keeping track of birthdays, etc. The grandparents serve to preserve the integrity of the whole family system. With the arrival of grandchildren, there may be more frequent contact between the parents and adult children than before, as well as renewed contact with other members of the family. The grandparents assume the task of keeping everyone up to date and therefore sustain familial ties.

Grandparents may also serve a more immediate need as family "stabilizers" or arbitrators. Not uncommonly, a youngster may turn to a grandparent to serve as a confidant or to settle a conflict between the parents and children. Grandparents should take care not to undermine a parent's authority by siding with the grandchild, but often just listening to the child and then suggesting that the youngster present his or her case to the parents will clear the air.

Although the role of grandparents may be changing, there is little doubt that it remains a satisfying one most of us hope we will eventually come to share. Still, we should avoid idealizing the role and having excessive expectations. While we may not always agree with the way a grandchild is being reared, it is important to recognize that this is the responsibility of the parents, not the grandparents. Advice may be offered when sought, but it is important to resist the temptation to interfere in the parental role.

❑ Divorce or Death of a Spouse

Certainly the most significant change that may come in middle or old age is the loss of a spouse through death or divorce. Suddenly, we are confronted with the restructuring of life at a time when we are already occupied with trying to cope with the normal stresses of aging. The personal loss of the spouse through death or divorce, difficult enough in itself, may also trigger dramatic changes in other areas of one's life: the family support network, finances, friendships and sometimes even one's geographical location.

▪ *Effect on Relationships*

It is well known that divorce or the death of a spouse has different effects on the lives of men and women. Women tend to have a stronger network of peer and family relationships than men. Adult children may rally around the wife, if only because she is usually the one who needs some sort of financial or practical assistance in the early stages. Thus, a woman's ties with certain family members may be strengthened after divorce or her husband's death.

Sometimes, however, widows or divorcées are afraid of becoming a burden on adult children and thus may hesitate to ask for help. When adult children feel that the mother needs financial or other help but find it difficult to provide that help, guilt or resentment may build up. And those adult children who may have been expecting financial aid from their parents often find that the newly widowed or divorced woman is no longer able to help out.

For a man, the loss of a spouse through death or divorce invariably weakens his social network—a sharp contrast to the strengthened network experienced by women. His relationship with the children and with his in-laws may be affected, and since it is typically the woman who has made the effort to maintain family contacts, he may even see members of his own family less frequently. We might expect these adverse reactions following divorce, but they seem to hold true for widowers as well. Studies show that widowers tend to become socially isolated from relatives, whereas widows typically receive support and assistance from family members. It is also common for the parents of the husband to lose contact with the grandchildren. Many states now have specific statutes that give grandparents visitation rights; if matters deteriorate to this point, grandparents should be aware that they do have a right to see their grandchildren.

Friendships, especially with other married couples, may be altered by divorce for both men and women. Married couples often find it difficult to sustain a relationship with both parties after the divorce and they are not always willing to include the divorced individuals, with their new status as singles, in their social activities. A similar situation often exists for a widow or widower, who suddenly finds she or he is no longer invited to "couples" events.

▪ *Remarriage*

Studies show that men are much more likely to remarry following a divorce than women. The stereotype of the middle-aged or older man who divorces his wife of many years to marry a younger women is all too true. Although attitudes are changing somewhat, an older woman is not nearly as likely to establish a relationship with a younger man. Since middle-aged and older women outnumber men of the same ages, the prospects of an older woman remarrying are significantly less than those for a man. For example, after the age of 65, remarriage rates are eight times as high for men as for women. Widows have a somewhat greater likelihood of remarrying than divorcées, but even so, most do not. By age 75, 70 percent of women are widows, while 69 percent of men who reach that age have spouses, according to 1980 U.S. Bureau of the Census statistics.

▪ *Economics*

Women frequently experience a dramatic drop in income after divorce or death of a spouse—an unfortunate circumstance that is not as common among men. Sometimes loss of economic support can further exacerbate the social isolation and loss of self-esteem. Divorced women are often less well off financially than widows and the fact that the majority of working women 50 or over are in poorly paying positions makes their financial futures uncertain. But fortunately a growing number of resources are responding to this situation by helping older divorced or widowed women achieve financial independence (see Table 8:4, Resources).

▪ *Establishing New Friends and Networks*

Many widowed or divorced women are reluctant to move out of their own little niches to establish new networks and relationships. Some men also may hesitate to start anew, but most have the advantage of having established a life and identity outside the home and family. An older woman who has been married for the last twenty or thirty years may be particularly hesitant about dating, especially under the "new" rules and mores, yet there may be little opportunity to meet potential partners in her present network of friends and family members.

Even if a woman has no intention of seeking a new mate or partner, it is a good idea to investigate new activities and interests that will introduce her to a new set of acquaintances. The old group of friends may find it difficult to adjust to her new identity as a single person but the new group will know only that identity, which may ease somewhat her transition into this new status. Men often can fall back on work colleagues; if

Resources

For the Older Woman:
Displaced Homemakers Network
1010 Vermont Avenue NW, Suite 817
Washington, DC 20005

Offers retraining programs and services to help older women reenter job market.

Older Women's League
1325 G Street NW, Lower Level B
Washington, DC 20005

Provides variety of information and services.

For Both Men and Women:
ACTION
806 Connecticut Avenue NW
Washington, DC 20525

Independent government agency that provides centralized coordination and administration of volunteer and other programs for older people.

American Association of Retired Persons
1909 K Street NW
Washington, DC 20049

Provides information, insurance and services for older people.

Legal Services for the Elderly
132 West 43rd Street
New York, NY 10036
212-595-1340

National Council of Senior Citizens
1511 K Street NW
Washington, DC 20005

Local offices or chapters of :
YWCA and YMCAs
Department of Aging
Small Business Administration
Social Security Administration

Table 8:4

not, they often face adjustments and problems similar to those of women.

When considering becoming involved with someone or remarrying, one of the most important things to keep in mind is that the new person should not be seen as a replacement for the old spouse but accepted as a unique person in his or her own right. Trying to "re-create" the former marriage is one of the surest ways to failure of the new one. Finding entirely new interests or moving to a new home are possible ways to avoid this trap. The expectations from the first marriage must not be carried over into the second. It is equally important not to be unduly influenced by other people's opinions, pro or con, about dating or marriage, whether they come from adult children or friends. Only the individual knows whether he or she wants to enter into a relationship and whether a relationship is right.

▪ *Extended Networks*

Although close family ties are important, they are not enough for an interesting and satisfying lifestyle. Friendships with people of one's own generation, with those who share similar interests and with those who are available to participate in social activities are essential to a full life. Older people who have ongoing friendships and who are able to establish new ones are more satisfied with their life than those whose contact with people is limited to family members. These friendships are particularly important during times of transition, such as retirement. Retirees, however, sometimes find it difficult to find friends to replace co-workers and other friends from the workplace. Since the older person may not have any other built-in social network, it becomes particularly important for him or her to develop other such networks now. Museums, libraries, senior-citizen centers, volunteer corps, adult education classes, foster grandparent organizations, churches or synagogues are only a few of the places where people can find others with like interests. Making an effort to join in new activities, to attend events at the community center and to renew old friendships that may have faded during the working years are all useful "networking" strategies.

❑ Coming to Terms With Change

All of life is marked by change; those that occur during old age are merely a continuation or extension of what has gone before. How we lived our youth will to a large degree determine how well we will cope with age. "I will never be an old man," the financier and statesman Bernard Baruch once said. "To me, old age is always fifteen years older than I am." Franz Kafka offered a wonderfully simple secret to lasting youth when he wrote: "Youth is happy because it has the ability to see beauty. Anyone who keeps the ability to see beauty never grows old."

In his book *A Good Age* (New York: Fireside Books, 1976), the noted gerontologist Dr. Alex Comfort stresses that "most of the handicaps of oldness in our society are social, conventional and imaginary. The physical changes [of age] are trifling by comparison. Old age as we see it exists only in societies which create it by the way they classify people."

History abounds with notable examples of older people who conquered new heights despite infirmities. At the age of 68, Thomas Jefferson, although physically ailing, resumed the study of mathematics. "I have forgotten much," he wrote, "and recover it with more difficulty than when in the vigor of my mind

I originally acquired it. It is wonderful to me that old men should not be sensible that their minds keep pace with their bodies in the progress of decay." Giuseppe Verdi composed his two greatest operas, *Otello* and *Falstaff,* while in his seventies; Claude Monet was 73 when he started his series of nineteen water lily paintings. Perhaps Ralph Waldo Emerson said it all when he wrote: "We do not count a man's years until he has nothing else to count."

9

LIFELONG LEARNING—THE KEY TO MENTAL FITNESS

The mind's capacity for learning knows no age restrictions. No matter what our age, our minds crave new challenges, interesting stimuli and variety to keep us curious, alert and capable people—to ourselves as well as to others. The marvelous thing about being human, Ashley Montagu writes in his book *Growing Young* (New York: McGraw-Hill, 1981), is that we are designed *throughout* our life to continue to explore, discover and change.

Studies have shown that learning is not only a potent mental stimulant, but helps promote a healthy body. The more mentally active a person is, in fact, the less likely he or she is to deteriorate physically. Researchers are trying to find out why this is true; the most popular theory is that the brain is more closely linked to the body's immune system than previously thought, and may play a role in other organ systems. Unfortunately, formal education has been traditionally viewed as a "chunk" of experience appropriate to the first three decades of life and not as a lifelong process. As a rule, "education" is thought to end when real "adult" life—work—begins. Although the setting and functions of education may vary at different times in life, stimulation, growth and learning are as necessary—and accessible—to the mind of a seventy-five-year-old as they are to a fifteen-year-old.

While the time it takes to react and solve problems appears to increase with age, it affects those who actively pursue new interests and continue to learn and exercise their minds to a lesser degree. Aging in itself does not affect learning ability, but learning does seem to have a positive effect on the quality of the aging process. Continuous learning opportunities and serial jobs, allowing every person the chance to explore multiple interests and learn new skills, would do much to avoid the gradual decline associated with boredom and inactivity in older persons.

❏ The Good News

A person's ability to learn, his or her creative drive, imagination and conceptual powers do not decline over the years. Studies have shown, contrary to much of accepted opinion, that intellectual performance in a healthy person continues undiminished until at least the seventies. In his book *A Good Age* (New York: Crown, 1976), Dr. Alex Comfort (whose real medical specialty is gerontology) notes that if the mind has not atrophied through disuse there is no reason to suspect that learning ability will decline until well into the ninth decade. The overwhelming majority of older people suffer no loss of mental function. When there is a decline, it is not the result of aging, but almost always is due to a physical cause, such as stroke. Ill health is much more likely than age to cause mental deficiencies.

In a long-term study involving members of a Seattle health maintenance organization there was virtually no decline shown in cognitive test performance up to age 60, with fewer than half of those tested at age 80 showing any measurable decline. Since most intelligence tests are designed for the young, their efficacy in testing older people may be limited. It is possible that aging brings benefits to intellectual performance in some areas, such as experience-based decision-making, interpersonal competence, and the ability to evaluate alternatives and set priorities.

The only tests in which older people may show a somewhat slower reaction are those that involve a time element. Because reaction time may increase with age, it may take an older person a little longer to solve a problem, but there is no decline in the ability to do the work.

Societal prejudices that assume older people are less competent, interesting or capable than younger ones are completely unfounded. Often this attitude is self-perpetuating; when adopted at an early age many people actually believe themselves capable of less as they age and will close off many of their options, initiating what Ashley Montagu calls "psychosclerosis," or hardening of the mind. Just as a limb can atrophy through disuse, so can the mind lose its ability to function for lack of exercise. The best way to ensure an alert, functioning mind at age 70 is to continue, throughout the years, to learn and entertain new ideas.

❏ Memory

To associate poor memory with aging is specious. There are many young people with poor memories and older people with very reliable ones. A 30-year-old man who forgets his raincoat in the office will simply pick it up the next day without wasting any time thinking about his "forgetfulness." If a 60-year-old man did the same thing, however, he and his associates would more readily attribute the lapse to "age." Research has shown that although some functions that affect memory may slow down with age, memory, for the most part, is not affected. Older people may have need for more frequent use of certain "memory strategies"—such as writing notes to prompt their memory—but there is no reason to believe that their recall capability cannot be as efficient as that of a young person. "Prospective memory"—remembering to do something at the right time—actually seems to improve with age. Other memory functions, such as short-term memory and world knowledge (specific information not tied to a time or event), remain stable over time.

Certain physical conditions can masquerade as memory loss: An undetected hearing or vision deficit, for instance, may cause a person to "forget" names or faces because he did not hear or see them correctly. Once the problem is corrected, such "memory problems" should disappear.

The accuracy of memory is linked to several factors: interest, motivation, education, health and the circumstances of the event. Because people with a lot of education have had to use their memory skills extensively, they seem to have better memories. Motivation is an especially important factor: If information has no particular relevance or use, it probably will not be remembered. A sports enthusiast, for example, will easily remember the week's baseball scores, while someone with no interest in the game, even if he or she has listened to the same broadcast, will not.

▪ *Making the Effort*

Memory depends, to a large degree, on whether or not a person tries to remember and employs effective strategies. Robin West, in her book *Memory Fitness Over 40* (Gainesville, Fla.: Triad, 1985), points out that the few effects age does have on memory can easily be overcome with consistent use of memory strategies. According to West, more cues may be needed for recall because the ability to concentrate and ignore distractions becomes more difficult with age, making it harder to remember things. West advises people to evaluate their memory to see what strategies they use most effectively and then to refine and expand upon them. People with good visual memories could use mental pictures as a memory aid. For example, many parking lots use a visual aid to help patrons remember what section they parked in—e.g., "My car is to the left of the cat sign." For those more verbally oriented, West suggests word and letter associations.

An organized routine and structured environment can be invaluable aids to memory. It is easier to remember an object when it is in a place that corresponds to its use. If, for instance, it becomes routine for you to check your desk (where your appointment calendar is) before lunch, you will be less likely to forget afternoon appointments or errands. Always laying reading glasses on the table next to the bookshelf will help to eliminate frustrating searches. One technique that seems to come naturally to many people is to leave what is important in the most visible place; for instance, leave a report that has to be taken to a meeting on top of the desk instead of in the file.

Researchers have found that older people have more difficulty not "finding" something already in its proper place than do younger people. Since, according to Yvette Tenney, a psychologist at Boston Veterans Administration Hospital, this is really a perceptual and not a memory problem, all that may be required is to slow down and look in the same place more carefully again.

Like all things worth doing, memory improvement takes effort. Once the proven techniques are learned, you should practice them as you would any other skill with the assurance that memory can be improved at any age and that the minor memory deficiencies that may result from age can be circumvented.

❑ Special Interests/Characteristics of the Older Learner

With his or her variety and depth of life experiences, the older person will bring fresh and valuable perspectives to any learning environment. In turn, the educational process will enrich the learner. New interests will grow out of old ones and be sparked by the interests of others.

Older people in record numbers are now realizing the rewards of, and their potential for, learning. The proportion of older Americans participating in educational programs is greater than ever and expected to increase. In addition, even as the number of people reaching retirement age in good health is increasing, the number of traditional-aged students seeking degrees is decreasing. With this shift in demographics, educational institutions and alternative educational programs are already adjusting some of their programs to respond to the needs and interests of the older learner.

The ability to learn is not what separates the older learner from the younger; it is rather the distinct difference in interests between the two. The older learner is usually motivated by personal interest in a specific subject. As their numbers grow, older students will find they exert more influence on the kinds and types of courses and programs most suited to their interests—whether they are learning woodworking or a new job skill, the study of philosophy, the stock market or a foreign language. Many institutions have already realized the potential of these new students and have designed programs for them (see below). Although they take varied forms, the programs share a common and very important element—input from participants. In some, the courses are taught by participants; in others they may be taught by regular college faculty who are chosen by participants. (See Table 9:1 for a list of resources.)

▪ *Social Aspects*

An added advantage of enrolling in a program under the auspices of an educational institution is the availability of extracurricular benefits—cafeterias, libraries, film programs, theater and sports centers. For some, these resources are incentive enough to participate. For others, just being on campus offers opportunities to converse with and meet others. For the retired, taking a class or going back to school might replace the social contacts and feeling of usefulness provided by the workplace. Being actively involved in a learning situation will help older people contradict false assumptions some younger people may have about the learning abilities and capabilities of the older generation. (See Table 9:2, Where to Go for Classes.)

Resources for Adult Learning

The National Home Study Council
1601 18th Street NW
Washington, DC 20009
202-234-5100

National University Extension Association
One Dupont Circle NW
Washington, DC 20036

Both of the above are sources of information on correspondence courses.

Gray Panthers
3700 Chestnut Street
Philadelphia, PA 19104

Institute of Lifetime Learning
American Association of Retired Persons
1909 K Street NW
Washington, DC 20049
202-872-4700

Association for Adult Education
1201 16th Street NW, Suite 230
Washington, DC 20036
202-822-7866

Elderhostel
80 Boylston Street
Suite 400
Boston, MA 02116

The Extension Service
National Gallery of Art
Washington, DC 20565

Division of Adult Education Programs of the U.S. Office of Education
Washington, DC 20202

National Alliance of Senior Citizens
2525 Wilson Boulevard
Arlington, VA 22201
703-528-4380

(continued)

Resources for Adult Learning *(continued)*

American Museum Association
2233 Wisconsin Avenue NW
Washington, DC 20037

Adult Education Action Council
4201 Cathedral Avenue NW
Suite 1205 East
Washington, DC 20016

American Association of Community and Junior Colleges
One Dupont Circle NW
Suite 410
Washington, DC 20036

National Retired Teachers Association
1909 K Street NW
Washington, DC 20005
202-872-4800

Administration on Aging
U.S. Department of Health and Human Services
330 Independence Avenue SW
Washington, DC 20201

National Senior Citizens Education & Research Center, Inc.
1511 K Street NW
Washington, DC 20005

National Association for Human Development
1620 I Street, Room 517
Washington, DC 20006

National Association of Mature People
2212 NW 50 Street
P.O. Box 26792
Oklahoma City, OK 73126

National Council on the Aging, Inc.
600 Maryland Avenue SW
West Wing 100
Washington, DC 20024

College Examination Board
P.O. Box 1824
Princeton, NJ 08544

Council of National Organizations for Adult Education
174 Broadway, 17th floor
New York, NY 10019

American Association of University Women
2401 Virginia Avenue NW
Washington, DC 20037

Books:

Bolles, Richard N.
The Three Boxes of Life
Berkeley, Calif.: Ten Speed Press, 1981.

Cross, Wilbur
The Weekend Education Source Book
New York: Harper & Row, 1976.

Freede, S. Robert
Cash for College
Englewood Cliffs, N.J.: Prentice-Hall, 1975.

Gross, Ronald
The Lifelong Learner
New York: Simon & Schuster, 1977.

Guide to Credit by Examination.
Office on Educational Credit & Credentials
Washington, D.C.: American Council on Education, 1981.

Jones, John
The Correspondence Educational Directory and Alternative Educational Opportunities
Oxnard, Calif.: Racz, 1984.

Paying for Your Education: A Guide for Adult Learners
Princeton, N.J.: College Board, 1983.

Thompson, Frances Coombs
The New York Times Guide to Continuing Education
New York: Quadrangle, 1972.

Table 9:1

▪ *Educational Opportunities for Different Needs*

One of the biggest problems an older person faces in signing up for classes is simply picking a manageable number from the wide range of what is available. As a first step, it may be advisable to sort out your objectives.

Learn new job skills. The right class can help you keep abreast of technological changes in your field or investigate a new endeavor, such as getting a real estate license or advising on investments. Retirement may liberate you from working for financial considerations, so that your definition of what work can be may broaden to include volunteer or community service. Many jobs, such as working with young children or in a hospital, or learning to read Braille books, require new skills which may, in turn, stimulate further interest in more intensive or specialized learning.

Explore a lifelong interest. As an adult learner, you are not necessarily constrained by what will be "useful" in terms of getting a job or what will look good on a résumé. You have the freedom to devote time and energy to whatever is of genuine interest—or to indulge a fleeting fancy. Colleges and universities now offer evening and weekend classes, certificate programs, noncredit courses and auditing options from which the adult student can choose the most appealing format.

Keep up with current affairs. Senior citizen centers, Ys and community organizations often offer discussion groups on books, theater, world affairs, new technology and other topics of current interest.

Self-help classes. These include courses on aspects of financial management, preventive health, nutrition, coping with stress, exercise, and more.

Combined interest programs. These allow you to match your skills with other interests. If you like to travel, for example, you may want to study photography or languages during a special-interest tour. Nutrition and gardening mate well with cooking; all can be enhanced by a class taken in any one of the subjects.

❑ DEGREE-ORIENTED LEARNING

It would be a mistake to assume that all adult education programs are necessarily divorced from degree or career-oriented programs. Because the retirement years offer an opportunity to do what finances, work or family responsibilities may have precluded in the past, someone interested in earning a high school or college degree or pursuing an advanced degree has many options from which to choose. There are many programs that make working on a degree feasible and convenient in the pre-retirement years.

Where to Go for Classes

- High schools and colleges
- Community centers, Ys
- Museums
- Libraries
- Churches, synagogues
- Senior centers
- Labor and professional organizations
- Correspondence courses
- Learning exchanges

(The local librarian also can direct you to other local learning centers.)

Table 9:2

Many colleges now offer discounts on tuition to senior citizens, both to those enrolled in a regular program and those interested only in specific courses. The Age Discrimination Act of 1975, which made discrimination based on age in any programs receiving federal funds illegal, applies to college and university admissions and financial assistance. The state attorney general's office can direct people who suspect discrimination as to their best course of action.

Life experience credit, now available at most schools, is especially attractive to the mature student working toward a degree because it recognizes the importance of experience and allows him or her to turn it into course credit. Each school evaluates skills/requirements that were fulfilled in the workplace or at home and assigns an appropriate credit for them. While it sounds easy, there is a catch: You must have documentation of the experience, which might be difficult to obtain for something done twenty-five years ago. Nevertheless, careful analysis of life experience and perseverance should yield at least moderate credits prior to registration.

The College Level Examination Program (CLEP), a national program sponsored by the College Examination Board, as its name implies, gives credit by examination. The prospective student submits the CLEP scores to the college admissions office, which will decide whether or not to accept the credit.

University Without Walls is an individually tailored program worked out by the student and the school as an alternative to the traditional degree program. For information, contact your local college.

As schools begin to recognize the needs of the older student, and as the older population begins to lobby for programs to meet those needs, more opportunities will become available. To date, community colleges have been particularly receptive to the needs of the older student, but some private schools have also been in the lead.

▪ *College at 60*

Although many adults hesitate to return to campus because they fear they will not be able to compete with younger students or that they have forgotten necessary study skills, experience has shown no basis for these fears. Older students have no trouble with the subject matter and are often more responsible, reliable and schedule-conscious than their younger colleagues.

Fordham University in New York City attempts to ease this anxiety by offering College at 60 (for those 50 and over), a program that introduces those who have never attended college to college-level courses and offers returning students a chance to reacclimate themselves in an academic environment of their peers. After four courses in the program, the student may enter Fordham's Liberal Arts College. Those on social security are eligible for a 50 percent reduction in tuition. Similar programs are being offered throughout the country. Information can be obtained by contacting admissions offices at the individual institutions.

▪ *The Learner's Advisory Service*

Many public libraries offer a learner's advisory service that provides information on available college programs, requirements, admissions policies and tuition grants, as well as alternative educational resources. Where it exists, this service can be one of the most comprehensive sources of information on education resources available and is invaluable not only to the adult returning to school, but to anyone seeking information on a special interest or an alternative learning program. If your local public library does not offer this service, information can be obtained from the Adult Services Division of the American Library Association at 50 Huron Street, Chicago, IL 60611.

▪ *Matching the Older Student with the Opportunity*

Those who find the plethora of alternatives in educational opportunities overwhelming may want to avail themselves of the services of a number of testing organizations.

Those who prefer a "high-tech" approach may want to try SIGI Plus, a computer-assisted guidance system developed for the Educational Testing Service in Princeton, New Jersey. The user puts in information about his or her skills and objectives and the computer generates a list of possible occupational or educational opportunities with information on the skills needed and advice on how to acquire those skills. (Laurence Shatkin, who helped design the program, is now working on a similar system for retirement planning.) The program is offered free through 480 colleges and universities. To find an affiliated school, call SIGI at 609-921-9000.

Although many adults in their middle or older years may feel that they already know what they want or are able to do, many are often surprised, not only at what emerges from an evaluation of aptitudes and interests, but at possibilities that never before occurred to them. Some people are unaware of skills that they possess or do not know which skills will transfer easily from one field to another. Many factors should be taken into consideration when choosing a new activity or finding the best way to fulfill an interest. For instance, what is the person's learning style? Does he or she learn best in a lecture environment? In a hands-on situation? In a peer discussion group? Is the person a visual or verbal learner? What skills are strongest—interpersonal? artistic? investigative? A person's experience, background, personal likes and dislikes, degree of commitment and motivation, along with a number of other things, all enter into the equation. When all these things are taken into consideration, they may lead to some unexpected and appealing opportunities.

❑ Life Review/Personal History

Reviewing one's life can give coherence and meaning to the past, help a person face the present and plan for the future. Colleges, community centers and senior centers recognize the importance and popularity of these projects and now offer courses and workshops in journal writing, oral history or autobiography. Sharing life events with others may give someone the necessary momentum for what is normally a solitary endeavor. Writing or recording a personal history ensures that cherished memories are passed on to children and grandchildren, providing a sense of continuity. The recorder will also benefit, if past events have been recorded honestly, by being able to view past relationships more clearly, with the hope that the examination will improve or strengthen present ones. At a time of transition, life review can give a person clues to his or her behavior. It can also be an excellent pre-retirement tool and, in the last years of life, can provide a sense of fulfillment and closure.

In his book *Preparing a Personal History* (Salt Lake City: Primer Publications, 1976), William G. Hartley suggests creating a family tree and writing a personal time line of major events. Sorting through old family records, talking to others, revisiting places from the past, and reading diaries and letters that have been saved through the year all provide a basis for this personal history.

❑ Special Programs

In recognizing the special requirements of the older student—the desire for student-directed classes, a clear definition of interests and an emphasis on a specific area of interest—many schools offer special programs specifically designed for the mature student.

Based on a participatory education model, The Institute for Retired Professionals (IRP) at the New School for Social Research in New York City, founded in 1962, is the precursor for other programs. Study groups, seminars and workshops are student led. Members of the IRP, who come from diverse professional backgrounds, study a variety of subjects from foreign languages to computers, music, economics and tai chi. Members benefit from more than simply the learning opportunities; the IRP is also a vital center for social contacts: New friendships are formed, coffee breaks and lunch provide opportunities for conversation, and extracurricular activities are regular features of the program.

Started in 1977, the Institute for

Learning in Retirement, part of Harvard University's Center for Lifelong Learning, was modeled after the New School's IRP. Student-led groups on a variety of topics are chosen by the members of the institute. The only requirements for admission are that the individual be retired or semi-retired, pay the very low fee each term and have a desire to learn. Members of the ILR, like those at the New School, report that the social side of the experience—the new network of friends, opportunities and activities—is as valuable as the educational aspect. Similar programs are offered at Duke University, UCLA, American University and Brooklyn College, and undoubtedly many more schools. Check your own local community colleges.

▪ *Elderhostel*

Founded in 1975 as a summer residential college program, Elderhostel offers noncredit courses in the liberal arts and sciences to people over 60. The program has expanded to include year-round and foreign study opportunities and is now found on eight hundred campuses around the country. Participants consider as important pluses the built-in social and interactive aspects of the residential format. For information, write Elderhostel, 80 Boylston Street, Suite 400, Boston MA 02116.

▪ *Interhostel*

Interhostel is a program for older adults that offers travel-study opportunities, generally of two-week duration. Lecture and field trips are arranged with educational institutions in the host country. For information, write Interhostel, University of New Hampshire, Division of Continuing Education, Brook House, Rosemary Lane, Durham, NH 03824.

▪ *TV as an Educational Medium*

With television reaching 99 percent of the population, it is not surprising that it is often used as a vehicle for education. The PBS Adult Learning Service, a national college credit service, is a cooperative program involving 285 public television stations and more than 1000 colleges and universities. After enrolling in the electronic college campus through their local college, students watch the appropriate shows and study at home, then go to the college campus for exams and occasional visits with professors. A variety of subject areas are included in the course offerings. The local community college is the best source of information.

▪ *Learning Exchanges*

For those who want specific knowledge on a variety of subjects, from learning a foreign language to auto repair, or who would like to get together with others to share views on a topic of interest, learning exchanges are valuable resources. They match those with a particular interest with either an individual who is knowledgeable in that field or with those sharing the same interests. The telephone directory, community center, library or community newspaper can help locate a learning exchange in your area.

▪ *Self-Teaching*

There is nothing written in stone that says learning can be accomplished only in group situations. While not for everyone, self-teaching offers the self-motivated the luxury of learning as quickly—or leisurely—as desired. Without the constraints of a curriculum, one has the freedom to explore tangential interests in depth. But for self-teaching to be effective, an individual must learn to locate and use available resources; learning to use the library profitably can be a course in itself. While self-education eliminates the social contact and exchange of ideas that make learning in a class or group situation so appealing, for the disciplined student with the right temperament and interests it can be a rewarding undertaking and provide a sense of accomplishment. (See Table 9:3, Educational Motivations.)

❑ GOING BACK

Many older adults who would like to return to the classroom hesitate to do so, fearing they will not fit in or that they will be embarrassed by their ignorance of a particular subject or skill. A 67-year-old retired lawyer recalls his horror at walking into a creative writing course and seeing a word processor set up on every desk. "My idea of writing was with a pad and pencil, and here the instructor insisted that we learn to write on a computer. I didn't even know how to type!" Instead of following his first instinct, which was to head for the door, he signed up for a typing–word processing course in addition to creative writing and ended up with a solid B+. A year later he sold his first short story to a literary magazine.

The secret of successful lifelong learning is not being afraid of new experiences. Of course it can be intimidating to walk into a library and find out that computers have replaced the old card catalogues that most of us grew up with. But you are not alone—and mastering the new skills yields a wonderful sense of accomplishment and self worth. Learning may be difficult, but it can keep you young in heart and mind—and that's well worth the effort.

Educational Motivations

- Personal interest
- Practical knowledge
- Learning for its own sake
- Formal degree credit
- Social contact
- Health/well-being promotion
- Stimulation/change in routine
- Improved or new job opportunities

Table 9:3

10

PLANNING FOR RETIREMENT

Retirement is one of those major life milestones that all of us face with mixed feelings. For some of us, it means the freedom to travel, return to school, take up new hobbies or devote more time to old ones, and do so many other things that we have not had time for while holding down a job. Others of us anticipate retirement with dread, fearing that it will mark the end of our usefulness. For still others, retirement is a little of both.

❑ THE NEED FOR RETIREMENT PLANNING

Today more people than ever before are retiring from the workplace, and today's retirees, for the most part, have greater financial security than past generations, thanks to improved pensions and social security benefits. But one of the most important aspects of successful retirement is the one that is the most neglected—namely, careful pre-retirement planning. (See Table 10:1, Retirement Strategy.)

We often hear horror stories of people who have been forced into retirement and ended up in a semi-vegetative state from boredom or who died shortly thereafter, also presumably due to boredom. While this may indeed happen occasionally, surveys of retirees show that most of them are content to be retired and that many are happier than when they were working. Still, those who cope the best and report the most satisfaction are the ones who have kept busy with fulfilling activities, and who have maintained a good relationship with a spouse or a network of friends. Richard Bolles sums up the ideal very nicely in his book *The Three Boxes of Life* (Berkeley, Calif: Ten Speed Press, 1981): retirement should be part learning, part working and part playing, although the "work" does not have to be what it was before. Those people who think that the word "retire" is a signal to stop doing, moving or trying are those who quickly become dissatisfied with retirement, and are also those who are most likely to develop health or mobility problems soon afterward.

Retirement Strategy

- Start early
- Consult with your spouse before making a plan
- Talk to recent and longtime retirees
- Investigate options
- Develop a plan
- Look into practical ways to implement plan
- Focus on long-term goals, but incorporate flexibility and alternative plans
- Have a backup plan
- Investigate options

Table 10:1

People can do a number of things to make retirement more enjoyable and less stressful. The first step is to start planning early, in the fifties or even the forties. Many people make the mistake of thinking that retirement planning entails only financial planning. Although finances are, of course, an important part of retirement planning, they are only one component among many. Retirement can provide that longed-for opportunity to pursue in depth a genuine interest, but effort and planning are still necessary to get the most out of the experience. Lifestyle planning is as important as financial planning in this respect.

Health maintenance should not be overlooked as an important part of retirement planning. Problems neglected or untreated when we are young often become serious or disabling with age. Commonsense practices such as not smoking, keeping weight under control and regular exercise all are important preventive measures.

Of course, retirement planning must involve both husband and wife. If one spouse looks forward to moving to the country and tending a garden and the other has always assumed foreign travel will be the focus of the retirement years, both will be in for an unpleasant surprise when the time for retirement arrives. A couple should come up with individual plans, compare and discuss them, and make compromises and alterations until they arrive at a formula that satisfies the requirements of both as much as possible.

A retirement plan should always be flexible enough to accommodate any unexpected changes in the economic picture, health or personal preferences—the arrival of grandchildren, for example. There should also be a backup plan in case the original one turns out to be less than ideal. If after a couple of months in the country, both people are going stir-crazy and longing to return to the city, then they should be able to do so without great stress or hardship. If possible, "safety systems" should be in place. The couple might, for instance, sublet their city apartment or suburban home for six months while they experiment with living in the country.

Making an inventory of the best and worst of the present situation is a good way to identify preferences. Life review and aptitude tests (see Chapter 9, Lifelong Learning) are also helpful. People who know that retirement is ten to fifteen years away should begin developing new interests and activities. Short-term projects, such as fixing up the house, will soon run out, leaving the retiree with a lot of unscheduled time. Many people plan to continue their lives after retirement more or less as they are, living near family and friends. Others may plan drastic changes.

▪ *Starting a New Career*

For the person whose life has been enjoyably work-oriented, retirement to a life of leisure may be a deadly prospect. Such a person may be happier finding some type of employment or even a new career after retirement. The work may be part-time, self-employment or volunteer service. The opportunities and possibilities are virtually limitless. A few examples: Several Florida senior citizen health clinics are staffed by retired physicians who work on a volunteer basis. Many school districts welcome retired teachers as tutors, substitutes or volunteers to work with special education programs or extracurricular activities. Retired executives, professors or people with special knowledge or skills are often sought out as highly paid consultants.

There are organizations that help place retired people with specific skills in the right positions. For example, SCORE—Service Corps of Retired Executives—matches people who can volunteer their knowledge to small businesses in need of their skills. RSVP—Retired Senior Volunteer Program—is a special program that seeks volunteers for community service programs. For information on RSVP, write:

ACTION–RSVP
806 Connecticut Avenue NW
Washington, DC 20525

For SCORE, write:

Small Business Administration—SCORE
1030 15th Street NW
Suite 250
Washington, DC 20417

Retirement can also provide an opportunity to work for a public service group or cause. Hospitals, charities, the Foster Grandparent Program (also run by ACTION) and political organizations are just a few of the possibilities.

Even for people who have a good idea of what they want to do, a pre-retirement course or workshop can be helpful. There are so many variables involved, from finances to what to do with leisure time, that it would be difficult to cover all the bases on one's own. Many companies are now offering some kind of in-house planning service. Retirement counseling may also be available at the local community college, community centers such as Ys or senior centers.

The National Council on Aging (NCOA) offers a multimedia package on retirement planning that may be purchased by any interested group—a person's company, for instance, or colleges or community centers. The council will train a staff member to present the program or will provide someone to conduct the session. The program is broken down into six parts: lifestyle planning, financial planning (including getting records together, fighting inflation, and savings and investment), healthful living, interpersonal relations, living arrangements, and leisure and work options. Workbooks are provided for spouses, to encourage people to participate as couples. The program material is appropriate for a wide range of ages, interests and occupations. Council officials recommend that people begin planning for retirement in their forties or early fifties.

The American Association of Retired Persons (AARP) also offers retirement counseling programs. The AARP will train a company representative to provide work-site retirement counseling or will send trained volunteers into a community at the request of individuals who do not have access to company-sponsored programs. These counseling sessions may be held at any available community site, such as the local library, church or synagogue.

The AARP advocates an overall "wellness" approach to retirement planning. Ideally, retirement planning should be an ongoing process incorporated into the lifestyle at an early stage, beginning, for example, right after graduation from college. Concrete planning should begin at around age 50 when a person is "within striking range of retirement." According to AARP, a good retirement plan should balance three essential elements—financial health, physical health and emotional health—with emotional health receiving the greatest emphasis.

A workbook on retirement planning is available from the local AARP office for $25. The workbook contains exercises to help the individual assess his or her status in the three important areas and his or her needs and goals for the future.

▪ *Financial Planning*

Some experts estimate the cost of maintaining the desired retirement lifestyle at somewhere between 60 to 70 percent of pre-tax income, adjusted for inflation. When people begin to assess their financial preparation for retirement, they should become familiar with all potential resources and probable expenses: pensions, IRAs, social security, life insurance, health insurance and cost of living. Changes in the tax laws are bringing about some changes in the way people plan retirement income and are placing more responsibility on the individual since 401k plans and IRAs will be less attractive.

A session with a tax accountant or financial planner can help a person assess future needs and begin making the necessary financial arrangements well in advance of retirement. Many colleges, companies, community centers, banks, brokerage houses and other organizations offer retirement counseling programs, money management workshops or computerized financial planning.

Many people who have a substantial amount of money turn to financial planners or money managers. Before taking this route, however, it is important to do prior checking and choose cautiously. Financial planning is a rapidly growing but vaguely defined and poorly supervised field. Checking the planner's credentials and background, speaking to other clients, going on the recommendation of tax lawyers or bankers and speaking to several consultants before making a choice are important tactics for choosing a trustworthy financial planner. Unfortunately, there are unscrupulous or incompetent planners who simply walk away after depleting a client's life's savings. (See Table 10:2, Checking Out a Financial Planner.)

Checking Out a Financial Planner

Before engaging a financial planner, ask for and check references. A call to the Better Business Bureau or regulatory body also may be worthwhile. Financial planners also should demonstrate credentials and qualifications. Here are some of the more common ones:

- *International Association for Financial Planning.* Membership simply signifies payment of a fee and agreement to respect a code of ethics.
- *Registry of Financial Planning Practitioners.* Maintained by the International Association for Financial Planning. Listing signifies the planner must have three years of financial planning experience, meet educational standards and pass a written examination.
- *Certified Financial Planner.* Signifies person has passed a series of examinations.
- *Chartered Financial Consultant.* Signifies person has passed an even more rigorous series of tests.

Table 10:2

▪ *Hasty Moves*

All too many people associate retirement with selling the house and moving to a sunny clime. This may be fine for some people, but a large number find that life in a Florida or Arizona retirement community is a far cry from what they had expected, and in a few months they are back "home." When asked why they returned, they will often say, "We missed our friends" or, "There wasn't anything to do" or, "We want to be near our grandchildren." Many find they do not enjoy the segregated feeling of living in a retirement community of mostly older people, while to others this may be exactly what they are looking for.

Before making any permanent move, a couple should thoroughly test the water first. A depressingly large number of older people end up living in a place that is unsuitable to their interests. Others are duped out of their life's savings by investing in real estate schemes or financially shaky retirement homes or communities. The lure of prepaid lifelong care is understandably attractive, but before signing any papers or investing a penny, check out the operation thoroughly with your lawyer, the Better Business Bureau, consumer protection agency and other appropriate groups.

If you are unsure where you want to live, try sampling several places before buying and selling. House exchanges, or renting out your present home and leasing one in an area you are considering, are low-risk possiblities. It takes more than a couple of weeks to really sample what living in a place may be like; it is better to give yourself several months or even a year's trial before making a major move.

PART III

A PREVENTIVE APPROACH TO DISEASES OF AGING

11

HEART DISEASE AND CIRCULATORY DISORDERS

Despite considerable medical gains made against heart disease during the last few decades, cardiovascular disease remains our leading cause of death, claiming about one million lives a year. Of these, heart attacks account for 547,000 deaths a year, followed by strokes with 156,000, hypertensive disease with 31,000 and miscellaneous other cardiovascular diseases accounting for the remaining 247,000-plus deaths. Of course, mortality figures are not the only important ones; a huge number of Americans—more than 63 million, according to the American Heart Association—live their day to day lives with some form of heart or blood vessel disease.

Although the risk of a heart attack and other cardiovascular diseases increases with age, about a fifth of the deaths occur among people under the age of 65. At one time, we assumed that heart disease was a factor of aging, but this is no longer true. Increasingly, experts are convinced that a large percentage of heart attacks, strokes and other forms of heart disease can be prevented by changing our lifestyle to avoid or minimize the factors that raise the risk of cardiovascular disease. Scores of studies conducted by researchers here and around the world have repeatedly identified these avoidable risk factors as:

Cigarette smoking. Smokers have more than twice the risk of a heart attack as nonsmokers, and smoking is the leading risk factor for sudden cardiac death. More than 350,000 cardiac deaths a year are linked directly to smoking, according to the United States Surgeon General's office. A smoker who has a heart attack is more likely to die of it, with death often occurring within an hour of onset. Stopping smoking, however, lowers the risk to normal within a few years.

High blood cholesterol. Too much blood cholesterol leads to atherosclerosis, the buildup of fatty deposits along the artery walls. When the coronary arteries are affected, blood flow to the heart muscle is reduced and, if a coronary artery becomes completely blocked by the fatty plaque or a clot, a heart attack occurs.

High blood pressure. People with high blood pressure, or hypertension, are more likely to have a heart attack, stroke, congestive heart failure and kidney failure than people whose blood pressure is normal. The risk is even greater among hypertensives who smoke, have high blood cholesterol or other cardiovascular risk factors. The risk can be reduced by normalizing blood pressure, usually by a combination of medication, diet and exercise.

Diabetes. Type II or adult-onset diabetes, the most common form of the disease, occurs in middle age, especially among overweight people. It may be present in the body for many years without causing symptoms, while still causing damage to the heart, blood vessels, kidneys and other vital organs. Controlling diabetes through diet, exercise and insulin or other diabetes medication, if needed, can reduce both the risk of a heart attack and complications of the diabetes itself.

Although these are the major avoidable risk factors linked to heart disease, a number of others that may not be so clearly associated with heart disease, but still important to control, have been identified. These include:

Obesity. A number of studies have found that markedly overweight people, defined as 20 percent or more above their ideal weight, have a higher incidence of heart attacks as well as a higher death rate from cancer and a number of other diseases. Added weight increases the risk of high blood pressure; it also increases the heart's workload.

Sedentary lifestyle. Although it has not been proved that lack of exercise increases the risk of a heart attack, studies have found that people who exercise regularly do have a lower incidence of cardiovascular disease. Exercise is important in weight control; it also strengthens the heart muscle and improves the efficiency of the cardiovascular system.

Type A personality and stress. It has not been conclusively proved that these are cardiovascular risk factors, but many experts think that personality type and our individual responses to stress may affect our vulnerability to heart disease. Type A people tend to be overly competitive, aggressive, time-driven and compulsive. They overreact to even very minor stresses by pumping out the stress hormones that prepare our bodies for a fight or flight response. Sometimes referred to as "hot responders," these people may have several episodes a day in which their blood pressure rises, their heart rate increases and their body goes through the involuntary changes intended to protect us from danger. Some researchers hypothesize that these surges of stress hormones can in some way damage blood vessels and may be a factor that initiates atherosclerosis. Even individuals who do not fit the Type A profile run an increased risk of heart disease from severe or prolonged stress. Reducing stress and developing effective coping techniques can help minimize this personality type, and its associated stress, as risk factors.

In addition to avoidable risk factors, other circumstances increase cardiovascular vulnerability over which we have no control. These include:

Heredity. A family history of early heart attacks, high blood pressure or strokes greatly increases the risk. Anyone whose parents or other close relatives have suffered heart attack or stroke before the age of 50 or 55 should make a special effort to minimize other risk factors.

Age. Although we commonly associate heart attacks with the striking down of young men in their prime, the fact is that the risk rises sharply with age. More than half of all heart attacks occur in people over the age of 65, and of those who die, 80 percent are 65 or older.

Sex. Men are much more likely to have a heart attack than women. Even after menopause, when women's risk of a heart attack begins to rise, the cardiovascular death rate of women is lower than that of men.

Race. Blacks have a higher incidence of hypertension than whites, which is believed to explain why blacks have a much higher death rate from heart attacks and strokes.

Socio-economic status. Greater use of alcohol, a higher prevalence of smoking and often chronic unemployment contribute to both physical and mental stress.

As might be expected, the more risk factors a person harbors, the greater his chance of suffering a heart attack, stroke or some other form of heart disease. Although one cannot change one's family history, age, sex or race, a person who falls into one or more of these high-risk groups is not necessarily fated to develop cardiovascular disease. But the presence of any unavoidable risk factor or combination thereof should serve as an extra incentive to modify or avoid those factors over which we do have control.

❑ How the Heart Works

To better understand how you can protect yourself from heart disease, it is important to know the basis of how this vital organ works. The heart is a simple yet marvelously engineered organ, about the size of two clenched fists and weighing 11 to 16 ounces in the average adult. It is situated between the lungs in the upper chest cavity.

The heart is made up mostly of muscle tissue, called myocardium. It is a hollow organ divided into four chambers. The upper two are the right and left atria—chambers where blood collects—and the lower two are the right and left ventricles, the pumping chambers. The right atrium receives the blood that has circulated through the body; this blood is low in oxygen and nutrients, high in carbon dioxide and the waste products that normally are expelled through the lungs. This "used" blood passes into the right ventricle, and is pumped to the lungs where the carbon dioxide and wastes are removed and fresh oxygen is added. This freshly oxygenated blood passes from the lungs into the left atrium, then through the mitral valve into the left ventricle. This chamber is the heart's "workhorse" because it must pump the blood through the aortic valve into the aorta—the body's great artery—to begin its journey through the body's circulatory system.

In a normal active adult, the heart beats about 100,000 times a day, in effect pumping the equivalent of more than 4000 gallons of blood through more than 60,000 miles of the body's blood vessels, an operation most of us are totally unaware of until something goes wrong. But despite the heart's prodigious workload, it is designed to last a lifetime. Autopsies performed on men and women in their eighties and nineties who have died of something other than heart disease have found that their hearts sometimes show little signs of wear and tear, despite the fact that the heart must beat regularly sixty to eighty times a minute (and more during exercise), without stopping, year in and year out. So despite popular notions to the contrary, it does not appear that heart disease is an inevitable part of aging; instead, it is a consequence of life-style or other as yet unidentified factors that many experts feel can be changed or controlled to prevent a large percentage of heart attacks, especially those that occur at relatively early ages.

The heart muscle itself is nourished by a network of coronary arteries that encircle the heart like a crown, hence the name "coronary." These vessels appear to be particularly susceptible to atherosclerosis, a narrowing or "hardening" caused by deposits of fatty plaque, or atheroma. These deposits are made up of cholesterol, fats and fibrous tissue. The cause of atherosclerosis is unknown, but it appears to start early in life and is a progressive disease. Particularly common among Americans, it has been linked to our high-cholesterol diet. Cigarette smoking, perhaps an autoimmune response to something in tobacco or smoke, is believed to be a possible initiating factor. Nicotine, a vasoconstrictor, narrows the coronary arteries, allowing clots to form, and carbon monoxide in the blood from smoking reduces the effective supply of oxygen to the heart muscle. Stress, an autoimmune process (a defect in the body's immune system that causes it to damage itself), and hormonal imbalances are among the other possible factors that have been linked to atherosclerosis. High blood pressure and diabetes accelerate the process.

About 5 percent of the body's total blood flow passes through the coronary arteries. As these vessels become progressively narrowed by atherosclerosis, the heart muscle may become "starved" for oxygen and other nutrients. This can result in episodes of angina—the chest pains that are characteristic of coronary disease. Since the heart muscle is extremely efficient in extracting oxygen from the blood, the coronary vessels can be markedly narrowed—as much as 70 to 90 percent blocked—before symptoms occur. Thus, a person can have severe coronary disease without knowing it. In a distressingly large number of cases, the first sign of heart disease is a heart attack or sudden death.

The rhythmic beating of the heart is controlled by a bundle of cells that generate electrical impulses to coordinate the heart's contractions. This natural pacemaker sometimes goes away, resulting in serious disturbances of the heart's rhythm. Drugs and artificial pacemakers may be lifesaving in such circumstances.

In order for the blood to travel through hundreds of miles of vessels throughout the body and deliver oxygen to every cell, a certain pressure must be maintained within the vessels. With each heartbeat, about three ounces of blood is pumped from the left ventricle into the aorta. You can feel this sudden surge of blood at any of a number of pulse points throughout the body. The force of the heart's beat is a determining factor in maintaining blood pressure. When blood pressure is measured, two readings are taken—for example, 120 over 80. The higher number is the systolic pressure, which is the peak pressure when the blood is forced from the heart during a contraction of the left ventricle. The lower number is the diastolic pressure, which is the force exerted on the artery walls when the heart is resting between beats. This diastolic pressure is controlled by the resistance to blood flow from the arterioles—the smallest arteries—into the capillaries, the microscopic vessels that feed the individual cells. If the arterioles are constricted or narrowed, diastolic pressure will rise, and this in turn forces systolic pressure up in order to ensure continued blood flow.

To ensure that blood moves in the right direction, we have a marvelously engineered system of valves in the heart and blood vessels. Sometimes the valves in the heart become damaged, either by congenital defects or diseases, such as rheumatic fever or other infections. Drugs, surgery and replacement with artificial valves now make it possible for many people with severe valvular disease to lead normal lives. More commonly, it is the tiny valves in the veins, especially those in the lower legs, that can become weakened or damaged. This can cause varicose veins and the pooling of blood in the lower extremities. Heredity, overweight and a sedentary lifestyle are possible causative factors. Other circulatory problems can be caused by a narrowing of arteries in the legs—a process similar to what happens to clogged coronary arteries.

❑ Common Forms of Heart Disease

▪ *Coronary Disease and Angina*

As the coronary arteries become progressively narrowed by atherosclerosis, many people experience angina pectoris, the medical term for chest pains behind the breastbone. Typically, a person does not have any problems while resting or carrying out moderate activities. But extra demands upon the heart—running to catch a bus, climbing a flight of stairs, experiencing an emotional upset, going out on a cold, windy day or eating a heavy meal—will produce chest pains and shortness of breath. The attack usually lasts for only a few minutes and is relieved by rest or drugs, such as nitroglycerin.

These pains are due to inadequate oxygen being delivered to the heart muscle, a condition called myocardial ischemia. Some people experience myocardial ischemia without pain, a condition referred to as silent ischemia. Others may have pain without significant narrowing of the arteries. Typically, people with this variant form of angina may experience pain when resting, and studies of their coronary arteries may find only minor narrowing. In these instances, the angina is thought to be caused by a spasm of the coronary artery, frequently at the site of atherosclerotic plaque.

It is sometimes difficult to tell pain caused by myocardial ischemia from those of other conditions, such as heartburn, a hiatal hernia, chest muscle pain and so forth. In general, the pain of angina starts in the center of the chest and is a persistent squeezing or pressing sensation that may spread to the shoulders or arms, usually on the left side although both sides may be involved, as well as the back, neck or jaw. Most people with angina can identify a triggering factor—exertion, a burst of anger—and the episodes usually pass with rest or taking a nitroglycerin tablet.

Anyone who suspects he or she is experiencing chest pains or shortness of breath related to the heart should see a doctor promptly. Most people with angina learn to adjust their lives to live with the condition. Stopping smoking, starting a program of gradual exercise conditioning, losing weight, lowering cholesterol and other cardiovascular risk factors, taking medication to prevent or minimize attacks, avoiding precipitating factors—all are commonsense measures that can minimize the problem. In some instances, however, the attacks come with increasing frequency and severity, often without provocation. This is called unstable angina and is often a prelude to a heart attack. More intensive treatment, such as drug therapy (see Table 11:1, Drugs to Treat Angina) or a coronary bypass operation, may be needed to prevent a heart attack.

▪ *High Blood Pressure*

Nearly 55 million Americans—or one out of every four adults—have high blood pressure, making it our most com-

Drugs to Treat Angina

Generic Name	Brand Name	Possible Side Effects
NITRATES		
isosorbide dinitrate	Isordil Sorbitrate Dilatrate-SR	*Headache,*† *flushing,* dizziness upon standing, nausea, vomiting
nitroglycerin	Nitro-Bid Nitro-Dur Nitrostat Transderm-Nitro	Same as above and rapid pulse
CALCIUM BLOCKERS		
verapamil HCL	Calan Isoptin	Dizziness, *headache,* low blood pressure, slow pulse, ankle swelling, constipation
diltiazem	Cardizem	Nausea, swelling, irregular heartbeat, *headache,* rash, fatigue
nifedipine	Procardia	Dizziness, light-headedness, headache, weakness, flushing, transient low blood pressure, palpitations, ankle swelling, nausea
BETA-BLOCKERS Action: Reduce heart rate and heart muscle contractility through action on sympathetic nervous system, which in turn reduces oxygen demand		
propranolol HCL nadolol atenolol* pindolol* timolol*	Inderal Corgard Tenormin Visken Blocadren	Slow pulse, weakness, low blood pressure, asthma attacks, fatigue, insomnia (Inderal), impotence
OTHER Action: Increases blood flow to the heart by dilating certain coronary arteries		
dipyridamole	Persantine	*Headache, dizziness,* weakness, nausea, flushing

*Commonly prescribed for this condition, but not listed as FDA indications.

†Italicized side effects are more common than others, which are relatively rare.

Table 11:1

mon cardiovascular disease. Often referred to as the silent killer, hypertension—the medical term for high blood pressure—is the leading cause of strokes and is also a major risk factor for heart attacks, congestive heart failure and kidney failure. It is called "silent" because it usually does not produce symptoms until its most advanced stages, and by that time, the heart, blood vessels and other organs may have suffered permanent damage.

In general, high blood pressure in adults is defined as consistent systolic readings of more than 140 millimeters of mercury (mm Hg) and/or a diastolic pressure of 90mm Hg. Not uncommonly, a person may have a high reading when blood pressure is measured in a doctor's office and normal readings at home or elsewhere. This is why several readings taken at different times and in different positions usually are needed to establish a diagnosis of hypertension, especially if it is in the mild to moderate range.

Many people mistakenly think that as we get older, blood pressure normally rises in order to get blood to the vital organs. This is not true: The higher the blood pressure, the greater the chances of having a heart attack, stroke or kidney failure, regardless of age. Hypertension usually develops between the ages of 30 and 45, and without treatment, becomes progressively higher with age.

In more than 90 percent of people diagnosed, no cause can be found for the high blood pressure; this is referred to as "primary" or "essential" hypertension. In a small number of cases, a cause for the hypertension *can* be identified; for example, some types of kidney disease, adrenal tumors, hormonal abnormalities, use of birth control pills and certain medications may raise blood pressure. In some of these cases, identifying and correcting the underlying cause will cure the hypertension. But this is unusual; the large majority of hypertension has no identifiable cause, and treatment usually must persist for life. Recent studies have found that some patients can eventually stop the drugs after years of treatment, but experts think these are exceptions rather than the rule, and many eventually must resume therapy.

Many people think that chronic tension or stress causes hypertension. Although stress can produce a temporary rise in blood pressure, it has not been proved that it actually causes the sustained elevations seen in hypertension. Still, some experts think that stress, or perhaps more accurately, poor techniques in coping with stress, may be a contributing factor.

Heredity appears to play a definite role in determining who will develop hypertension. Children in families in which one or both of the parents have hypertension are more likely to have blood pressures at the high end of the scale, and have an increased risk of developing hypertension as adults. Obesity also appears to be a factor: Overweight people have a higher incidence of hypertension than their normal-weight peers. In this country, blacks have a much higher incidence of hypertension than whites. The reasons for this are unknown, although heredity, poverty, stress and high-salt diets have been suggested as possible explanations.

The role of sodium as a possible cause of high blood pressure is a matter of continuing debate among doctors and researchers. There is no clear evidence that consuming large amounts of sodium—the major ingredient in table salt—will cause hypertension among people who are not predisposed to the disease. But among those with a genetic predisposition, it appears that sodium consumption is a major contributing factor. And restricting sodium often will lower blood pressure in hypertensives. In fact, before the development of modern antihypertensive drugs, severe salt restriction, such as the famous rice diet developed at Duke University Medical Center, was about the only treatment for high blood pressure.

Recent studies have found that regular consumption of alcohol, even in moderate amounts of one or two drinks (or glasses of wine or beer) per day, increases the risk of developing high blood pressure. And among people with high blood pressure, alcohol consumption increases the incidence of strokes.

Once a diagnosis of hypertension has been established, it is important to bring the high blood pressure into the normal range. Often this can be accomplished with weight loss, lowered salt intake, increased exercise and development of improved techniques for dealing with stress, especially if the hypertension is in the mild to moderate range (140–160/90–95). But if this conservative approach fails to normalize blood pressure in three to six months, most doctors will prescribe antihypertensive drugs.

These medications have truly revolutionized the treatment of high blood pressure. Just a few decades ago, malignant hypertension—a particularly severe form of the disease that killed President Franklin D. Roosevelt—was a fairly common disorder; today it very rarely occurs. There are now a large number of different drugs (see Table 11:2 on drugs used to treat high blood pressure) that can be prescribed to lower high blood pressure; so many, in fact, that most cases can be brought under good control without undue side effects. If side effects occur, it is important to talk to your doctor; frequently, the dosage can be adjusted or the medication changed to eliminate or minimize side effects and still control the high blood pressure.

Some possible side effects of reactions to commonly used blood pressure–lowering drugs that may be experienced by a small percentage of people taking these medications

Generic Name	Brand Names*	Possible Side Effects
thiazide diuretics	Hydrodiuril Esidrix Saluron Hygroton Zaroxolyn	Weakness, muscle cramps, joint pains (gout), impotence
furosemide	Lasix	
indapamide	Lozol	
rauwolfia drugs	Reserpine Raudixin	Stuffy nose, nightmares, depression
alpha methyldopa	Aldomet	Drowsiness, depression, impotence, fever
BETA BLOCKERS:		
propranolol HCL	Inderal	Insomnia, nightmares, slow pulse, weakness, asthmatic attacks, cold hands and feet, impotence—varies with different drugs
metoprolol	Lopressor	
atenolol	Tenormin	
nadolol	Corgard	
timolol	Blocadren	
pindolol	Visken	
labetalol†	Normodyne or Trandate	

Generic Name	Brand Names*	Possible Side Effects
hydralazine	Apresoline	Headaches, rapid heartbeat, joint pains
minoxidil	Loniten	Headaches, rapid heartbeat, excessive hair growth, fluid retention
guanethidine	Ismelin	A form of impotence, dizziness
clonidine	Catapres	Dry mouth, drowsiness, fatigue
guanabenz	Wytensin	Same
prazosin	Minipress	Sudden faintness after first few doses
captopril	Capoten	Skin rash, loss of taste, kidney problems

*Various combinations of drugs listed below are also available.
†Also has some other effects.

Source: From *High Blood Pressure and What You Can Do About It* by Marvin Moser, M.D., a Benco Edition published by The Benjamin Company, Inc. Copyright © 1986. Used by permission.

Table 11:2

Although modern drugs can bring high blood pressure under control, they are not a cure for the disease. Almost always, one must take the medication for many years or even for the rest of one's life. Many people make the mistake of taking the drugs for a few weeks or months, and then, when checkups show normal readings, just stopping the medication. This can be a potentially life-threatening mistake: Some drugs cannot be stopped abruptly without a rebound effect in which the blood pressure soars higher than ever. More specifically, abrupt cessation of beta-blocking drugs may precipitate a heart attack.

Although hypertension can be a fatal disease, when properly treated the vast majority of patients live perfectly normal lives. In fact, no one would even suspect they have a serious cardiovascular disorder. The outlook today for people with high blood pressure is excellent—so long as they continue their treatment. Anyone with high blood pressure should see his or her doctor regularly, usually every six to twelve months once blood pressure has been normalized, to make sure that the disease is under control. Many doctors also advise patients to periodically measure blood pressure at home. This may be done with the regular cuff and stethoscope that your doctor uses, or one of the newer electronic monitors with a digital readout. (See Table 11:3, How to Take Your Own Blood Pressure.)

How to Take Your Own Blood Pressure

Monitoring your blood pressure at home is helpful to both you and your physician. By keeping track of daily and weekly changes in blood pressure you can acquire a more complete record of readings under a variety of conditions. Often, patients find that readings taken in a doctor's office will be higher than those taken at home. Home monitoring will assure you that your blood pressure is under control and lets the doctor monitor your medication accordingly.

Several automatic blood pressure–reading machines (sphygmomanometers) are available at most pharmacies. These devices have a built-in sensing device that removes the need to use a stethoscope. The readings obtained with these machines are not as accurate as the readings taken by your doctor or even at home, but they are easy to use and directions are usually printed on them.

Following is a procedure for taking your blood pressure with a nonautomated sphygmomanometer and stethoscope:

- Be sure you are in a quiet place. You have to be able to hear your blood flow.
- Take your reading in the same position each time. Blood pressure readings will vary depending on whether you are sitting or lying down.
- Rest your forearm flat on a table. Your upper arm (where the cuff will be placed) should be at the same level as your heart, to avoid deviations in readings.
- Roll up the sleeve to expose the upper arm. If the sleeve is rolled tight, slip that arm free of the sleeve.
- Place the stethoscope on the brachial artery in the crook of your elbow. You can locate it by feeling for your pulse with your fingertips.
- Slip the deflated cuff onto your upper arm. Use the ring and Velcro wrap to make the cuff snug. (Keep the stethoscope over the artery as you fit the cuff.)
- Place the pressure gauge (manometer) where you can see it easily.
- Put the ear tips of the stethoscope in your ears. (You may have to reposition the stethoscope on your arm to get a better sound.) Inflate the cuff about 30 points (millimeters of mercury) above your expected systolic pressure. This value is determined by trial and error or you can use the last reading taken at your doctor's office.
- Once the cuff pressure is greater than your systolic pressure, the cuff will act as a tourniquet, cutting off the blood supply. You should not hear any sound in the stethoscope. Keep your eye on the gauge and gradually release the pressure in the cuff using the release on the bulb. (Ideally, you should release the pressure slowly, about 2 to 3 points per heartbeat.)
- As soon as the arterial pressure drops below the cuff pressure, you will hear a pulse. Note the reading on the pressure gauge at the first sound of your pulse. This reading is your systolic pressure.
- Continue to release air from the cuff. The sound of your pulse will increase as more blood is allowed through the artery. Then, as the cuff pressure approaches your diastolic pressure, the sound will begin to fade. Listen carefully until the pulse disappears. The gauge level at the last sound you hear is your diastolic reading.
- Record both the systolic and diastolic reading as well as the date and time of the measurement.
- If you want to check this reading you can do so by taking it again. Wait a minute before you repeat the measurement. This time, adjust your initial cuff pressure to exactly 30 points above your previous systolic pressure.
- If you can, record your weight and pulse, in addition to unrelated events such as any arguments, physical exertion or medications you have taken which might affect your readings. This will help you and the doctor to interpret any changes in pressure.

Table 11:3

▪ *Heart Attacks*

More than 1.5 million Americans each year suffer a heart attack, and about 550,000 of them die. Understandably, a heart attack is a very serious and frightening event, but it need not mean the end of a productive life. More than 4.7 million living Americans have had a heart attack, and most return to their jobs or former activities, even though some restrictions may be necessary. Today's improved treatments mean that ever more people are surviving heart attacks—and with less lasting damage than in the past.

The medical term for heart attack is myocardial infarction, which means death of heart muscle. A heart attack occurs when a coronary artery becomes blocked, cutting off the supply of blood to the nearby muscle (see Figure 11:1). Any prolonged or extensive obstruction of a coronary artery can lead to irreversible injury to the heart itself, and de-

What Happens During a Heart Attack

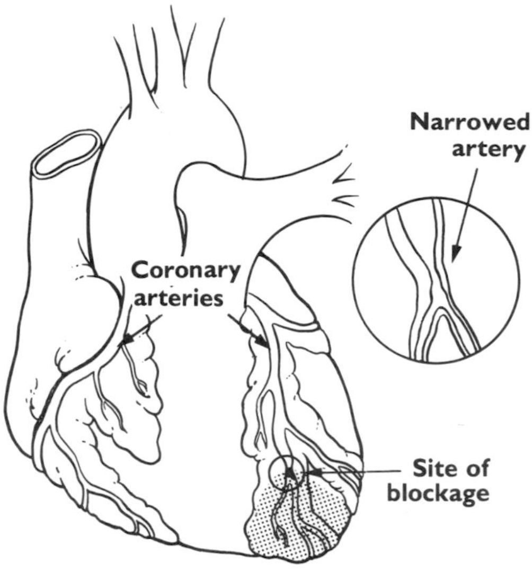

Figure 11:1
During a heart attack one of the coronary arteries becomes completely blocked, resulting in death of the surrounding heart muscle, as indicated by the shaded area in the lower portion of the heart.

pending upon the location and extent of the damage, this can result in death or disability. Early treatment of a heart attack with new drugs that dissolve the obstructing clot now makes it possible to avoid much or even all of the damage that usually occurs during an infarction. But for this to work, treatment must be administered within the first few hours of the attack.

All too often, a heart attack victim delays seeking medical help, frequently with fatal results. Most heart attack deaths occur in the first 2 hours, yet studies have found that many people wait 4 to 6 hours before getting to an emergency room. Warning signs of a heart attack are listed in Table 11:4. NEVER IGNORE THEM.

After a heart attack it is normal to be depressed and afraid. Many people fear that this means the end to their holding a job, enjoying a normal sex life, participating in all of the things that make life worthwhile. This is why rehabilitation after a heart attack is so important. A heart attack causes some permanent heart damage, but the extent of this damage varies widely from person to person. In some, it may be barely noticeable; in others it can be severe enough to impose some limitations. But the vast majority of people who survive a heart attack are able to resume an active, normal life. Unfortunately, far too many heart attack patients opt for disability rather than rehabilitation. Most heart attack patients are able to return to their regular job, but some whose job is particularly strenuous or stressful may need reassignment. Increasingly, cardiac rehabilitation programs include attention to occupational rehabilitation.

Activity is the key to any successful rehabilitation effort. This usually entails exercise conditioning, both to improve cardiovascular function and to retrain weakened muscles. Typically, today's heart attack patient will be sitting up in a day or two, walking around the hospital room or corridor as soon as the danger of serious rhythm disturbances and other complications is past—usually in four or five days—and ready to go home by the end of the second week (or even earlier). The prospect of leaving the safety of the hospital is very difficult for many heart attack patients. Many hospitals now give a modified exercise test before discharging a heart attack patient. This shows the patient that he or she can safely engage in a certain amount of physical activity; it also enables a doctor to draw up a specific exercise prescription. Typically, the patient will be instructed to walk; slowly at first, and gradually building up both distance and speed. At first, the person may feel weak and shaky; this is due more to the weakness that follows any stay in bed rather than to the heart attack itself. But after

Warning Signs of a Heart Attack

- Uncomfortable pressure, fullness, squeezing or pain in the center of the chest that lasts 2 minutes or longer.
- Pain spreading to the shoulders, neck or arms.
- Severe pain, dizziness, fainting, sweating, nausea or shortness of breath.

Not all of these warning signs occur in every heart attack. If some of these symptoms do occur, however, GET HELP IMMEDIATELY.

Be Prepared: Know What to Do:

- Know which hospitals in your area have 24-hour emergency cardiac care.
- Determine in advance the hospital or medical facility that is nearest your home and office, and tell your family and friends to call this facility in an emergency.
- Keep a list of emergency rescue service numbers next to your telephone and in your pocket, wallet or purse.
- If you have chest discomfort that lasts for 2 minutes or more, call the emergency rescue service.
- If you can get to a hospital faster by going yourself and not waiting for an ambulance, have someone drive you there, but don't drive yourself or exert yourself by chasing a cab, for example.
- If you are with someone who is showing signs of a heart attack, and the warning signs last for 2 minutes or longer, act immediately.
- Expect a "denial." It is normal for a person with chest discomfort to deny the possibility of anything as serious as a heart attack. Don't take "no" for an answer, however. Insist on taking prompt action.
- Call the emergency rescue service, or
- Get to the nearest hospital emergency room that offers 24-hour emergency cardiac care.
- Give CPR (mouth-to-mouth breathing and chest compression) if the person's heart and respiration have stopped and if you are properly trained.

Source: Reproduced with permission. © 1986 Heart Facts. American Heart Association.

Table 11:4

a few weeks most people find they again feel physically fit, and those who were sedentary before may be surprised to find they actually are in even better shape than before their heart attack. (See Chapter 2, Exercise, for a more detailed discussion.)

Sex is a topic that all too many patients and physicians alike avoid discussing, but it is a question that is uppermost in the minds of heart attack victims and their partners. A recent study by researchers at Massachusetts General Hospital found that heart attack patients who resumed sexual relations had a lower incidence of subsequent heart attacks and death than those who did not, even though their physical conditions were comparable. An optimistic attitude as well as maintaining close personal relationships is an important but often neglected factor in the recovery process.

Contrary to popular belief, sexual intercourse requires only a modest amount of extra cardiovascular effort. Most doctors agree that a heart attack patient who can climb a flight of stairs or walk a block has enough physical stamina for normal sexual relations. Most sexual problems following a heart attack are due to fear (on the part of both the patient and his or her partner), not to cardiac disability. Some of the drugs used to treat heart disease also may interfere with sexual function; if this is a problem, it should be discussed with one's doctor, who may be able to adjust the drug dosage or prescribe an alternative medication that will not have this side effect.

Obviously, life is not exactly the same after a heart attack; chances are, healthy changes are in order. Stopping smoking, losing weight, increasing physical activity, avoiding unnecessary stress are all commonsense lifestyle changes that most of us could benefit from. But it often takes something as drastic as a heart attack to prod us into action.

SURGERY TO TREAT CORONARY DISEASE

Nearly 200,000 Americans undergo coronary bypass surgery each year. A growing number are having angioplasty, instead of a bypass. This is a newer treatment that involves using a catheter and inflatable balloon-like tip to flatten the fatty deposits in coronary arteries. These operations are adding more than $5 billion to the nation's annual medical bill—a cost that a growing number of critics are questioning. In addition, even more costly procedures such as heart transplants are being done with increasing frequency. And experimental treatments, such as development of an artificial heart, continue to capture our imagination and attention.

In the last few years, a number of physicians have questioned the long-term value of many of these operations, and there is still disagreement among experts as to whether patients with certain types of coronary disease should be treated with drugs and exercise rather than surgery. Some studies have found little or no difference in survival rates among people who have a bypass versus those who are treated medically—i.e., with drugs, exercise, lifestyle changes, etc. Some doctors even think that coronary bypass operations will become obsolete in a few years. At present, however, many people with severe coronary disease are undergoing bypass surgery, including second and even third operations for people who had their first bypass five to ten years ago.

In a bypass operation, segments of healthy blood vessels, usually a vein from the leg, are grafted onto the heart's surface to bypass clogged areas of coronary arteries. (See Figure 11:2.) An alternative is to use the internal mammary artery, which is near the heart. Studies have shown this vessel is more likely to stay open than transplanted veins; the operation is more difficult than the traditional bypass, however, and is done only in a few medical centers.

During a bypass operation, which usually takes two to four hours, the heart is stopped and circulation is maintained by a heart-lung machine. Afterward, most patients spend two or three days in an intensive-care recovery room, and an additional week to ten days in the hospital. The objective is to restore normal blood flow to the heart muscle, thereby eliminating or minimizing anginal attacks and, hopefully, preventing heart attacks.

The operation is not without risks: A small percentage of patients, 1 to 3 percent nationwide, die during surgery or before leaving the hospital. In addition, a small percentage suffer a heart attack, stroke or other serious complication during or immediately after the operation. The operation is not a cure for coronary disease; in fact, the grafted vessels seem to become clogged by the same atherosclerotic process that damaged the original coronary arteries, only even faster.

Coronary Bypass Operation

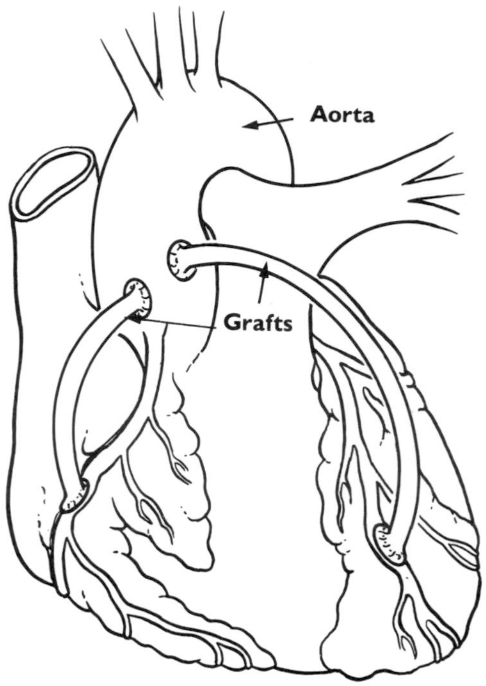

Figure 11:2
Portions of veins from elsewhere in the body are grafted to coronary arteries to bypass severely blocked areas.

Despite these very real drawbacks, large numbers of heart patients unquestionably benefit from coronary bypass surgery, especially in terms of overcoming the symptoms and disability of severe coronary disease. If an operation is called for, however, it should be done in a hospital which does at least 100 to 150 such operations per year.

Balloon Angioplasty

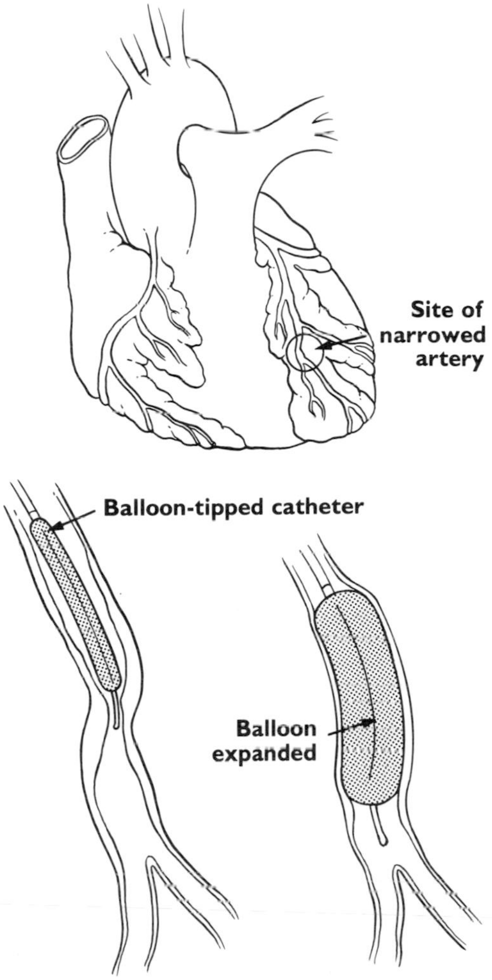

Figure 11:3
In balloon angioplasty, a catheter with a balloon tip is passed through the coronary arteries to the site of blockage. The balloon is then inflated, flattening out the fatty deposits along the artery wall to allow more blood to flow through the vessel.

Angioplasty is less costly and safer than coronary bypass surgery, but it, too, has its limitations and drawbacks. Angioplasty is the passing of a balloon through the artery and expanding it at the site of narrowing. (See Figure 11:3.) Not all clogged coronary arteries can be treated with angioplasty. The results also tend to be temporary; many patients who undergo angioplasty eventually require a second procedure or bypass surgery. Still, the technique is constantly being improved, and it is likely that angioplasty will eventually replace many of the bypass operations now being done. To be sure about the value of one of these operations, seek a second opinion, from a board-certified cardiologist.

Experiments to use lasers and other advanced technology to unclog coronary arteries and other blood vessels are beginning to show promise. Already new enzyme-drugs are being used to dissolve coronary clots in the first few hours after a heart attack. Lasers, which are concentrated beams of light instead of a surgical scalpel, are being used in a number of surgical procedures, including delicate eye surgery and gynecologic operations. Many heart researchers think it is only a matter of time before lasers will be used to clean out atherosclerotic plaque from coronary arteries.

▪ *Strokes and Mini-Strokes*

The incidence of stroke has dropped dramatically in the last twenty years, due largely to increased detection and treatment of high blood pressure. Even so, it remains a major cause of death and disability; about 500,000 Americans suffer a stroke each year, of whom approximately 156,000 die. Of the nearly 2 million living stroke victims, many have significant disabilities.

During a stroke the blood supply to part of the brain is cut off, resulting in death of brain tissue in the affected area.

Most strokes are caused by a cerebral thrombosis, in which a clot blocks one of the arteries serving the brain. Strokes also may be caused by bleeding or hemorrhage, usually when a weakened blood vessel bursts. This type of stroke also may be caused by a head injury or an aneurysm—a weakened section of blood vessels that balloons out from the artery wall.

In addition to high blood pressure, the risk of a stroke may be increased by:

- A high red blood cell count
- Heart disease
- Diabetes
- Being black
- Being male
- Use of birth control pills.

Frequently a stroke is preceded by mini-strokes, or transient ischemic attacks. These are temporary symptoms caused by reduced blood flow to the brain, and they are important warning signs that should never be ignored. (See Table 11:5, Warning Signs of a Stroke.) Prompt treatment at this point often can prevent a full-blown stroke.

Treatment of strokes and mini-strokes depends upon severity and the source of blockage. Often, the blockage occurs in the carotid artery in the neck, frequently causing mini-strokes. Surgery to remove the atherosclerotic plaque or bypass the clogged area may be sufficient to prevent a stroke. As with coronary bypass surgery, a second opinion is valuable, since the operation has its own risks.

Warning Signs of a Stroke

- Sudden, temporary weakness or numbness of the face, arm and/or leg on one side of the body.
- Temporary loss of speech, or trouble speaking or understanding speech.
- Temporary dimmed vision, or loss of vision, particularly in one eye.
- Unexpected dizziness, unsteadiness or sudden falls.

Table 11:5

If the blood vessel is blocked by a clot, drugs may be given to dissolve it and to prevent the formation of new clots. Some of these anticlotting drugs must be given in a hospital setting and be carefully monitored to make sure that the blood does not become too thin, resulting in hemorrhaging. On a long-term basis, a low dose of ordinary aspirin, usually one half to one aspirin per day, seems to prevent the formation of potentially lethal clots. People who have had heart valve replacement also are at a high risk of strokes because clots tend to form in and around the artificial valves. This can be prevented by taking anticlotting medication.

Rehabilitation is a vital part of stroke treatment. Contrary to popular belief, most people who have had a stroke can be successfully rehabilitated, though this, of course, depends upon the extent of brain damage. The attitude and cooperation of the patient and family members also is very important, as is the timing and quality of the rehabilitation program. Ideally, rehabilitation should start as soon as the immediate crisis is passed. The part of the brain damaged by the stroke determines the physical consequences (see Figure 11:4). Often, little can be done to overcome some of the paralysis, memory loss and other problems, but increasingly, we are learning more about retraining the brain to enable a stroke victim to learn new skills and relearn old ones.

▪ *Heart Valve Disease*

A system of four valves—one for each chamber—ensures that blood moves in the right direction as it passes through the heart. For example, the tricuspid valve allows blood to pass from the right atrium into the right ventricle; the blood is then forced from the right ventricle into the lungs via the pulmonary valve; oxygenated blood goes from the lungs into the left atrium, where it passes through the mitral valve into the left ventricle, the heart's main pumping chamber. Finally, blood being pumped from the left ventricle goes through the aortic valve into the aorta, where it begins its trip through the body's circulatory system.

Possible Effects of a Stroke

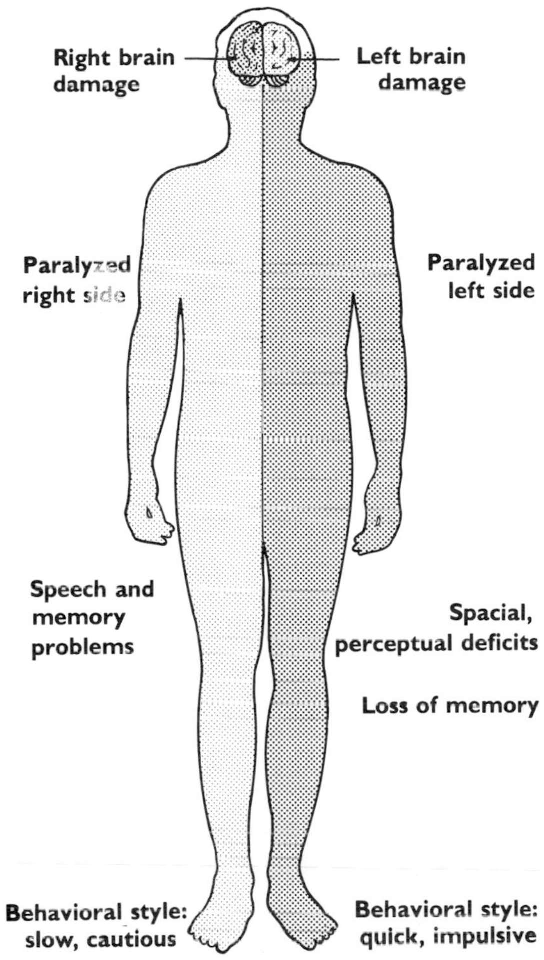

Figure 11.4
Brain damage affects opposite side of the body.

Sometimes, for instance, in a quiet moment after exercising, you can actually hear your heart making a thumping sound. This is the sound of the heart valves closing. The valves work in close synchronization with each other; when the heart beats (or contracts), the pulmonary and aortic valves open to allow blood to pass into the lungs and aorta, respectively; between beats, the tricuspid and mitral valves open to let the blood from the atria into the pumping chambers.

Heart valve disorders usually fall into one of two categories: valvular stenosis, in which the valve becomes thickened and narrowed, preventing it from opening properly and impeding the outward flow of blood; or valvular incompetence, in which the valve is weakened and does not close properly, permitting a backflow of blood. Congenital defects, heart attacks and aging all can lead to valvular disease. Heart valves also may be damaged by infection, such as rheumatic fever, which is caused by a streptococcal bacteria; or bacterial endocarditis, a serious heart infection that is most common among intravenous drug users. In the past, syphilis was the major cause of valvular heart disease, but this is now rare because of early treatment with antibiotics.

When valves become defective, the heart has to work harder to pump blood through the body. Eventually this can lead to congestive heart failure or disturbances in the heart rhythm. Sometimes a defective heart valve is discovered during a routine examination; a doctor detects a murmur or other unusual sound when listening to the heart through a stethoscope. More frequently, the problem will be discovered after producing symptoms. Shortness of breath and fatigue are common signs of valvular disease. A bluish tinge to the fingers or lips and fainting also are possible signs of heart valve disease.

Diagnosis of a valvular problem can be confirmed by echocardiography, an examination that uses sound waves to map the structures of the heart; or cardiac catheterization and angiography. Most valve problems can be treated by drugs. Digitalis or other medications may be prescribed to slow the heartbeat and increase its output. Diuretics and a salt-restricted diet may be added to prevent a buildup of fluid. Since diseased heart valves commonly provide a favorable site for clots to form, low-dose aspirin or other anticlotting drugs are often needed as a preventive measure. Beta-blockers or other antiarrhythmic drugs may be needed to prevent irregular heartbeats. Prophylactic antibiotics also are important in long-term treatment of heart valve disease. Defective valves are particularly susceptible to bacterial endocarditis; to prevent this, antibiotics should always be taken before any surgical or dental procedure in which bacteria may enter the bloodstream.

If a heart valve becomes so damaged that it seriously hampers the flow of blood or is causing congestive heart failure, it may be replaced with an artificial valve. In recent years, a number of efficient and durable replacement valves have been developed; some of these are made from animal parts, others, from plastic and/or metal. Valve replacement should be done by a surgeon who does a large number of these operations each year. The hospital team should also have regular experience in the technique. Following heart valve replacement, antibiotics and blood-thinning drugs may be permanently prescribed to prevent infection and clot formation.

A person with severe valvular disease may need to avoid very strenuous activities or include rest periods throughout the day. But with proper treatment, most can live reasonably normal lives.

▪ *Heart Rhythm Disorders*

The average adult heart beats regularly sixty to seventy times per minute. The rhythm slows during sleep and speeds up during exercise. Normally, we are unaware of our heart's rhythm; our sympathetic nervous system automatically regulates the heart's breathing. All of us now and then experience a skipped heartbeat or even a series of fast beats, or palpitations. These occasional disturbances in heart rhythm usually are benign, but there are a number of diseases in which cardiac arrhythmias, or irregular heartbeats, are potentially serious.

When the heart beats too fast, it is referred to as tachycardia; too slow, as bradycardia. Cigarette smoking, excessive caffeine consumption, anxiety and certain drugs all can affect the heart's rhythm. An overactive thyroid can cause tachycardia, and too little thyroid hormone results in bradycardia. Some types of heart disease, such as coronary or heart valve disorders, also cause heart arrhythmias.

Most arrhythmias are temporary and harmless, but some can be life-threatening. Ventricular fibrillation, for example, is a common cause of sudden death. When this happens, the heart beats in a shallow, quivering, disorganized fashion and fails to pump any blood. The quivering is caused by severe disturbance in the heart's electrical impulses. If the fibrillation is not stopped almost immediately, at least within two or three minutes, and the heart's normal rhythm restored, the affected person will die. If you like TV medical dramas, you have probably seen emergency room doctors using electrical defibrillators—paddle-like devices that administer an electrical shock to the heart to interrupt the disturbed electrical pattern and restore a normal one. When ventricular fibrillation occurs outside a hospital setting or where emergency help is not quickly available, it can result in sudden death.

Another common and potentially serious arrhythmia is atrial fibrillation. In this disorder, the atrium beats 500 to 600 times a minute, causing the ventricles to beat irregularly, at a slower rate of 170 to 200 beats per minute. Atrial fibrillation often occurs after a heart attack and in other types of heart disease. Once established, it lasts for life, but it can be controlled by drugs. (See Table 11:6, Drugs to Treat Cardiac Arrhythmias.)

Some cardiac arrhythmias arise in the heart's pacemaker cells—specialized cells that conduct electrical impulses. The heart may beat either too fast or too slow; if the problem is severe and cannot be controlled by drugs, an artificial pacemaker may be needed. This is a device that provides electrical impulses to ensure a steady heartbeat. Some pacemakers work on demand; that is, they send out impulses only when the heart rate falls below a certain predetermined level. They do not send impulses when the heart is beating normally. Other pacemakers work constantly, sending out impulses at a fixed rate regardless of whether the heart is beating too fast or too slow.

People who are prone to cardiac arrhythmias should avoid caffeine, tobacco and drugs that cause the heartbeat to speed up. Although most cardiac arrhythmias are relatively harmless, some can develop into serious problems; therefore, all should be investigated by a doctor.

Drugs to Treat Cardiac Arrhythmias

Generic Name	Brand Name	Possible Side Effects
DIGITALIS PREPARATIONS		
digoxin digitoxin	Lanoxin Crystodigin Purodigin	Headache, slow pulse, anorexia, nausea, vomiting, blurred or yellow vision, weakness
BETA-BLOCKERS		
propranolol HCL nadolol atenolol* pindolol* timolol* and others in this family	Inderal Corgard Tenormin Visken Blocadren	Slow pulse, weakness, low blood pressure, asthma attacks, fatigue, impotence
OTHERS		
bretylium tosylate	Bretylol	Low blood pressure, dizziness upon standing, nausea, vomiting
procainamide HCL	Pronestyl Procan SR	Anorexia, nausea, bitter taste, weakness, hives, itching, mental depression
QUININE PREPARATIONS		
quinidine gluconate	Quinaglute	Ringing in the ears, headache, visual disturbances, nausea, vomiting, diarrhea
quinidine sulfate	Quinidex Quinora	

*Commonly prescribed for this condition, but not listed as FDA indications.

Table 11:6

▪ *Congestive Heart Failure*

Congestive failure occurs when the heart is unable to pump enough blood through the body, even during rest or periods of very modest activity, to enable the body to carry out normal functions. This results in a buildup of blood volume, causing an accumulation of fluids, or congestion.

A frequent early sign of congestive failure is difficulty breathing when lying down. Typically, the person will waken with a feeling of breathlessness. This is caused by an accumulation of fluid in the lungs, which is eased by sitting up. Many people with congestive failure end up sleeping upright in a chair or propped up in bed with several pillows. Swelling legs is another common early sign of congestive failure, as is a rapid pulse, which is caused by increased pumping action as the heart attempts to meet the body's demand for the oxygen normally carried in the blood.

Congestive heart failure may be the result of damage to the heart muscle during a heart attack or from chronic high blood pressure. Cardiomyopathy, a disease of the muscle, and diseased heart valves are other causes of congestive failure. Early diagnosis and treatment of valvular disease or high blood pressure are important in preventing congestive failure. Chronic infection with fever, severe anemia and extreme vitamin B deficiency are still other causes of congestive failure.

The earlier diagnosis and treatment of congestive failure is made, the better the outlook. Often, identifying and correcting the underlying cause will improve the heart's pumping ability. For example, treating high blood pressure or valvular disease will make the congestive failure easier to manage.

Several drugs are used to treat congestive failure. Digitalis, which slows the heart's rate and increases the strength of its contractions, thereby enabling it to pump more blood, is a standard drug in treating congestive failure. Diuretics are often prescribed to reduce the accumulation of fluid in the legs, lungs, liver and other tissue. Captopril, a drug used to treat hypertension, may sometimes be prescribed when diuretics and digitalis are not effective. Vasodilator medications may also be prescribed to ease the heart's workload. Weight loss, salt restriction and frequent rest periods throughout the day are among lifestyle changes that may be necessary to overcome problems caused by congestive failure. Moderate exercise aimed at improving cardiovascular function may help the body make more efficient use of available oxygen and ease the feelings of breathlessness, but any exercise program should be carried out under a doctor's direction.

▪ *Circulatory Disorders*

Most of us immediately think of the heart when we talk about cardiovascular disorders, overlooking the blood vessels and other facets of circulatory function. Often, circulatory problems are related to heart disease, but in many instances, they are independent disorders. The more common are described below.

VARICOSE VEINS

Varicose veins are very common, especially among older women who have had several children. Varicose veins are caused by weakened valves in the veins that help keep the blood flowing toward the heart. Blood that circulates to the legs and feet must travel upward, against the force of gravity, to get back to the heart and lungs. Blood pressure aids in promoting this upward flow, as does the constriction of leg muscles as a person moves about. These forces are aided by a series of one-way valves, flaplike leaflets that lie flat against the wall of a vein when blood is moving toward the heart, and that billow outward if the blood starts to flow backward. These valves help ensure that the blood flows in one direction.

If some of these valves become weakened, a backflow of blood may result. The blood will seep backward until it is stopped by a properly functioning valve. The blood will accumulate in this spot, causing the vein's walls to expand outward. Over time, this will result in the twisted and swollen vessels characteristic of varicose veins.

Some people have an inherited tendency to develop varicose veins. Pregnancy, overweight and standing in one position for long periods are among the other factors promoting varicose veins. Women may be more susceptible than men because their leg muscles may not be as well developed. The varicose veins that often develop during pregnancy are caused by the increased abdominal weight and extra blood flow, as well as the downward pressure of the fetus. These usually disappear after the baby is born, but a woman who has had repeated pregnancies and varicose veins may be more susceptible to developing them later in life.

Swelling and darkening of vessels in the leg are the first symptoms of varicose veins. There is often a feeling of tightness or heaviness in the lower legs, tenderness, muscle cramps and weakness, and sometimes ankle swelling. In severe cases, bruising, infection and swelling may form at the site of the varicosities.

Exercise is very important in both preventing and treating varicose veins. People whose job demands that they stand for long periods—barbers, traffic police officers and surgeons, among others—should make it a point to move their legs frequently. Standing with one leg elevated on a short stool may help; taking a break now and then to sit with the legs raised to promote blood flow is also recommended. Avoid sitting with the legs crossed—this hinders blood flow in the legs.

Walking and cycling are particularly good activities for people with varicose veins. Wearing elastic support hose also may be recommended; to get the maximum benefit, however, the hose should be the prescription type, which offers better support than regular support hose. Of course, anyone with varicose veins should avoid wearing tight shoes, garters or other garments that restrict blood flow. And they should lose weight if they are heavy. Veins that are supported by firm muscle, instead of soft fat, are less likely to swell.

For people who are not helped by conservative methods, medical treatment may be needed. One common approach entails injecting the vein with a solution that causes it to harden, thus sealing off the vessel and forcing the rerouting of blood to other healthier vessels. This may provide temporary relief, but it usually is not a permanent cure. In severe cases, surgical removal of the damaged vessels may be necessary. This also forces a rerouting of blood and improves circulation in the lower legs.

PHLEBITIS AND THROMBOPHLEBITIS

Phlebitis refers to inflammation of a vein; this often results in formation of a clot, or thrombus, at the site of inflammation—a condition called thrombophlebitis. There are two kinds of thrombophlebitis: inflammation and clotting in a superficial vein; and deep thrombophlebitis, which occurs in a vessel located deeper within the leg. Superficial thrombophlebitis is uncomfortable but rarely life-threatening; in contrast, a part of a deep thrombophlebitis may break off and travel through the circulation to the lungs with often fatal results. Deep thrombophlebitis is most common among people who have chronic heart or lung disease, or who are confined to bed following surgery, stroke or a broken bone. Signs of a deep thrombophlebitis include heaviness and pain in the leg, especially when it is down, swelling and a bluish cast to the skin, which also may feel warm to the touch. Diagnosis is made by injecting a dye and following its course by X-rays.

Superficial thrombophlebitis often occurs in people with varicose veins. It usually can be treated by periodic resting with the leg elevated and anti-inflammatory drugs to ease the inflammation and pain. Warm compresses and elastic stockings also may help. It is important to stay active and to avoid long periods in bed or in one position. In severe cases, however, bed rest with the leg elevated may be required. If these measures do not work, the patient may need surgery to remove the clot and inflamed lining of the vessel.

Deep thrombophlebitis always requires prompt medical treatment. Anticoagulant drugs to prevent further clotting are usually needed. People taking these medications need to have their blood tested frequently to make sure that it is not being thinned too much. They also should avoid taking aspirin or any other drug that further inhibits clotting or may cause bleeding. Bed rest with the leg elevated also may be required; wearing elastic stockings, even when in bed, will help promote circulation.

Since phlebitis has a tendency to recur—remember President Richard Nixon's recurrent bouts with phlebitis?—it is important that a person be aware of the warning signs and seek prompt medical attention should they appear.

ARTERIOSCLEROSIS OBLITERANS AND OTHER OBSTRUCTIVE DISEASES

Arteriosclerosis—progressive hardening and narrowing of the arteries—can occur in many parts of the body. When it affects the lower legs, the condition is called arteriosclerosis obliterans. Typically, it strikes men over the age of 50 who smoke and have high blood cholesterol. High blood pressure and diabetes also increases the risk.

As the major arteries that carry blood to the legs and feet become progressively narrowed by fatty deposits, smaller collateral vessels attempt to take over a greater circulatory function. But these vessels usually are inadequate to meet the demands. At first, the person may be troubled by leg cramps, aching or muscle fatigue in the legs when exercising. This is called intermittent claudication. The site of the pain and other symptoms is determined by the area of narrowing. For example, if the femoral artery, which runs down the thigh, is blocked, pain is likely to occur in the calves.

Typically, the person will notice that he has to stop and rest his legs after walking a block or two or climbing a flight of stairs. As the narrowing worsens, pain is likely to occur almost constantly, even when resting. Eventually, the skin—deprived of oxygen and other nutrients—weakens and begins to break down, resulting in ulcers. In severe cases, gangrene may develop, requiring amputation. Fortunately, this can usually be avoided by early treatment. Stopping smoking, lowering cholesterol and high blood pressure, and if diabetes is present, keeping blood sugar in the normal range, are all important first steps in controlling obstructive arterial disorders. There are other causes of intermittent claudication, such as a degenerative spinal disc. It is important to see a doctor to determine the cause of the problem so proper treatment can be initiated.

Exercise, even though it may be painful, is a vital part of treatment. Patients with arteriosclerosis obliterans and intermittent claudication usually are instructed to walk or use a stationary bicycle for 15 to 30 minutes several times a day. Patients should rest when pain occurs, but continue when it eases. A program of graduated walking and exercise improves collateral circulation and, for many patients, can ease the symptoms.

If the problem persists or worsens, vascular surgery may be attempted to improve circulation. This may entail using grafts—either taken from healthy vessels elsewhere or synthetic material—to bypass the blocked area(s), and endarterectomy, during which the diseased vessel will be opened and the fatty deposits that are clogging it removed. Angioplasty—the procedure in which a balloon-tipped catheter is used to flatten the fatty deposits and widen the artery—

is increasingly replacing endarterectomies. Researchers also are studying the use of lasers to "clean out" these blocked vessels, noting that the leg is better suited to this type of surgery than the heart.

ANEURYSMS

An aneurysm is a weakened segment of an artery or other blood vessel that fills with blood and balloons outward. Congenital weakness in the blood vessel walls, high blood pressure, infection, arteriosclerosis and injuries are among the more common causes of aneurysms.

Very often, a person can have an aneurysm without knowing it. These symptomless aneurysms may show up on an X-ray or be felt during a physical examination. Some, however, will produce symptoms, depending upon their severity and location. Sometimes an aneurysm will press on an internal organ, causing pain or other problems. A person may feel a pulsating sensation; for example, an aneurysm of the large abdominal aortic artery may be felt as a pulsation in the abdomen.

Rupture is the major danger of an aneurysm. Depending upon the location and amount of bleeding, a ruptured aneurysm can produce shock, loss of consciousness and death. A ruptured aneurysm in the brain can cause a stroke. Sometimes an aneurysm leaks blood without actually rupturing; this can cause pain without the shock and rapid onset of other symptoms seen with a rupture, but it is still potentially life-threatening. Aneurysms also increase the danger of blood clotting, which can result in a heart attack or stroke. Sometimes an aneurysm will bleed into the wall of an artery and block some of its branches. This happens most often in the aorta.

Sometimes an aneurysm can be surgically repaired or removed; in other instances, treatment may consist of lowering blood pressure and keeping it at a low level to prevent extra strain on the weakened vessel.

12

CANCER

Despite considerable gains in the last two decades, cancer remains our second leading cause of death, second only to heart disease, and many people still harbor the mistaken notion that a diagnosis of cancer means unrelenting pain and an automatic death sentence. The fact is, using present treatments and technology, half or more of all cancers can be cured. Three million of the 5 million living Americans who have had cancer were treated five or more years ago, and most of these are considered cured of the disease.

As for the question of cancer pain, while it is true that some cancers are painful, many produce little or no pain, and for most patients, what pain does exist can be controlled with aspirin or other prescription drugs or self-help techniques. In fact, the pain of chronic arthritis is considered more unrelenting than the pain of many cancers.

A comprehensive discussion of the many forms and implications of cancer is beyond the scope of this book. In this chapter, we will present an overview of the changing picture of modern cancer detection, prevention and therapy, as well as brief discussions of some of the more common cancers.

❑ Changing Attitudes

Fortunately, the social stigma and many of the groundless fears that were associated with cancer in the past seem to be disappearing, but many misconceptions remain. For example, many former cancer patients still find employers reluctant to take a chance and hire or promote them, even though studies have found that recovered cancer patients do not have as much job absenteeism as people with heart disease or diabetes. Cancer rehabilitation remains a largely neglected aspect of treatment, even though most cancer patients can resume normal, productive lives if given the opportunity.

Cancer prevention is another area largely neglected by the general public.

Experts contend that the majority of cancer cases—some say as many as 85 percent of some of the more common cancers—could be prevented simply by avoiding known carcinogens, such as tobacco. Despite available information on the relation of cancer or survival after cancer to such factors as smoking, diet and early detection, attention to cancer prevention does not seem to be a personal priority with the American public. But as more information is made available and as evidence to support some claims about risks and benefits grows stronger, health-care professionals and other concerned individuals hope to see a movement away from health-endangering practices toward health promotion. The fact is, an informed, participatory public is the best equipped to prevent cancer from happening in the first place.

It may seem difficult to correlate the fact that cancer causes so many deaths with the statistics that show that survival rates for cancer have been steadily improving over the past decades. In the 1940's only one in four patients was cured of the disease, cure being defined as being alive and free of the disease five years after diagnosis. Today three out of eight achieve this goal. The increase in number of deaths despite the improved survival percentage rate is due largely to an increase in the number of new lung cancer cases that occur each year, particularly among women who smoke cigarettes.

Survival—being symptom-free for five years following treatment for cancer—has improved for a variety of reasons, among them improved forms of therapy and methods of getting treatments directly to malignant tissue, more sophisticated screening techniques leading to earlier detection, and heightened public awareness, which can also lead to earlier detection.

❑ What Is Cancer?

Cancer is a "family" of disease that includes over a hundred types. Basically, cancer is uncontrolled cell growth. Normal cells have a specific function in the maintenance of the body and a regulated growth process that controls the ratio of old or dying cells to new cells. Cells can be divided into three types as far as their growth potential is concerned: *static* cells, such as muscle and nerve tissue, which do not divide or grow after they have reached a specific size; *committed* cells, which stop growing when the organ or tissue achieves its normal size, though they may be reactivated if damage occurs to the tissue or organ; and *stem* cells, which are continually dying and being replaced, but which appear to have an internal control system that maintains a balance between new and old cells.

Cancer cells, on the other hand, do not serve any assigned function in the body and do not obey any such regulatory process. They grow, therefore, without restraint, and they do not die or "shed" as do normal cells. Cancer cells live longer than normal cells and divide also more often during their life span, thus fueling the growth of tumors which may start to encroach on neighboring tissue.

Another distinguishing characteristic of cancer cells is their ability to migrate from their original site to other parts of the body through the blood or lymph systems, forming metastases (new cancer growths). Initially, this spread may be confined to one region of the body, but depending on the type of cancer and the time in which it is left untreated, the disease may eventually spread throughout the body.

Cancer is not contracted the way a cold or stomach virus is. Some cancers tend to run in families, and are assumed to have a genetic predisposition. Typically, cancer develops slowly, over a period of many years, but some come on very suddenly. There may be a substantial gap between exposure to a cancer-causing agent and the first symptoms, or diagnosis, of cancer—the time-bomb effect. It is possible that many cancers develop by means of a two-stage process: first, exposure to *initiators,* substances that may "pave the way" for cancer; and then exposure to *promoters,* carcinogens, or cancer-causing agents.

❑ Improving the Odds

The risk of cancer substantially increases with age. Studies have shown that your risk of developing cancer approximately doubles in every decade you reach past the age of 25.

Knowledge and action are the keys to lowering these statistics. To achieve this, cancer awareness must replace cancer fear in the public's mind as the first step toward prevention and early detection.

Treatment methods are improving and survival rates for some cancers are rising steadily. Continued research is essential, but a better understanding and application of prevention techniques can also do much and is obviously the preferred alternative. Some experts estimate that environmental factors—including overexposure to sun, smoking, alcohol, diet and exposure to other carcinogenic substances—account for the majority of cancers in this country, and that a majority of those cases could be avoided by responsible attention to health promotion by everyone.

▪ *Smoking*

If the claim that reducing cancer risk substantially is within the power of the general population sounds extravagant, a look at the statistics on lung cancer may provide supporting evidence. Of the 144,000 annual cases of lung cancer—a cancer with one of the lowest five-year survival rates, at 13 percent—the American Cancer Society estimates that 100,000 could be prevented if no one smoked. Lung cancer is now the number-one cancer killer of both sexes, having recently surpassed breast cancer in women, because of an increase in smoking among women. Tobacco is commonly blamed as the primary cause of lung cancer, but it is also implicated in cancers of the mouth, throat, larynx, esophagus, pancreas and bladder. And cigarette smoking enhances one's risk to other environmental hazards. Asbestos exposure, for example, places a person at risk for lung cancer, but in conjunction with smoking, that risk is substantially increased. The same is true for smoking, combined with exposure to other substances that may contribute to lung cancer, including coal, iron ore and nickel dust, to name a few. (See Table 12:1, Agents Associated with Lung Cancer.)

Not only the simple incidence of lung cancer but the death rate from lung cancer is higher among smokers; those who smoke two or more packs of cigarettes a day face a 15 to 25 percent higher mortality rate than nonsmokers. Risk increases with the number of years the person has smoked, the number of cigarettes smoked per day, and the tar and nicotine content of the cigarettes. There-

Agents Associated with Lung Cancer

Although cigarette smoking is implicated in the large majority of lung cancers, other agents that increase susceptibility include:

- radioisotopes
- mustard gas
- asbestos dust
- polycyclic aromatic hydrocarbons
- halogen ethers
- nickel dust
- chromium dust
- inorganic arsenic
- iron ore
- wood dust
- leather-tanning agents
- isopropyl oil
- vinyl chloride
- printing ink (possibly)
- textile dye (possibly)

Table 12:1

fore, the single most effective strategy for preventing lung cancer is unquestionably to stop smoking.

Although cigarette smoking is the primary factor in lung cancer, cigar and pipe smoking substantially increase the risk of other cancers, such as those of the mouth, lip, tongue, pharynx, larynx and esophagus. Smokeless tobacco—moist "dip" tobacco and loose-leaf chewing tobacco—significantly increase the risk of mouth and throat cancers.

PASSIVE SMOKING

Evidence is mounting that those who are around smokers suffer health risks as well. Nicotine has been found in the saliva and urine of nonsmokers who were exposed to smoke in a work environment. Some studies have suggested that the spouses of heavy smokers have twice the risk of developing lung cancer as those of nonsmokers, but the data is not yet conclusive and further studies are needed.

A SAFE CIGARETTE?

Although the risk of lung cancer increases with the number of cigarettes smoked, there is no "safe" level of smoking. The risk of cancer for a light smoker is always greater than that for a nonsmoker, although somewhat less than that of a heavy smoker. The introduction of low tar and nicotine (less than 15 milligrams of tar per cigarette) and ultralow-tar (0 to 10 milligrams of tar per cigarette) brands may have given some people a false sense of security about their smoking habit. Although the low-tar brands may carry a lower risk than the high-tar brands, the difference is one of degree, not substance. And there is evidence that those who smoke the low-tar brands smoke more cigarettes, inhale more deeply and take more puffs per cigarette, thus negating whatever benefit might have come from the low-tar cigarette.

SMOKELESS TOBACCO

Many people, especially young athletes, have the mistaken notion that snuff or other forms of smokeless tobacco are safer than cigarettes. Research has found that, on the contrary, in addition to being highly addictive—some people find it is harder to quit using smokeless tobacco than to give up cigarettes—snuff and other forms of chewed tobacco are associated with a high risk of mouth and throat cancers.

STOPPING

True or False: If a person smokes, the damage to his or her body has been made and therefore he or she will derive no benefit from ceasing to smoke.

False. Such reasoning is absolutely groundless. It is immediately beneficial to stop smoking. Studies have shown that even if some damage from smoking has taken place, if the smoker quits, the body is able to repair damaged cells with normal ones. In general, the risk reduction experienced by ex-smokers will be related to their number of tobacco-free years. "Complete" recovery seems to take ten to fifteen years, at which time ex-smokers may have only half the risk of dying from lung cancer as smokers, although they will still be at slightly higher risk than those who have never smoked. Various methods and strategies for stopping smoking are given in Chapter 3, Breaking Bad Habits.

▪ *Caffeine*

A preliminary study at the University of California at San Diego suggests that drinking more than two cups of coffee a day increases the risk of colorectal cancer, especially in older people. Since tea and soft drinks that contain caffeine do not seem to have the same negative effect, it appears that another subsance in coffee may be responsible. More research is needed in this area before any definite conclusions can be drawn.

▪ *Sun Exposure*

Overexposure to the sun is considered to be a factor in almost all cases of non-melanoma skin cancers, of which there are 400,000 cases a year in the United States. These cancers—basal cell carcinoma and squamous cell carcinoma—are almost always cured once correctly diagnosed. Caucasian heritage, fair complexion and living near the equator are also risk factors (see Table 12:2). Sun exposure has also been shown to be a factor in malignant melanoma, a relatively rare cancer that has been increasing dramatically in the United States in recent decades (see Table 12:3). The mortality rate from melanoma, which strikes those over 45 most frequently, is about 20 percent. People at high risk of skin cancer can observe simple protective measures listed in Table 12:4.

▪ *Radiation*

Exposure to ionizing radiation can come from diagnostic radiology (X-rays), nuclear medicine and radiation therapy. Medically, X-rays are invaluable diagnostic aids and can reveal the need for lifesaving interventions. Mammography (X-ray examination of the breast), for example, can detect very early a tumor that is too small to show up on physical examination. Computerized tomography helps identify the location of brain tumors. For this reason, no one should refuse any necessary X-ray procedure recommended by a physician. But in response to the overall increase in use and types of diagnostic radiology, guidelines to limit unnecessary X-ray exposure have been developed. (See Table 12:5, Avoiding Unnecessary X-ray Exposure.)

Nuclear medicine, which uses radioactive chemicals to diagnose abnormalities in organs and tissues, exposes the whole body to short-term radiation and should be used only when it is essential to the diagnosis, not as an extra test.

Radiation therapy should be used only when there is a confirmed diagnosis of cancer and the radiation therapist and physician have evaluated its usefulness.

Skin Cancer and Sun Exposure

Skin Type	Reaction	Susceptibility
I	Always burns, never tans	Highest
II	Always burns or tans less than average	High
III	Mild burn, tans about average	Average
IV	No burn, tans more than average	Low

Table 12:2

Warning Signs of Malignant Melanoma

Melanomas may develop from moles or pigmented cells known as melanocytes. Experts recommend monthly at-home skin examinations using a good light source and spouse or friend to check areas that cannot be seen. Early signs of melanoma include:

- Asymmetrical moles
- Irregularly defined borders
- Multicolored skin growths. Colors may vary in a single area from tan to brown or black. Red, blue or white areas may also be present
- Moles having a diameter larger than 6 millimeters—about the size of a pencil eraser
- Spread of pigmentation from the edge of mole onto the skin
- Scaling, crusting, ulceration or bleeding of skin
- Persistent itching, tenderness or pain in or near a mole
- Sudden appearance of new moles or skin spots

Table 12:3

Protective Measures Against Skin Cancer

- Avoid sunbathing between the hours of 10 A.M. and 3 P.M., when the sun's rays are strongest.
- Wear protective clothing such as a hat and long-sleeved shirt.
- Use a sun-blocking agent such as PABA (para-aminobenzoic acid) with an SPF (sun-protector factor) rating of 15 or higher. Sunscreen should be applied one hour before going out in the sun and reapplied after swimming or perspiring heavily.
- Examine your skin regularly and have a doctor check any suspicious moles or sores that do not heal.

Table 12:4

Avoiding Unnecessary X-ray Exposure

- If abdominal or intestinal X-rays are needed, the sexual organs should be shielded whenever possible
- The X-ray film should not be larger than the area to be examined and the beam should fall only on the film.
- Dental X-rays should be done only on an "as needed" basis and the patient always should wear a protective lead shield. The dentist or dental technician should also follow protective techniques.
- Many patients view an X-ray as the first step in a diagnosis. But often diagnoses are made using a patient history, physical exam or blood testing. Let the physician decide whether an X-ray is appropriate, rather than requesting one yourself.
- Keep a record of when and where X-rays were taken as well as the purpose.
- If you live in a state where X-ray records are destroyed after seven years, be sure to request that the X-rays or reports be sent to your home. If you will be changing physicians, make sure your previous doctor releases the records to the new one.
- Fluoroscopy, in which a contrast material is used to provide a clearer outline of selected areas, delivers a larger dose of radiation than X-ray film does. Alternate means should be considered unless this test is an essential part of a procedure, such as in an upper GI series or barium enema.
- X-rays should be taken only by an accredited X-ray technician or a radiologist.

Table 12:5

▪ *Occupational Carcinogenic Hazards*

Awareness and caution are the keys to limiting risk from occupational exposure to carcinogens. (See Table 12:6, Occupational Groups Associated with High Risks for Cancer.) The Occupational Safety and Health Administration (OSHA) issues and enforces workplace standards, conducts on-site inspections and deals with complaints about violations from workers.

Employees have an obligation to become familiar with the safety standards of their company and to comply with all health and safety rules. Workers must also be careful not to carry hazardous materials home on their clothing or body. Protective clothing worn in the workplace should not be brought home to be washed.

Occupational Groups Associated with High Risks for Cancer

Occupational Group	Site(s)
Benzoyl chloride manufacture	Lung
Chemists	Brain Lymphatic and hematopoietic (blood-forming) tissue Pancreas
Coal miners	Stomach
Coke by-product plant workers	Colon Pancreas
Foundry workers	Lung
Leather workers	Bladder Larynx Mouth Pharynx
Metal miners	Lung
Oil refinery/ petrochemical workers	Blood (leukemia) Brain Esophagus Lung Multiple myeloma Stomach
Painters	Blood (leukemia)
Printing workers	Lung Mouth Pharynx
Rubber industry workers	Bladder Blood (leukemia) Brain Lung Prostate Stomach
Textile workers	Nasal cavity and sinuses
Woodworkers	Lymphatic tissue Nasal cavity and sinuses

Source: Adapted from Daniel Miller, M.D., "Cancer Prevention: Steps You Can Take," in *The American Cancer Society Cancer Book* (New York: Doubleday, 1986).

Table 12:6

Any possible violations or health hazards should be reported to a supervisor and/or to OSHA. Questions about the safety of a particular chemical may be directed to OSHA. To further ensure employee safety, many states now have "right to know" laws that require the employer to divulge the makeup of chemicals used in the workplace upon an employee's request. If there is a question about the safety of a chemical, contact OSHA.

▪ *Heredity*

In addition to age and environmental hazards, heredity can influence a person's cancer risk quotient. Again, if a person's family history places him or her in a high-risk category, it is simply another reason for increased vigilance, not panic. A person with a family history of cancer has even more reason to take steps to avoid known cancer-causing substances, such as tobacco, and to arrange with the physician for special cancer screening.

Certain cancers seem to show more of a hereditary connection than others: cancer of the breast, colon and rectum, endometrium, lung, prostate, stomach and possibly the ovaries. Hereditary risk increases with the number of close relatives a person has who have developed cancer. Some studies have shown that a woman whose mother or sister had cancer in both breasts has a much greater risk of developing cancer than if the relative had cancer in only one breast. Recent research suggests that people may inherit a susceptibility to certain cancer-causing agents.

There are some cancers for which a clear genetic tendency has been identified: retinoblastoma, a rare cancer of the eye thought to be due to an absence of two protective genes; and medullary carcinoma, a rare cancer of the thyroid. Familial polyposis, also rare, is a condition that predisposes people to develop polyps in the colon and eventually to develop colon cancer. Hereditary malignant melanoma is signaled by the development of moles on the body. People at risk must routinely scrutinize any moles and report any change in color or size immediately to a physician.

The importance of individual responsibility borne by a person with a known genetic tendency to develop cancer is illustrated by the risk for lung cancer in those with a family history of the disease. The risk for such an individual—one whose parent, sibling or child has had lung cancer—is approximately three times more than that of the general population. If that person also smokes cigarettes, however, his risk may be fifteen times greater than that of the general population.

The influence of heredity makes an accurate medical and family history extremely important. With this information on hand, the physician and patient can investigate lifestyle changes that may reduce the risk of cancer and initiate screening programs that will help detect cancer in the early stages. A woman whose mother or sister has had breast cancer, for instance, should have more frequent mammograms than a normal-risk woman and should have her breasts examined twice yearly by a physician, in addition to a careful monthly self-examination.

All of the above factors—personal habits, heredity, environmental influences—affect a person's individual tendency to get cancer; therefore anything that falls into the "risk" category, such as smoking or heavy drinking, should be made known to the physician. Early detection of cancer is a joint project between physician and patient—but the success of such a project rests heavily on the patient.

▪ *Nutrition and Cancer*

The precise role of nutrition in cancer is unknown, but many experts think that dietary factors can increase the risk of some types of cancer among susceptible people. Both the American Cancer Society and the National Cancer Institute have proposed dietary guidelines aimed at lowering cancer risk (see Table 12:7). These guidelines are very similar to the

Dietary Guidelines

In addition to avoiding obesity and reducing fat intake, dietary guidelines recommended by the American Cancer Society include:

- Eat more high-fiber foods. In the past, some people have interpreted this as a call to add large amounts of bran to food. This should be avoided; recent studies indicate that an excess of bran may actually promote rather than prevent colon cancer. A balanced consumption of whole-grain cereals and breads, fruits and vegetables will provide a variety of fiber, as well as essential vitamins and minerals.
- Include foods rich in vitamins A and C in the diet. Dark green and deep yellow vegetables and yellow fruits are rich in beta carotene, a form of vitamin A. Studies indicate that this may be protective against cancer of the larynx, esophagus and lung. People who consume adequate vitamin C (ascorbic acid) have a lower incidence of stomach and esophageal cancers. Ascorbic acid blocks production of nitrosamines, which are carcinogenic. A word of warning, however: These vitamins should come from the diet instead of high-dose supplements. Megadoses of vitamin A can be highly toxic; excessive vitamin C may increase the risk of urinary irritation.
- Include cruciferous vegetables—members of the mustard family, such as broccoli, Brussels sprouts, kohlrabi and cauliflower—in the diet. These foods are believed to lower the risk of cancers of the gastrointestinal and respiratory tracts.
- Be moderate in consumption of alcoholic beverages. Heavy drinkers, especially those who also smoke, are at high risk of developing cancers of the mouth, larynx and esophagus. Alcoholism is also associated with an increased risk of liver cancer, as well as of cirrhosis and other liver diseases.
- Be moderate in consumption of salt-cured, smoked or nitrate-cured foods, such as hams, bacon or smoked fish. These foods absorb some of the tars that result from incomplete burning during smoking. The tars are similar to those found in cigarettes. Charcoal broiling deposits cancer-causing substances, such as benzopyrene, on the surface of foods, and also should be used in moderation.

Table 12:7

dietary recommendations of the American Heart Association and also are in line with what is recommended for people with diabetes.

A high-fat intake, as it is in heart disease, appears to be the dietary factor with the strongest established association with cancer. Diets high in animal fats or saturated fats are associated with an increased risk of cancers of the heart, prostate, large bowel and colon. Some laboratory studies indicate that total caloric intake may be at least as important as the amount of fat, and restricting calories may inhibit tumor growth.

Obesity increases the risk of developing many health problems, including cancer. Cancers of the colon, rectum and prostate are more common in obese men, and cancers of the gallbladder, bile passages, breast, cervix, ovaries and uterus are more common in obese women. Some studies indicate that the location of fat may be more significant than its quantity: Fat centered around the waist, abdomen and upper body appears to present greater health risks than fat in the hips or thighs. Fat in these areas is believed to be more "mobile"—it is more readily broken down—and also contributes more to high serum cholesterol than fat located elsewhere in the body.

High levels of protein in the diet may be associated with some cancers, although the data is not conclusive. Since most diets very high in protein are also high in fats, it is difficult to isolate protein as the cancer link. Alcohol may contribute to development of cancers of the gastrointestinal tract, liver, head, neck and esophagus. Excessive beer drinking has been associated with risk of colorectal cancer.

The American Cancer Society emphasizes that "the optimal diet cannot yet be defined, but there is abundant evidence that the usual American diet is not optimal and this is adequate reason to recommend modification."

Several other nutrients have been linked to a possible lowered risk of cancer, but not enough evidence is available to say for certain that they are beneficial. For example, vitamin E blocks the production of cancer-causing nitrosamines as well as provides other necessary functions. Vitamin E and selenium, both natural antioxidants, are being studied for their ability to inhibit tumor production, particularly in chemically induced cancers. Many health-food stores and faddists urge that people take vitamin E and selenium supplements, but a well-balanced diet contains abundant sources of both nutrients and taking large amounts of any vitamin or mineral can be hazardous.

Although there is no indication that high iron intake has a preventive effect against cancer, iron deficiency has been associated with cancer of the upper alimentary tract and possibly gastric cancer. Since iron is important to overall health, the diet should provide adequate sources of this mineral.

❑ Detection and Screening

The older person should regard his or her increased risk of cancer not as a reason for fatalism or an excuse to let nature take its course, but instead as an incentive to be particularly alert and responsible regarding health maintenance. Early detection is the next best thing to prevention. The long-term survival rates for patients with localized cancer are dramatically higher than in those with regional spread, a testimony to the effectiveness of early detection.

As a rule, patients with widespread cancer have the lowest chances of survival. Although the nature of the specific cancer also affects how fast it spreads, most adult tumors are slow-growing. Therefore, delay in seeking diagnosis or treatment must be singled out as the major obstacle to early detection and a contributing factor to mortality.

Early detection affects not only the cure rate for cancer but can also have an impact on the treatment. Depending on the stage (extent) of the cancer, treatment may be short-term and relatively nonintrusive, or radical and intrusive.

Early Warning Signs of Cancer

- Change in bowel or bladder habits
- A sore that does not heal
- Unusual bleeding or discharge
- Thickening or lump in breast or elsewhere
- Indigestion or difficulty in swallowing
- Obvious change in wart or mole
- Nagging cough or hoarseness

Table 12:8

Two components in a successful early detection program are the individual's self-monitoring program and the periodic cancer screening undertaken by health professionals as part of a regular health maintenance regimen. Everyone should be familiar with the warning signs of cancer publicized by the American Cancer Society (see Table 12:8).

If any of these symptoms are present, medical attention should be sought immediately. Delay or denial can greatly increase risk of death if cancer is present, and can cause needless apprehension if the symptom does not turn out to signal cancer. Eighty percent of breast lumps detected by women during self-examination, for instance, are noncancerous.

However, these symptoms are not necessarily signs of an *early* stage of cancer. That's the value of a regular cancer-screening program: It may detect cancer *before* symptoms appear, when the cancer is in a *very* early stage and chances of cure are highest.

Smoking, diet and sun exposure are environmental factors that are within a person's control. Others, such as radiation, occupational hazards and heredity, may not be completely within individual control but merit your attention and can usually be improved on. It is important to know if you are in a high-risk category and to inform your physician of any special aggravating conditions or predispositions you may have to cancer, so that a special screening program can be initiated on your behalf.

Cancer Therapies

Three major types of treatment for cancer exist, all of which may be used singly or in combination. The nature of the cancer, the stage at which it is discovered, the likelihood of spread, and a person's age and degree of risk all influence the treatment approach.

Surgery

Surgery is considered the most effective treatment when the cancer is localized and there is the possibility of completely removing the tumor. Surgery may also be used to reduce the size of a tumor so that it will respond more effectively to radiation and chemotherapy. Advances in surgical techniques have led not only to an improved cure rate for some types of cancer but have made some cancer surgery less disfiguring and traumatic than it was in the past. The therapy is not appropriate for widespread cancer or for cancers involving vital organs, such as the heart, although it may be used in advanced cancer to reduce the size of a tumor and relieve symptoms rather than as a cure.

Depending on the location and extent of the cancer, the consequences of surgery may require major accommodations from the patient. The physician should thoroughly explain what the results of the surgery will be before the operation and any adjustments the patient will have to make to it. If the bladder, colon or rectum is involved, for instance, an ileal conduit (an opening in the abdomen for urine) or a colostomy (an opening for feces) may be required. If a mastectomy is performed for breast cancer, a prosthesis or breast reconstruction is often desirable. The patient should make sure he or she understands what is involved in the procedure and why it is necessary. The physician should also inform the patient of the availability of any support groups responding to his or her particular type of cancer and anticipated treatment.

Radiation

Although it has been known for some time that radiation can kill cancer cells, refinements in technique have made this method more effective and have reduced side effects. Radiation therapy may be delivered in the form of beams of X-rays from a machine directed at the tumor or as implants of radioactive substances placed into a body cavity or tumor, either permanently or temporarily. Radiation therapy destroys the cancer cell's ability to reproduce. Some cancers, such as that of the lymph nodes, are more responsive to radiation therapy than others.

Although this treatment is sometimes the sole therapy, it is most often used in conjunction with surgery and/or chemotherapy. Surgery, for instance, is often used to remove a large cancerous mass and then followed with radiation treatments to destroy the individual cancer cells left behind. Radiation is also used when the tumor cannot be removed surgically because it is too large or has involved vital organs. Preoperative radiation is currently being used on occasion to reduce the chance that cancer cells will spread through the bloodstream during or after surgery.

The goal of treatment is to deliver the largest amount of radiation to the tumor while causing minimal damage to normal tissue. To do this, the beam is directed at the cancer itself in divided doses given over several sessions rather than in one large dose, which would cause lethal damage to the whole body. Computerized tomography (CT scan, formerly called CAT scan) and ultrasound are developments that help the therapist verify the exact location of the tumor, thus providing a more precise target for radiation and reducing unnecessary exposure of other tissues. Lead shields are also used whenever possible to protect surrounding tissues.

COPING WITH SOME COMMON SIDE EFFECTS

Some people fear cancer treatment such as radiation as much as they do the disease. The complications and discomfort one experiences, however, have been blown out of proportion. Over the years, improved techniques have minimized side effects and strategies have been developed to deal with those that do occur. (See Table 12:9, Overcoming Side Effects of Radiation Therapy.)

▪ *Chemotherapy*

Chemotherapy is the use of anticancer drugs, usually in combination, to kill cancer cells throughout the body. It is given orally in pill or liquid form or intravenously. It may be used alone, for instance in the treatment of leukemia, or in combination with surgery and/or radiation to treat other cancers. Different anticancer drugs disrupt cell function in different ways. (See Table 12:10, Major Types of Anticancer Drugs.) They are used together to increase the overall effectiveness of the attack on the cancer cells and to reduce the chance that cancer cells will be resistant in some stage of their development to one class of drug. Combining the drugs also helps balance out the toxicity of individual agents. Since chemotherapy attacks rapidly growing cancer cells during the cell division process, it is most effective against small, fast-growing tumors (see Table 12:11). Large tumors, which have

Overcoming Side Effects of Radiation Therapy

Nausea/vomiting
- Antinausea drugs
- Self-hypnosis
- Relaxation techniques
- Small, frequent feedings rather than regular meals

Mouth sores
- Avoid irritating liquids such as alcohol, orange or grapefruit juice. Instead, drink water, grape juice, apple juice—and eat bland foods that are neither too hot nor too cold
- Use lip balm
- Gentle but thorough oral hygiene using soft nylon toothbrush and baking soda solution rather than harsh toothpaste

Skin problems
- For red skin, use vitamin A and D ointment or mild hydrocortisone cream, if physician approves
- For dry peeling, use cornstarch
- For moist peeling, use mild saline soaks and gentle soap and water to remove dead skin
- Use sun-blocking agent to prevent burning if sun exposure cannot be avoided
- Wear soft, loose-fitting clothing to avoid irritating friction

Postirradiation cataracts
- Wear protective eye covering during treatments

Table 12:9

Major Types of Anticancer Drugs

- *Alkylating agents.* Interfere with cell division by damaging the genetic material in the cell.
- *Antimetabolites.* Substitute for substances required for cell growth, impairing the cancer cell's ability to divide.
- *Antibiotics.* Disrupt cancer cell function by altering the manufacture or repair of genetic material. Antibiotics used in cancer treatment are highly toxic and not given to fight bacterial infections.
- *Plant alkaloids.* Derived mainly from periwinkle plants; prevent cell division by inhibiting the formation of proteins necessary for reproduction.

Table 12:10

Cancers That May Sometimes Be Cured with Chemotherapy

- Acute lymphocytic leukemia (ALL) in children
- Acute myelogenous leukemia (AML)
- Burkitt's lymphoma
- Choriocarcinoma
- Diffuse histiocytic lymphoma
- Embryonal rhabdomyosarcoma
- Ewing's sarcoma
- Hodgkin's disease
- Nodular mixed lymphoma
- Ovarian carcinoma
- Testicular carcinoma
- Wilms's tumor

Table 12:11

more resting or nondividing cells, may be resistant to this treatment. Chemotherapy is also sometimes used in cases of advanced cancer, not as a curative therapy but rather to relieve discomfort and symptoms.

Adjuvant chemotherapy, given after surgery, for example, is used as a precautionary measure taken when it is unclear whether or not the cancer may have spread.

COMMON SIDE EFFECTS

Today researchers have learned that different ways of administering chemotherapy may reduce toxic side effects of certain drugs. For example, one antibiotic, Adriamycin (generic name, doxorubicin), used in treating a number of cancers, is far less damaging to the heart muscle when given very slowly over a longer period of time than when given faster over a shorter period. However, most anticancer drugs commonly have adverse side effects regardless of the way in which they are administered. For example, most cause nausea and vomiting (see Table 12:12), although this tends to be temporary and can be controlled in most patients.

Bone marrow suppression usually begins immediately after a session of chemotherapy and builds over a period of days or weeks. Bone marrow normally produces white blood cells to fight infection, red blood cells and platelets; these functions are hindered after chemotherapy. A person with bone marrow suppression is at high risk for infection, anemia and, possibly, serious bleeding. A second course of chemotherapy is generally not given until the blood count—an indication of bone marrow function—returns to normal.

Many patients find that hair loss, although temporary, is one of the most personally devastating effects of cancer therapy, and it may occur with both radiation treatments and chemotherapy. The rapidly growing hair cells are a natural target for the chemotherapeutic agents. Patients will experience different degrees of hair loss, from a slight thinning to complete loss of hair. Hair usually begins to grow back within just a few weeks after the last course of chemotherapy. With radiation, however, the loss of hair roots in the radiated area may be permanent. Some new techniques may minimize hair loss, depending on the drugs being used and the type of cancer: A cold compress, or "ice turban," restricts circulation to the head and will help keep the drugs from reaching scalp hair follicles. Scalp tourniquets have also been used. (See Table 12:13, Protecting Your Hair During Chemotherapy.)

Some Strategies to Overcome Nausea During Cancer Chemotherapy

- Use antinausea drugs
- Practice self-hypnosis
- Practice relaxation techniques
- Take small, frequent feedings rather than regular meals
- Time chemotherapy at night rather than during the day
- Avoid preparing food yourself
- Eat food that is cool or at room temperature, to minimize food odors

Table 12:12

Protecting Your Hair During Chemotherapy

When chemotherapy is ongoing and after hair starts to grow back in, measures can be taken to protect the hair:

- Have hair cut in an easy-to-manage style.
- Use a mild protein-based shampoo, cream rinse and conditioner every four to seven days.
- Avoid using electric hair dryers, or use only at the coolest setting.
- Avoid electric curlers, curling irons, hair clips, elastic bands, hair or bobby pins, hair spray and dye.
- Avoid excessive brushing and combing; they put stress on the hair.

Table 12:13

Hormonal Therapy

High doses of natural and synthetic steroid hormones may be used to treat cancers such as lymphomas, certain breast cancers and some leukemias. They may also be used to relieve symptoms of other cancers due to swelling of tissues. Alternatively, hormone-blocking drugs may be used to treat cancers that are dependent on hormones for growth, or that occur in hormone-producing glands. Side effects of steroid hormones include increased blood sugar, hypertension, swelling of the face and extremities, easy skin bruising, loss of bone density and increased susceptibility to infection.

Staging of Cancer

An essential part of the diagnostic process involves determining how far the cancer has spread into regional tissues or distant organs. (See Table 12:14, Staging of Cancer.) Staging is a factor in deciding which type of treatment is most appropriate. Surgical removal is generally considered curative for a localized tumor, for instance, but chemotherapy is the preferred alternative for widespread cancer cells. Staging also helps predict the future course of the disease. In the past, patients with a certain type of cancer may have been diagnosed at a certain point in the disease where there may have been undetectable metastases. Therapy to attack such residual cancer cells will now be automatically prescribed for new patients with the same stage cancer. Diagnostic procedures that help identify the stage may include X-rays, computerized tomography, biopsy and laboratory tests.

Staging of Cancer

Numerical	Degree of Spread	Alphabetical
I	No spread to regional lymph nodes or distant organs. The primary tumor is designated T and followed by numbers to describe size.	A
II	Primary tumor, T, plus spread to regional lymph nodes, N, followed by numbers to describe extent.	B
III	Primary tumor, T, with or without spread to lymph nodes, N, and spread to distant organs, or metastases, M, followed by numbers to describe extent.	C

Table 12:14

Experimental Therapies/New Directions

Cancer research branches out into several directions—prevention, efforts to improve cure rates (including techniques for early detection) and efforts to improve the quality of life of cancer patients (including the development of effective but less mutilating surgical procedures, more potent pain control methods and techniques for reducing the side effects of treatments). A variety of techniques and substances now being studied in the research phase are showing promise for future effectiveness.

IMMUNOTHERAPY

Research in this area focuses on ways to activate the body's own ability to fight off and control maligant cells without damaging normal cells, either by strengthening the body's immune system or by developing vaccines to the same end.

Interferon comes under the category of immunotherapy. A natural product of the body's cells that aids in resisting viral infection, interferon also has a regulatory effect on the growth of cells, called an antiproliferative effect. There is some evidence that this twofold ability to confer immunity and control cell growth may make interferon an effective cancer therapy. Interferon has been approved by the Food and Drug Administration for the treatment of a rare type of leukemia, hairy-cell leukemia. Previously very expensive and in short supply, interferon is now being produced through genetic engineering. Despite the heavy media attention this potential therapy has received, it is important to realize it is still in the experimental stage. Evidence to support its efficacy is promising in some areas and disappointing in others.

HYPERTHERMIA

Research has shown that cancer cells are more susceptible to the effects of changes in temperature than are normal cells. Hyperthermia therapy is the use of heat to kill malignant cells. The use of total body hyperthermia is limited because extreme heat may also injure normal cells—although not at the same rate as cancer cells—and because it is extremely uncomfortable for the patient. The effect of heat in combination with chemotherapy and radiation is under investigation.

However, *localized* hyperthermia directs heat to a specific area using techniques such as diathermy, ultrasound, radio waves and microwaves. By confining the heat to the tumor area, many of the negative side effects of whole-body hyperthermia can be avoided. Both methods are still considered experimental, but they look promising for the future.

MONOCLONAL ANTIBODIES

One experimental therapy that seems to hold out hope of the broadest potential for use in cancer management is monoclonal antibody technology. These laboratory-developed antibodies combine a normal antibody-producing cell, known as a plasma cell, with a cancerous cell. The resulting hybridoma, as it is known, seeks out specific targets on cancer cells. When successful, hybridomas will produce large quantities of site-specific antibodies (depending on the initial antibody used) for a long period of time. Most hybridomas today are produced from mouse antibodies.

Monoclonal antibodies have potential in both the diagnosis and treatment of cancer. Specific antibodies for a certain type of cancer can be made with a radioactive iodine which is injected into a patient's bloodstream. The antibodies should attach themselves to the cancer cells and thus reveal the location of the cancer when x-rayed.

Treatment possibilities include using monoclonal antibodies to destroy or damage cancer cells, to deliver anticancer drugs directly to cancer cells and to deactivate the growth substance that is secreted by cancer cells.

There are still many unanswered questions in monoclonal antibody research. For one thing, most monoclonal antibodies have been derived from mice and could cause serious side effects or death if injected into humans. Researchers are working on producing human hybridomas, but there are many problems to be resolved. Nevertheless, this field of investigation offers many far-reaching possibilities.

▪ *Other Advances*

Cancer researchers are exploring numerous other areas that promise improvements in diagnosis and treatments in the next few years. These include:

- Improvements in the technique of bone marrow transplantation for patients with leukemia
- More effective methods of pain control
- Research into interrupting the two-stage process of cancer development
- Infection control
- Identification of HTLV (human T-cell leukemia virus) and research into a

vaccine to prevent this type of cancer
- More refined techniques for early detection (thermography, ultrasound, diaphonoscopy)

Questionable Therapies

Over the years claims of cancer "cures" have been made for a variety of substances, ranging from apricot pits to carrot juice, and techniques, ranging from relaxation and imagery exercises to the Orgone Energy Accelerator. Even otherwise harmless claims are dangerous in the long run if people refuse traditional, proven treatment in favor of the unproven and thus give the cancer time to spread unchecked. Moreover, many of these alternative cancer treatments are offered in settings or in forms that free them from institutionalized consumer protection regulations, leaving the consumer open to exploitation and experimentation. Many alleged cancer preventives and/or cures are marketed in ways that, while in accordance with the letter of the law, contradict its spirit. For instance, it is illegal for unproven claims to appear on a product. As a result, in many "alternative" stores, pamphlets promoting certain substances are found on shelves in one part of the store and the corresponding products in another part. The American Cancer Society reviews unproven methods of cancer treatment and will make its evaluation of the method available to you on request. Check with your local chapter.

Laetrile therapy has received the most public attention in recent years. Made from the extract of apricot pits, laetrile contains cyanide and is supposed to "kill" cancer cells. A national clinical trial conducted by the National Cancer Institute offered no support for this theory. And some individuals who have gone the laetrile route have shown signs of cyanide poisoning.

Nutritional gimmickery seems to provide the richest source for these "instant cures." Many health-food stores or mail-order houses package a specific nutrient as a cancer cure, for instance, vitamins A or C. The problem is, the research indicating possible health benefits from these sources is usually based on studies using sensible portions of foods containing the nutrients; the findings are perverted by the mail-order house to suggest that concentrated megadoses of the vitamin are even more helpful. On the contrary, such "therapy" may be toxic.

EVALUATING CLAIMS FOR UNKNOWN THERAPIES

Dr. Victor Herbert, a noted nutritionist, hematologist and authority on medical fraud, suggests asking the following questions to determine whether an unconventional cancer treatment is legitimate:

- Is the therapy based on personal observation or can it withstand examination by other scientists?
- Was it tested in controlled studies against a placebo to rule out patient suggestibility? Could the "effect" be attributed simply to the expected course of the disorder or to the fact that the patient really did not have cancer?
- Has its safety been tested? Is the risk-to-benefit ratio worthwhile?
- Has research on the therapy been published in scientific journals and reviewed and verified by professional peers?

Some suggested therapies do no damage in themselves and may indeed be helpful with certain aspects of cancer management, particularly the psychological stress associated with the disease and some treatments. The Simonton technique is of the "mind over matter" variety and consists of a series of mental exercises that will supposedly help the patient control his or her cancer. Biofeedback can alter brain waves and blood pressure, and the theory is that the immune system, too, may be influenced by mental control. Although patients who have a fighting attitude toward their disease seem, in some studies, better able to cope, there is no current conclusive evidence that the immune system responds to positive thinking. Relaxation and visual imagery techniques, when used in conjunction with standard cancer treatments, may be helpful in controlling the psychological distress and even some of the physiological side effects, such as nausea. On the other hand, people should not accept the idea that they have had some part in causing their cancer, due to some personality trait or pattern of thinking.

Your physician, your local branch of the American Cancer Society, the National Cancer Institute and the Food and Drug Administration are all good sources of information regarding unfamiliar treatments. Your next-door neighbor, a clerk at the health-food store and magazine advertisements are not.

❑ Living with Cancer

One of the effects of improved treatment methods and higher cancer survival rates is that more attention is finally being paid to a significant aspect of cancer that was often ignored or underemphasized in the past—the psychosocial aspect of living with a cancer diagnosis, either one's own or a family member's. With increasing frequency, health-care professionals and patients themselves are redefining cancer care as something more than the medical management of the disease. Since cancer can now be considered more as a chronic illness than a death sentence, its impact on the daily routine of living, on the patient's interactions with those around him, on work, and on future plans must now be considered an important part of cancer management. A person with cancer now often has to deal with the disease and the stresses of treatment while maintaining as normal a lifestyle as possible. Techniques for coping, support services, counseling and attention to financial and social concerns are now a major part of cancer therapy.

Fear and anxiety are normal responses to any illness, but especially to cancer when, at first, the outcome is uncertain. Hopefully, this fear will motivate the patient to seek out and follow through on medical advice. Sometimes, however, excessive fear can lead to denial of the disease or rejection of needed treatment. Information and open communication are the keys to dispelling unwarranted fears about cancer and to developing constructive coping strategies. The health-care team is a primary source of information. The patient should openly express any fears, concerns or questions to the physician, nurse or hospital social worker. Some physicians prefer to discuss aspects of the patient's condition and treatment with a family member present to encourage discussion and prevent misunderstandings.

The patient with cancer should also look to family members for support and discuss his or her concerns and expectations with them honestly, as well as listen to theirs. If family members have moved away or died, close friends can provide the needed communication network. People from work, social, community or church groups may turn out to provide unexpected support.

Numerous organizations will provide information and counseling to cancer patients as well as help with transportation and financial advice. (See Table 12:15, Sources of Help.) Many of them will put the cancer patient in touch with someone who has already experienced what the patient is going through. Facts and

Sources of Help

American Cancer Society
National Headquarters
90 Park Avenue
New York, NY 10016
212-736-3030

Local chapters are listed in the white pages of the telephone directory. The following organizations, sponsored by the society, can be contacted by calling your local A.C.S. chapter; or for those with national headquarters, at the addresses listed:

I Can Cope
Educates patients and families about cancer and how to deal with psychological stresses.

CanSurmount
Uses volunteers to provide patients and families with current information.

Reach to Recovery
Volunteer organization staffed by former breast cancer patients. Volunteers make in-hospital and home visits to women who have had mastectomies and provide both emotional support and practical information on breast reconstruction and other aspects of rehabilitation.

International Association of Laryngectomees
Information on resources; members visit hospitalized patients.

Ronald McDonald Houses
℅ Golin Harris Communications, Inc.
500 North Michigan Avenue
Chicago, IL 60611
312-836-7129
Provides a place for children and/or their parents to stay during treatment. To locate one near you, call or write A. L. Bud Jones, International Coordinator, at the address above.

The Candelighters Childhood Cancer Foundation
2025 I Street NW, Suite 1011
Washington, DC 20006
202-659-5136
An international organization of self-help groups of parents of children and adolescents with cancer. To locate a group near you, call or write the national office.

Corporate Angel Network
Westchester County Airport, Building One
White Plains, NY 10604
914-328-1313 (nationwide)
Provides free air transportation to and from treatment centers for cancer patients and an accompanying family member on private corporate airplanes. (For patients capable of walking without assistance only. Subject to availability.)

Leukemia Society of America, Inc.
733 Third Avenue
New York, NY 10017
212-573-8484
Provides financial assistance and consultation service.

United Ostomy Association
2001 West Beverly Boulevard
Los Angeles, CA 90057
213-413-5510
Network of volunteers who have an ostomy provides practical advice and emotional support.

Office of Cancer Communications
National Cancer Institute
Building 31, Room 10A18
Bethesda, MD 20205
301-496-5583
Information about the disease, treatment and local resources. Toll-free number for questions about cancer operated by National Cancer Institute: 1-800-4-CANCER

Cancer Care, Inc.
National Cancer Foundation
1180 Avenue of the Americas
New York, NY 10036
Provides counseling on physical and emotional effects of cancer on patients and families.

United Cancer Council, Inc.
650 East Carmel Drive, Suite 340
Indianapolis, IN 46032
Provides financial assistance with medication and treatment costs.

Foundation for Dignity
Cancer Patient's Employment Rights Project
37 South 20th Street, Suite 601
Philadelphia, PA 19103
Provides public and professional information and works to protect legal rights of people with cancer.

Encore
A nationwide program sponsored by the YWCA for women who have had breast cancer surgery. Volunteers provide information, peer support groups and postsurgery exercise programs.

The American Society of Plastic and Reconstructive Surgeons
233 North Michigan Avenue
Chicago, IL 60601
312-856-1834
Provides a patient referral service for those considering reconstructive surgery following cancer or other potentially disfiguring surgery.

Cancer Research Institute, Inc.
144 East 58th Street
New York, NY 10022
212-688-7515
Provides information regarding effects of nutrition in maintaining health and fighting cancer; free nutritional guides and immunological information is also available.

American Society of Clinical Hypnosis
2250 East Devon Avenue
Des Plaines, IL 60018
312-297-3317
Can supply the name of trained clinical hypnotists in your area (psychiatrists, psychologists and social workers).

Table 12:15

perspective ring truer when they come from someone with personal experience of the disease. Also, it may be easier to discuss certain concerns with objective, sympathetic outsiders than with family members or friends.

▪ *When the Diagnosis Comes*

The diagnosis of cancer is a difficult one to absorb at any age, but for middle-aged or older adults, there are some additional burdens to contend with. Middle-aged adults are already dealing with major life changes—changes in physical appearance, the "empty nest" syndrome, the death of parents and/or peers. The older person may be coping with the stresses of retirement and his changing image in his own eyes and in society's, and dealing with aging as well as changes in body image. When a diagnosis of cancer comes at this time of life, it adds to the already present stresses and brings new concerns about financial security and maintaining independence. If a person has successfully adjusted to the changes of middle or old age, he will be in a better position to deal with a diagnosis of cancer. If, however, he or she is still in the process of, or has not been able to face up to, these adjustments, coping with cancer will be an especially difficult task.

People react to a diagnosis of cancer in different ways. Some may want all the information they can get, others may refuse to accept the truth, still others may be able to absorb only small amounts of information at a time. Doctors need to be honest in telling the patient what he or she can expect, but they also need to tailor what they have to say according to the individual's readiness to hear it.

Periods of denial, anger or depression are normal responses to a cancer diagnosis. Counseling and mild tranquilizers may be necessary to help the patient through this initial adjustment period.

It is important to note that no one can accurately predict how long a particular patient will live with cancer. Patients often react to a time limit—for example, "you have six months to live"—as if it were a sentence of death. Doctors should avoid making such statements and patients and family members should refrain from pressing for a time limit. There are numerous cases in which a person given six months or a year to live is doing well long after that.

PAIN—AN OFTEN UNWARRANTED FEAR

Many people believe that cancer will always bring severe pain. In fact, the majority of cancer patients do not have pain or have mild to moderate pain that is easily controlled by drugs. Studies have found that, overall, about 30 to 40 percent of patients have pain, but that this is almost always controlled by readily available medications. Patients with terminal cancer are more likely to experience severe pain than others.

For most effective pain control, medication should be given on a round-the-clock basis, rather than allowing pain to become intense. Due to individual differences, some people metabolize drugs faster than others and may require more frequent medication to keep pain from building up.

Sometimes cancer patients hesitate to ask for pain control drugs because they are afraid of becoming "addicted," or because they feel they would be "giving in" to the pain, or because they are afraid that if the pain medication works now it will be ineffective if the pain gets worse later. Although patients can develop tolerance to a drug, requiring ever-larger doses for the same relief, they do not have the underlying psychological dependence that characterizes addiction. Tolerance can be overcome by switching to another medication from the wide range of available drugs. Besides medication, nerve-blocking measures—injections of local anesthetic, alcohol or severing the nerve—may also be appropriate. The patient and his or her physician should discuss pain control options just as they discussed treatment options in order to come up with a plan that meets the patient's physical and psychological needs. A number of medical centers now have specialized pain clinics to help people with intractable pain. Consult your doctor or major medical center in your area for information. (See Table 12:16, Organizations That Specialize in Pain Control.) Taking medication for mild pain is not "giving in," but can be an important part of coping with cancer. A person who is not in pain will eat better, be more active and generally have a better outlook, which can all contribute to a positive outcome. For terminally ill patients with severe pain, relief can be obtained, while at the same time leaving the individual alert and in contact with others.

REHABILITATION

Rehabilitation after cancer treatment must be both psychological and physical. A short period of "mourning" or depression is normal following any kind of surgery that has changed a person's physical appearance or ability to function. A cancer patient needs some time to reflect on what has happened to him and incorporate it into his life. But if this phase persists, counseling should be sought. The cancer patient needs to begin making the transition back to a normal, active life. Former cancer patients can be of valuable service at this point, offering practical tips on day-to-day living and an understanding ear for the patient's concerns.

Fear of recurrence after successful cancer treatment is not uncommon. The patient should not hesitate to call the physician or other support service if he or she has any questions or simply needs reassurance. This anxiety is normal and will gradually diminish if family and health-care staff respond to the patient's concerns at this time.

Observation indicates that patients who struggle to survive, who cooperate and participate in their treatment and who focus on maintaining a normal existence deal better with cancer. A good attitude and the use of available support services are important.

Organizations That Specialize in Pain Control

American Pain Society
340 Kingsland Street
Nutley, NJ 07110

Committee on Pain Therapy and Acupuncture
American Society of Anesthesiologists
515 Busse Highway
Park Ridge, IL 60068

Committee on the Treatment of Intractable Pain
2001 S Street NW, Suite 302
Washington, DC 20009

International Association for the Study of Pain
Department of Anesthesiology RN-10
University of Washington School of Medicine
Seattle, WA 98195

Table 12:16

❑ Major Types of Cancer

▪ *Breast Cancer*

Until recently breast cancer was the major cancer killer among women. (Lung cancer now claims that distinction.) The breast is still the most common cancer site among women. It is estimated that one out of eleven women will develop breast cancer at some time and women over 50 are at particular risk. (See Table 12:17.) Like many other cancers, the cure rate for breast cancer is directly linked to early detection. The American Cancer Society guidelines for breast cancer screening in asymptomatic, normal-risk women is as follows:

- Monthly breast self-examination (see Figures 12:1–12:3)
- Annual breast exam by physician
- Annual mammogram (X-ray examination of breast) for asymptomatic women over the age of 50

Most breast cancer begins in the milk ducts or in the milk-secreting glands known as lobules. Cancer confined to the inside of the duct or lobule is carcinoma *in situ* and is almost 100 percent curable by surgery. The cancer may remain dormant in this stage for years before spreading through the lymph ducts and nodes or through the bloodstream.

Factors That Increase Breast-Cancer Risk

- Mother or sister with breast cancer
- No completed pregnancy or first baby after age 30
- High-fat diet
- Obesity
- Previous breast cancer
- Long menstrual history (early menstruation with late menopause)
- Age over 50
- Possible but not proven link to DES (diethylstilbestrol), prescribed from the late 1940's to the 1960's to prevent miscarriage, and oral contraceptives containing estrogen

Table 12:17

DIET

A high-fat diet and excess pounds have been linked to an increase in a woman's risk of developing breast cancer, but definite proof of this is lacking. The general dietary guidelines recommended by the American Cancer Society are designed to reduce the amount of fat in the diet and provide a good basic plan to follow.

Recent studies indicate that excess weight may be more directly related to breast cancer than fat intake. In addition, results of a long-term study by researchers at Harvard Medical School implicate regular alcohol consumption—even as little as one or two drinks a day—to an increased risk of breast cancer. A prudent course to follow, especially for women with a strong family history of breast cancer, would include a low-fat, low-calorie diet and only occasional alcohol consumption.

DIAGNOSIS

If a lump is found by the woman or her doctor, if warning signs are present (see Table 12:18), or if a mass shows up in a routine mammogram, a biopsy is the next step. Suspected cancer can be confirmed only with a biopsy.

A needle biopsy done under local anesthetic is often the first step. In this procedure, a hollow needle is inserted into the lump to withdraw fluid or tissue and is sent for laboratory analysis. If fluid is withdrawn and the lump disappears or collapses, it is probably a benign cyst. If no abnormal cells are found on analysis, no further tests will be needed. This technique is inexpensive, relatively painless and has a low risk of infection.

However, if fluid was not withdrawn or if the lab report is positive, a surgical biopsy will be necessary. Women with large breasts who have a small lump near the chest wall or those whose mammograms indicate a possible lump that

Breast Self-Examination

All women should examine their breasts each month. For menstruating women, this should be a week after the start of a period; postmenopausal women can select an easy-to-remember date.

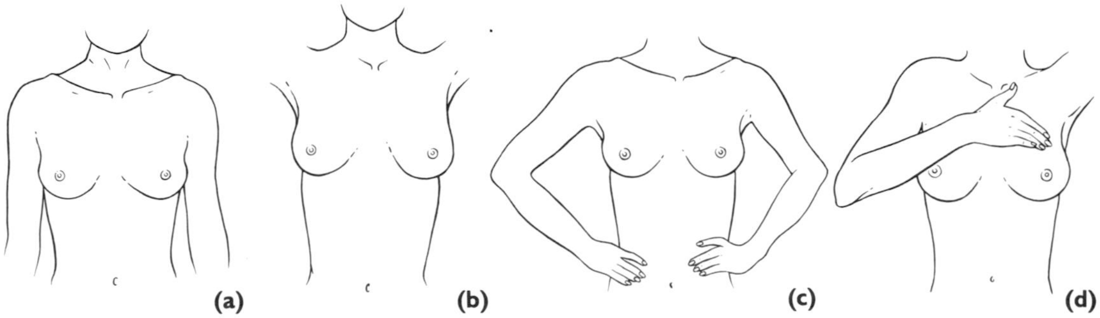

Figure 12:1
Start by standing in front of a mirror with arms at your sides. Look for any changes, such as puckering of the skin. Do the same with arms raised overhead, and then finally with hands on the hips and chest muscles tensed.

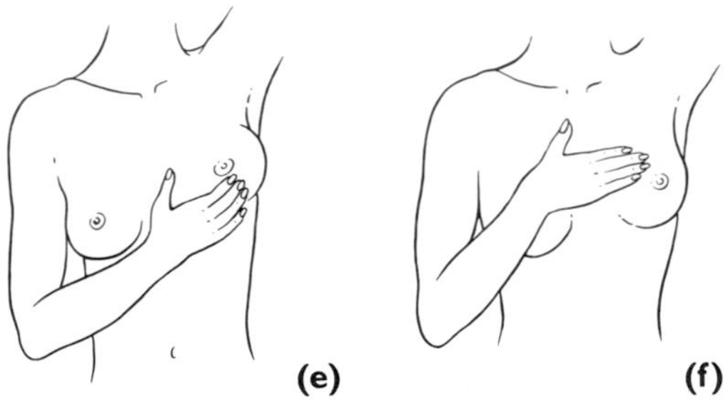

Figure 12:2
Next, lift one arm up behind your head and, using the other hand, examine the entire breast, moving counterclockwise and from the outer portion toward the nipple. (Alternatively, the breast can be examined in horizontal strips.) Repeat this procedure on the second breast, raising the opposite arm over your head. Feel for any unusual lump or thickening.

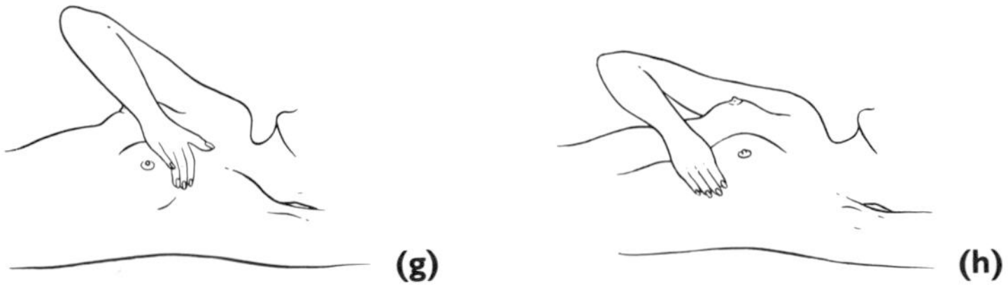

Figure 12:3
Then lie down and place one arm under your head, and using the other hand, examine the entire breast, moving clockwise and from the outer portion toward the nipple. Repeat this procedure on the second breast, placing the opposite arm under your head.

Make sure to cover the entire area from under the armpit across to the breastbone and up to the collarbone.

Finally, squeeze each nipple to see if there is a discharge. Any lump, change, discharge or other unusual finding should be checked promptly by a doctor.

Warning Signs of Breast Cancer

- A lump that does not go away
- Thickening of tissue
- Dimpling or peeling of skin
- Change in breast or nipple shape or contour
- Nipple discharge
- Retraction or scaliness of nipple
- Pain or tenderness

Table 12:18

cannot be felt will have to have a surgical, or excisional, biopsy in which the lump is removed for laboratory analysis. An estrogen-receptor test should be done at the same time to see if the tumor is stimulated by estrogen.

The majority—eight out of ten—breast lumps are not cancerous. If the lab tests do indicate cancer, however, then the woman should discuss treatment options with her physician.

TREATMENT

In the past a one-stage approach to diagnosis and treatment of breast cancer was standard policy. The biopsy was done under general anesthesia, the tissue examined immediately, and if the results were positive, a mastectomy would be performed at that time. This approach is no longer common. Now the biopsy is done as a preliminary procedure and the woman has the opportunity to find out the diagnosis, discuss options with her physician and, if desired, get a second opinion on the best course to take. The time between diagnosis and treatment can provide a valuable adjustment period and give the woman the opportunity to look into available resource groups that can provide information and support during this stressful period. (See Table 12:19, Breast Cancer Staging.) Currently physicians may differ on how to treat breast cancer as new techniques and modified approaches are constantly evolving.

Surgery is still the most common treatment, but there are various techniques within this realm. The traditional Halsted radical mastectomy removes the breast, underlying muscle and axillary lymph nodes. The modified radical mastectomy removes the breast and axillary lymph nodes. Simple mastectomy involves removing only the breast. Surgeons differ in their opinions on which method offers the best chance of cure, and the extent of the disease often determines which surgical procedure is appropriate. (See Figure 12:4, Types of Mastectomies.) Simple mastectomy is usually used for Stage I or II disease. A recent study supported by the National Cancer Institute indicates that simple mastectomy is as effective as radical mastectomy in most cases. In this study, lymph nodes were removed or irradiated after simple mastectomy if they were found to be cancerous, and no difference was found in survival rates between those receiving radical mastectomy and those receiving simple mastectomy and follow-up radiation treatment.

Breast Cancer Staging

STAGE I
Small tumor (less than 2 centimeters, or .78 inch). No spread to lymph nodes or evidence of metastases.

STAGE II
Tumor between 2 and 5 centimeters with no spread to lymph nodes or metastases *or*
Tumor smaller than 5 centimeters across with spread to lymph nodes but no metastases.

STAGE III
Tumor larger than 5 centimeters *or*
Any tumor seen with invasion of skin or wall of the chest or other "grave signs" *or*
Tumor with spread to lymph nodes of collarbone, but no distant sites.

STAGE IV
Any tumor with distant metastases, whether or not lymph nodes are involved.

Table 12:19

Another encouraging finding of a study supported by the National Cancer Institute is that lumpectomy, or removal of the cancer and surrounding tissue

Types of Mastectomies

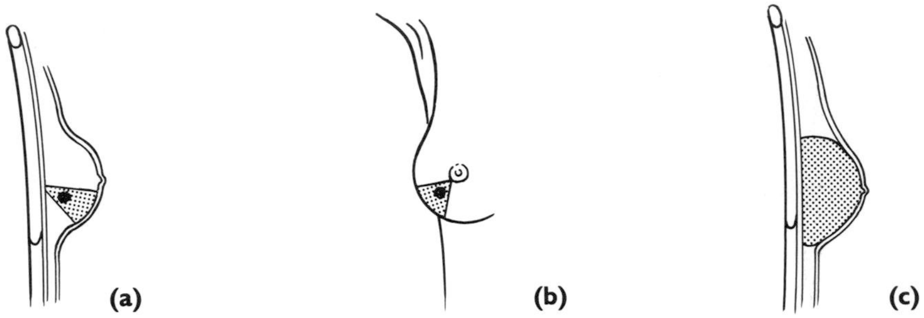

Figure 12:4
(a, b) Lumpectomy or segmental mastectomy, showing removal of the cancer and surrounding tissue.

(c) Subcutaneous mastectomy, showing removal of breast but not the nipple and skin. (Since this procedure is usually done prophylactically, no tumor is shown.)

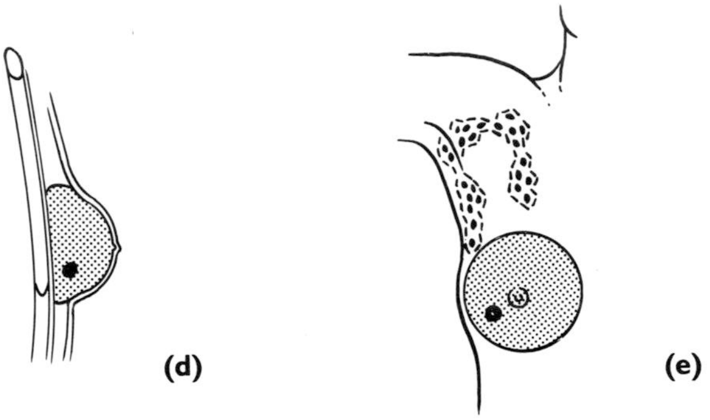

(d) Simple mastectomy, showing removal of breast, nipple and skin but not lymph nodes or muscle.

(e) Modified radical mastectomy, showing removal of breast, lymph nodes and surrounding tissue but not the underlying muscle.

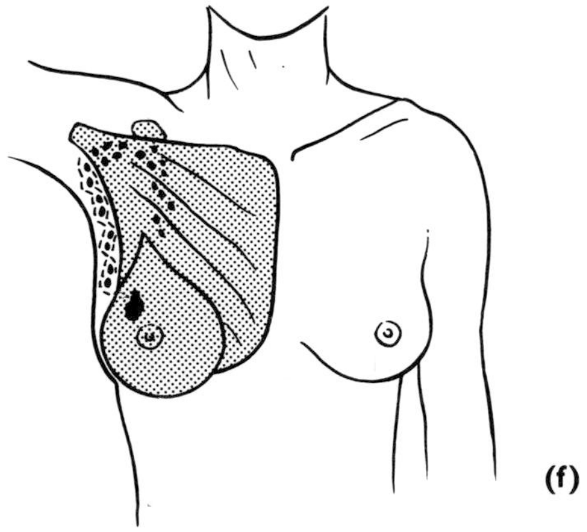

(f) Radical mastectomy, showing removal of breast, lymph nodes and surrounding muscle.

Shaded areas indicate what is removed in each procedure. The cancer is designated by the blackened lump.

with the rest of the breast left intact, followed by radiation therapy (and adjuvant chemotherapy when nodes are positive), seems to be as effective in treating small, localized cancers as total mastectomy. This procedure, however, is still controversial and some surgeons feel more information is needed before it can be recommended as an effective treatment.

Radiation therapy is usually used as an adjunct to surgery. Only for those patients with Stage IV cancer, for whom mastectomy would be ineffective, or those too ill for surgery, is radiation used as the only treatment. Radiation is used most commonly following lumpectomy; it is not considered necessary, as a rule, when a mastectomy has been performed. Radiation treatments are given four or five times a week over a four- to six-week period.

Chemotherapy is also used in conjunction with surgery and/or radiation, primarily for those patients whose cancer has invaded the lymph nodes and who are therefore at risk for further spreading of the cancer. A combination of drugs is usually given over a period of a year or longer. Chemotherapy does not seem to offer any advantage if the lymph node is not involved.

Hormone therapy has been found to be effective in estrogen-receptor positive tumors. The estrogen- and progesterone-receptor tests done at the time of biopsy help determine whether the cancer's growth rate is affected by these hormones. Previously, estrogen production was blocked in premenopausal women by removing the ovaries or exposing them to radiation, but the current approach uses drugs to block or halt estrogen production. Sometimes removal of the adrenal and pituitary glands is recommended. One of the adrenal glands produces androstenedione, a male hormone, which the postmenopausal woman converts to estrogen, and the pituitary produces hormones that stimulate the ovaries. In postmenopausal women, estrogen levels may be reduced satisfactorily by removal of the adrenal glands alone. If the adrenal glands are removed, the woman will have to take replacement cortisone and possibly Fludrocortisone (Florinef) to regulate salt processing; taking Pitressin, a synthetic form of the hormore vasopressin, to conserve water, may also be necessary.

Alternatively, many estrogen-receptor positive tumors in women who are five years or more beyond menopause respond to *adding* estrogen or other hormones.

There are many variables to take into consideration when making the choice of treatment. Treatment may depend on the stage of the disease, estrogen-receptor status, whether the woman is in a risk category, whether she is pre- or postmenopausal and the preferences of both the patient and the physician. Whatever the circumstances, the woman should make sure that she understands the rationale for the choice of some therapies or elimination of others before going ahead with a decision. A second opinion from a well-qualified breast specialist will often be helpful in reaching a decision. This almost always can be arranged without incurring undue delay.

BREAST RECONSTRUCTION

Options for breast reconstruction should be investigated when treatment options are discussed. Knowing beforehand about the alternatives available to her may help to reduce a woman's anxiety about breast surgery. Breast reconstruction is a possibility even for those who have had a radical mastectomy. (See Table 12:15, Sources of Help, back on page 190.) Usually, a soft silicone prosthesis is implanted under the skin or pectoral muscle. (See Figure 12:5.) An alternative method involves using tissue removed from the abdomen or other part of the body to construct a breast.

▪ *Lung Cancer*

Lung cancer is responsible for more deaths in the United States than any other form of cancer. The majority of lung cancer cases are found in the 55- to 65-year-old group. (See Table 12:20.) It is unfortunately very difficult to diagnose in an early stage; the warning signs usually indicate a relatively advanced stage of the disease. (See Table 12:21.) Lung cancer begins with precancerous cellular changes in the lung which produce no symptoms but gradually evolve into cancer. There is evidence that a smoker who develops these early precancerous changes can still circumvent the normal progression of the disease. If the smoker quits immediately, the damaged bronchial lining will often repair itself. The American Cancer Society estimates that cigarette smoking is responsible for 85 percent of lung cancer cases among men and 75 percent among women.

FOUR TYPES OF LUNG CANCER

Squamous cell carcinoma. Squamous cell carcinoma arises in the central part of the lung, in the larger bronchi, or air passages leading to and through the lungs. This is the only type of cancer that has a detectable precancerous stage that may last for years. During this phase abnormal cells will show up in the sputum on examination. If abnormal cells show up, the bronchial tree can be examined with a fiber-optic bronchoscope, a flexible instrument, in an attempt to locate the source of the cells. No tumor will show up on X-ray until later stages. Squamous cell cancers do not spread as rapidly as other lung cancers and thus respond to surgery and radiation treatments more successfully. Squamous cell carcinoma has a better prognosis than other forms of lung cancer.

Adenocarcinoma. Adenocarcinoma refers to glandular structures composed of

Breast Reconstruction

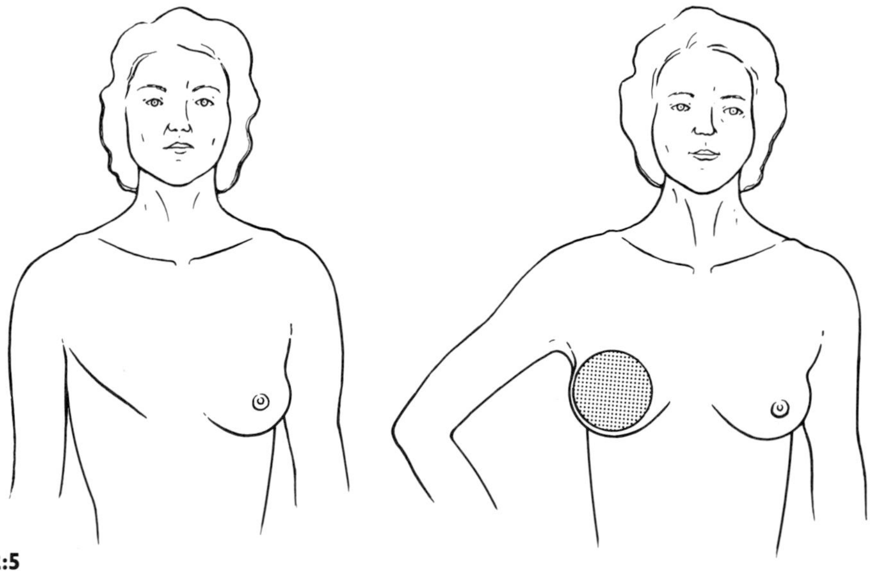

Figure 12:5
Gray area shows position of implant after a mastectomy.

People at Risk for Lung Cancer

- Cigarette smokers, especially those who have smoked twenty years or more
- Those exposed to industrial carcinogens such as asbestos, especially smokers
- Those with a history of tuberculosis
- Possibly those whose family members or ancestors have had lung cancer, suggesting a genetic link
- Possibly those with a dietary deficiency of vitamin E

Table 12:20

Warning Signs/Symptoms of Lung Cancer

- Persistent cough
- Blood-streaked sputum
- Chest pain
- Recurring attacks of pneumonia or bronchitis
- Wheezing unrelated to asthma
- Weight loss

Table 12:21

tumor cells (*adeno* means gland) starting in the smaller bronchi and often spreading into the pleural spaces between the lung and chest wall. The most common lung cancer in women, adenocarcinoma has a lower cure rate than squamous cell carcinoma. Surgery, sometimes followed by radiation therapy or chemotherapy, is the standard treatment. *Bronchioloaveolar carcinoma* is a subtype of adenocarcinoma that is not associated with smoking and may have a better prognosis. (Squamous cell and adenocarcinomas account for the majority of lung cancer cases.)

Small cell or "oat cell" carcinomas. Made up of cells that resemble oat grains under the microscope, this type of cancer is the most invasive of all lung cancers. The cancer has often spread to distant parts of the body by the time of diagnosis, making surgery an ineffective form of treatment. Ten years ago, only half of those patients diagnosed with this type of cancer were given more than two months to live. Recently, combination chemotherapy has enabled many patients to survive for up to two years and some are expected to reach the five-year mark. This type of cancer is responsible for approximately 20 percent of lung cancer cases.

Large cell lung carcinomas. These are rare cancers that resemble adenocarcinomas in their behavior. Treatment is also similar. There is some question about whether this is a distinct classification or a variation of squamous cell and/or adenocarcinoma.

DIAGNOSIS

Except for squamous cell carcinoma, early diagnosis is difficult. The National Cancer Institute has studied the effectiveness of periodic chest X-rays and sputum cell examinations for high-risk individuals—heavy smokers over 45. Although unsuccessful in early diagnosis of small cell lung cancer, the screening programs do seem to detect a higher percentage of early squamous cell and adenocarcinomas than is found in the general public. Thus, some experts recommend that heavy smokers over the age of 45 or 50 have periodic sputum cell analysis and chest X-rays.

Although the overall outlook for lung cancer survival is poor, advances are slowly being made. Prevention, especially quitting smoking, is obviously the best measure.

▪ *Colon and Rectum Cancer*

Cancers of the large bowel, which includes the colon and rectum, follow cancers of the lung and breast on the list of leading cancer killers. The cure rate for this cancer is currently only about 50 percent, but when detected at an early stage, the cure rate can rise as high as 87 percent. (See Table 12:22.)

The incidence of colorectal cancer increases in those over 40 but, unlike lung cancer, the cancer can be easily detected in the early stages. (See Table 12:23.) Early diagnosis is a very realistic goal.

Signs That May Increase Risk for Colorectal Cancer
▪ Family history of the disease ▪ Polyps in the colon ▪ Possible link to high-fat, low-fiber diet ▪ Ulcerative colitis and other inflammatory bowel diseases

Table 12:22

Warning Signs of Colorectal Cancer
▪ Change in bowel habits, either diarrhea or constipation ▪ Blood in stool ▪ Rectal bleeding ▪ Lower abdominal pain

Table 12.23

However, many people, even some physicians, ignore or avoid the basic screening procedures essential for early detection. The American Cancer Society recommends:

- An annual digital rectal examination for everyone over the age of 40, with or without symptoms. Many bowel cancers begin in the rectum and can easily be felt by the physician. This simple examination could save many lives.
- An annual stool guaiac test to detect occult blood for everyone over age 50. Simple, inexpensive kits, available in many drugstores, contain specially treated paper or slides on which the individual smears a small amount of stool. The kit is then sent to a laboratory for analysis.
- Proctosigmoidoscopy (examination of the rectum and colon with a flexible lighted tube) every three to five years after the age of 50, provided that two consecutive annual examinations were negative. Any suspicious area can be biopsied at the time of examination.

If any of these tests indicate suspicion of cancer, further examinations may be needed, such as a barium enema, in which a chalky substance containing barium to outline the colon on an X-ray is infused into the rectum, or colonoscopy, which uses a long, flexible tube inserted into the colon to allow the mucous membranes to be observed. Samples can be removed for biopsy at the time of colonoscopy.

TREATMENT

If cancer is found, further tests may be done to determine if it has spread to the kidneys, ureter, bladder or other parts of the body. Surgery is the most effective treatment. The aim is to remove the tumor and adjacent colon and lymphatic tissue. The ends of the intestine are then rejoined (an anastomosis), restoring function of the colon. Sometimes a temporary colostomy, an opening between the colon and the surface of the body, will be needed if the intestine cannot be repaired at the time of the operation. Occasionally, a permanent colostomy will be necessary in cases of rectal cancer. However, the development of more sophisticated surgical techniques has made this unnecessary for most patients. Only about one out of seven patients with rectal cancer will need a permanent colostomy.

Radiation therapy may be used either before or after surgery in some cases, depending on the size and nature of the cancer. Adjuvant chemotherapy is sometimes recommended for those patients with very large tumors or for those whose cancer is suspected of having spread to other parts of the body.

Delay in seeking diagnosis or treatment is, as with most other cancers, a major obstacle to survival. If procedures for early detection are followed, some estimates of subsequent cure rates go as high as 90 percent. Many people are fearful of the surgery and its consequences and wait until long after they first suspect a problem before obtaining medical advice. Frequently, an early diagnosis would have resulted in less mutilating surgery and virtually no long-term aftereffects. But even if a colostomy is required, most patients are able to live normal, full lives. There is no reason to curtail work, travel or sexual activity. As with many things, fear and the imagination can conjure up images that are much worse than the reality.

▪ *Prostate Cancer*

Cancer of the prostate is the second most common cancer in men. Average age at diagnosis is 73. Since the cause of prostate cancer is unknown, there are no established guidelines for prevention, but men can greatly reduce their risk of death if they have regular examinations of the prostate. (See Table 12:24.) Because early prostate cancer produces no symptoms, early detection depends on having a digital rectal examination of the prostate once a year after the age of 40.

The prostate gland is about the size of a walnut and encircles the top of the urethra, which carries urine and ejaculate from the body. The first symptom of prostate cancer is usually difficulty in urination because the enlarged prostate can obstruct urine flow. However, this symptom does not appear until the cancer has reached an advanced stage.

Other late symptoms include pain or a burning sensation on urination or a weak or interrupted urine flow. These symptoms may also indicate benign disorders, but they should always be evaluated. Back or other bone pain is also a common symptom because of the spread of advanced cancer to the skeleton.

Higher-Risk Indicators for Prostatic Cancer

- History of venereal disease
- History of prostate infection
- Age over 50
- High-fat diet (possibly)
- Risk is also much higher among black men

Table 12:24

If swelling or nodules are found during the rectal examination, a biopsy is done to determine whether or not cancer is present. If the biopsy is positive, further studies to determine the extent of the disease will be done, including blood tests, X-rays of the skeletal system, bone marrow cell study and a bone scan using radioactive isotopes.

TREATMENT

Treatment for prostate cancer varies depending on the extent of the cancer, the patient's general health status and his psychosexual needs. Sometimes no treatment is considered necessary for those with Stage A_1 disease, which is confined to one or two microscopic areas of the gland. Surgery or radiation is the preferred treatment for those with Stage A or B disease, in which the cancer is confined to the prostate. Surgery, a radical prostatectomy, used to lead frequently to impotence because the pelvic nerves were severed during surgery. Recent advances, however, have made it possible to preserve sexual function. Radioactive implants have also been used, with a resulting 5 percent incidence of impotence. External radiotherapy is another alternative, but it has demonstrated a lower rate of success and a higher incidence of impotence.

More advanced stages of the disease are treated with radiation and hormone therapy, often to prolong life and relieve symptoms even if a cure is not possible. Removing the testes or administering estrogen, a female hormone, will suppress the production of testosterone, which is known to influence prostate function. However, estrogen therapy is associated with impotence, breast swelling, fluid retention and an increased incidence of cardiovascular disease. Another form of hormone therapy—the use of analogues to control the production of luteinizing hormone, which stimulates testosterone secretion—has been effective in halting testosterone production without producing the negative side effects of estrogen therapy. Anticancer drugs have also been used in the treatment of advanced stages of cancer to slow tumor growth and relieve symptoms.

▪ *Cervical Cancer*

Because the symptoms of cervical cancer are not necessarily early warning signs but may signal advanced disease, regular screening examinations that include a Pap test are essential. (See Table 12:25.) The Pap test is a smear or sample of epithelial, or lining, cells shed from the cervix that are mounted on a slide, stained and examined by a laboratory for signs of abnormal cell changes. The American Cancer Society and National Institutes of Health recommend a Pap test every three years after two consecutive yearly tests have been negative. The American College of Obstetrics and Gynecology still recommends annual pelvic examinations and Pap tests. The frequency of testing should be decided by the woman and her physician, bearing in mind risk factors and personality traits such as a tendency to procrastinate. (See Table 12:26.) A physician would not want to schedule an exam every three years for someone who is likely to stretch that out to five.

The overall five-year survival rate for cervical cancer is 65 percent. It rises to 80 to 90 percent for those patients whose cancer is diagnosed early—and for carcinoma *in situ*, or localized cancer, the cure rate is virtually 100 percent. (See Table 12:27.)

Warning Signs of Cervical and Endometrial (Uterine) Cancer

- Intermenstrual or postmenopausal bleeding
- Unusual discharge
- Abdominal pain

Table 12:25

Women at Risk for Cervical Cancer

- Intercourse at an early age
- Multiple sexual partners
- Family history
- History of syphilis or gonorrhea
- Possibly, papilloma virus (related to genital warts)

Table 12:26

Stages of Cervical Cancer

- Dysplasia (abnormal growth): changes in some cells of the cervix. This is a precancerous stage and in many cases the cells will return to their normal state without treatment. Dysplasia can be detected by a Pap test.
- Carcinoma *in situ*: abnormal cells that do not invade neighboring tissue. This condition is considered preinvasive cervical cancer and may persist for eight to ten years. It can be detected by a Pap test and treatment can produce a complete cure.
- Invasive cancer: the cancer cells have spread to surrounding tissue, lymph channels and blood vessels, and then to lymph nodes and distant organs. Most cases of invasive cervical cancer are found in women between 45 to 55 years old. Invasive cancers are further subdivided according to the extent of the spread.

Table 12:27

TREATMENT

Preinvasive cervical cancer is usually treated by the following methods, which do not require extensive surgery and need not affect reproductive ability.

Conization is the removal of cancerous tissue in a cone-shaped wedge. General anesthesia and a short hospital stay are necessary. Careful follow-up including semiannual pelvic exams and Pap tests are recommended after conization.

Cryosurgery kills cancerous cells by freezing them with carbon dioxide, and is used to treat dysplasia and preinvasive cancer. This procedure requires no anesthesia and may be performed in the doctor's office. Vaginal discharge lasting two to four weeks is common following treatment. Sexual intercourse should be avoided for ten days. If abnormal cells remain or return, conization will probably be necessary. Laser therapy is an experimental therapy that may replace cryotherapy eventually.

Invasive cervical cancers are treated with surgery or radiation, or a combination of the two. Stage I cancers (confined to the cervix) are usually treated by radical hysterectomy, which involves removal of the uterus, the upper vagina, and ligaments supporting the uterus and adjacent lymph nodes. In women approaching or past menopause, the ovaries are sometimes removed to prevent the occurrence of ovarian cancer.

Stage II cancers (extending to the upper third of the vagina or tissue around the uterus but not the pelvic wall) are treated with radical hysterectomy, sometimes followed by radiation therapy.

For more advanced cases, radiation is the usual therapy. Radiation is preferred over surgery for patients in whom surgery would pose a threat, such as the elderly, diabetics or those debilitated by some other condition. Radiation therapy may be given in the form of X-rays or radioactive implants placed in the vagina or uterus. The implants usually stay in place two to four days, during which time the woman remains hospitalized.

▪ *Endometrial Cancer*

Endometrial cancer, or cancer of the lining of the uterus, usually occurs in women between the ages of 50 and 65. Over recent decades, the incidence of endometrial cancer has steadily increased. (See Table 12:28.) It is now more common than cervical cancer. Survival rates for endometrial cancer are quite high: 84 percent overall and 91 percent when the cancer is diagnosed early.

Indicators That Increase Risk for Endometrial (Uterine) Cancer

- History of infertility
- Failure to ovulate or other menstrual irregularities
- Prolonged estrogen therapy unaccompanied by progesterone
- Obesity
- Late menopause
- Family history

Table 12:28

CONTRIBUTING FACTORS

Estrogen is known to be involved in endometrial cancer, and a number of studies have shown that postmenopausal estrogen therapy increases the risk of endometrial cancer. The degree of risk appears to be dose-related; the longer the period of medication and the higher the dose, the greater the risk. In the past, estrogen was prescribed on a daily basis. Now some doctors recommend that the smallest possible dose be given for three out of every four weeks. Hormone replacements that contain both estrogen and progesterone do not increase the risk.

Obesity's link to endometrial cancer is well established. One possible explanation is that fat cells manufacture a certain amount of estrogen and thus overweight women have a natural source of excess estrogen. Women with diabetes and high blood pressure seem to have a higher incidence of this cancer, but it is unclear whether these conditions are actually associated with the cancer since women with these conditions are usually also overweight.

DETECTION/DIAGNOSIS

A Pap test is not highly accurate in detecting endometrial cancer. If there is reason to suspect the presence of endometrial cancer, cells from the uterine lining will be obtained by using an aspirator. It is recommended that women at high risk have an endometrial tissue sample taken at the time of menopause. Women on estrogen therapy—which should always include progesterone—should have a pelvic examination and Pap smear every 6 or 12 months and endometrial tissue sample taken every year or two. If the endometrial tissue sample indicates cancer, another procedure, dilation and curettage (D&C), is done to confirm the diagnosis. During a D&C the cervix is widened or dilated and a curette is used to scrape the lining of the uterus. This procedure requires light anesthesia and is usually performed in a hosptial. An alternative procedure is an aspiration curettage, which uses a long pump to withdraw cells. This procedure can be done without anesthesia in a doctor's office.

Although the cure rate for endometrial cancer is quite high, early diagnosis and treatment are still important to prevent the cancer from spreading to other organs. (See Table 12:29.)

Stages of Endometrial Cancer

- Stage 0 (overgrowth or adenomatous hyperplasia of the endometrium). This is a precancerous stage that may be effectively treated with hormone therapy or a D&C. However, if the hyperplasia persists, a hysterectomy may be recommended.
- Stage I (cancer confined to the body of the uterus). This is treated with a hysterectomy, removal of tubes and ovaries. This may be the only therapy needed.
- Stage II (both cervix and uterus are affected). This usually requires removal of the uterus, ovaries and sometimes lymph nodes, cervix and part of the vagina in addition to radiation therapy.
- Stages III and IV (cancer has spread beyond reproductive organs). Treatment depends on which organs are affected. Therapy will probably include a combination of surgery and radiation and possibly chemotherapy.

Table 12:29

13

ARTHRITIS

Arthritis is a general term that applies to any disorder involving inflammation of the joints and surrounding tissue. In its various forms, arthritis is one of the most common disorders in the United States and it is also the disease most frequently associated with old age in the public's mind. In fact, more than 36 million people (one in seven) in this country have some type of arthritis, according to the Arthritis Foundation. Most kinds of arthritis can occur at any age. However, since many kinds of arthritis are chronic and progressive in nature, older people frequently suffer from joint disorders. (For what a normal joint looks like, see Figure 13:1.)

Just as there are many types of arthritis, there also are many causes. (See Table 13:1.) Many types of arthritis have no cure, although most can be managed sufficiently to minimize pain and prevent major disabilities. Early diagnosis and appropriate treatment are keys to how well a person will do in living with arthritis. The person most likely to have long pain-free periods or to be able to maintain an acceptable level of activity despite chronic symptoms is the one who consulted a physician early and then cooperated fully in the recommended plan of care. Procrastination not only permits symptoms of pain and discomfort to persist, it can result in permanent joint damage that can hinder a person's mobility, comfort and quality of life. In the following sections, the major types of arthritis particularly common among older people are discussed.

Structure of a Normal Joint

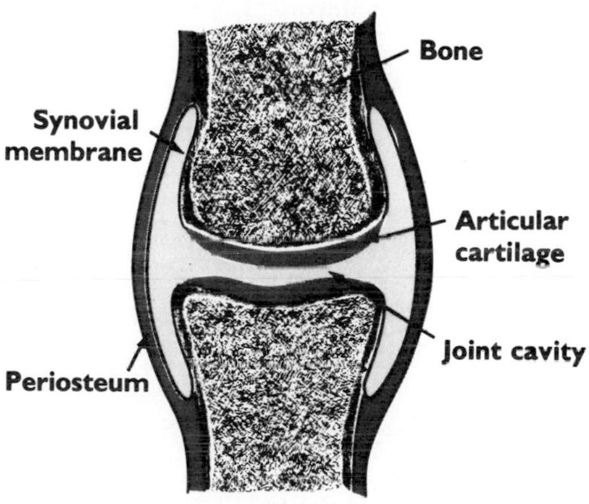

Figure 13:1

Causes of Arthritis

The precise cause of many kinds of arthritis is unknown, but a number of contributing factors have been established. These include:

- *Wear and tear on the joints.* The most common manifestation of this is osteoarthritis, also referred to as degenerative joint disease. Injuries or excessive stress on a joint—for example, the knees of football players and other athletes—also can lead to arthritis.
- *Genetic predisposition.* Some forms of arthritis, such as gout, rheumatoid arthritis or osteoarthritis, appear to run in families.
- *Biochemical or metabolic abnormalities.* Gout, which is due to excessive uric acid in the blood, is a prime example.
- *Endocrine disorders.* Hormonal imbalances can result in inflammation, joint deformities and other factors leading to arthritis. Rheumatoid arthritis, for example, invariably goes into a remission during pregnancy, and recent studies have found a lower incidence among women who take postmenopausal estrogen replacement.
- *Infection.* Both viral and bacterial infections may play a role in arthritis. Untreated gonorrhea, for example, can lead to a painful form of arthritis that clears up with antibiotic treatment.
- *Complications of other diseases.* Men with hemophilia, for example, often develop arthritis due to bleeding into the joints.
- *Drugs.* Some drugs—for example, thiazide diuretics used to treat high blood pressure—may provoke gout or other forms of arthritis characterized by biochemical imbalances.
- *Possible immune system defects.* There is growing evidence that several types of arthritis are autoimmune disorders in which the body's defense system turns on itself and destroys its own tissue.

Table 13:1

❑ Osteoarthritis (Degenerative Joint Disease)

This is the type of arthritis most closely associated with aging. Other types may occur in early years, and because of their progressive nature, grow worse as time goes by, but osteoarthritis develops primarily because of the passage of years.

Osteoarthritis is the gradual degeneration of cartilage, the shock absorber in a joint. Eventually, the cartilage may disappear completely, leaving the bone surfaces without a cushion. Inflammation, the major symptom in most other kinds of arthritis, is at worst a minor problem in most osteoarthritis. Although this condition can be caused by overuse of a joint or repeated injury to a joint—ballerinas' ankles, for instance, or pitchers' shoulders are often affected—it is generally the result of the repetitive use of joints over time. Therefore, just about everyone will eventually develop some degree of osteoarthritis with age, although it will not usually be severe enough to cause any noticeable symptoms or discomfort. This degenerative disease may be present in its early stages in people in their twenties or thirties, but it does not usually produce any symptoms until people reach their fifties. There are exceptions, however. Some people are stricken early in life while others may not be affected until old age.

Although use and aging contribute to development of osteoarthritis, it is also possible that people may be born with a predisposition to the disease. Researchers believe that some people may have defective cartilage or that their joints may not fit together correctly. These abnormalities would not cause any apparent defects but might eventually contribute to degeneration of the joints.

The joints most commonly affected by osteoarthritis are the fingers, vertebra, knees, hip and neck. Symptoms usually entail discomfort in and around the joint and stiffness. Typically, the pain and stiffness are absent or relatively mild in the morning and progress as the day wears on. Hot, swollen joints, characteristic of other forms of arthritis, usually do not occur in osteoarthritis.

As a rule, osteoarthritis does not affect the whole body; instead, it is usually found in one or two specific joints. As a rule, only when the spine or weight-bearing joints such as the hip or knee are affected is there any severe pain or incapacity. The hands are the most frequent site of osteoarthritis, with the ends of the fingers and base of the thumb usually being involved. Osteoarthritis typically produces bony spurs, new bone growth, in the joints. When these are confined to the ends of the fingers (Heberden's nodes), they rarely cause pain or interfere with use of the hands, although they may make the hands somewhat unsightly.

In the spine, bony spurs can cause considerable pain because they exert pressure on sensitive nerves, producing symptoms similar to those of a ruptured disk. Therefore, even though the effect on the joints themselves is not that serious, osteoarthritis of the spine can be severely painful and incapacitating.

▪ *Treatment*

There is no single treatment for osteoarthritis; an individual patient's regimen will depend upon severity of the disease and the joints affected. To minimize the effects of osteoarthritis on weight-bearing joints, a person should maintain ideal weight; obesity puts extra stress on the joints and can hasten their degeneration. Exercise is also vital. Stretching and range-of-motion exercises help maintain mobility, but activities that put excessive stress on joints (for example, jogging if you have bad knees) should be avoided. Good posture is important, as is wearing properly fitted shoes. Many people have one leg slightly longer than the other without even knowing it; this can lead to osteoarthritis of the hip and knees. Wearing a properly fitted shoe lift to even out the leg lengths can prevent further damage.

Particular attention should be paid to protecting the vulnerable joints. Strategies range from simple, commonsense ones such as warming up before exercise, using a long-handled mop to wash the floor instead of scrubbing on hands and knees, and avoiding activities that will put pressure on joints, to more specific and sophisticated ones that require the recommendation and supervision of a physician or physical therapist. And, of course, controlling weight is one of the most effective ways to relieve stress on joints.

In some instances, canes, walkers or other aids may be needed to reduce pressure on the joints. Many self-help devices are available that can make daily functioning easier. *The Self-Help Manual for Arthritis Patients,* available from the local chapter of the Arthritis Foundation, is a catalogue of such devices and includes many useful tips.

DRUGS

The goal of drug therapy in arthritis is to reduce pain and control inflammation. Thus the major drugs used are anti-inflammatory agents, namely aspirin, nonsteroidal anti-inflammatory drugs (NSAIDs) or antiprostaglandins, and cortisone. (See Table 13:2, Drugs to Treat Arthritis.)

HEAT/COLD

Dressing warmly and applying heat packs or swimming in heated pools will help relieve pain. Many people find that paraffin baths, in which a painful hand is placed in warm, melted paraffin, is helpful. Extreme cold seems to aggravate pain.

REST

Although many people with osteoarthritis experience pain and stiffness when they first get up, after moving

Drugs to Treat Arthritis

Drug	Action	Possible Side Effects
ASPIRIN	Relieves pain Counters inflammation	Excessive blood thinning, gastrointestinal bleeding, ringing in the ears, nausea, heartburn, diarrhea, hearing loss, fast pulse
NSAIDs: indomethacin (Indocin); diflunisal (Dolobid); fenoprofen calcium (Nalfon); ibuprofen (Motrin, Rufen or the over-the-counter forms, Advil, Nuprin, etc.); meclofenamate sodium (Meclomen); naproxen (Naprosyn); piroxicam (Feldene); sulindac (Clinoril); and tolmetin sodium (Tolectin). Phenylbutazone (Butazolidin) is rarely used to treat chronic arthritis, but may be used for acute gout.	Relieves pain Counters inflammation Suppresses prostaglandins	Nausea, heartburn, blood thinning, gastrointestinal bleeding, rash, itching, dizziness, ringing in the ears, fluid buildup, blood and liver abnormalities
CORTICOSTEROIDS: betamethasone (Celestone); Cortisone acetate; hydrocortisone (Cortef and others); dexamethasone (Decadron); methylprednisolone (Medrol); prednisone (Deltasone); triamcinolone (Aristocort)	Fights inflammation	Muscle weakness and shrinking, bone thinning, fluid retention, ulcer, gastrointestinal bleeding, impaired healing, skin thinning and bruising, menstrual irregularities, weight gain and fat redistribution (Cushinoid changes), cataracts, glaucoma
GOLD: injectable: gold sodium thiomalate (Myochrysine); oral: auranoflin (Ridaura)	Fights inflammation May induce remission	Dermatitis, itching, rash, hair loss, ulcers, gum inflammation, blood disorders, nausea and gastrointestinal upsets, eye disorders, jaundice
PENICILLAMINE: (Cuprimine or Depen)	Reduces inflammation May induce remission	Serious blood disorders (blood to be checked biweekly for first six months); kidney and liver disorders, myasthenia gravis, rashes, ulcers, dietary deficiencies, possible increased cancer risk
ANTIMALARIALS: chloroquine (Aralen, Chloroquine); hydroxychloroquine (Plaquenil)	Reduces inflammation	Headache, itching, nausea, diarrhea, ringing in the ears, visual disturbances

Table 13:2

around a bit this usually subsides. However, pain and stiffness often seem to get worse as the day wears on, especially if the joints are being used a good deal. Occasional rest periods will help relieve the pain. It is, therefore, important to have a schedule that incorporates planned rest periods throughout the day. When nerves in the cervical or neck area are affected, bed rest and traction may be needed. A cervical collar can help reduce strain on the neck.

SURGERY

Hip joint replacement surgery is often successful for those whose disease has progressed to an advanced stage. The surgery does restore function but is considered only for those whose movement is severely restricted by the disease, since the artificial joint may eventually wear out and have to be replaced.

Several knee operations may help osteoarthritis patients. The insertion of an arthroscope—a hollow instrument with viewing devices—into the knee joint and microsurgery to remove particles that are damaging the cartilage is a new procedure that is gaining popularity over older surgical methods. In recent years, improved artificial knee joints have been developed and knee replacement is becoming increasingly popular.

Other joints that are candidates for repair or replacement include the fingers and shoulders. There are also new procedures using cartilage transplants, but these are still experimental and reserved for very severe cases. Still another new procedure entails withdrawing some of the joint fluid if it is found to contain tiny crystals that are shed from the bone. These crystals can cause irritation and inflammation; removal of the joint fluid, followed by an injection of cortisone into the cavity, can provide marked relief.

▪ *Outlook*

Most people with osteoarthritis do very well. There may be periods when the joint pain flares up, but these generally do not last long and can be relieved with drugs, rest and heat.

❑ Rheumatoid Arthritis

Rheumatoid arthritis is one of the more disabling forms of the disease, and this is the type that generally comes to mind when someone says he or she has arthritis. In this country, it afflicts more than 7 million people, making it the most common form of disabling arthritis. Although rheumatoid arthritis may occur at any age, it usually first appears in the thirties and forties. It is three times more common in women than men.

Rheumatoid arthritis is a systemic disease and may affect many organs in addition to the joints. It is usually bilateral; if one knee or finger joint is affected, for example, the same joint on the opposite side usually will be similarly attacked. The most frequent sites are the knees, hands, feet, neck and ankles, although the disease can attack any joint.

The initial symptoms include:

- Swelling in one or more joints
- Early-morning stiffness
- Recurring pain or tenderness in any joint
- Inability to move a joint normally
- Obvious redness and warmth in a joint
- Unexplained weight loss, fever or weakness combined with joint pain

▪ *Predisposing Factors*

The cause or causes of rheumatoid arthritis are unknown, but certain factors suggest a pattern of development and predisposing factors. These include:

Autoimmune disorder. The first symptoms of rheumatoid arthritis often follow a viral infection, which may suggest that an immune response has been triggered by the infection. This response may promote the inflammation of the joint lining and lead to rheumatoid arthritis.

Rheumatoid factor. This is a gamma globulin or antibody that is present in the blood and joint fluid of the majority of patients with rheumatoid arthritis. It acts against a person's normal gamma globulin, in effect making the body allergic to itself. Rheumatoid factor is manufactured by synovial cells and released directly into the joint cavity. When it comes into contact with the normal gamma globulin, an immune complex is formed. In the body's attempt to protect itself, a substance called complement attracts inflammatory cells to destroy the immune complexes. Inflammation is the body's natural protective reaction to injury or the presence of viruses or bacteria. Normally, after the immune system attacks and repairs the problem, the inflammation subsides. But in arthritis, the protective mechanism seems to backfire; the inflammation response releases enzymes that can destroy joint tissue. A circular process results: Inflammation, the body's response to the damage caused by the enzymes, produces more destructive substances, leading to more damage and then to another inflammatory reaction.

There are various theories on what causes the rheumatoid factor to develop, including an infection or viral agent, but no explanation has been established. It is also possible that the immune complexes are only part of the disease process of rheumatoid arthritis and not an initiating cause.

Genetic predisposition. Obviously not everyone who has an infection or virus or whatever the triggering agent is develops rheumatoid arthritis. One theory is that some people have a genetic tendency to develop rheumatoid arthritis. This theory has been bolstered by discovery of a genetic marker, HLA-DR4, a tissue type similar to a blood type. A person with this tissue type is at higher risk for developing rheumatoid arthritis.

▪ *How the Disease Progresses*

Since rheumatoid arthritis is a systemic disease, it can produce symptoms throughout the body. In the early stages, people may feel tired, feverish or weak. Lack of appetite and weight loss are common. In addition to joint symptoms, a person may complain of inflamed eyes, pleurisy, generalized inflammation of heart muscle, blood vessels and other tissues. Rheumatoid nodules, which are lumps under the skin, may form, but they usually do not cause any major problem. Some people have an initial severe attack of rheumatoid arthritis and then have no symptoms for a prolonged period, but the symptoms usually do reappear eventually. Indeed, periods of flare-up followed by remission are a major characteristic of rheumatoid arthritis, which is a lifelong disease.

Initially, inflammation is confined to the joint lining, the synovium. (See Figure 13:2.) As the synovium becomes enlarged and thickened, it attacks the articular cartilage, leading to possible deformity of the joint. Fluid accumulates in the joint cavity. Both the inflammation of the joint lining and the fluid accumulation produce pain. In response to the pain, the body attempts to rest the joint, producing muscle spasm or stiffness. The stiffness makes movement of the joint even more difficult and painful. If the disease progresses unchecked, the articular cartilage may be destroyed and, with the cartilage, the edges of the bones may fuse together. Although the inflammation process, and thus the pain, will stop, the fusion results in a loss of joint function.

▪ *Diagnosis*

Early diagnosis and treatment can make a significant difference in the long-term outcome of rheumatoid arthritis. The Arthritis Foundation estimates that, on average, people wait four years after symptoms first appear to seek out medical advice. Because arthritis is progressive, the longer it goes untreated, the greater the damage it can do. Medication, exercise or other treatments can go a long way toward maintaining joint mobility, but if too much time elapses, surgery and joint replacement may become the only effective treatment.

Progression of Rheumatoid Arthritis

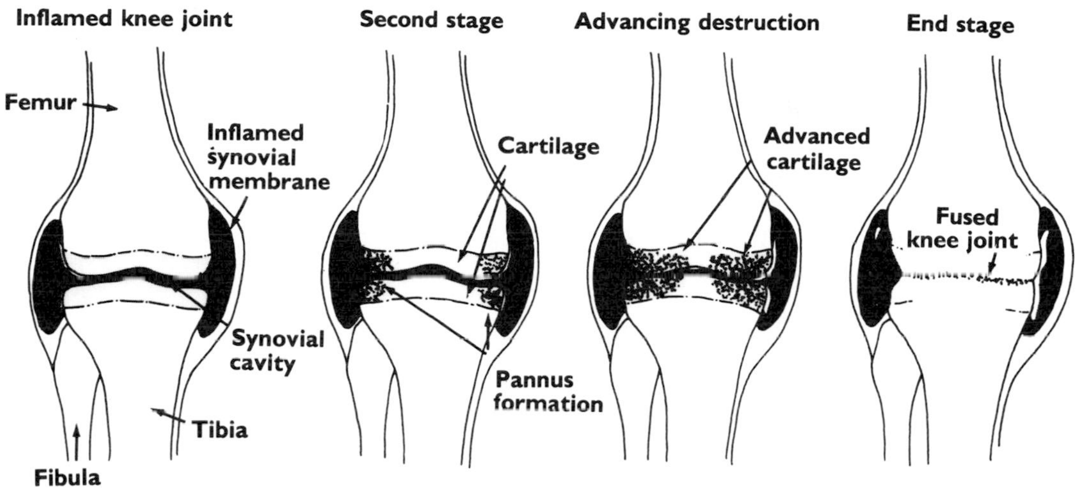

Figure 13:2

A diagnosis of rheumatoid arthritis is based on the person's medical history, a physical examination, the presence of characteristic symptoms and certain laboratory tests. Often the doctor will request a sedimentation rate test, which measures the rate at which red blood cells fall within one hour. An elevated rate indicates inflammation somewhere in the body. Blood tests to detect anemia and the presence of rheumatoid factor may also be made. X-rays may be taken to determine change in the joint.

▪ *Treatment*

Many people with rheumatoid arthritis have only mild symptoms that do not interfere with daily functioning in any significant way. Others may have occasional severe attacks with long symptom-free periods. For a minority of those with rheumatoid arthritis, however, the disease becomes progressively more severe and the periods between attacks, shorter. Whatever the degree of the disease, however, various methods of treatment can prevent or delay serious damage to the joints. Appropriate treatment will depend on the degree of joint pain and damage and the other systemic symptoms. As a rule, a combination of treatments are recommended that can offer relief from pain and increase mobility.

DRUG THERAPY

Aspirin is the mainstay of treatment for rheumatoid arthritis. Its anti-inflammatory effect is important in controlling rheumatoid arthritis. A much higher dose of aspirin is needed to activate the anti-inflammatory property than is needed for pain control. Recommended dosage for headache pain, for example, is two regular tablets (5 grains, or 325 milligrams) of aspirin every four hours. For control of the inflammation of arthritis, the dose may be anywhere from sixteen to twenty-four tablets a day.

Many people think that because aspirin is used for so many relatively minor aches and pains and is a nonprescription medication, it is not effective against a disease as serious as rheumatoid arthritis. Or alternatively, they may think that it is harmless and resort to self-medication without supervision of a physician. Both of these attitudes contain basic flaws: Although it is true that aspirin is taken for just about any kind of minor ailment, it is also one of the most effective, safest and cheapest arthritis medications available. But it is not without potential side effects. Also, the dosage and length of therapy can determine how successful aspirin is in controlling inflammation. Therefore, it is essential that a physician monitor the effectiveness and progress of therapy.

If side effects do occur, they should be brought to the attention of the physician without delay. High-dose aspirin can cause stomach irritation, gastrointestinal bleeding, nausea, ringing in the ears and thinning of the blood. A number of different aspirin products are available, but these tend to be much more expensive than regular aspirin and are not any more effective. Buffered aspirin, for example, also contains an antacid. The same effect can be obtained by taking regular aspirin with an antacid or glass of milk. Coated and time-release aspirin also are available to reduce stomach irritation, but these products may not be absorbed as efficiently as plain aspirin. High-strength aspirin preparations for arthritis may be more convenient for some people but are usually more expensive; the same effect can be achieved simply by taking three regular aspirin. Table 13:3 offers suggestions to reduce side effects.

Aspirin compounds, except for buffered aspirin, are generally not appropriate to arthritis treatment, especially those that contain caffeine or phenacetin. Aspirin substitutes such as acetaminophen (Tylenol, etc.) may relieve arthritis pain, but do not have adequate anti-inflammatory action to qualify as adequate for treatment.

Tips on Taking Aspirin

Side Effects	Action
Ringing in the ears	Reduce dosage slightly
Nausea/vomiting/gastrointestinal irritation	Try taking more frequent but smaller doses Take aspirin with milk, an antacid or food, such as crackers and milk Drink a glass of water after each dose Try taking aspirin in suspension by dissolving tablets in half a glass of milk or water, followed by another half glass Avoid taking aspirin with orange juice or other acidic foods, which increase irritation
Bleeding	Do not take aspirin with other drugs that thin the blood Decrease dosage Avoid alcohol use while taking aspirin

Table 13:3

OTHER ANTI-ARTHRITIS DRUGS

Although aspirin is the mainstay drug used in treating rheumatoid arthritis, a number of other medications are available and may be prescribed when aspirin is ineffective or for people who cannot tolerate it. These drugs include:

Nonsteroidal anti-inflammatory drugs, or NSAIDs. These relatively new medications are often prescribed as alternatives to aspirin. They are highly effective against inflammation and some are believed to have other beneficial effects, such as inducing a remission. NSAIDs interfere with the production of prostaglandins, hormone-like substances that contribute to the inflammation process. Although all NSAIDs are chemically similar, their effect varies with the individual. It is sometimes necessary to try several NSAIDs before finding the one that works. Generally, a week or ten days of therapy is necessary before it is clear whether the drug is effective or not. If one particular NSAID becomes ineffective after long-term use, another can usually be substituted. NSAIDs should be taken only under the supervision of a physician and any adverse effects should be reported promptly. (See Table 13:2, Drugs to Treat Arthritis, on page 208.)

Corticosteroids. When it was discovered in the 1950's that cortisone could produce dramatic relief of arthritis pain and inflammation, corticosteroids were hailed as a new miracle cure for the disease. The miracle proved to be very short-lived, however.

Although corticosteroids can produce a dramatic reduction in inflammation and pain, the effect is temporary and the accompanying side effects of prolonged use of steroids can be severe, including lowered resistance to infection, thinning of bones and gastrointestinal problems. Generally, corticosteroids are used only if pain or inflammation cannot be controlled by aspirin or other drugs, and then only for short periods. Some of the systemic side effects can be avoided by injecting the steroid directly into the joint, but this cannot be done repeatedly because it may actually cause joint damage.

Gold preparations. When the symptoms of rheumatoid arthritis are severe and do not seem to respond to aspirin or other treatments, injection of gold salts is sometimes effective. Gold therapy is slow-acting: it may be several months after therapy is initiated before any benefits are felt. Previously, there were often serious side effects from gold therapy, but with usage has come a better understanding of proper dosage and the incidence of side effects has declined. It is not known exactly why gold works, but when it is effective it reduces early-morning stiffness and swelling and increases strength and mobility. The benefits of gold therapy may gradually disappear over time, and since it is impossible to know beforehand if the treatment will work, it is not recommended except in cases where other treatments have been unsuccessful. New oral gold preparations reduce the side effects somewhat, but they may not be as effective as the injections.

Penicillamine. Like gold, penicillamine is used only when other standard treatments have failed to bring relief. Penicillamine is a chelating agent—a substance that removes excess lead, copper or other "heavy" metals from the body. It requires several months to take effect, but when it works the results can be dramatic. Penicillamine does have potentially serious side effects and must be used only under the close supervision of a physician.

Antimalarial agents. Chloroquine and hydroxychloroquine, drugs normally used to treat malaria, also control inflammation. Like gold and penicillamine, these drugs are slow-acting but they are usually well tolerated. Anyone taking one of these drugs should have regular eye examinations since serious damage to the retina is a possible side effect.

Gold, penicillamine and antimalarial agents are usually taken in combination with another anti-inflammatory (aspirin or an NSAID) to achieve an additive effect, and also to produce relief while waiting for the slower-acting medications to work.

NON-DRUG TREATMENTS

Rest and exercise. Although most people don't think of rest and exercise as being specific treatments, they are very important in the overall management of rheumatoid arthritis. Both are necessary to maintaining mobility, but neither must be taken to excess. Since fatigue is a common component of rheumatoid arthritis, specific rest periods are all the more essential in being able to carry out normal activities. Daily exercise is vital to maintain joint mobility and function, but too much activity can backfire, increasing pain and joint inflammation.

Arthritis patients should learn to organize their daily schedules to provide rest periods that will relieve stress on joints, but timed so that they will not interfere too much with normal activities. Caffeine or other drugs that may interfere with sleep patterns should be reduced. If fatigue is persistent, anemia may be responsible and treatment should be for the disease, not the fatigue.

Remember, too, that arthritis is a disease with ups and downs; there are days when you feel terrific with nary a twinge, and other times when it takes real effort just to get out of bed in the morning. As much as possible, try to keep your schedule flexible enough to take advantage of good periods and to pamper yourself during flare-ups. This does not mean letting the disease rule your life, however; common sense should be the rule.

Exercise helps keep joints flexible and muscles toned, providing more support for joints; it is also good for morale and promotes enhanced feelings of well-being. Exercise that puts gradual pressure on the joint helps nourish the cartilage by stimulating lubrication of the joint. Although there may be some pain at the beginning of the exercise program, exercise is probably the most effective way to avoid severe long-term pain. Many people have found that with regular exercise their pain diminishes to the extent that they can cut down on medication.

Since pain is a warning signal sent by the body, it is important not to exercise shortly after taking painkillers; you may go overboard because you simply won't feel the masked warning messages from the body. Gentle stretching or range-of-motion exercise, however, can be done even when painkillers are being taken. (See Table 13:4.) An exercise program tailored to your specific needs should be developed cooperatively by your physician and you and possibly a physical therapist. The Arthritis Foundation offers a guide to physicians on appropriate exercise.

The exercises that are most helpful for people with arthritis are those that help maintain the joints' full range of motion and apply gradual pressure rather than sudden stress to the joints. Swimming, especially in a heated pool, is one of the most effective therapies. Warm-water exercise programs are available at some local chapters of the Arthritis Foundation, and many hospitals have special arthritis clinics where information on exercise programs may be obtained.

How to Prepare for Exercising

1. A nice, slow, general stretch lying in bed is a good way to begin the day. Stretch like a cat that is getting up. Stretch one arm up, then the other, pull knees up and do a few bicycle turns in the air. Stretch legs out straight, roll to the side, swing the legs off the edge of the bed, using the momentum to help you sit up.
2. To maintain function, each joint in the body must be put through its full range of motion each day. Remember, stiff painful joints did not develop overnight and relief will not come quickly either.
3. If no exercise-induced pain lasts for more than two hours, then exercise time and activity can be increased.
4. Applying heat, taking a warm bath or soaking stiff joints all can aid in relaxing joints and muscles prior to exercise.
5. Experiment with different activity. Every exercise doesn't work for every person. Give an activity two weeks to a month for first results, then choose another exercise if results are not forthcoming.
6. Exercise daily unless you are having a flare-up with hot, painful joints. Some arthritis symptoms may be due to stiff, unused muscles. It is important to keep muscles in strong, supple condition. Muscle strength will help keep joints stable.

Table 13:4

Exercises Appropriate for Arthritis Patients

Recommended	Not Recommended
Swimming	Running
Cycling (use caution if knees are affected)	Skiing
Isometrics, which increase muscle tone without putting stress on joints	Jumping rope
Moderate weight lifting	Jogging
Yoga	Tennis
Walking	Racquetball
Stretching	

Table 13:5

The key to benefiting from exercise is frequent repetition: 10- or 15-minute sessions performed three or four times a day are best. Exercising aggressively for one hour is not only ineffective but may be counterproductive, causing even more joint damage. Exercising when the joint is inflamed can aggravate the inflammation. It is best to rest to reduce inflammation and then exercise. Still, even when inflammation is a problem some sort of exercise program, such as simple stretching or range-of-motion exercises, should be followed. Table 13:5 lists Exercises Appropriate for Arthritis Patients as well as those that are not.

HEAT/COLD

Heat treatment can help relax muscles and relieve pain and stiffness. Many people find that a warm bath or shower helps reduce early-morning stiffness. Heat, whether in the form of a shower, heat pack or heat lamp, can also be helpful after exercise. Paraffin baths, in which a painful hand, for example, is immersed in melted wax, relieves pain for many patients. Care should be taken that the wax is not scalding hot. Warm compresses that are changed frequently can have a similar effect.

Cold packs applied directly to the painful area can numb the area and relieve pain. Cold can also inhibit transmission of pain impulses to the brain and cool down "hot" joints.

JOINT PROTECTION

Canes and walkers can reduce stress on joints, and a physical therapist can teach methods of using joints with the least possible strain, such as using hands with the fingers extended whenever possible and closing doors with the whole hand rather than with the fingertips. Splints to hold joints in proper position may be recommended for use either at night or during the day. Splints, usually made of lightweight plastic with foam padding, allow joints to rest and help keep surrounding muscles and ligaments limber.

SURGERY

In cases of advanced disease, surgical repair of joints may be advised. In some of these procedures, diseased synovium is removed and the joints are realigned. Both large and small joints are now being repaired using these techniques. Removal of the diseased synovial membrane also reduces the inflammation of the synovitis but is usually done only when drug therapy has been unsuccessful or when one joint is significantly more inflamed than others.

Increasingly, joint replacement surgery is being used to restore function for people who are severely handicapped. Joints that are candidates for replacement include the hip, fingers and knees. In considering joint surgery, make sure that the surgeon is experienced in repairing or replacing the joints in question. A skilled hand surgeon may not be the best choice to operate on the knees or hips, and vice versa. When in doubt about the need for surgery, the type of operation, or the best surgeon, a second opinion can be helpful.

▪ *Practical Aspects to Living with Rheumatoid Arthritis*

It would be folly to imply that people with rheumatoid arthritis can go about their daily life giving little or no consideration to the disease. Even though in most instances the disease can be controlled, and its victims lead rewarding, productive lives, adjustments and compromises are often needed. Chronic diseases are by nature difficult, particularly those that are both painful and disabling.

Many people make the mistake of thinking that a stiff upper lip is all that is needed. Determination is important, but in dealing with arthritis, common sense is perhaps even more essential. Sometimes simple household or personal tasks, such as opening a jar or putting on panty hose or getting up off a low toilet seat, can be very difficult if not impossible. A variety of gadgets are available that make it easier to perform ordinary tasks. Surgical supply houses or arthritis specialists usually have catalogues. Physical and occupational therapy also are valuable in learning new skills.

Arthritis also takes its toll on family members and personal relationships. Many arthritis patients find they avoid sexual relations because at the end of the day they are fatigued or they fear anything that may produce pain. While sexual intimacy may not be the most important factor in a relationship, it certainly is an important one, and there is no reason the arthritis patient should be denied a warm and loving association. Often, simply timing sexual activity to coincide with the "best" part of the day—perhaps in the morning after a shower to get limbered up, or after an afternoon nap—solves the problem. Experimenting to find positions that are comfortable and do not put stress on painful joints also helps.

People with chronic diseases often resort to becoming manipulative and complaining. This is understandable, but it does not make life pleasant for those who live with the patient. The person with arthritis should not hesitate to ask for help when it is needed, and to accept offers of help. But this is quite different from becoming overly demanding or dependent. Take time to assess what is really important and, if need be, reorder priorities. A housewife may want a spotless house, but does it really matter that every speck of dust is removed from hard-to-reach places? Instead of wearing yourself out doing a massive cleaning and then spending a couple of days in bed, it is far better to do a little each day and to encourage (not nag) other family members to do their share.

In recent years, there have been major advances in the long-term management of rheumatoid arthritis. It is now rare for a person to become severely crippled from the disease, and even those with considerable disability can learn to be self-sufficient.

❑ Gout

Also called crystal arthritis, gout is one form of arthritis that almost always can be kept under good control to avoid periodic flare-ups. It is also the one form of arthritis for which the cause is well established. People with gout have an inborn metabolic error that causes crystals from excessive uric acid in the blood to form and settle in the joint space, resulting in inflammation and severe pain.

We often associate gout with the gluttony of King Henry VIII or the wisdom of Benjamin Franklin—two famous sufferers—but there is nothing inherent in these traits to predispose a person to gout. The disease almost always occurs in men, with the first attack usually coming in middle age. Typically, an attack comes on without warning. A big toe is the favored site; within hours, the joint will be red, swollen and inflamed, as well as extraordinarily painful. Gout sufferers describe the pain of an attack as much worse than the most severe toothache. Even the slightest touch or the weight of a sheet will send waves of extreme pain through the foot and leg. If untreated, an attack usually lasts for several days, and then the sufferer may not have another episode for several months. As time goes by, the attacks usually become more frequent, and more joints—usually the elbow, ankles, knees or fingers—may be affected. It is understandable that in time past, gout sufferers became preoccupied with their disease and lived in dread of the next attack.

Fortunately, times have changed. The vast majority of gout patients can now live without attacks; several drugs can eliminate the cause—namely, excessive uric acid in the blood. Uric acid is normally filtered from the blood through the kidneys. The conditions that lead to gout arise when there is an overproduction of uric acid or when, for some reason, the kidneys cannot eliminate uric acid adequately. As a result, uric acid crystals form in the joint space, irritating the joint lining and causing a severe inflammatory reaction. The inflammation affects the nerve endings in the joint, which accounts for the severe pain.

Sometimes people with high uric acid will have large deposits of crystals, or tophi, in soft tissue (such as the outer ear), without having the usual symptoms of gout. Many also will develop urate kidney stones, which are made up of uric acid. In such instances, the first indication of high uric acid may be the development of a kidney stone. Hyperuricemia (excess uric acid) in itself does not need to be treated if it causes no symptoms, but people with elevated uric acid levels should be tested regularly for signs of kidney damage. People with high uric acid also tend to have an increased incidence of heart attacks, but it is not known if there is a relationship between the uric acid and heart disease, or if other common characteristics of gout patients, such as being overweight, account for the rise.

Gout appears to be linked to a genetic factor: Some people have a predisposition to develop hyperuricemia. In addition, diet, infections and certain drugs, especially diuretics used to treat high blood pressure, can precipitate gout. In susceptible people, frequent aspirin use also can cause hyperuricemia.

▪ *Treatment*

Gout is one of the most successfully managed forms of arthritis. If the treatment regimen is followed carefully, it can almost always be kept under control. It is also one of the few forms of arthritis for which aspirin is not appropriate. Drug therapy for gout is two-pronged: an analgesic other than aspirin, such as acetaminophen (Tylenol) or codeine for the pain, and an anti-inflammatory drug to control inflammation. Colchicine is the traditional drug used during the acute phase. It is an ancient drug, derived from the autumn crocus or meadow saffron, which has been used in folk medicine to treat gout since the sixth century. Benjamin Franklin is reputed to have been treated with colchicine during his European travels and is said to have introduced the drug to American physicians. Colchicine has remarkable anti-inflammatory action, but it seems to work only for gout and not for other forms of arthritis. The major problem with colchicine is its extreme toxicity. Indeed, the ancients recognized it as a poison and hesitated to give it to humans as medicine. Typically, a gout patient will be instructed to take a 1 milligram tablet of colchicine at the first sign of an attack, and 0.5 milligram every two or three hours until the pain abates or diarrhea, nausea, vomiting or abdominal cramps develop. This is a sign that a toxic level has been reached, and the patient should take no more of the drug. If the colchicine is continued, severe diarrhea and intestinal hemorrhaging may occur. As little as 7 milligrams of colchicine may be fatal, so it is very important that the patient recognize when it is time to stop the drug. Why is such a toxic medication prescribed? Mainly because even a small dose produces dramatic relief: A person who is writhing in pain and unable to bear even the slightest touch to the inflammed joint may be up and walking about, free of pain, in a few hours.

Patients who cannot tolerate colchicine may be given potent nonsteroidal anti-inflammatory drugs (NSAIDs) as an alternative. The two used most often are phenylbutazone (Butazolidin) or indomethacin (Indocin). Phenylbutazone is perhaps the more effective, but it also has a long list of potentially serious side effects, including serious blood disorders, liver damage, nausea, vomiting, gastrointestinal bleeding and kidney damage.

It is generally prescribed for only a short time, and the patient should have frequent blood tests. Indomethacin is less likely to cause severe blood disorders and is also effective in treating acute gout. Both drugs take longer than colchicine to end an attack, but most patients will experience relief within a couple of days.

After the acute phase of the gout attack has passed, the physician will look into the underlying cause. If medications, such as diuretics, are responsible, alternative drugs may be prescribed. If there does not appear to be a secondary cause, treatment depends on how frequent and intense subsequent attacks are. For chronic gout, where the attacks are frequent, colchicine is sometimes given in low doses as a preventive. If the side effects of colchicine, even in low doses, are too severe or if the attacks persist, a uricosuric agent—one that lowers the level of uric acid by blocking its reabsorption as it filters through the kidney—may be tried. Probenecid (Benemid) or sulfinpyrazone (Anturane) works in this manner. Alternatively, a drug that blocks production of uric acid, such as allopurinol (Zyloprim or Lopurin), may be prescribed. Allopurinol also may be given in combination with either probenecid or sulfinpyrazone. These drugs are never given during an acute attack of gout; they may, in fact, make the attack worse. They are given to prevent attacks of gout by altering the conditions that can lead to it.

NON-DRUG THERAPY

Diet. It has long been known that certain foods can precipitate an attack of gout. These include foods rich in purine—organ meats, sardines, anchovies, dried peas and legumes—which can increase the level of uric acid. Wine, beer and sometimes other alcoholic beverages also can precipitate an attack of gout. Patients with mild gout or elevated uric acid often are advised to avoid these foods. Ironically, many gout patients develop strong cravings for the very foods that are responsible for their disease.

Weight Reduction. Obesity not only puts a strain on the affected joint, producing more pain, it can also be responsible for the hyperuricemia. Therefore, weight reduction is sometimes the only treatment needed for gout. It is important, however, to follow a sensible weight-loss plan that produces a gradual reduction because a sudden dramatic drop in calories can actually cause an attack.

Gout patients should make sure they drink lots of nonalcoholic fluids to increase urine output and flush out the excessive uric acid. Since even the slightest pressure during an attack of gout is so very painful, using a bed frame to keep sheets and blankets off the affected foot may help. Most gout patients cannot tolerate wearing regular shoes; sandles or roomy soft shoes, such as sneakers, may be more tolerable.

❑ Pseudogout

Pseudogout is caused by crystals of calcium pyrophosphate dihyrate (CPPD) in the joint space. Pseudogout is more common in men than women and its incidence increases with age. The knee, rather than the toe (as in primary gout), is the most frequent site, although the fingers, toes, hips, shoulders, elbows and ankles may be affected. Sometimes there are no acute attacks, as in true gout, but the disease may result in chronic inflammation and calcification of joint cartilage. In this stage, pseudogout may be confused with rheumatoid arthritis or inflammatory osteoarthritis.

Pseudogout usually can be treated effectively with nonsteroidal anti-inflammatory drugs. Cortisone injected directly into the joint may be used for acute attacks.

❑ Infectious Arthritis

Sometimes arthritis may be a complication of another disease caused by a virus, bacterium or fungus. Microorganisms enter the joint, causing infection and inflammation. Infectious arthritis is the only arthritis for which there is really a complete cure, provided the infection is diagnosed in time and treated with the appropriate antibiotic. If the infection is not treated promptly, however, the joint may be permanently damaged and a chronic arthritis may develop. People who have used steroids for long periods or who have a lowered resistance to infection for some other reason may be at risk for infectious arthritis. In addition, those with rheumatoid arthritis seem to be at risk for bacterial arthritis. If a person with rheumatoid arthritis is persistently bothered by one joint, even when the disease is in remission elsewhere, bacterial arthritis should be suspected.

Staph infections, gonorrhea, tuberculosis, rheumatic fever, osteomyelitis (bone infection) and a variety of viral and fungal infections all can cause infectious arthritis. In recent years, a good deal of publicity has been given to Lyme arthritis, a disease carried by deer ticks and named for the Connecticut town in which it was discovered. In all types of infectious arthritis, treatment involves identifying the causative agent and then prescribing the appropriate antibiotic or antifungal drug.

❑ Soft-Tissue Rheumatism

A number of conditions affect the muscles, tendons, ligaments or tissue surrounding joints that may cause pain and stiffness. Although the individual may misinterpret the symptoms as arthritis, these disorders actually fall into another category of rheumatic disease, soft-tissue rheumatism. Treatment for some of these conditions may be similar to treatment for arthritis, but a specific diagnosis will lead to the best course of therapy. Some of these conditons are not chronic in the same sense that arthritis is, but recurrence may be a problem with some.

Disorders classified as soft-tissue rheumatism may be either localized, confined to a specific joint or two, or diffuse.

Some of the more common localized conditions include:

Bursitis. Inflammation of the bursae, small fluid-filled sacs around the joint space. It occurs most commonly in the shoulder, hip, knee and elbow. Pain is localized and the area may be hot and red. It frequently follows an injury to the area or excessive use of the joint; for example, tennis players often develop bursitis in their shoulders.

Capsulitis. Inflammation of the joint capsule, most commonly the shoulder.

Costochondritis. Inflammation of cartilage outside the joint. The ribs are commonly affected.

Fasciitis. Inflammation of the membrane covering the muscles, the fascia. Plantar fasciitis occurs in the heel. Other sites include the neck, back, thigh, hands and feet.

Ligamentitis. Inflammation of ligaments, the bands of fibrous tissue that connect bones. This may be caused by improper joint motion, particularly in the knee and ankle.

Nerve-entrapment syndrome. A condition caused by swelling of a ligament that puts pressure on an adjacent nerve. Carpal tunnel syndrome, for example, causes hand and wrist pain because of pressure on the nerve that passes through the carpal tunnel in the wrist.

Tendinitis. Inflammation of the tendons (the tissue that connects muscle to bone) and their sheaths often caused by overuse or injury. Tennis elbow is a form of tendinitis. Shoulders, wrists, hips, knees, ankles and fingers, as well as elbows, may be affected.

Diffuse conditions include:

Fibrositis. Symptoms include pain in muscles, ligaments and tendons, difficulty in sleeping and local tenderness in any of several trigger points, primarily on shoulders, back or hips. Tingling, numbness, fatigue and anxiety are common. Since X-rays reveal no changes in muscles or other tissue, in the past the person suffering from fibrositis was often misdiagnosed or the symptoms were dismissed as psychological. Now the characteristics of the condition are more widely recognized.

Giant cell arthritis. A rare disorder involving inflammation of the blood cells that can lead to severe headache, fever, weight loss, anemia and blindness.

Polymyalgia rheumatica. Characterized by stiffness and pain in shoulder and hip area. It affects older people primarily. Treatment usually involves a combination of rest, exercise and drug therapy.

Arthritis may also be associated with other diseases. For example, people with psoriasis often develop psoriatic arthritis; ulcerative colitis may also be accompanied by arthritis.

14

MATURITY-ONSET DIABETES

An estimated 10 million Americans suffer from maturity-onset diabetes, the most common form of this endocrine disorder. Maturity-onset diabetes, also known as Type 2 or non-insulin–dependent diabetes, comes on gradually and is most common after the age of 40 and among people who are overweight. Type 2 diabetes usually can be controlled by diet, in contrast to juvenile diabetes, also known as Type 1 or insulin-dependent diabetes, which requires insulin injections. (For the sake of consistency, we will use the terms Type 1 and Type 2 diabetes.) Some people with Type 2 diabetes may eventually require insulin shots; also, some adults develop Type 1 diabetes, characterized by a failure of the pancreas to produce insulin.

Diabetes is a widespread and serious but manageable health problem; altogether, the two forms of the disease and its complications are responsible for approximately 334,000 deaths annually. But through early diagnosis and careful adherence to diet, medication regimes and other methods of self-care, people with diabetes can greatly reduce the chances of disability and life-threatening illness.

Type 2 diabetes arises when the body is unable to make effective use of insulin, a hormone produced by special islet cells in the pancreas. Among other functions, insulin is essential to the body's metabolism. Without sufficient insulin, the body is unable to utilize blood sugar, or glucose, its major fuel. Carbohydrates are the major source of glucose; insulin is also important in the metabolism of proteins and fats, and performs other vital functions.

In contrast to Type 1 diabetes, in which the pancreas secretes little or no insulin, patients with Type 2 diabetes often have normal or even high levels of the hormone, but for some reason the body is unable to use it. This may be due to a larger amount of insulin-resistant fat tissue (about 80 percent of Type 2 diabetics are overweight), a reduced number of receptors that enable insulin to enter the cell, abnormal receptors or other factors. This resistance may also be due to a defect in which the body's immune system perceives its own insulin as "foreign" and attacks it. Current research on drugs that suppress selected parts of the immune system, correcting the defect while allowing the rest to carry out defensive functions, may someday be used in the treatment of Type 2 diabetes.

In addition to being overweight, having a close relative with the disease greatly increases the risk of diabetes in adults 40 and older. Certain drugs, disorders of the pancreas and endocrine system and stress also may produce diabetes, usually Type 1.

Symptoms of Diabetes

Older adults who are either overweight or have a family history of the disease, or both, should see a physician for the following symptoms which may indicate diabetes.

- Extreme hunger or thirst
- Frequent need to urinate
- Marked weight loss
- Nausea and vomiting
- Fatigue or drowsiness
- Blurred vision
- Impotence in males
- Irritability and mood swings
- Itching
- Frequent vaginal infections
- Frequent infections of small skin abrasions which heal slowly
- Numbness, tingling or pins-and-needles sensations in hands or feet
- Slow-to-heal cuts, particularly on the feet

Table 14:1

❑ How Diabetes Is Diagnosed

Regular physical examinations including blood and urine testing are important in detecting Type 2 diabetes, which may not produce symptoms in its early stages (see Table 14:1). Diabetes is characterized by high levels of blood glucose because the body is unable to use it for fuel. Eventually, some of the excessive glucose will be secreted by the kidneys in the urine. Detecting glucose in the urine is a warning sign of diabetes, but since other factors can produce this symptom, blood tests to measure the level of glucose are a more accurate diagnostic tool.

To diagnose diabetes, blood sugar is measured before breakfast in the morning, after an overnight fast. Two separate readings of more than 140 milligrams of glucose per deciliter of blood are generally considered indicative of diabetes. If the blood sugar is only slightly elevated, the physician may order an oral glucose tolerance test (OGTT). In preparation, the individual must eat sufficient carbohydrates (100 to 150 grams per day) for three days preceding the test and then fast the night before. He or she is then given a sugar drink and blood samples are taken every 30 minutes for two to three hours. In nondiabetic people, blood sugar rises for as long as one hour after the drink and then gradually drops. Those with diabetes will have higher blood sugars at the one-hour point and not show the expected drop. The results of these tests can be thrown off by many factors, including alcohol abuse, liver disease, prior gastrointestinal surgery and decreased activity levels. Many medications, including antidepressants, steroids and certain other hormones, thiazide diuretics and the anticonvulsant drug Dilantin may also either raise or lower blood glucose.

❑ Controlling Type 2 Diabetes

Numerous studies have demonstrated that most cases of Type 2 diabetes can be successfully controlled by diet and exercise. The diet entails strict reduction of calories and weight loss. In practice, however, most people with the disease simply do not adhere to the dietary restrictions. Anyone who has tried to lose weight knows only too well that cutting down on calories is difficult. For diabetic patients, cutting calories may be even harder because they often feel hungry most of the time. Even though the person is overweight and has high levels of blood glucose, the body is unable to make proper use of this fuel. The brain especially requires a steady supply of glucose; if this is not forthcoming, it will send out powerful hunger signals. This explains why extreme hunger is one of the major symptoms of diabetes: The brain is being starved and is trying to protect itself by signaling it needs more food. So it takes even greater willpower to lose the excess weight; if this can be achieved, however, the body is able to make better use of its insulin and the hunger will then abate.

Of course, not all people with Type 2 diabetes are overweight, and there are instances in which weight loss alone is not sufficient to control the diabetes. In such patients, if blood sugar still remains high, or in the case of overweight diabetic patients who cannot lose weight, medication may be prescribed. This usually entails taking pills from a family of drugs known as oral hypoglycemics, although for some patients, insulin injections may be needed. (Insulin cannot be taken orally because it is a protein hormone and would be rendered useless by the digestive process.)

▪ *Achieving Weight Loss*

Maintaining normal weight will usually control Type 2 diabetes, but it is not a cure; if the lost weight is regained, chances are the blood sugar will rise and any previous symptoms may recur. To prevent complications, normal weight must be maintained for life. To plan for safe weight loss, the patient should work with a dietitian to come up with a satisfactory eating plan—one that the patient can live with and still control the blood sugar.

Older individuals who have a lifetime of bad eating habits may need much support in changing them. Additionally, being diagnosed with an incurable chronic disease often leads to anger or denial of the illness and results in self-destructive behavior patterns, including gorging on forbidden foods. Groups such as Weight Watchers and Overeaters Anonymous and techniques such as hypnosis and behavior modification may facilitate weight loss. Individual counseling or a diabetes support group may help the newly diagnosed diabetic cope with his or her disease.

▪ *Exercise*

Regular exercise combined with cutting calories offer a faster and less painful way of losing weight than dieting alone. Aerobic activities, such as brisk walking, jogging, swimming and cycling, are most important. These activities exercise the large muscles, which reduces insulin resistance and rapidly burns glucose. This form of brisk prolonged activity also helps condition the cardiovascular system, increasing the heart's efficiency and reducing the risk of coronary artery disease and heart attacks, which are associated with both Type 1 and Type 2 diabetes. Aerobic exercise also helps reduce stress and lower cholesterol and possibly hypertension—major risk factors in the development of heart disease.

Older adults—in fact, anyone over age 35—who have not practiced regular, vigorous exercise should consult a physician before embarking on such a program. Heart disease, even a previous heart attack, is not a contraindication for strenuous exercise, as long as the program is properly tailored to meet the individual's health status.

To design a safe yet effective regimen,

the physician may recommend a stress test that measures how the heart performs during vigorous exercise. In this procedure, pulse, blood pressure and a continuous electrocardiogram are taken while the individual rides an exercise bicycle or walks a treadmill. Test results are then read by a physician.

Anyone starting an exercise program should begin gradually and work up to a heart-conditioning level. The routine should be done at least three or four times a week. (See Chapter 2.)

▪ *Medications*

Even though most people with Type 2 diabetes can be treated by weight loss alone, in practice many end up taking an oral hypoglycemic medication. These drugs are also called sulfonylureas because they are related to the sulfa drugs. They lower blood sugar by stimulating the pancreas to produce more insulin and possibly decreasing insulin resistance. Although they all belong to the same family of drugs, they have somewhat different actions; some may be either short- or long-acting, have different times of peak action and dosage schedules. (See Table 14:2, Drugs to Treat Type 2 Diabetes.)

Although people who take oral medications are not at as great a risk for developing excessively low blood sugar as those taking too much insulin, this reaction can occur. Skipping a meal or not eating enough, alcohol consumption, concurrent use of certain drugs and overexercising may bring on excessive low blood sugar, or hypoglycemia (see Table 14:3, Symptoms of Hypoglycemia). Persons with adrenal insufficiency (Addison's disease) or liver, kidney or pituitary gland disorders and the elderly may require careful dose adjustments to prevent hypoglycemia.

If hypoglycemic symptoms occur, the individual should immediately take a quick source of sugar—for example, a glass of orange juice—followed by a protein source for sustained glucose release. Diabetic patients should always carry hard candies for a quick sugar source when away from home.

Although a controversial study has shown that oral hypoglycemic drugs may carry some increased risk of death from heart disease, complications of uncontrolled diabetes are usually considered to more than offset this possible risk.

Drugs to Treat Type 2 Diabetes

Generic Name	Brand Name	Usual Daily Dose	Time of Peak Action
tolbutamide	Orinase	2–3	3–4 hours after taking
tolazamide	Tolinase	1–2	3–4 hours after taking
chlorpropamide	Diabinese	1	3–6 hours after taking
acetohexamide	Dymelor	1–2	4–5 hours after taking
glyburide	DiaBeta, Micronase	1–2	4 hours after taking
glipizide	Glucatrol	1–2	1–3 hours after taking

Table 14:2

Symptoms of Hypoglycemia

- Headache
- Extreme fatigue
- Sudden drowsiness or change in alertness
- Nervousness or tremulousness
- Confusion or personality change
- Hunger
- Profuse perspiration
- Cold feeling
- Clammy skin
- Pallor
- Blurred or double vision
- Rapid pulse or palpitations
- Ringing in the ears
- Numbness or tingling in lips, nose or fingers

Note: The drug propranolol (Inderal) may mask symptoms of hypoglycemia.

Table 14:3

❑ Complications of Diabetes

Diabetes can affect many organ systems through changes in the blood vessels, nerves and other less clearly understood mechanisms. Although complications are somewhat more common in Type 1 diabetes and are usually related to poorly controlled blood sugar and/or duration of the disease, people with good control may also suffer these, while those with long-standing diabetes may be spared. Even with this somewhat unpredictable outcome, strict control of blood sugar and regular medical follow-up of any early signs of concurrent disease is vital to minimize the risk of complications.

▪ *Eyes*

Diabetes is the chief cause of new cases of blindness in adults, according to the American Diabetes Association. Most commonly, diabetes affects the retina and lens of the eye. People with hypertension are especially at risk since this disease can cause hemorrhaging and other abnormal changes in the retina and optic nerve.

The retina lies at the back of the eyeball and contains the color- and light-sensitive cells that transmit electrical impulses to the brain, resulting in visual perception. In diabetic retinopathy, the walls of the capillaries nourishing the retina weaken and burst, or become constricted and die. Resulting small hemorrhages and decreased supply of oxygen and other nutrients to the retina can result in visual impairment.

More seriously, fragile new blood vessels can develop in the retina, leaking blood into the jelly-like vitreous humor that fills the eyeball. The bleeding can initially cause temporary dimming of vision or blindness; eventually fibrous scar tissue forms, leading to permanent vision loss and retinal detachment which can result in blindness. Advances in laser surgery and microsurgery, used to destroy weakened or excess blood vessels and repair a detached retina, now reduce the chance of permanent damage. Patients who suffer loss of sight resulting from bleeding into the vitreous humor may be helped by having this substance replaced by an artificial solution.

Diabetic patients are also sometimes subject to an early and rapidly developing form of cataracts that closely resemble those often found in the elderly. Research suggests that the lens may become clouded because glucose combines with lens proteins or because enzymatic changes related to high blood sugar occur. Treatment is the same as for other cataracts—removal of the lens followed by special glasses, contact lenses or insertion of an intraocular lens to restore vision.

People with diabetes should promptly report blurred vision, evidence of bleeding or other visual changes to an ophthalmologist. In addition, regular eye examinations (every six months to one year, or more often) are vital to prevent or minimize loss of sight.

▪ *Heart Disease*

Multiple changes in the cardiovascular system put diabetic patients at an increased risk for diseases affecting the blood vessels and heart. People with diabetes are more likely to develop arteriosclerosis (hardening of the arteries) and atherosclerosis (fatty buildup in the arteries) both earlier and at a faster rate than the general population. High blood pressure and increased blood cholesterol and triglyceride levels—major risk factors for stroke and heart attack—are also more common. The characteristic thickening of capillary membranes that result in impaired blood flow to the heart also affects the limbs, particularly the lower legs and feet. As a result, diabetics are vulnerable to skin ulcers, infection and gangrene. In fact, diabetes is the leading cause of amputation in this country.

In addition to changes in both large and small blood vessels, people with poorly controlled diabetes have an abnormal type of hemoglobin as well as the normal form. Excess sugar in the blood attaches to hemoglobin, resulting in a combined molecule which carries less oxygen to the tissues.

The increased risk of heart disease may also be due to the attraction of platelets, blood particles responsible for normal clotting, to the walls of arteries that have been injured by diabetes-related factors. When platelets accumulate and clump together, they can trap other cells and the LDL cholesterol that forms fatty plaque to clog blood vessels, resulting in decreased circulation. (Aspirin taken daily in small doses has been shown to reduce clumping of platelets.) The high, but ineffective, levels of insulin found in many people with Type 2 diabetes may also increase the risk of atherosclerosis by promoting fat synthesis and rapid cell growth within the artery walls. (However, insulin injections needed by Type 1 and some Type 2 diabetics have not been shown to increase this risk.)

To minimize the chance of developing cardiovascular disease, people with diabetes should reduce or eliminate the following risk factors:

Smoking. Nicotine stimulates the release of substances that increase blood pressure, constrict the blood vessels and, in general, make the heart work harder. Toxic gases in cigarettes decrease the amount of hemoglobin available to carry oxygen and may increase formation of fatty plaques.

Obesity. In addition to making cells resistant to insulin, being overweight is associated with high blood cholesterol, triglycerides and hypertension. Weight loss has the added advantage of reducing or eliminating the need for medication in many Type 2 diabetics.

Hypertension. Diabetic patients should closely observe any restrictions on salt and calories, as well as medication schedules. Although relatively easy to control, hypertension is dangerous because there are often no symptoms or feelings of being "sick." Since there are no symptoms, many patients do not think they have a serious disease and stop taking their medication to lower blood pressure.

Impaired circulation joins with two other complications of diabetes—nerve damage and susceptibility to infection—to vastly increase the risk of gangrene. Cold feet, numbness or tingling in the toes, leg cramps when walking or climbing stairs, dry or shiny skin and loss of hair from the feet and toes are symptoms of circulatory/nerve damage and may indicate poor control of blood sugar. Diabetic patients should practice meticulous foot care (see Table 14:4) to avoid serious foot infections, ulcers and perhaps eventual amputation.

▪ *Diabetic Neuropathy*

High blood sugar is thought to cause damage to a variety of nerves affecting many parts of the body. For example, injury to peripheral sensory nerves—those that carry impulses from the skin to the brain and spinal cord—can result in altered sensations described earlier. Injury to peripheral motor nerves—those that carry impulses from the brain and spinal cord to muscles and glands—can cause muscular deterioration and weakness. Damage to the autonomic nervous system—nerves that affect smooth muscle, the heart and glands—can result in impotence, gastrointestinal and urinary tract problems, dizziness on standing (orthostatic hypotension) and irregular heartbeats.

Foot Care for People with Diabetes

1. Inspect your feet daily, watching for the following potential danger signs:
   - Redness or discoloration, especially near corns, calluses or at pressure points (heel, big toe, ball of foot)
   - Cracked, peeling or dry skin
   - Swelling, tenderness, warmth or other signs of infection
   - Thickening or discoloration of toenails
   - Ingrown toenails
2. Wash your feet daily in warm, not hot, water. If you are unable to test water temperature with your feet because of impaired sensation, use your elbow or a thermometer. Use a gentle soap and a soft brush, sponge or fine pumice stone to remove dead skin. Avoid alcohol, coarse pumice stones and other agents that may damage skin. To avoid drying out skin, limit soaking time to 10 to 12 minutes. Dry your feet and surfaces between toes thoroughly with a soft towel. Use a lanolin-based or other lubricating lotion to soften dry skin.
3. Protect your feet from injury by always wearing shoes, slippers or, when in the water, swim sandals. If you are wearing soft or open-toe shoes, watch where you step to avoid stones and other sharp objects.
4. Buy comfortable, well-fitting shoes. If you have a foot deformity that cannot be accommodated in a ready-made shoe, it is wise to invest in a custom-made one. (In some states, Medicaid may cover orthopedic shoes ordered on a doctor's prescription form.) Avoid very high heels, sharply pointed toes and constricting boots. Choose shoes made of materials that let the feet "breathe." Have at least two pairs and alternate them so each has the chance to dry out. Break in new shoes gradually and be on the alert for signs of irritation during this period.
5. Wear cotton socks or stockings and change them daily—more often if your feet are sweating. Do not wear garters or socks with tight elastic bands, which can reduce circulation to the feet.
6. Do not self-treat corns, calluses or fungal infections such as athlete's foot. If a corn or callus is developing, soak the foot in warm water for 10 minutes and scrub gently with a soft brush. Apply a lubricating lotion to the area when dry. Check your shoes to see what part may be rubbing or putting pressure on the area. Switch to another pair or protect your foot by using a piece of lamb's wool or moleskin over the affected area. Any redness or discoloration around a corn or callus should be brought to the attention of a podiatrist. All corn removal products contain harsh substances that can contribute to skin breakdown; corns and calluses should be removed by a podiatrist or other foot specialist.
7. Trim your toenails regularly. File them or use nail clippers, not scissors, straight across the top, being careful not to damage underlying tissue. Do not cut into the corners as this can cause ingrown toenails. Moisten the cuticles with oil and gently nudge them back with an orange stick. People who have poor vision or limited hand flexibility should have their toenails trimmed by someone experienced in diabetic foot care.
8. Promote good circulation. If you must sit with your legs crossed, cross them at the ankle rather than the knee. Keep your feet raised when sitting to avoid pooling of blood. Flex your feet or shift your weight from one foot to the other to increase circulation when sitting or standing for long periods.

Table 14:4

Widespread nerve damage, or neuropathy, may cause few symptoms in some people, while producing disabling problems in others. It may begin early in the course of the disease, long before any symptoms appear. Nerve damage often produces some form of pain, ranging from mild discomfort to severe stabbing or aching sensations. Although many parts of the nervous system may be affected, often it is the legs and feet that show the most obvious damage.

Some diabetic patients are troubled by dizziness or fainting when they suddenly change position, such as when getting out of bed in the morning or when rising from a chair. This is caused by othostatic hypotension, a temporary drop in blood pressure that occurs when going from a lying or sitting position to an erect one. The problem usually can be controlled by avoiding sudden changes in position; for example, sitting up for a minute or so before getting out of bed in the morning. Wearing elastic stockings to reduce the pooling of blood in the legs, which contributes to the drop in blood pressure, also may help. Weakness or other functional impairment in the arms and legs may be compensated for by braces or other assistive devices.

Research indicates that keeping blood sugar in the normal range while observing meticulous skin care can prevent or minimize neuropathy and the risk of gangrene. Patients who experience pain should consult their physician for appropriate pain medication.

▪ *Impotence*

For some men, impotence is one of the first signs of diabetes. The problem is caused by nerve damage, which makes it impossible to achieve an erection. The problem usually cannot be cured, but new techniques using special penile prostheses can restore sexual function. Some of the devices have balloon-like structures that are inflatable; others are more rigid and hold the penis in a more or less permanently erect position. (See Chapter 6, Midlife Crisis—The Man's Side.) Diabetic men troubled by impotence should consult a urologist who can determine the most appropriate type of prosthesis.

▪ *Kidneys*

Diabetes is one of the most common causes of kidney failure in the United States. The kidneys serve, among other functions, as a filter for wastes carried in the blood. Exposure to high glucose levels causes the membranes of blood vessels supplying the kidneys, as well as other organs, to thicken and lose the ability to filter waste. Arteriosclerotic changes in the capillaries result in partial blockage, further contributing to kidney damage and perhaps eventual kidney failure. Increased susceptibility to infection adds to the potential for damage.

Although the kidneys have vast reserve capacity—the body can function successfully on only one—diabetes damages both organs. Dialysis and kidney transplants may add years to the lives of those whose kidneys have failed; however, dialysis is expensive and time-consuming and kidneys for transplant are in short supply. In addition, research indicates that healthy kidneys develop symptoms of disease when transplanted into diabetic patients.

Once again, good control of blood glucose is essential to prevent or reduce damage to the kidneys. Studies have shown that reducing blood sugar to normal levels may even reverse kidney damage if started early on. Additionally, diabetic patients should seek medical attention at the first sign of a urinary tract infection. Symptoms include pain or burning on urination; frequency, urgency or difficulty in voiding; and cloudy, blood-tinged or foul-smelling urine.

▪ *Infection*

People with diabetes are susceptible to infection from many sources—the common cold, bacteria that invade a simple cut, normally harmless microorganisms that live in the mouth. Infections and colds tend to last longer in diabetics and require antibiotic therapy. And infection upsets the body's hormonal and metabolic balance, resulting in increased resistance to insulin. Women with diabetes may be particularly susceptible to vaginal yeast infections.

Diabetes somehow hampers the ability of the immune system to combat infection, possibly by interfering with white blood cell function. People with this disease should avoid coming into contact with those who might transmit an infectious illness. When this is not possible, good hygiene, particularly handwashing, may prevent the spread of bacteria. Diabetic patients should also be immunized against pneumonia, as well as get yearly shots against influenza and a tetanus booster shot every ten years.

People with diabetes should promptly seek medical attention when infection does set in so that prompt treatment can be started to shorten the duration of illness and bring blood sugar back to normal.

❑ Monitoring Blood Sugar

Traditionally, urine testing has been the only way diabetic patients could monitor their disease at home. Urine testing still has its place, but in addition, diabetic patients are now taught to do home blood sugar measurements. Although some physicians have not felt this necessary for patients with Type 2 diabetes, anyone who wants to ensure good control of blood glucose should learn this simple test. Blood glucose testing can also serve as a positive reinforcement for the majority of Type 2 diabetic patients who are overweight; as weight loss is achieved, lower blood sugar levels become evident. There are now a number of highly accurate, relatively inexpensive machines patients can use for home glucose testing. Patients should ask their doctor to show them how to use a home machine. By keeping daily records of blood sugar measurements, both a patient and physician can quickly spot patterns of poor control and take steps to correct them. (See Table 14:5.)

How to Do Home Blood Glucose Testing

There are two methods for home glucose testing:

1. Visual strip method. A drop of blood is placed on a chemically treated strip and compared against a color chart representing different sugar levels.
2. Glucose meter method. A drop of blood is placed on a chemically treated strip, which is inserted in an electronic glucose meter that analyzes reflected light from the strip. The blood sugar level is indicated in a digital reading.

The visual method is the less expensive of the two, but it is also less reliable. For example, it may be difficult to accurately judge the color that appears, especially for those with vision problems. Glucose meters are available for under $200 and may be covered by insurance if the physician certifies the need for testing.

Check with your doctor as to when and how often to test your blood sugar. The normal range for blood glucose in a fasting state and before meals is lower than that obtained one to two hours after meals. Below are the basic steps for monitoring blood glucose using a meter. Ask your physician to teach you how to use your particular device and then double-check your technique.

1. Calibrate machine according to the manufacturer's instructions.
2. Wash your finger with soap and water and dry thoroughly.
3. Squeeze finger for several seconds to stimulate blood flow.
4. Prick side of fingertip with sterile lancet and wipe the first drop of blood onto a gauze pad.
5. Apply second drop to test strip.
6. Observe any time interval specified by manufacturer and then blot strip onto specially supplied blotter paper.
7. Insert strip into slot on meter, read glucose level from digital readout and record in notebook.

Table 14:5

❑ The Long-Term Outlook

A diagnosis of diabetes often comes as a shock, and since most people know that it is a potentially life-threatening disease, it is understandable that the news can be depressing. There is a bright side, however. Type 2 diabetes is much less threatening than Type 1, and with proper diet, exercise and medication, if needed, blood sugars can be brought back into the normal range. This greatly reduces the chances of serious complications, and many experts believe that so long as blood sugar is kept within a normal range, a person with diabetes should expect to live a full, productive life. The development of computerized insulin pumps that are implanted in the abdomen and computerized to deliver insulin as needed offer hope for better control and management of Type 1 diabetes. Several promising new oral drugs for Type 2 diabetes also are being tested. Researchers also are developing techniques to transplant islet cells from fetuses under the skin of Type 1 diabetics, where the cells start producing insulin as though they were in the pancreas. On these and other fronts there is increasing hope for better control of diabetes. Sources of further information are listed in Table 14:6.

Resources

The American Diabetes Association
National Headquarters
2 Park Avenue
New York, NY 10016
1-800-232-3472
212-947-9707 (New York residents)

Organization with many local offices nationwide. Specializes in patient education, increasing public awareness of diabetes and funding diabetes research. Publishes literature on all aspects of diabetes, much of which is available at little or no cost.

Books

Lauffer, Ira J., M.D., and Kadison, Herbert.
Diabetes Explained: A Layman's Guide.
New York: Dutton, 1976.

Mirsky, Stanley, M.D., and Heilman, Joan Rattner.
Controlling Diabetes the Easy Way.
New York: Random House, 1981.

Subak-Sharpe, Genell J.
Living with Diabetes.
New York: Doubleday, 1985.

Home Glucose Monitoring

LifeScan, Inc.
1025 Terra Bella Avenue
Mountain View, CA 94043
1-800-227-8862
1-800-982-6132 (California residents)

Table 14:6

15

CHRONIC LUNG DISEASES

Breathing is the most essential function of the body; deprived of oxygen the body will die within 5 to 10 minutes. The respiratory (pulmonary) system, responsible for the vital transportation of air into the lungs, also filters out infectious agents and provides the air necessary for speech.

Air pollution, noxious fumes, smoking and overcrowded living conditions where infections are easily spread all take a heavy toll on the body's breathing mechanism. Every day the average person inhales about 3000 gallons of air; if it is contaminated with poisons, irritants and toxins, the simple act of breathing can reduce the life span and cause debilitating effects as one ages.

❑ How the Pulmonary System Works

Air, breathed in through the nose or mouth, passes through the windpipe (trachea) to the bronchial tubes, which divide into smaller branches called the bronchioles. From there air enters the thin-walled alveoli, the air sacs of the lungs where inhaled oxygen, vital to nourishing all tissues, is exchanged for waste carbon dioxide, which is then expelled by the lungs. (See Figure 15:1.) The chest muscles, together with the diaphragm, act as a bellows, expanding to allow the lungs to inflate and pull in air and contracting to expel the stale air.

The lower respiratory tract (comprised of the bronchial tubes, their branches and the lungs) is protected from invasion by foreign bodies by a variety of defenses, beginning with filtering hairs in the nose and continuing into the upper part of a muscular tube known as the pharynx. Next is the epiglottis, the flap of skin that covers the larynx, or voice box, when you swallow to prevent food or other foreign particles from entering the trachea, or windpipe.

The next barriers are the mucous secretions and cilia, minute hairs on the cells lining the respiratory tract that trap microorganisms and sweep them back up into the throat. Coughing helps to

The Pulmonary Tree

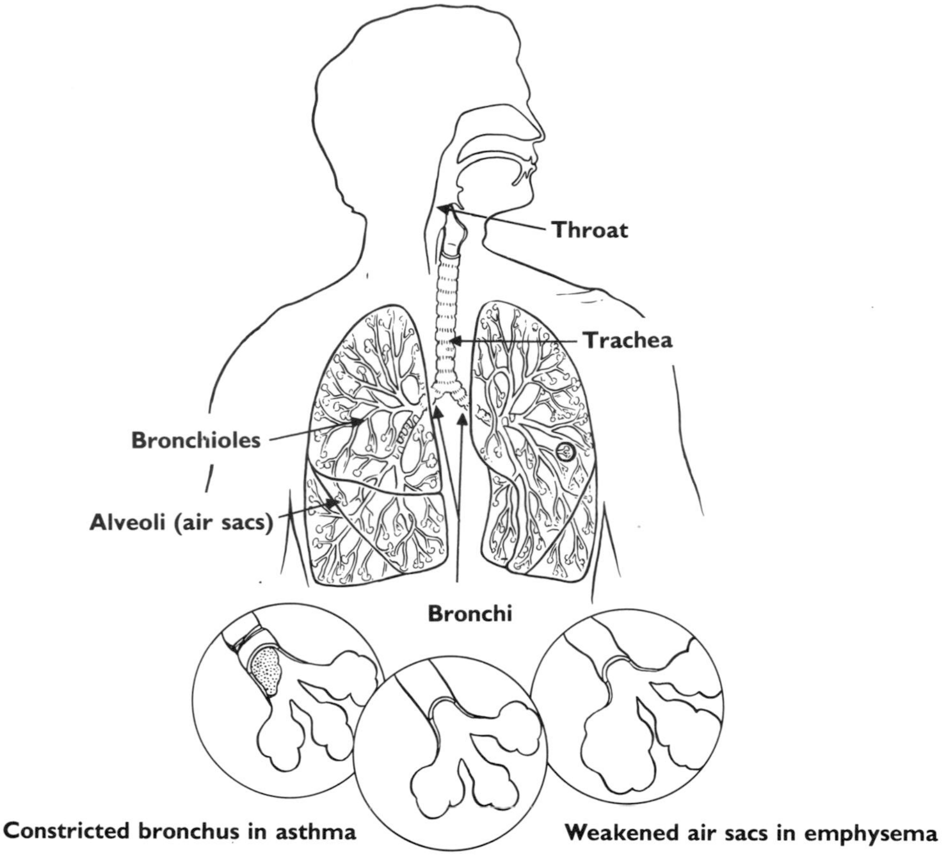

Figure 15:1

expel intruders from the bronchial tubes. The last in the line of defense are macrophages, white blood cells in the air sacs that destroy foreign invaders.

Assaults on the respiratory system can weaken these defenses: Viral and bacterial infections can carry diseases into the lungs; cigarette smoking and upper respiratory infections can partially paralyze the cilia, clogging the air passages with debris and causing further irritation; heavy alcohol intake, surgical anesthesia, prolonged bed rest and large doses of barbiturates or immune suppressants can also hinder respiratory controls and reduce the lung's ability to take in air. Chronic asthma may also eventually cause lung damage.

When the respiratory system is impaired, the oxygen supply to the organs is diminished. The heart overextends itself as it compensates for the oxygen deficiency by pumping more blood and may become enlarged.

Severe oxygen depletion can lead to cyanosis, a slightly blue skin discoloration. Always a serious symptom, cyanosis frequently accompanies certain cardiac conditions and sometimes pneumonia and chronic bronchitis.

The state of the lungs is one good indication of general health. Anyone

How to Check Your Lung Function

The Snider Match Test:

- Be sure the room is draft-free.
- Light a match from a matchbook and let it burn halfway down.
- Hold it 6 inches from your mouth and try to blow it out *with your mouth wide open.*

If you cannot extinguish the match, it usually indicates your lungs are not in the best of condition, possibly as the result of a lung disorder.

Chest Expansion:

- Take your chest measurement. (Men should measure around the nipples; women just under the breast.)
- Take a full breath and measure again. The second measurement should be at least 1.5 inches greater than the first, with variations according to size and sex. Expansion that is less than 1.5 inches, regardless of gender or size, suggests weak lungs. A medical checkup would be worthwhile.

Timed Exhalation:

- Take a deep breath.
- Time yourself as you exhale as rapidly as possible. Time only the exhalation.

If it takes you 3 to 4 seconds or less to exhale a normal amount, your lungs are healthy. It if takes longer, this may indicate the possibility of emphysema or another lung disorder.

Table 15:1

troubled by coughing, wheezing or shortness of breath, or who is prone to constant respiratory infections and other lung disorders, needs to know the cause of the breathing difficulty, how to increase maximum oxygen intake and decrease respiratory irritants. (See Table 15:1 for lung self-tests.)

❑ Chronic Obstructive Pulmonary Disease

Chronic bronchitis and emphysema are banded together under the term "chronic obstructive pulmonary disease," which doctors often refer to simply as COPD.

During air pollution disasters, in creased mortality occurs largely among elderly individuals suffering from these diseases. Although much is known about the causes of chronic obstructive pulmonary disease, no cure has been found. Depending on whether emphysema or bronchitis is more prevalent, symptoms may include excessive mucus, impaired clearance of mucus, chronic cough, increased susceptibility to respiratory infections, obstruction of the smaller airways, swelling and rupture of the lung's alveoli resulting in difficult breathing, insufficient oxygen in the blood and easy tiring.

Those who smoke half a pack of cigarettes a day are five times as likely to die from chronic obstructive pulmonary disease as are nonsmokers, while those who smoke two packs a day are twenty times as likely to succumb from the disease.

Although quitting smoking will not completely reverse all lung damage, it will usually reduce the frequency of symptoms, particularly the phlegm-producing cough. While most authorities agree that the risk of chronic obstructive pulmonary disease is greater from cigarette smoking than from environmental pollution, the risk from environmental factors still exists.

The severity of the disease increases with age and varies with the individual, his or her place of residence, heredity and innate resistance. Environmental pollution can be controlled by the individual only minimally by such means as the use of air filters to clean the air in the home, but obviously most air pollution problems will have to be addressed on a national or global scale.

▪ *Exercise*

Prolonged inactivity leads to excessive disability in patients with chronic obstructive pulmonary disease. As long as there is no severe cardiac disease, there should be a regular exercise program prescribed by a physician. If the patient is severely disabled, the program should be supervised by a physical therapist.

Breathing exercises may be helpful for anxious patients who develop an excessively rapid breathing rate during exertion.

▪ *Emphysema*

COMMON CHARACTERISTICS

Emphysema is a pulmonary disease in which progressive damage to the millions of tiny air sacs in the lungs causes difficulty in exhaling, a fatiguing cough, breathlessness from slight exertion and, sometimes, a barrel-shaped chest as the lungs try to compensate.

In more than 80 percent of all cases, emphysema, commonly called air hunger, is a direct consequence of smoking. Presently, men are about eight times more susceptible than women, but with more women smoking, the ratio will likely change. The disease usually appears between the ages of 50 and 60. In the United States, half of those afflicted are over 65, while nearly all the rest are over 45.

During the respiratory process, the alveoli expand and contract in unison as air is inhaled and exhaled. As emphysema develops, these tiny grapelike clusters of air sacs lose their elasticity, become distended and eventually rupture.

Under normal conditions there is an efficient exchange of oxygen and carbon dioxide in the alveoli. When the chambers become damaged, carbon dioxide cannot be expelled completely and waste-laden air accumulates. As breathing becomes shallower and requires more effort, the muscles of the neck, chest and diaphragm work harder to get enough oxygen into the bloodstream, and respiration increases to twenty-five inhalations a minute instead of the normal fifteen.

CAUSES

Advancing age, heavy smoking or a hereditary predisposition can promote the disease. The leading cause is smoking, particularly over a long period. The risk for heavy smokers exposed to pollutants on the job and elsewhere is very high. However, even light smokers can sustain tissue damage; studies show emphysema is not uncommon among them.

DIAGNOSIS

In its early stages, emphysema cannot be detected by X-ray, but airway function can be measured by a test done in the doctor's office with a spirometer that measures the amount of air that can be expelled from the lungs with maximum effort. When measurements detect residues of carbon dioxide remaining in the lungs, there is reason to believe that the cause is impairment of the air sacs. Lung scans using radioactive isotopes are also useful in diagnosing and evaluating the extent of lung damage.

TREATMENT

To stop progression of the disease, it is mandatory that all patients quit smoking. If environmental pollutants are the cause, a change of job or early retirement with compensation for the disability should be strongly considered.

Tips on Breathing More Efficiently

Deep breathing, moving the diaphragm rather than the upper chest, can help people with chronic obstructive pulmonary disease take in more oxygen and reduce breathlessness. The American Lung Association suggests the following steps be practiced often throughout the day to make diaphragmatic breathing "second nature."

- Relax your upper body, letting neck and shoulders droop.
- Place both hands on abdomen above waist and breathe in through your nose. If you are breathing with your diaphragm, your hands will move outward as the abdomen expands.
- Exhale slowly through pursed lips and repeat entire procedure. If you feel dizzy, take a few breaths using the upper chest and then try going back to breathing through the diaphragm.

Table 15:2

Self-treatment should include avoiding exposure to wet and windy weather and respiratory infections, having flu shots and a pneumonia immunization and, if necessary, losing weight. Drinking plenty of liquid to keep sputum loose, and taking prescribed antibiotics at the first sign of bronchitis or other upper respiratory infections (which may include colds), may also help. The physician may also prescribe drugs to dilate the bronchial passages, making breathing easier. In severe cases, oxygen therapy may be needed. (See Table 15:2, Tips on Breathing More Efficiently.)

▪ *Acute Bronchitis*

COMMON CHARACTERISTICS

Bronchitis, generally a self-limiting disease, is an inflammation of the bronchial tree caused by a virus or bacteria, inhalation of chemical pollutants and cigarette smoke. The microorganism or irritation causes a heavier secretion of mucus which, in turn, causes the characteristic phlegm cough. While complete healing and return of function is possible, bronchitis can be serious for debilitated patients and to the elderly if it is prolonged and develops into chronic bronchitis and possibly pneumonia.

▪ *Chronic Bronchitis*

Chronic bronchitis is a degenerative disease in which the walls of the bronchial tubes become thickened, inelastic and constricted, and the respiratory cilia are irreparably damaged. The mucous membranes of the bronchi are permanently inflamed and the airways become filled with a sticky mucus. There is a chronic or recurrent mucus-producing cough that lasts three or more months and recurs year after year. Chronic bronchopulmonary diseases impair the mucus-clearing ability of the lungs.

Chronic bronchitis may result from a series of attacks of acute bronchitis, or may evolve gradually owing to heavy smoking or the inhalation of air contaminated with other pollutants in the environment. Airway obstruction can result as a consequence of the mucus buildup, thickening and narrowing of the bronchial walls resulting from frequent respiratory infections and, in some cases, spasms of the bronchial muscles. Coughing, though distressing, is essential to the elimination of bronchial secretions and to clear the airways. (See Table 15:3, Getting the Most from Your Cough.)

Getting the Most from Your Cough

Mucus buildup in the airways can stimulate the urge to cough to expel it, but with chronic pulmonary disease, the individual may not be able to generate enough force to bring up the mucus for a so-called productive cough. The result is an unproductive, hacking cough or coughing spell which leaves the person fatigued, frightened and short of breath. Cough medicines should not be used unless allowed by the physician. The American Lung Association suggests the following steps for making a cough productive:

- Sit with your feet on the floor and head bent slightly forward.
- Breathe in deeply.
- Hold your breath for a few seconds.
- Cough twice, first to loosen the mucus, then to bring it up.
- Breathe in by sniffing gently.
- Spit out mucus; swallowing it can upset your stomach.

Table 15:3

TREATMENT

Removal of the bronchial irritants is essential in treating chronic bronchitis. Smoking must be stopped and the patient should avoid any environment in which irritants or noxious fumes are present. Antibiotics are recommended when there is pus in the sputum or when high fever persists, with some pulmonary specialists advising they be taken prophylactically at the first sign of cold or upper respiratory infection. Carbon dioxide retention and cyanosis may require the use of oxygen therapy. Slight

How to Make Lungs More Efficient

- Practice "pursed-lip breathing," exhaling slowly while keeping your lips in a whistling position, to relieve breathlessness.
- Do exercises that strengthen the diaphragm and abdominal muscles.
- Organize your time to allow rest periods between activities requiring exertion.
- Clear the lungs of excess mucus by lying in special positions, known as postural drainage, that help mucus drain from the lungs. If your physician approves, have a physical therapist or visiting nurse teach a family member how to "clap" on your chest to further loosen mucus.
- Build strength by taking a short walk every day.
- Use appropriate combinations of medicines, breathing aids and living patterns to make life more comfortable.

Table 15:4

to moderate breathlessness may be helped by breathing exercises. (See Table 15:4, How to Make Lungs More Efficient.) Postural drainage may be used to help remove secretions from the bronchial tree. Drinking plenty of liquids, especially chicken soup, remaining indoors and using nebulizers and vaporizers may also be helpful.

A NOTE ABOUT SMOKING

A smoker faces a four to twenty-five times greater risk of death from chronic bronchitis than a nonsmoker. By quitting, the cough and sputum may disappear within a few weeks, lung functions can improve and deterioration of the respiratory tract will be retarded. (See Chapter 3, Breaking Bad Habits.)

❑ Asthma

Asthma, characterized by an oversensitivity of the bronchi, is a chronic, often disabling disease that affects adults as well as children. Attacks can be provoked by numerous factors, including exposure to allergy-producing substances, and irritants such as dust, tobacco smoke or other pollutants, vigorous exercise, infection and stress. Sulfites used in food preservation have also been associated with severe asthma attacks.

Frequently, a person who has suffered childhood asthma will notice it disappear, seeming to outgrow it during adolescence, only to have it return in adulthood. The attacks may be precipitated by an infection or by exposure to a triggering factor, such as cigarette smoke or an allergen.

During an asthma attack both large and small airways become narrowed owing to inflammation and spasm of the bronchial muscles. Thick mucus further blocks the airways, leading to wheezing, coughing and difficulty breathing. Attacks vary widely in duration, intensity and frequency.

▪ *Treatment*

Because asthma can lead to life-threatening emergencies or permanent lung damage, it is important to learn how to control the disease. People whose asthma is brought on by a particular allergen should avoid that source wherever possible. Sometimes, desensitization shots are available for offenders such as molds, pollen and certain grasses. Exposure to cigarette smoke, environmental pollutants and household dust should be avoided. Most people with asthma are advised not to keep cats or dogs; even if the pets do not seem to provoke attacks, their dander is an irritant that increases vulnerability to bronchospasms.

During an acute asthma attack, bronchodilator drugs usually bring relief. People who have frequent attacks may be placed on preventive medications such as theophylline or cromolyn sodium, or a combination of drugs. Severe or prolonged attacks require prompt medical attention. The individual should remain as calm as possible at the start of an attack—something that is often easier

Relax to Breathe More Easily with Asthma

Learning to relax while breathing can help prevent the nervousness and anxiety which compounds breathlessness and traps more air in the lungs. The American Lung Association suggests practicing the following technique for 5 minutes twice a day, or whenever you feel yourself becoming short of breath.

- Sit up straight in a chair with your arms dangling at your sides.
- Breathe deeply, slowly and evenly through all the following steps:
  1. Tense your upper torso by simultaneously clenching your fists, shrugging your shoulders and tightening your arms. Hold the tension while counting to 2.
  2. Release tension, letting your shoulders drop, hands open and arms hanging relaxed. Count to 4.
  3. Tighten your legs and feet. Count to 2.
  4. Relax your legs and feet, keeping your upper body relaxed at the same time. Count to 4.

Table 15:5

said than done. Sitting down and leaning forward, with elbows or arms resting on a table, may be the most comfortable position. (See Table 15:5.)

Many asthma patients never learn the correct way of taking their medication. To relieve an attack, it is important to open the smallest of the airways. The inhalant medicines should be diluted and inhaled very slowly to enable the particles to penetrate deeper into the lungs and open the tiny passages. (See Figure 15:2.)

▪ *Complications and Precautions*

Chronic, poorly controlled asthma can lead to emphysema. The continued stretching of the air sacs during attacks by accumulations of stale air can cause them eventually to lose their elasticity and cease to function. Shortness of breath is a serious symptom and should be evaluated by a physician. Cardiovascular problems may sometimes accompany lung diseases and improve with medications, relieving shortness of breath.

How to Use a Nebulizer

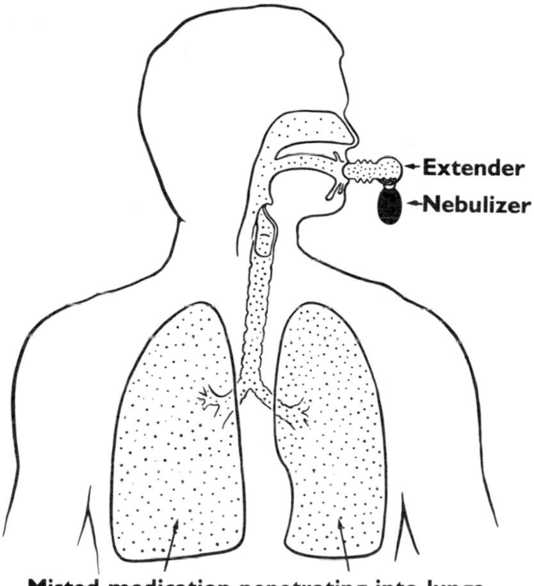

Figure 15:2
Nebulizers deliver tiny droplets of medicine deeply within the lungs. The smaller the particles of medicine, the deeper they will penetrate into the small airways, opening them up. To properly use a nebulizer, the medication should be diluted and an extender, or flex-tube, added to the end of the nebulizer. This helps break the droplets into a fine mist.

To inhale the medicine, take the biggest breath possible to ensure that the medication will penetrate as deeply into the lungs as possible. Breathe slowly, as if you are sipping hot soup, which also helps the medication get to where it is needed most. Be sure to "trigger" or squeeze the nebulizer just *after* you begin breathing in, not *before* you take your deep breath.

❑ Occupational Lung Disorders

▪ *Common Characteristics*

Respiratory diseases are widespread and figure among the most serious health problems originating in the workplace. Each year about 65,000 Americans develop some respiratory disease related to their work environment and 25,000 die from it. Since these diseases may take twenty or more years to develop, however, it can be difficult to trace their original causes.

The common factor in a variety of occupational lung disabilities is long-term exposure to microscopic and submicroscopic dusts, from inorganic (minerals and metals) or organic (cotton, moldy hay, mushroom spores) sources.

Although some occupational lung disorders may take the form of chronic bronchitis, emphysema or cancer, most are now grouped under the single heading of dust disease, *pneumoconiosis* ("dusty lung").

Symptoms of the disease are shortness of breath, abnormal fibrous tissue in the lungs, wheezing and coughing with or without phlegm (if serious, the phlegm will be bloody). All of these diseases can eventually lead to pneumonia and lung cancer, and can increase the risk of developing tuberculosis.

▪ *Treatment*

Treatment for pneumoconiosis can only relieve symptoms. The unhealthy environment that caused the condition should be avoided and smokers should quit.

▪ *The Dust Diseases*

SILICOSIS

Because of the number of industries that place workers at high risk for this, silicosis, caused by the inhalation of silica dust, is the most widespread of the dust diseases. Fibrous nodules develop and shortness of breath results as the amount of functional lung tissue declines. Silicosis increases the risk of tuberculosis and leads to heart failure.

BLACK LUNG DISEASE

Officially known as coal worker's pneumoconiosis, black lung results from the inhalation of bituminous or anthracite coal dust. Some cases develop into a condition known as progressive massive fibrosis, which destroys blood vessels and airways, and is likely to lead to premature death.

BROWN LUNG

Byssinosis, or brown lung, is a progressive debilitating disease caused by an allergy-like response to inhaled dusts from cotton, hemp and flax. Unlike some other dust diseases, byssinosis cannot be identified by changes in lung tissue nor does it show up on X-rays. An individual's susceptibility to the allergy-producing properties of the dust may determine the acuteness of the reaction, although it is not clear whether the disease truly represents an allergy. When the dust triggers a release of histamine in the lungs, the result is broncho-constriction, usually described as a feeling of "tightness" in the chest.

The disease pattern starts with something resembling an asthma attack. Because the air has difficulty moving out of mucus-clogged passages, a wheezing sound is produced. With the increasing frequency of these attacks chronic bronchitis sets in and eventually, when the air sac walls become irreparably damaged, emphysema results.

FARMER'S LUNG

Farmer's lung is the best known of the lung disorders caused by the inhalation of organic dusts (usually fungus spores). Farmer's lung attacks only people who are allergic to a fungus found in dust from moldy hay. Typical symptoms include a cough, shortness of breath, chills and fever. Continued exposure to offending spores leads to destruction of elastic tissue within the lung.

ASBESTOSIS AND ASBESTOS-INDUCED CANCERS

Asbestos is a generic term covering a variety of mineral silicates—naturally occurring mineral products that can be separated into microscopic fibers. Once these minuscule fibers are released into the air, they can remain suspended for long periods and inhaled into the lungs, where they become lodged in the tiny air passages deep within the lung. Asbestosis is the formation of fibrous tissue that eventually impairs the exchange of oxygen and carbon dioxide, resulting from asbestos inhalation. A dust-free environment is the only prevention.

Far more serious is the development of lung cancer and mesothelioma, a highly fatal cancer of the pleural lining of the lungs. Of persons diagnosed with mesothelioma tumors, 80 percent were exposed, often quite briefly, to asbestos twenty or thirty years previously. Although other forms of lung cancer may respond to chemotherapy and surgery, mesothelioma is highly invasive and often recurs after surgery. Smoking among workers exposed to asbestos compounds their risk of cancer.

❑ Smoking

Smoking, for even a short while, impairs the respiratory system. Smokers have reduced lung capacity and are more vulnerable to infections than are nonsmokers. Smokers have less endurance, less oxygen and a buildup of carbon dioxide in their lungs. (For a more detailed discussion as well as guidelines on quitting smoking, see Chapter 3, Breaking Bad Habits.)

In addition to the harm smokers do themselves, there is growing evidence that passive smoking also is harmful, especially to people with chronic lung disorders. Tremendous numbers of people are sensitive or allergic to tobacco smoke and the microscopic particles that contain irritating substances. The lung responds to irritating smoke with chronic mucus secretion and coughing, both common symptoms in smokers. Nonsmokers who are prone to respiratory infections are particularly sensitive to secondhand smoke.

❑ Pneumonia

▪ *Common Characteristics*

Pneumonia is not a single disease but a group of diseases that are caused by different bacterial or viral infections, irritation of delicate lung tissue by inhalation of poisonous liquid or gas, such as chlorine, or the blockage of a section of the lung caused by inhaling a tiny bit of food or vomit. The general term "pneumonia" refers to the infection, and resulting inflammation of lung tissues and alveoli. Treatment varies with the cause of the infection.

If pneumonia is not treated it can be fatal. But even with treatment, mortality runs from 5 to 10 percent, with most deaths occurring in the over-50 age group. Among people over 65, it is one of the five leading causes of death. Those whose lungs have been weakened as a result of being bedridden for long periods for other ailments are also vulnerable. The course of the disease in older persons does not follow the same pattern as it does in younger age groups, with one difference being that there is less response to medication.

The number of pneumonia cases and deaths reaches a peak in the months between December and March. In closed rooms, viral infections, which weaken the respiratory system's normal defense system, are spread easily from one person to another. Pneumonia often accompanies flu and bronchitis attacks. In 73 percent of flu patients age 70 and over, pneumonia occurs; in 36 percent of patients between the ages of 60 to 69, pneumonia and bronchitis occur together.

▪ *Symptoms*

Pneumonia either begins as, or is preceded by, an upper respiratory infection like a cold, accompanied by fever and a cough, often with pus-filled sputum.

Sweating, sharp pain in the chest, difficulty breathing and cyanosis may also be present. The patient feels weak, has muscle aches and loss of appetite, often accompanied by stomach distress. As the illness progresses, an initially dry cough may produce sputum, ranging from green to yellow or rusty in color (which indicates bleeding). Not all symptoms appear in everyone, but the presence of a number of these signs should always serve as a danger signal.

If left untreated, certain microorganisms responsible for pneumonia may spread to other parts of the body, causing infection in the lining of the heart (endocarditis) or membranes in the brain (meningitis).

▪ *Treatment*

Once a diagnosis is confirmed by chest X-ray and blood and sputum cultures, the physician will prescribe an antibiotic if the pneumonia is due to a bacteria. For viral pneumonias, treatment is to relieve symptoms. Cough medicines and mild painkillers may be used to relieve a cough or chest pain. To help reduce fever, aspirin and lukewarm sponge baths may be recommended. In severely debilitated patients, pneumonia may require hospitalization.

▪ *Prevention*

Nutrition and exercise, especially aerobic, are important to maintain general health and a strong respiratory system resistant to viral infections. Lung irritants and tobacco smoke should be avoided. Prompt treatment of any upper respiratory infection can help prevent pneumonia. Additionally, a vaccine against pneumonococcal pneumonia is usually recommended for all persons over 65 and for younger people with diabetes or chronic heart or lung diseases. Those who have already had a pneumococcal polysaccharide vaccine should not receive a second one. Individuals whose immune systems are weakened, such as those with AIDS, and those who are being treated with immunosuppressive drugs are vulnerable to other forms of pneumonia, such as *Pneumocystis carinii,* and should take particular care to avoid outside sources of infection.

▪ *Legionnaires' Disease*

Legionnaires' disease, a recently discovered form of pneumonia, is caused by the *Legionella pneumophila* bacteria present in contaminated humidifiers and air-conditioning systems. The disease was first recognized after a group of American Legion members meeting in Philadelphia in 1976 became ill; however, the bacteria has caused disease outbreaks since 1965.

The disease affects men more than women with an average age of 56. After an incubation period of two to ten days, the victim (who often has a history of other debilitating lung and heart diseases) develops fever, generalized weakness and loss of appetite, chills, diarrhea, dry cough, sore throat, and sometimes headaches and confusion. Fever rises over several days and hospitalization is necessary.

Treatment with antibiotics cures Legionnaires' disease; however, patients with compromised immune systems who are not placed on antibiotics have a high mortality rate.

❑ Flu and Flu Vaccines

Three different classes of influenza viruses, types A, B and C, are responsible for flu. Flu, also called the grippe, tends to come in epidemics and, periodically, worldwide pandemics. Type A flu occurs most commonly with widespread epidemics about every three years. Outbreaks of type B flu occur every five years or so, while type C flu viruses are localized and cause only minor sporadic outbreaks of mild illness.

Older people who get the flu have a greater tendency to develop a more serious illness and/or pneumonia. If fever, cough and sore throat continue for more than four days, pneumonia should be suspected, especially if there is shortness of breath, blood in the sputum, a second rise in temperature or a relapse in which the cough intensifies. Because of the possibility of developing pneumonia as a secondary infection, flu is especially serious for people already in a weakened state.

▪ *Symptoms*

The effects of flu infection can differ from person to person. Sometimes flu will not cause obvious symptoms. Often, however, the patient will feel weak and will develop a cough, headache and sudden rise in temperature. Other symptoms include aching muscles, chills and red, watery eyes.

Because of the additional risk of pneumonia in the elderly, doctors recommend that everyone over 65 and anyone with chronic heart and respiratory disorders, cancer, diabetes, kidney disease, anemia or conditions that affect immunity get a flu shot. The flu vaccine carries a low risk of side effects; however, people who are allergic to eggs should not take the shot. Also, someone who is acutely ill should wait until he or she is better before taking a flu shot.

❑ PLEURISY

▪ *Common Characteristics*

Pleurisy is an inflammation of the pleura, the two-layered membrane that encases the lungs and rib cage. It is caused by any disease that also inflames the lung, such as pneumonia, tuberculosis or a tumor, and can be triggered by flu, a severe cold, rheumatic fever, bronchitis or kidney disease.

Pleurisy in its early stages may be fibrous, or dry, with inflamed membrane surfaces rubbing against each other, but often the inflammation leads to a seepage of fluids between the membranes, a condition known as pleural effusion. In dry pleurisy, the symptoms are either mild or sharp chest pains aggravated by coughing and pains in the abdomen, neck and shoulders. There may also be a crackling or harsh grating sound on respiration. In a pleural effusion, pain subsides or disappears completely, but breathing becomes difficult.

▪ *Treatment*

Treatment consists of finding the underlying cause of pleurisy and resolving this. Aspirin may be recommended to relieve pain and it is important to prevent pneumonia from developing by trying to cough up secretions that may accumulate. To minimize pain, the doctor may suggest holding a pillow against the chest while attempting to cough.

▪ *Complications*

Empyema, or the buildup of purulent fluid in the pleura, is the most serious complication, but it responds to antibiotic treatment and careful surgical drainage of the fluid.

❑ PULMONARY TUBERCULOSIS

▪ *Common Characteristics*

In the United States, tuberculosis, now a rare disease with a low mortality rate, usually occurs among elderly people, impoverished individuals living in unsanitary housing, and malnourished persons such as alcoholics. Recently, however, there has been a rise in its incidence in some parts of the country that is attributable to the influx of immigrants from areas such as Southeast Asia, Mexico, and Central and South America, where tuberculosis is common. In addition, malnourished homeless people, as well as those with immune deficiencies such as AIDS, are susceptible to tuberculosis.

In adults, early signs of this bacteria-caused disease may be totally absent or resemble the flu. Gradually, weight loss, fatigue and a slight fever are seen. A cough may be dry at first but then produce increasingly large amounts of yellow or green sputum and may contain blood. Difficulty breathing, pleural chest pains and night sweats may also accompany tuberculosis.

▪ *Treatment*

Once tuberculosis is diagnosed by chest X-ray and sputum culture, the disease can be treated on an outpatient basis with a combination of drugs, which may include isoniazid (in conjuction with vitamin B_6), streptomycin, ethambutol and rifampin. Rest and nutritious diet are vital to recovery. Antituberculosis drugs may be required for one to two years *after* the person has recovered to prevent recurrence or complications. Many patients stop taking the drugs too soon, especially if they are feeling well. This increases the risk of further spread of the disease. Regular checkups for at least two years after recovery are recommended. Since tuberculosis remains a serious and highly infectious disease, anyone living with a patient should be examined for infection as soon as possible. Older persons with lung disorders who live in a home with young children should also have themselves thoroughly checked.

❑ PULMONARY EDEMA

This swelling of the lungs because of fluid accumulation is a life-threatening symptom of heart failure. Inefficient pumping by the left ventricle of the heart results in a backup of blood in the vessels, increased pressure and rapid filling of the alveoli with the liquid part of the blood known as plasma.

Symptoms include extreme difficulty breathing, cyanosis, anxiety accompanied by a feeling of suffocation, a dry or sputum- or blood-filled cough, pallor and sweating. The person should be taken immediately to the nearest hospital emergency room.

▪ *High-Altitude Pulmonary Edema*

This form of pulmonary edema occurs when a person travels to an oxygen-deficient high altitude faster than the body can adjust. Heavy exertion before this adjustment increases the risk, as does chronic lung disease and age. The symptoms, which appear within 24 to 72 hours after ascent above 10,000 feet, include shortness of breath, rapid heartbeat, slight fever, a cough that may become bloody and cyanosis. Oxygen should be administered at once and the patient brought to a lower altitude. The best prevention is gradual ascent and moderated physical activity during the adjustment period.

❑ COUGH

Although a cough can free the respiratory tract from harmful secretions and foreign matter in the bronchial tubes, it can also be a symptom of a serious pulmonary problem. Coughing up bloody phlegm, with or without chest pain, can indicate pneumonia, tuberculosis, pulmonary edema, a blood clot in the lungs or cancer in the respiratory tract. If the bloody cough is accompanied by pain in the lungs, it could signal pneumonia, pulmonary tuberculosis, a lung abscess or lung cancer. A cough that appears for the first time in the middle-aged individual who smokes could be a sign of lung cancer. Persistent coughs accompanied by purulent sputum, chest pain or sputum containing blood should be evaluated by a doctor.

❑ Foreign Objects

In adults, inhaling foreign objects most often occurs while eating, when under the influence of alcohol or when holding objects such as screws or nails in the mouth. First-aid measures are necessary only if the person is unable to clear the object by coughing and if the airway is severely obstructed. If the individual can speak or cough effectively, he or she should be left to clear the object without assistance. If the person cannot talk or is turning blue, the Heimlich maneuver should be applied. Foreign bodies that cannot be cleared spontaneously or with the Heimlich maneuver must be promptly removed by a physician. People who have been revived by the Heimlich maneuver should also be seen by a physician to check for the possibility of damage to internal organs from the abdominal thrusts.

❑ Breathing Aids

People with chronic lung diseases sometimes require specialized equipment to deliver medications, oxygen or moist air deep into the lungs to help clear mucus out of the airways or ensure a sufficient supply of oxygen in the blood. If your physician orders a breathing aid for you, a respiratory therapist, technician or community health nurse will demonstrate its use.

▪ *Nebulizers*

Nebulizers produce a fine spray of medicine that is breathed deeply into the lungs. Some require the user to squeeze a bulb to power the spray. Other nebulizers plug into electric outlets and operate with compressed air or oxygen. In a metered-dose nebulizer, the medication is prepackaged in a spray container. Nebulizers can be used before or after postural drainage.

▪ *Intermittent Positive Pressure Breathing (IPPB)*

IPPB machines use pressure to push additional air into the lungs when the individual inhales. During exhalation there is no pressure and the individual breathes out normally. A physician must specify that the patient needs IPPB, which is meant for intermittent use only. *The Merck Manual*, a reference text for physicians, states that although the machines are widely used, they have not been shown to help raise mucus secretions or improve the overall condition of patients with chronic obstructive pulmonary disease who are able to remain somewhat active.

▪ *Oxygen*

The physician may prescribe home oxygen therapy for patients who have chronically low levels of oxygen in the blood, or for those whose levels drop when they begin an exercise program. Oxygen is prescribed at a specific rate of flow per minute which should not be changed by the patient; too much oxygen can damage the lungs and interfere with the body's mechanism for ridding the blood of carbon dioxide.

A respiratory therapist, technician or community health nurse will instruct you on how to set the flow rate, when and for how long to use oxygen and procedures for reordering supplies.

For safe use, *never* smoke in a room where oxygen is being used. The American Lung Association recommends that the tank should be at least 10 feet from open flame, gas, stove, pilot lights in water heaters and furnaces, wood-burning stoves and electrical equipment that may spark.

▪ *Humidifiers and Vaporizers*

Inadequate fluid intake and a dry room environment can make mucus more viscous and harder to cough up. A humidifier, vaporizer or even pans on a radiator filled with water add moisture to the air, which helps soften and loosen the mucus so it can be coughed up. As with other breathing aids, humidifiers and vaporizers must be cleaned carefully, according to the manufacturer's instructions, to avoid spreading infections.

Those living in areas with poor air quality, or who have allergies in addition to lung disease, might consider an air filter or air purifier. Devices which produce ozone gas should be avoided.

❑ Traveling

Millions of people with disabilities are traveling. With some precautions and planning, there is no reason that an older person with a chronic lung disorder cannot take an enjoyable trip. The amount of preplanning depends on specific conditions, medications and any need for equipment. (See Table 15:6, Tips for Travelers with Lung Disease.)

Since flying involves many stresses that affect the respiratory system, individuals suffering from an upper respiratory infection should delay their departure until they are well, and those suffering from asthma or emphysema should seek medical advice before getting on an airplane. Major airlines may supply oxygen equipment if the passenger is preapproved by the company's medical department and has a note from his or her physician. Arrangements should be made well in advance of the trip.

Tips for Travelers with Lung Disease

Before You Leave:

- Get extra medicines and prescriptions to carry with you. Keep some of your medicines in carry-on baggage in case your luggage is lost.
- Write out your daily schedule for taking medicines and treatments; it is easy to forget old routines in new surroundings.
- Ask your physician for the name of a doctor in the areas you will be visiting. If you will be traveling to a non-English–speaking country, a number of organizations have physical referral lists available, often at a reasonable charge.
- If you will need oxygen, arrange in advance with the airline. Airlines won't allow you to use your own oxygen equipment, but they will supply oxygen for a fee to selected patients. (Take your own equipment with you in your baggage.)
- If traveling to a country with a different voltage system, buy adapters (available in radio-electronics stores) that will allow you to plug any machines into foreign outlets.
- Check with your local health department for any forecasts of potential flu epidemics in the areas you plan to visit.

While Traveling:

- Plan a realistic schedule and be sure your traveling companion is prepared to go at your pace.
- In cities or areas with high pollution, travel at night or early in the morning, if possible, when emissions are likely to be lower.
- Those with allergies should check for potential problem substances, such as feather pillows.

Table 15:6

16

MENTAL FUNCTIONING IN AGING

All too many people still view becoming "senile" as an inevitable component of old age. Contrary to this popular, albeit mistaken belief, the vast majority of people retain their intellectual faculties well into the later years and, indeed, to the end of their lives. There are examples of accomplishments of famous and not-so-famous people in their seventies, eighties and even nineties and hundreds. If an individual's expectations about remaining intellectually fit are positive, and there are no men tally disabling diseases present, he or she can remain intellectually "alive" indefinitely.

There are, however, certain disorders that do affect mental function and are more commonly associated with aging. Most of these respond to treatment, once the underlying cause is discovered. However, some researchers believe that nearly a third of the people diagnosed with dementia—the irreversible deterioration of mental function—have other, more treatable conditions. This is why it is imperative to make absolutely sure that the diagnosis is accurate before assuming that a person has Alzheimer's disease or some other disabling brain disorder. There are numerous examples of older people who have been institutionalized with what was thought to be an irreversible brain disease only to discover later that the real problem was malnutrition, depression or some other treatable disorder.

❑ DEPRESSION

Many people think of depression as simply being "down in the dumps" or sad, and that a depressed person can "snap out of it" if he or she will only try to be a bit more cheerful. All of us feel sad from time to time, and we may even describe ourselves as being depressed. In reality, however, true clinical depression—or affective disorder, to use its medical name—is an organic illness involving biochemical changes in the body.

According to the National Institute of Mental Health, approximately 10 to 15 percent of older Americans suffer from significant depression—that is, depression severe enough to require treatment. Some experts, however, think that even this is a low estimate. Dr. Barry Gurland, a Columbia University authority on mental health in the aged, has found that 26 percent of persons over the age of 65 who seek medical attention suffer from a treatable clinical depression.

Often, depression will produce different symptoms in an older person than in a young person. For example, a younger person may complain of a variety of physical symptoms, while, in an older person, depression may mimic symptoms of senility—memory loss, confusion or disorientation, inattention to personal needs. Delusions and other signs of intellectual impairment are relatively common. This form of depression, called depressive pseudodementia, is thought to account for about 15 percent of the depression occurring among elderly people. The mental deterioration found in this form, as well as the forgetfulness and inability to concentrate characteristic of more typical depression, disappears when properly treated. But since this disorder can mimic dementia, it is important to know how they differ. (See Table 16:1, Major Differences Between Depression and Dementia.)

The cause of clinical depression is often unknown. We tend to think of depression as an emotional response to a misfortune or sad event, and occasionally, this type of normal sadness or grief may trigger clinical depression. More often, however, there is no identifiable cause of the depression, although research indicates that a biomedical imbal-

Major Differences Between Depression and Dementia

Depression	Dementia	Depression	Dementia
Comes on in a short period of time with full-blown symptoms. Medical attention sought soon after onset.	Usually comes on gradually and patient and family may not be aware of symptoms or seek help until later.	Patient appears depressed.	Patient has mood swings, shows little emotion or may be depressed.
Patient can describe decline in function in great detail; may state how bad memory is, how confused he or she feels.	Patient vague in describing symptoms; denies problems in remembering or feelings of confusion.	Variable performance on test items of similar difficulty.	Consistent performance on test items of similar difficulty.
Patient shows little motivation in completing tasks on performance tests; however, objective performance is better than own accounts of decline.	Patient tries hard to complete task, at least in early stages; objective performance is worse than own accounts of decline.	Impaired social relations early in course of illness. Insecure around others.	Impaired social relations later in course of illness. Demanding around others.
Ability to attend to task and concentrate generally good.	Ability to attend to task and concentrate generally poor.	Patient able to answer most questions of orientation and general knowledge—e.g., age, date, address, current President's name.	Patient cannot answer most questions on orientation or general knowledge.
Prior history of depressive episode in patient or family.	No prior history of depressive episode.	Able to cook for self, dress, do household chores. Able to find way home.	Unable to perform these activities of daily living without difficulty. Gets lost in own community or neighborhood.

Table 16:1

Diagnostic Criteria

During an episode of depression, at least three of the following symptoms are present:

1. Insomnia or excessive sleepiness
2. Loss of appetite, weight loss or excessive eating and weight gain
3. Loss of libido
4. Low energy level or chronic tiredness
5. Feelings of inadequacy, loss of self-esteem or self-depreciation
6. Decreased effectiveness or productivity at school, work or home
7. Decreased attention, concentration or ability to think clearly
8. Social withdrawal
9. Loss of interest in or enjoyment of pleasurable activities
10. Irritability or excessive anger
11. Inability to respond with apparent pleasure to praise or rewards
12. Less active or talkative than usual, or feeling slowed down or restless
13. Pessimistic attitude about the future, brooding about past events or feeling sorry for self
14. Tearfulness or crying
15. Recurrent thoughts of death or suicide

Source: Reprinted from *Health & Nutrition Newsletter,* vol. 2, no. 10, Columbia University School of Public Health.

Table 16:2

ance is a likely possibility. Some researchers hypothesize that suppressed anger may in some way upset the brain's biochemistry and lead to the depression.

Anyone showing signs of persistent mental impairment should be seen by a physician. If depression is suspected, the doctor may order psychological testing to help either confirm the diagnosis or point to another cause. Depression is often difficult to diagnose since there is no simple blood test or foolproof examination to take that pinpoints the disease. Frequently, the diagnosis is based on a constellation of symptoms (see Tables 16:2 and 16:3).

▪ *Importance of Treatment*

Sometimes depression will end spontaneously without treatment, but this may take six or more months. If left untreated, especially in an older person, the condition may progress to such a state of hopelessness that the victim is totally unable to function or may even commit suicide.

Depression is commonly treated by a combination of drugs and psychotherapy. Recent studies have found that in some cases of depression, psychotherapy may be just as effective as drug therapy, but drugs may produce quicker results. The most used drugs are called

How to Tell If It's True Depression

Sometimes it is hard to distinguish normal grief or sadness that is a reaction to a major loss or life event from clinical depression. The following table lists some of the more common differences.

Feature	Normal Sadness	Clinical Depression
Recent difficult or tragic life circumstance	Common	Unusual
Family history of depression	Absent	Present
Mood variation	Depression worse late in the day	Depression worse in the morning
Sleep disturbances	Difficulty in falling asleep, but then stays asleep	Middle-of-the night or early-morning insomnia
Appetite	May be increased or decreased; mild or no weight loss	Little interest in food; rapid weight loss
Physical ailments	Fewer and less severe	Many and more severe
Physical and mental activity	Mild slowing; more rarely, agitation	Moderate-to-severe slowing
Attitude, Feelings	Self-pity, pessimism, but no loss of self-esteem	Self-blame, remorse, guilt, complete loss of self-esteem
Interest	Mild-to-moderate loss, but usually able to work	Pervasive loss of interest or pleasure in everything
Suicidal behavior or thoughts	Relatively uncommon	Common

Source: Reprinted from *Health & Nutrition Newsletter,* vol. 2, no. 10, Columbia University School of Public Health.

Table 16.3

tricyclic antidepressants, so named because of their three-ring chemical structure. The drugs are believed to work by increasing the activity of the brain's catecholamine neurotransmitters, thereby restoring normal chemical balance.

The choice of antidepressant drug depends upon the type of symptoms. Some, such as amitriptyline (Elavil) or doxepin (Sinequan), are sedatives and may be the best choices for people who suffer from anxiety or sleeping problems in addition to the depression. Imipramine (Tofranil) and desipramine (Norpramin) are not as sedating and may be better choices for people who are excessively sleepy.

Monoamine oxidase (MAO) inhibitors, such as tranylcypromine (Parnate) and phenelzine (Nardil), also increase the action of the brain's catecholamine neurotransmitters, but these drugs usually are not prescribed unless the tricyclic antidepressants fail to produce an adequate response. Anyone taking a MAO inhibitor must be particularly careful about drug and food interactions that can cause a dangerous, even fatal, rise in blood pressure. Drugs that must be avoided include those that affect the sympathetic nervous system; these include amphetamines, cocaine, dopamine, epinephrine, methyldopa or related compounds. Prohibited foods include any high-protein food that has been chemically aged, fermented, pickled or smoked. These include cheeses, especially the aged varieties such as Cheddar; pickled herring; beer; wine; liver; yeast extract; dry sausages such as Genoa or hard salami or pepperoni; fava beans; and yogurt. Excessive caffeine and chocolate consumption also should be avoided.

Lithium salts may be prescribed on a long-term basis to prevent the extreme mood swings of manic depression. However, the dosage must be very carefully adjusted to avoid lithium toxicity; elderly patients often will develop signs of lithium overdose at amounts that are normally well-tolerated by a younger person.

Severe cases of depression may be treated by electroshock therapy. Unfortunately, electroshock therapy is widely misunderstood by the general public, largely because of highly distorted accounts of how it is administered. Contrary to popular belief, patients undergoing modern electroshock treatments do not feel any "shock," thanks to pretreatment with muscle relaxants and sedatives. There will be a slight twitching of the eyelids or muscles in the arm, but this is the only visible sign of electrical current passing through the brain. There is a temporary loss of memory, but this quickly passes; the kind of permanent amnesia or brain injury depicted in movies and other sensationalized depictions of the therapy rarely occurs. Although electroshock treatments are reserved for severe depression, they have a distinct advantage over drug therapy in that they produce much quicker results. Antidepressant drugs may take several weeks or even months to produce results, whereas electroshock treatments work much faster. Thus, electroshock may be the preferred treatment for people who are suicidal or for whom drugs are not working quickly enough. Often a single treatment will suffice, although some patients require more.

Psychotherapy is an important component in the treatment of depression. In the early phase, psychotherapy may provide needed emotional support while the patient waits for antidepressant drugs to take effect. After the acute phase has ended, psychotherapy may be useful in helping the patient understand his or her disease and develop coping techniques to avoid future episodes.

Physical activity is still another important aspect of long-term treatment. Research has found that regular vigorous exercise—for example, jogging, cycling, brisk walking, swimming—increases catecholamine activity in the brain and helps overcome or prevent depression.

❑ Other Causes of Mental Impairment

Although depression is one of the more common causes of mental impairment among older people, there are nearly a hundred different conditions or medications that can cause depression, memory disturbance, confusion or even psychosis. (See Table 16:4.) When the cause is discovered and promptly treated, the person usually regains normal mental capabilities.

In tracking down possible causes of mental problems in an older person, start by looking in the medicine cabinet and refrigerator. Drugs and/or nutritional deficiencies are among the most common causes of mental impairment among the elderly. Many people have chronic diseases requiring several medications which, alone or in combination, have adverse effects. In addition, most drugs are broken down by the liver and eliminated by the kidneys. As we grow older, these organs cannot handle drugs and other potentially toxic substances as efficiently; the drugs may remain longer in the body and build up to toxic levels. Very often, an older person will require special drug dosage adjustments, and even then, his or her risk of adverse effects may be greater than in a younger person.

Very often, a physician may have to try a different medication or even eliminate one or more drugs to reduce side effects. People taking certain drugs which have a narrow margin between a therapeutic and a toxic dose—for example, digitalis—should have periodic blood tests to measure drug levels. (See Table 16:5 for steps to reduce drug-related mental changes.)

Conditions That Cause Mental Impairment

Brain disorders
Advanced syphilis
Brain abscess
Brain injuries
Brain swelling
Concussion/contusion and other brain injuries
Meningitis
Stroke and mini-strokes
Tumors

Cardiovascular
Conjestive heart failure
Hardening of the arteries
Heart attack
Irregular heart rhythms

Miscellaneous Other Diseases
Anemia
Chronic lung disease
Disturbances in body chemistry
High blood sugar
Kidney failure
Liver failure
Low blood sugar
Low blood volume
Overactive adrenal glands (Cushing's syndrome)
Thyroid disorders
Underactive pituitary

Others
Adverse drug reactions
Alcoholism
Anesthesia or surgery
Arsenic, lead or mercury poisoning
Carbon monoxide poisoning
Deficiency of nutrients such as vitamin B_{12}, folic acid or niacin
Dehydration
Depression
Environmental change and isolation
Excessive drop in body temperature
Infection
Pain
Sensory deprivation states such as blindness or deafness

Source: Adapted from National Institute on Aging Task Force, 1980.

Table 16:4

Nutritional deficiencies are common among the elderly. Many older people, especially those who live alone, see little point in cooking for themselves and

Steps You Can Take to Reduce Drug-Related Mental Changes

To reduce the chances of intellectual impairment, anyone taking multiple medications should:

- Have all prescriptions filled at the same pharmacy so that the pharmacist can be on the alert for adverse interactions. Some pharmacies have a computerized record-keeping system that makes detection easier.
- Make a list of all medications, both the generic and brand names and doses, and carry it with you to all doctors' appointments. Don't overlook nonprescription drugs and any vitamin or mineral supplements you may be taking in making your list.
- Take medications only as prescribed. For example, if you are told to take a drug three times a day, do not take all three pills at once.
- Do not use alcohol in combination with drugs affecting the central nervous system—sedatives, tranquilizers, barbiturates and others. This restriction applies to nonprescription cold pills and sleep medications as well as to prescription drugs.
- Avoid chronic use of laxatives; they can cause chemical imbalances leading to confusion.

Table 16:5

subsist on tea, toast, sweets and the like. Others simply may not be able to afford fresh fruits and vegetables and the other essentials of a healthful diet. Lack of cooking facilities, inability to get to a supermarket because of physical disability or fear of crime in the neighborhood, lack of teeth or poorly fitted dentures, a sluggish appetite and alcoholism are among the myriad other factors that may contribute to malnutrition among older people. Limited fluid intake and use of diuretic medications can lead to dehydration, compounding existing deficiencies. Learning how to plan a balanced diet using inexpensive foods, taking advantage of food stamp programs, supermarket delivery services and programs such as Meals on Wheels can all help you meet your nutritional needs. Trying to eat at least one meal a day in a social setting—for example, a senior citizen center—helps to relieve loneliness and may stimulate your appetite at the same time. Very often, once the nutritional deficiencies are corrected, the mental symptoms will abate.

❑ Alzheimer's Disease

In recent years, all of us have become much more conscious of the tragedy of Alzheimer's disease. On the one hand, it is beneficial for more people to be aware of Alzheimer's and its impact on the victim and his or her family. On the other, the disease is not as widespread as many people have been led to believe. In fact, Alzheimer's disease is a relatively rare condition that affects between 2 and 2.5 million Americans and accounts for only 20 percent of people confined to nursing homes.

Although Alzheimer's disease was given its name only eighty years ago, it is not a new disease. Throughout history, there have been instances of dementia and senility that undoubtedly were caused by what we now call Alzheimer's, after the German physician who first described the disease in the medical literature.

Alzheimer's disease is responsible for at least half of all senile and pre-senile dementia, the progressive, usually irreversible deterioration of all intellectual ability. The condition usually appears after age 65, but in rare instances it has been known to develop in people as young as the mid-forties. It starts slowly, with mild memory loss and depression or moodiness. But unlike the normal mild forgetfulness that most people will experience regardless of age, in Alzheimer's disease forgetfulness progresses until the victim becomes unable to remember the most commonplace data: his or her address, birth date, names of children and lifelong friends. Eventually, the person loses the power of speech and the ability to take care of the most basic bodily functions. Abnormalities in the cerebral cortex of the brain are responsible for loss of memory, the power to think rationally, learning ability and the changes in personality and sense of judgment that characterize this disease.

Alzheimer's disease is a common contributing cause of death, but it usually does not kill directly. Instead, its victims die from accidents and the consequences of extreme disability, such as the inability to eat, found in the later stages of the disease. Older adults rarely survive more than five years beyond their diagnosis. Younger patients may live ten to fifteen years with the disease.

▪ *Importance of Diagnosis*

Eventually, a simple diagnostic test may lead to quick diagnosis of Alzheimer's disease. At this time, however, conclusive diagnosis of Alzheimer's disease can be made only at autopsy, after the brain is examined for the changes distinctive to the disease. Tentative diagnosis is currently based on results of psychological and mental testing, CT scanning, a patient history and evidence of continuing mental deterioration. (See Table 16:6 for a list of mental function tests.)

Researchers believe that there is more than one type of Alzheimer's disease, leading certain patients to deteriorate more rapidly than others. Those who suffer from psychiatric symptoms such as hallucinations or delusions, Parkinson's-like slowed, rigid movements, or involuntary muscle contractions known as myoclonus fall into this group.

▪ *Possible Causes: The Prime Suspects*

Discovering the cause and finding an effective treatment for Alzheimer's disease are among the top research priorities in the United States today. Because it is now known that the disease directly affects only a small, specific area of the brain, scientists think they are close to finding the cause, or causes.

Three areas are of particular interest to the researchers—genetics, immunology and the study of viruses. One of the most important new findings is the discovery of a protein, designated ALZ-68 antigen, that appears only in the brain of Alzheimer's patients and people with Down's syndrome, a disorder caused by an extra chromosome. It is not known whether ALZ-68 antigen and the gene, or genes, producing it is a cause; however, if the protein appears in the spinal fluid, as scientists suspect, it may lead to the development of a simple and specific test for the disease.

Mental Function Tests

Testing for progressive memory loss as well as other signs of intellectual decline should include a complete physical, psychiatric and neurological examination. The workup may include:

Detailed medical history. This may be acquired from the patient or a family member if the patient's recall is not reliable. A family history of certain hereditary disorders, or past events, such as head injuries or mini-strokes, may be responsible for current symptoms. Previous work exposure to toxic substances may also be a factor.

Laboratory tests. Blood, sputum and urine studies may show an imbalance of hormones, vital chemicals, toxic levels of medications or evidence of viral or bacterial infection—all possible causes of mental symptoms.

X-ray studies. An X-ray may show an infection, mass or head injury. A CT (computerized tomography) scan may show a tumor or structural abnormalities in the brain.

Electroencephalogram. This test measures the electrical patterns in the brain and may be used to detect brain tumors, infections, stroke damage or other brain abnormalities.

Psychological testing and mental status examination. These tests may be useful to rule out emotional disorders and to test memory and mental awareness.

Table 16:6

In the general population there is little definite pattern of Alzheimer's disease running in families. However, in a small number of patients, inheritance plays a definite role, and someone who is an identical twin has a nearly 50 percent chance of developing the disease if the other twin is affected. But having a parent, child or sibling with Alzheimer's disease does not significantly increase the risk.

The presence of ALZ-68 antigen in the brains of Down's syndrome patients also suggests a possible genetic link, since people with Down's have a high frequency of early-onset Alzheimer's disease.

The immune system may also be involved in the development of Alzheimer's disease. Down's syndrome patients are more likely to develop autoimmune diseases, in which immune cells attack the body's own tissues, and certain cancers, such as acute leukemia. Researchers hypothesize that an immune system defect might also make it easier for some form of microorganism to enter the brain, resulting in the abnormal formations typical of Alzheimer's disease.

Viral suspects in Alzheimer's disease include the so-called slow viruses, which result in damage to the brain or central nervous system many years after initial infection. Creutzfeldt-Jakob disease, a very rare, progressive, inevitably fatal illness which causes dementia and strikes men and women in their late fifties, is caused by a slow virus. However, there has been no evidence that Alzheimer's disease can be transmitted from one person to another.

Evidence has been found both for and against aluminum as a suspect in causing Alzheimer's disease. However, scientists state that using aluminum cookware poses no risk in developing the disease.

▪ *Brain Changes*

Changes in the cerebral cortex, or the "gray matter" of the brain responsible for intellectual functions such as thought, memory and language, cause the symptoms of Alzheimer's. Although patients eventually lose the ability to walk and talk, areas of the brain controlling these functions are not affected.

The brain of an Alzheimer's patient contains microscopic areas of degeneration known as neuritic or senile plaques, and abnormal fibers called neurofibrillary tangles. Although the brains of many elderly people show some of these changes, those with Alzheimer's disease have a greater number of abnormal areas, and the amount of intellectual decline is proportional to the size of the affected area.

The chief feature of Alzheimer's disease is the deficiency of certain enzymes needed to synthesize acetylcholine, a neurotransmitter. Neurotransmitters are chemicals which carry nerve impulses across the tiny gaps between nerve cells known as synapses. This defect of the acetylcholine system is particularly evident in nerve cells in the prefrontal cortex and the hippocampus, an area important in memory. People who develop this disease in their forties or fifties may have defects in other neurotransmitter systems as well as acetylcholine.

▪ *Current Research*

Although there is no cure for Alzheimer's disease, researchers have made great strides in understanding how the brain creates and retains memories. For example, it is now known that the memory of an event is stored in more than one place in the cortex. Acting on developments in brain research, drug companies are devoting extensive resources to memory-improving drugs that will probably be available to the public within several years.

Their emphasis is on developing drugs that either mimic acetylcholine or prevent it from being destroyed. Although such drugs hold great promise, more time and research is needed before we will have agents that are both safe and effective. To date, experimental agents have helped improve memory to a modest degree on performance tests; however, test performance may not always predict everyday functioning. Effects of these drugs may be short-lived or effective only in mildly or moderately impaired patients. Some, such as physostigmine, can cause serious side effects and must be given under close medical supervision.

Another type of drug, the nootropics (meaning "mind-turning" in Greek), has been found to improve mild memory loss in both animal and human experiments. Medical researchers are also working to develop drugs to help the brain use oxygen and glucose more efficiently and to stimulate electrical impulses inside the brain with chemicals already present in the neuron.

Other treatments have had mixed results or demonstrated only slight improvements in Alzheimer's patients. One drug, Hydergine, is available by prescription and may slightly improve mood and intellectual performance in some moderately impaired patients. One of the problems of developing drugs for brain ailments, however, is finding a way for an oral medication to cross the blood-brain barrier, a closely joined layer of capillaries and connective tissue designed to protect the brain from the penetration of foreign substances.

▪ *Caring for the Alzheimer's Patient*

Until a cure for Alzheimer's disease can be discovered, there is much family members can do to maximize the quality of life for their loved one. The patient should be seen regularly by a psychiatrist, neurologist or family physician or internist who consults with a neurologist. Maintenance of otherwise good health will prevent additional confusion from other causes. Pick a physician who will spend time with you and answer questions. (Table 16:7 lists sources of help.)

Sources of Help for Alzheimer's Disease

Organizations:

Alzheimer's Disease and Related Disorders Association, Inc.
70 East Lake Street
Chicago, IL 60601
1-800-621-0379

Has chapters in forty-three states and the District of Columbia that furnish information on family support groups and operates a referral network to locate homemaker and legal services, among others. Runs public education programs, lobbies for increased government spending for the disease and funds research programs.

Medic Alert Foundation International
P.O. Box 1009
Turlock, CA 95381-1009
1-800-344-3226

Sells bracelets or necklaces with diagnosis, operates a 24-hour collect telephone emergency answering service, and provides wallet identification card with medical and personal information.

Publications:

"Caring: A Family Guide to Managing the Alzheimer's Patient at Home," by Fredericka Tanner and Sharon Shaw. (Available by sending a check for $8 marked "Fund for Aging Services/Alzheimer's" to Alzheimer's Resource Center, 280 Broadway, Room 214, New York, NY 10007.)

Heston, Leonard L., and June A. White.
Dementia: A Practical Guide to Alzheimer's Disease and Related Illnesses.
New York: W. H. Freeman and Company, 1983.

Mace, Nancy L., and Peter V. Rubins, M.D., Ph.D.
The 36-Hour Day: A Family Guide to Caring for Persons with Alzheimer's Disease, Related Dementing Illnesses and Memory Loss in Later Life.
Baltimore, Md.: Johns Hopkins University Press, 1981.

Roach, Marion.
Another Name for Madness.
Boston: Houghton-Mifflin, 1985.

Table 16:7

Although the disease itself is not curable, certain conditions which may accompany it are helped by medication. Symptoms of restless, agitated behavior and paranoid delusions respond to drugs used to treat psychoses. Sleeping medications may be helpful to reduce agitation and the confusion that comes from lack of sleep. For reasons not yet understood, approximately 25 to 30 percent of Alzheimer's disease patients show signs of depression in addition to the disease. Although treatment with an antidepressant does not usually produce any striking improvement in intellectual function, the physician may prescribe such a drug to improve mood.

Of the two major types of medications used to treat depression, the MAO inhibitors may be more suitable for Alzheimer's patients than the tricyclic antidepressants. This may be because the elderly, and especially those with Alzheimer's, have higher levels of monoamine oxidase (MAO), an enzyme that destroys two neurotransmitters whose low levels have been associated with depression. MAO inhibitors (Marplan, Nardil, Parnate) allow these neurotransmitters to reach more normal levels. (See discussion of these drugs in the earlier section on Depression.)

DAY-TO-DAY CARE

Understandably, Alzheimer's disease takes a tremendous emotional and physical toll on family members and others who are close to the patient. It is important for anyone taking care of the individual to contact any local groups dealing with this disease. The Alzheimer's Disease and Related Disorders Association (ADRDA) can supply a list of local chapters that offer support groups for relatives, furnish information on how to care for the patient, and provide referrals to agencies offering assistance. Some communities have adult day-care centers offering programs for Alzheimer's patients.

In the early stages of the disease, both patient and family should plan how they will manage finances needed for future care. Retaining a lawyer knowledgeable in Medicare, Medicaid and social security law can prove helpful in setting up joint bank accounts, power of attorney and other ways to handle finances.

The course of Alzheimer's disease may be one of long, stable periods at progressively lower levels of functioning or one of a steady, rapid decline. Family members should assist the patient in staying as independent as possible during each period. Good nutrition, maintenance of sight and hearing, and a stable, familiar environment help the patient to cope. Above all, make it simple for the patient to understand what is being asked.

In the early stages of the disease when there is only mild memory loss, list-making may be enough to assist with daily activities. If the individual takes medications, a divided pill box labeled with the days of the week and an alarm clock set to ring at the same time each day will help jog the memory.

Encourage the person with Alzheimer's to use whatever talents or abilities remain to him or her. Someone who may no longer have the attention span to read a book, for example, may still be able to play a familiar musical instrument. Even the severely impaired person who cannot speak a coherent sentence may enjoy dancing or listening to music.

A well-balanced diet and plenty of fluids will help prevent vitamin deficiencies and dehydration. Severely impaired people may refuse to eat certain foods, and a good deal of coaxing and trial and error may be needed to provide a good diet. Avoid any alcoholic beverages, which serve only to confuse the patient.

As the disease progresses, more supervision and memory aids will be needed. Keep family photos around and label them if the individual has trouble remembering names. A blackboard with the day of the week and date on it may help the patient become aware of his or her surroundings. The Alzheimer's Disease and Related Disorders Association suggests posting signs around the house—for example, "FLUSH" over the toilet or "TURN OFF" over water faucets. Make sure the patient can safely use the stove before letting him or her do so alone. Keep clutter to a minimum. A busy environment is confusing to the patient.

Familiar people and surroundings are important in keeping confusion to a minimum, but even so, Alzheimer's patients often wander from home and may need constant watching. Kindly but firmly insist that the patient remain inside with you until it is time to leave the house. Alert neighbors to the individual's condition so they can report any wandering to you. People with Alzheimer's disease should wear an ID bracelet, available from Medic Alert, with their diagnosis and an emergency phone number on the back. Make sure that the individual carries very little, if any, money to prevent him or her from taking a taxi or public transportation out of the immediate neighborhood.

If it is necessary for you to be away from home for several days or longer, find a relative or friend whom the patient knows well and have that person stay at your house, rather than moving anyone with Alzheimer's. If the patient will be spending time in a new environment, such as an adult day-care center, a family member should accompany him or her on the first few visits to make the transition easier.

Since the Alzheimer's patient cannot retain new information, any activity in which he or she will be involved should be presented as simply as possible just before the event itself. For example, the Alzheimer's Disease and Related Disorders Association suggests that a family member should tell the patient of a visit to the doctor just before it is time to leave.

To allow for decision-making, yet minimize confusion, put the individual's clothing in a separate closet and only give him or her a choice of several items to wear. Similarly, when planning a menu, say, "Would you like chicken or fish?" rather than, "What would you like for dinner?"

Alzheimer's patients who cannot or will not brush their teeth are at risk of cavities and/or gum disease. This is especially true if the person is taking an antidepressant, which may decrease the flow of saliva. To brush the patient's teeth, use a long-handled or angled brush or an electronic toothbrush.

Urinary incontinence is often found late in Alzheimer's disease. Make sure the patient knows how to get to the toilet or, if he or she is unable to find the way, make the trip to the bathroom with the patient within an hour or two after drinking fluids.

To minimize bowel incontinence, provide a high fiber diet and plenty of fluids. The patient should be taken to the bathroom at about the same time a bowel movement would usually occur. If these techniques are not successful, have the doctor check for hemorrhoids, blockages or any medications which may be causing a problem.

Many Alzheimer's patients are restless and spend a lot of time pacing. If your loved one is losing sleep because of this, try darkening the room and setting an example by lying down as if to take a nap. At bedtime, warm milk may induce sleep and a nightlight may reduce anxiety. If sleeplessness and agitation continue to be a problem, notify the physician who may prescribe medication.

On the other hand, some Alzheimer's disease patients have difficulty moving about as the disease progresses. A cane or walker may help the patient to walk. Encourage exercise, even when sitting. Check with the doctor to see if any medications may be interfering with the ability to move.

Alzheimer's patients at all stages of the disease feel frustration, anger and despair; they know that something is wrong. A friendly grasp of the shoulder or any similar affectionate physical touch helps the patient maintain contact with others, even when he or she can no longer speak.

GETTING OUTSIDE HELP

The relative of the Alzheimer's patient should get help at home to ease the burden of care. Agencies listed in Table 16:7 can serve as referral sources. At this time Medicare does not pay for adult day care or for home care for anyone with a chronic disease such as Alzheimer's. Depending on the state where you live, Medicaid may pick up some or all of the expenses, if the individual meets their stringent financial guidelines. A social worker will be able to help you plan for care.

Eventually the individual with Alzheimer's disease may become too difficult to care for at home, and placement in a nursing home is necessary. Although this is often the best course for both patient and family, most people feel tremendous guilt when they come to this decision. But rather than postpone placement, the family should seek advice from the physician early in the course of the disease, since some nursing homes are reluctant to take a severely deteriorated patient who needs total care. Some large insurance companies, including Blue Cross/Blue Shield and Metropolitan Life, have policies covering nursing home stays.

❏ NORMAL MEMORY CHANGES

Many people who experience an occasional lapse in memory needlessly fear that it is a sign of Alzheimer's or an indication of some other mental deterioration. The fact is, we all forget things from time to time, and some people with perfectly normal brains are more forgetful than others.

As we age, changes in the brain contribute to a fall-off in certain areas of recall. A decrease in the number of nerve cells and changes in some of their prop-

Memory Changes That Come with Age

Normal changes include:

- *Slowed thinking processes.* This may be particularly apparent when dealing with new problems or a problem requiring an immediate reaction.
- *Reduced attention span.* Many people find they have difficulty paying attention and ignoring distractions in the environment.
- *Decreased use of memory strategies.* Older people do not make as much use of associations and pictorial cues as younger people, even though they may have an increased need for such cues.
- *Longer learning time.* This is especially true when an older person is confronted with new information.

Areas of memory that do not normally change include:

- *Immediate or short-term memory.* For example, remembering the name of someone you were just introduced to.
- *World knowledge or semantic memory.* Familiar information such as who is President, your children's birthdays, how to get to the supermarket. World knowledge is actually likely to increase with age.
- *Susceptibility to interference.* Newly learned information in a specific area competes with original information, making it hard, for example, to break old habits. This characteristic is present in both old and young people.
- *Retaining well-learned information.* The old forget no faster than the young.
- *Searching for stored information.* Older people may take longer to come up with the information, but the search technique does not change with age. Searching occurs automatically as well as with conscious effort.

Table 16:8

erties, a decrease in the flow of blood which supplies the brain with oxygen and other nutrients, and a slowing of electrical activity as measured by an electroencephalogram are some of the natural changes. Normal changes are summarized in Table 16:8, Memory Changes That Come with Age. It should be stressed that normal changes do not mean a person can no longer learn or retain new information; indeed, an older person is just as adept at learning as a younger one. As we grow older, however, we may need to practice memory exercises. For a more detailed discussion, see Chapter 9, Lifelong Learning.

17

SAVING YOUR EYES, EARS AND TEETH

Of all the senses, vision and hearing are probably the two that keep us most in touch with the world, and consequently, the two that we fear the loss of most. With age, we all experience normal changes in vision and hearing. Many people also lose some or all of their teeth, but this loss usually can be forestalled by good preventive dental hygiene and regular visits to a dentist. Similarly, most people can adjust to the normal changes in vision and hearing, and proper preventive care usually can avert total loss of these senses.

❑ The Eyes

▪ *Normal Vision Changes That Come with Age*

If you don't already need glasses to read this page, you probably will someday. It is a perfectly normal part of growing older, but it can be frustrating.

Often vision changes are the first sign of aging. Perhaps you have always had 20/20 vision, or maybe you have had the same corrective lens prescription since you were in your twenties. But as you enter your forties, fifties or sixties, you notice that you have to hold the newspaper at arm's length to focus on the page or that you need to take off your glasses to see close up. You may notice that your eyes get tired or that you develop headaches after only short periods of close work.

Vision changes due to the aging process may occur gradually and may start at different ages in different people. At first, you may be able to adjust to the changes by reading in short stints or avoiding small print. But sooner or later nearly everyone needs reading glasses.

The condition is called presbyopia, from the Greek meaning "old eye." Normally, long muscle fibers relax or contract to change the shape of the lens in the eye according to whether you are focusing on a near or distant object. The lens, which consists of elastic fibers, thins or flattens to see a distant object; it becomes rounder and wider to focus on an object close up.

As a person grows older, additional fibers accumulate in the lens. Although some experts estimate that the process may start as early as age 10, when the eye reaches its full size, most people do not notice the effects until the mid-forties. The increased number of fibers gradually reduces the lens' elasticity, making adaptation for close work more difficult. It may also take more time to change focus from one object to another.

The solution is simple: corrective lenses to do the work the lens of your eye can no longer do itself. If you have never had to wear glasses before, you may resent their imposition now. Indeed, most people put off getting glasses until they can no longer keep up day-to-day activities without them. But most everyone finds that once they get glasses, the pleasures of reading and being able to see close objects clearly again are worth the minimal trouble of toting and keeping track of the pair.

If you already have corrective lenses for another condition, bifocals or trifocals may be necessary to see both far and near without changing glasses. Some people who need glasses only for reading prefer bifocals with clear top lenses so that they can look up from their book to a distant object without taking their glasses off. Bifocals and trifocals may take some getting use to, but nearly everyone does adjust to them, given time and persistence. (See Table 17:1, Tips for Wearing Multifocal Lenses.) Since the lens fibers continue to accumulate throughout life, your corrective lens prescription may have to be increased, perhaps as often as every year.

Over-the-counter, ready-to-wear reading glasses may appear tempting to those who wish to avoid the expense and time of a visit to the optometrist or ophthalmologist. However, they are not a viable alternative to proper eye care. Besides prescribing lenses specifically for the individual's needs (with different lens powers for each eye and corrections for astigmatism), the eye examiner should check for early warning signs of eye diseases that, if undetected, could lead to blindness. In addition, uniformly made glasses cannot provide adequate correction and may cause the wearer more problems than if he or she wore no glasses at all. (See Fig. 17:1.)

Another normal effect of aging on vision affects the pupil. The pupil controls the aperture of the eye, growing larger in the dark to let in as much light as possible and becoming smaller in the presence of bright light in order to protect the eye. But as one grows older, the pupil is unable to open as wide or to adapt as quickly as it did previously. The result is that older people need more light in order to see clearly. According to the American Optometric Associa-

Tips for Wearing Multifocal Lenses

Bifocals, trifocals and even quadrafocals can open up fields of vision for people who need different corrective lenses for different situations. Proper placement of the lens segment is essential for comfortable and safe use of these glasses. Invisible bifocals, in which the prominent line between segments has been eliminated, may be more cosmetically appealing to some people but can cause problems for some wearers. In any case, getting used to multifocal lenses takes some time and patience. The American Optometric Association offers these tips for wearing multifocal lenses:

- Look straight ahead, not at your feet, while walking.
- Lower your eyes, not your head, to read out of the lowest part of the lens.
- Move reading material to accommodate your head, not vice versa. Folding the newspaper in halves or in quarters may be helpful. Hold reading material close to your body.
- Wear your lenses continuously for the first few weeks, even for tasks that do not require them, so that you get used to shifting your eyes from lens segment to lens segment.
- Keep lenses properly positioned by making sure the frames are tightened and adjusted for your face.
- Be especially careful walking down stairs when wearing new glasses or your reading glasses.

Table 17:1

How Glasses Correct Visual Problems

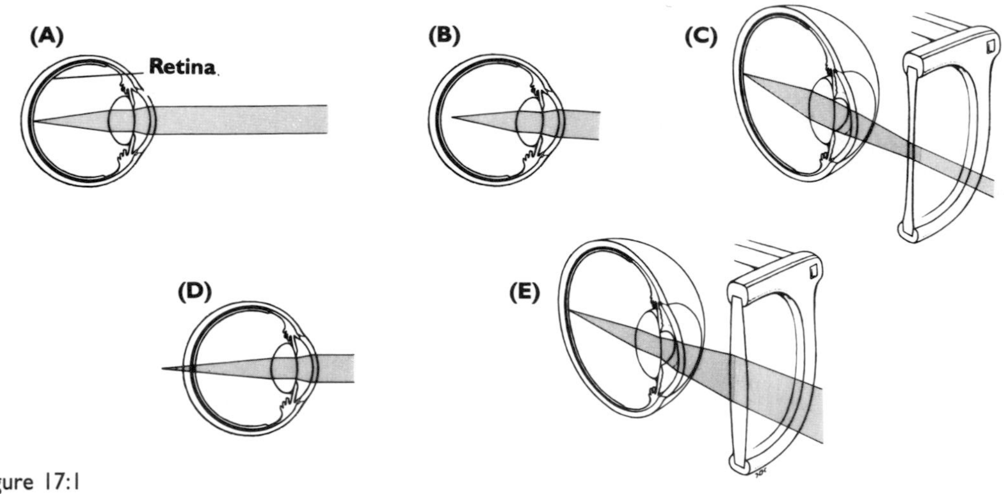

Figure 17:1

In order to see properly, light rays entering the eye are refracted by the lens and cornea to come to focus on the retina. If the rays come into focus in front of or behind the retina, you will have an "astigmatism," and will be either near or far sighted. These disorders are easily corrected with glasses that bring the light rays into focus on the proper place on the retina. In these drawings, A shows normal (20/20) vision, with the rays coming into sharp focus on the retina. In B, the rays focus in front of the retina, resulting in near-sightedness, which can be corrected by a concave glass lens, as shown in C. In D, the light focuses behind the retina, causing far sightedness. This is corrected with eyeglasses with convex lenses, as in E. (Drawing courtesy Neil Hardy.)

Safe Driving Tips for Older People

About 90 percent of the decisions made on the road are based on information received through the eyes. Therefore, any change in vision will have an effect on driving habits. Being aware of the changes that may occur with age, and taking them into account while driving, can prevent accidents. The following tips from the American Optometric Association are good, commonsense recommendations for drivers of all ages, but especially for those over 50:

- Have regular eye examinations to determine day and night vision capabilities. If corrective lenses are prescribed, be sure to choose frames that do not block peripheral vision. You may be able to pass the eye test for a driver's license without corrective lenses, but it is safer to wear them, especially for night driving. Take time to adjust to the lenses before attempting to drive with them. On bright days, wear quality sunglasses; gray lenses are recommended by many optometrists.
- When possible, drive at speeds and on roads where you feel comfortable. Keep pace with the traffic flow, driving neither too fast nor too slowly. Make use of mirrors but be aware of blindspots. If you have difficulty seeing over the dashboard, sit on a pillow to raise yourself. Move your head as well as your eyes to keep track of traffic on either side of you. Arthritis in the neck or stiff muscles which make it difficult to turn your head can combine with decreased peripheral vision to limit your line of sight. Be particularly careful when backing out. Convex mirrors placed opposite blind driveways on hills or curves are helpful in seeing oncoming traffic.
- Because adult eyes need more light to see properly, never wear sunglasses or tinted lenses while driving at night. A clear windshield is preferable to a tinted one. If night vision is impared, limit driving to well-lit, familiar roads. Make sure head and taillights are working correctly. Dusk and daybreak actually provide the most troublesome light conditions for driving; if possible, avoid driving at these times.
- Do not smoke or eat while driving. It can distract your attention from the road and impede vision if smoke gets in your eyes. Nicotine can also interfere with night vision. If you are taking any prescription or nonprescription medication, ask your doctor or pharmicist or read the label carefully to determine driving recommendations. And, of course, never drink and drive.

Table 17:2

tion, the average 60-year-old needs seven times as much light as a 20-year-old in order to see the same object clearly. For this reason, it is inadvisable for older people to wear tinted lenses for fashion purposes or to wear sunglasses at night. (See Table 17:2, Safe Driving Tips for Older People.)

The reduced ability of the pupil to open and let light into the eye can lead to trouble distinguishing colors. If the eye is like a camera, then the retina, which lines the back of the eyeball behind the vitreous humor, is the film. The rods and cones within the retina are the cells that perceive light and color and transmit their perceptions via a complex series of nerves to the brain, which analyzes the data.

The problem is that the cones, which perceive color, need much more light than the rods, which perceive light and dark. With the reduced amount of light that is let in by the aging pupil, it becomes progressively more difficult for older people to distinguish subtleties of color difference. Blues may appear as varying shades of gray. Pastel colors are usually the most difficult to discern. The ability to distinguish bright, "warm" colors, such as red and yellow, is not usually affected to the same degree.

All of these vision changes are normal aspects of the aging process. Not everyone will experience them to the same degree, and some people may not experience them at all. Corrective lenses and using more light will solve most of the problems. Some ophthalmologists suggest that exercises may forestall presbyopia in some people, but glasses are the standard recommendation.

Presbyopia is the most common and easily treatable of the eye conditions associated with aging, but more serious eye problems are likelier to occur in the second fifty years of life. Incidences of glaucoma and cataracts also increase with age, although both diseases may occur in infants and young adults as well. Fortunately, if caught early enough, permanent damage from glaucoma can be avoided. Surgery restores vision lost due to cataracts. Other serious eye problems that are more likely to occur after age 50 are macular degeneration and diabetic retinopathy.

▪ *Glaucoma*

The key to controlling glaucoma is early detection and treatment. Although it is estimated that 2 million Americans suffer from this disease, only half of them are aware of it and run the risk of becoming one of the 62,000 people in this country who are legally blind due to glaucoma.

The structures of the eye are protected from impact by a fluid called the aqueous humor. Normally, this fluid collects in the anterior chamber between the cornea and the lens (see Figure 17:2, Structures of the Eye) and is drained from the eye through Schlemm's canal. In the normal eye, fluid production and drainage maintain the correct amount of fluid in the eye.

In one type of glaucoma, Schlemm's canal becomes gradually or, less often,

Structures of the Eye

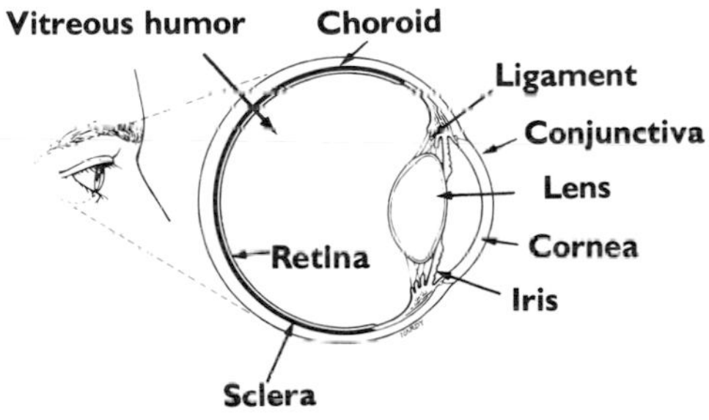

Figure 17:2

suddenly blocked, trapping the fluid in the anterior chamber. The intraocular pressure (pressure inside the eye) increases, and blood vessels within the eye may be pinched, cutting off the blood supply that keeps the optic nerve alive. Eventually, the nerve will be destroyed, causing loss of peripheral vision and, if untreated, blindness.

In the overwhelming majority of glaucoma cases, the buildup is gradual and insidious. In chronic open-angle glaucoma, almost no symptoms become obvious until irreparable damage has been done. The first signs of disorder may be blurred vision, colored circles around lights or decreased peripheral vision, which may never be totally regained.

However, if the increased pressure is detected before the nerves become choked and die, medications that lower intraocular pressure can prevent impaired vision. Taken orally or in the form of eye drops, two types of drugs are prescribed. One type reduces production of the aqueous humor, and the other facilitates the flow of the fluid out of the eye. These medications do not cure glaucoma, but they do prevent the damage to the optic nerve caused by the buildup of pressure. Treatment must be continual and lifelong in order to prevent reduced vision.

In a small number of cases, an attack of glaucoma comes on suddenly when Schlemm's canal becomes completely blocked. This blockage may be caused by injury to the eye, but more often the cause is unknown, although the disease does tend to run in families. The symptoms of closed-angle, or acute, glaucoma are a reddened, hard eyeball, vision disturbances and pain, which may be quite severe. Acute glaucoma is a medical emergency requiring prompt attention to prevent blindness. After an initial attack, surgery may be performed that can prevent subsequent episodes.

Since once the damage of glaucoma is done, it is irreparable, routine screening for early warning signs is the best preventive measure. An instrument called a tonometer is used to measure intraocular pressure. The device is placed directly onto the eyeball, which has been treated with anesthetizing drops. A new and widely used type of tonometer has been developed that uses an air jet to measure pressure. Since the instrument itself does not touch the eye, no anesthesia is needed. Both methods are simple and painless and useful in the early detection of glaucoma. A pressure reading of 14 milliliters of mercury is considered normal, well below the danger range. If a reading of 18 to 20 is obtained, follow-up examinations should be repeated every six months. A pressure reading of over 21 milliliters of mercury indicates glaucoma. People should receive the first glaucoma examination by the age of 35; those over 50 should be examined at least every two years, or at every eye exam, unless previous screening indicates high risk. Clinics and other organizations offer free testing in some neighborhoods. However, any suggestion of a high reading should be followed up on by an ophthalmologist.

Although an optometrist may perform the examination, anyone who receives a high reading should be examined by an ophthalmologist. Treatment for glaucoma must be prescribed and administered only by an ophthalmologist.

▪ *Cataracts*

The most common condition of the eye associated with growing older is cataracts, a clouding of the lens of the eyes. Experts disagree as to the cause; some say it is a normal part of the aging process for some people; others contend that overexposure to ultraviolet rays from the sun may play a prominent role.

Eye injury, X-rays, infrared rays and microwaves can induce the development of cataracts. People with conditions affecting their blood sugar levels (such as diabetes) are also at a higher risk for cataracts. Those suffering from a chronic cancer such as leukemia may be at risk for fulminating cataracts.

A cataract is an opacity of the lens of the eye which becomes progressively worse, although at varying individual rates. As with many diseases which are thought to be purely a product of aging, they may not necessarily reflect this, but be due to a pathological process related to another disorder. As the fibers comprising the lens become less elastic, they may also become discolored. Normally the lens is completely clear, but in a cataract the fibers may turn yellow, blocking out light and blurring vision.

The cataract may start as a small spot on the lens and then may grow until the whole lens is obscured. Left untreated, cataracts lead to blindness. This deterioration of sight may progress at varying rates in different individuals.

The usual treatment is surgical removal of the clouded lens. Eye drops to open (dilate) the pupil may improve vision somewhat if surgery must be delayed, but they will not solve the problem. Diet and exercise can do nothing to improve the condition. There is evidence that wearing sunglasses that block out ultraviolet rays may decrease the risk of developing cataracts later, but once the clouding process begins, only surgery will cure it.

It is not necessary to wait until the cataract is "ripe" to do surgery, but as soon as insufficient vision interferes with daily activities and the quality of life the cataract should be removed.

The operation may be done under general or local anesthesia. Local is preferred by some doctors because it enables surgery to be performed on even elderly patients. There are several different procedures for the operation. Your doctor should discuss with you which method is best suited to your needs, depending on the location and severity of the cataract and the presence of other health problems. If both eyes are affected, the more severe cataract will be removed first, followed by a second operation to remove the other once the first is healed.

After the lens is removed, a replacement is necessary in order to focus clearly. The eyeglasses originally used for this purpose were extremely thick and difficult to adjust to. Contact lenses are now the most common lens substitute. The patient may be fitted for the lenses once healing is completed, several weeks after surgery. Recent improvements in contact lenses make them easier to use and more effective.

In some cases, a plastic intraocular lens will be implanted in the eye. This may be done either at the time of the original surgery or in a second operation. Although these permanent lenses are the most convenient alternative for the patient, especially for those for whom contact lenses would be a problem, there is a slight increase in the risk of complications. Also, since the procedure is relatively new, there is insufficient data on how long the implants will last and function. The procedure may pose a special concern for very young patients with cataracts.

Overall, the outlook for cataract patients is quite positive. About 95 percent of patients undergoing surgery will have their vision improved as a result. The surgery is very safe and can involve a short hospital stay but may even be done on an outpatient basis. Ignorance and an irrational fear of surgery are the only obstacles to improved vision for most cataract sufferers. However, general anesthesia always involves some risk and should not be undergone unless failing eyesight has adversely affected the quality of life.

▪ *Macular Degeneration*

An estimated 3000 Americans become legally blind each year due to deterioration of the macula, a portion of the retina.

Because of the large number of rods and cones (light and color receptors) in the macula, it is the part of the retina responsible for the perception of fine details and the central field of vision. The most common cause of macular degeneration is reduced flow of the blood that nourishes the eyes, leading to separation of the area from the back of the eyeball. It may occur in one eye or in both eyes simultaneously.

If detected early enough, the degeneration may be repaired or arrested by laser surgery that seals the retina and reattaches it to the back of the eyeball. Surgery has the best chance for success if performed immediately after the deterioration process has begun—before symptoms become obvious to most people.

Since immediate action is so crucial, a daily self-test is recommended for people over 50 and those at high risk for the condition. With one eye at a time, focus on a straight line. If the line appears wavy, or broken, macular damage may be indicated. See your eye doctor for a complete examination.

If degeneration is not arrested by immediate surgery, complete loss of the central field of vision may occur. Fortunately, since peripheral vision is retained, most are able to care for themselves. Many people learn Braille after 65 to retain the ability to read. Special devices are being perfected to enable those with peripheral vision to read normally.

▪ *Diabetic Retinopathy*

Retinopathy refers to the degeneration of the retina, usually in association with poorly controlled Type 1 diabetes. Diabetes may lead to changes in the blood vessels of the retina, causing them to weaken and burst. New blood vessels also form on the retina, interfering with the transmission of light coming through the vitreous humor. These blood vessels are likely to hemorrhage and cause "spots in the eyes." Also, without sufficient nourishment from the blood, the retina begins to detach from the back of the eyeball. If the degeneration is detected early enough, laser surgery may be used to reattach part of the retina. Patients with diabetes should therefore have their eyes examined frequently and report any vision problem immediately to an ophthalmologist. (A more detailed discussion of diabetic retinopathy may be found in Chapter 14 on diabetes.)

❑ THE EARS

▪ *Normal Hearing Changes That Come with Age*

Normal hearing is a complex process of chain reactions. Sound starts as a vibration—a door slamming, hands clapping. The vibration causes a disturbance of the air molecules, making them disperse in a wavelike pattern. These sound waves enter the external ear, specially designed to funnel and concentrate the sound waves as they enter the ear canal. When they strike the tympanic membrane (eardrum) it vibrates, setting in motion the tiny bones called ossicles—the malleus (hammer), incus (anvil) and stapes (stirrup)—within the middle ear. This process further modifies the sound so that the inner ear will perceive it more clearly. From the stapes, the sound is transferred to the cochlea, a fluid-containing structure shaped like a snail

Structures of the Ear

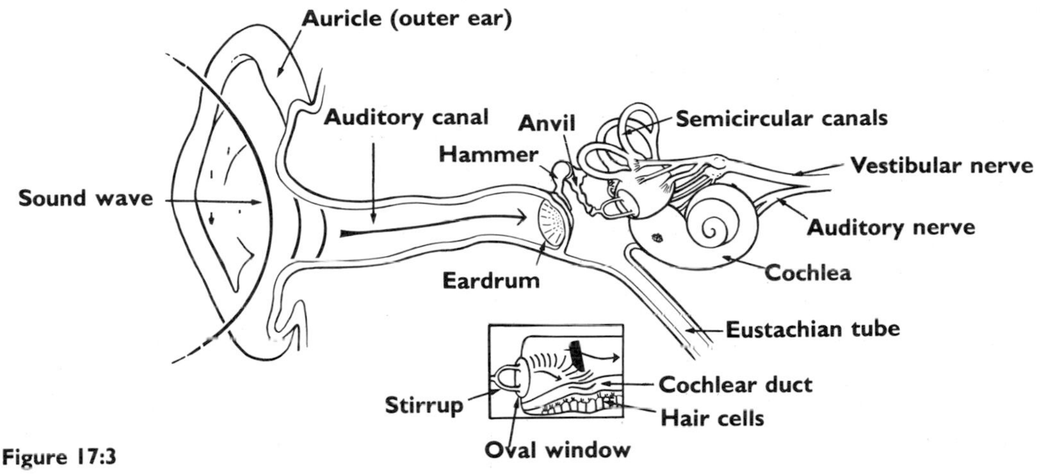

Figure 17:3

shell. Tiny hair cells inside the layers of the cochlea are set in motion by vibrations transmitted through the fluid. Hair cell vibrations are then converted into electric nerve impulses which are conducted to the brain via the eighth (auditory) nerve. (See Figure 17:3.)

As we grow older, these tiny hair cells begin to deteriorate, probably because of lifelong exposure to noise, and do not conduct the sound messages as efficiently. Because this hearing loss is due to the deterioration of these hair cells, and not the structures that conduct the vibrations, it is referred to as a sensorineural (perceptive) hearing loss. This condition, sometimes call presbycusis (from the Greek meaning "old hearing"), affects most people over 65 to some degree. The process of degeneration may start as early as one's middle thirties, but usually does not become noticeable until the mid-sixties. For reasons not known, men are more commonly affected than women, perhaps because men have jobs that expose them to high noise levels. Since women are now more likely to be employed in positions once thought of as exclusively male, we may come to see an upsurge in hearing loss in women over 65.

The first sounds to be affected are most commonly the higher frequencies. The frequency is determined by the rate of vibration; the quicker the vibrations, the higher the sound. In the cochlea, the hair cells that perceive sound are divided into three categories: those that perceive low-frequency sounds (located in the top region of the structure); those that perceive middle-frequency sounds (located in the center of the cochlea); and those that perceive high-frequency sounds (located at the base of the cochlea). The cilia at the base of the structure are usually the first to deteriorate to the point that sounds are not perceived correctly and incorrect or incomplete messages are sent to the brain. As a result the person cannot correctly interpret the sound message.

Because the human voice falls within the range most often affected by presbycusis, hearing loss may take a serious emotional toll on people when socializing becomes more difficult and frustrating. The inclination to avoid such occasions and isolate oneself may be hard to resist.

Although older people are more likely to be affected by this sensorineural hearing loss, conductive problems may occur as well. The ossicles, like other bones, may become stiff and less responsive to the vibrations of the eardrum. The eardrum itself may become thicker and less flexible. A hereditary condition call otosclerosis, in which one of the ossicles, the stapes (stirrup), becomes fixed by an overgrowth of the bone, is most common in older people. This condition is usually correctable by surgery in which the overgrown stapes is removed and replaced with a metal prosthesis.

Some experts now believe that some of the hearing loss experienced by older adults may be the result of circulatory problems such as heart disease, high blood pressure or diabetes, which diminish the supply of blood to the region. An acute infection can cause hearing loss. Certain medications such as some antibiotics, antihypertensive drugs and large doses of aspirin are also associated with hearing loss, loss of balance and ringing in the ears. Prolonged exposure to noise may also hasten deterioration of the hair cells in the inner ear. In some parts of the world—for example, in the African Sudan, where noise and stress levels are minimal and high blood pressure, heart disease, ulcers and asthma are almost nonexistent—the people do not suffer from hearing loss in old age. Although definite conclusions cannot yet be drawn from this information, it seems apparent that hearing loss is not inevitable for all people; that our noisy, stressful, industrialized society predisposes us to the condition. As noise becomes more prevalent in our automated, machine-oriented world, and as more people live past 65, adult hearing loss is bound to become more of a problem.

▪ *Treatment of Adult Hearing Loss*

It is important to determine the underlying cause of hearing loss before seeking treatment. Despite all of the pathological effects which cause hearing loss, the most common reason is the simple accumulation of ear wax. Simple, over-the-counter softening agents may be purchased to assist in removal. Inserting the wide end of an *intact* paper clip carefully into the canal, without excess pressure, may bring out the wax. Do not use a swab or other small, straight object that can penetrate too deeply. If the accumulation is at all difficult to remove, see a physician for professional cleaning. Some conditions that cause hearing loss, such as otosclerosis, are curable by surgery; others are best handled by use of a hearing aid. Still others may not improve with surgery or hearing aids. People with these conditions will benefit from training in lipreading and other techniques. Before purchasing a hearing aid, therefore, it is essential to have a complete hearing examination to determine the cause and best treatment for the hearing loss.

Very often the initial hearing examination is performed by the family practitioner. After age 65 a hearing test should be incorporated into the yearly physical examination. If hearing loss is detected, the doctor should check to be sure that there is no medical reason for it. Ear infection is a common cause of temporary hearing loss and hearing should return when the condition is eradicated. However, if no medical reason for the hearing loss is detected, or if after a medical condition has been successfully treated the hearing loss continues, the family practitioner may make a referral for further testing. This may be done by an otologist (physician specializing in disorders of the ears), otolaryngologist (physician specializing in disorders of the ears, nose and throat) or audiologist (certified hearing specialist). Tests may include a tympanogram (to detect conductive problems in the eardrum and middle ear), acoustic reflex test (to check reaction to loud noises), audiogram (to measure the ability to hear pure tones and discriminate speech) and audiometry (to determine the ability to hear sounds at various frequencies). In certain cases, X-rays and other laboratory tests may be ordered. Based on the results of these tests, recommendations will be made for the best treatment. (See Table 17:3, Communication Tips for Older People with Hearing Loss.)

HEARING AIDS

Not all hearing problems can be solved with a hearing aid; different impairments require different types of hearing devices. (Those with total hearing loss due to nerve deafness will not be helped by a hearing aid.) Essentially, all hearing aids are designed to do the same thing: amplify sound. It is important to remember that a hearing aid will not restore normal hearing. These devices work best in one-to-one situations; it is difficult to localize sound in a large group of people, one of the reasons President Ronald Reagan wears two hearing aids (for stereo sound). As the sound is amplified, it is also distorted. A consultation with an otolaryngologist or audiologist should acquaint you with the devices available and what you can expect from them. Taking some time to get used to the hearing aid will help you better judge whether it is the solution for you.

The type of hearing aid recommended will depend on the patient's hearing loss and any special needs. Basically, all hearing aids are made up of several elements: a microphone to receive the sound; an amplifier to make it louder; a receiver that transmits the sound into the ear; a volume control to adjust sound level; and a battery, which powers the device. The ear mold is not part of the amplifying mechanism but plays an im-

Communication Tips for Older People with Hearing Loss

When used effectively, lipreading and speechreading can help make communication with others less difficult. Lip movements, facial expressions and gestures can all be used as visual clues to follow conversation.

One-on-one or in small groups of people:

- Be sure lighting is adequate.
- Ask people to face you when they speak and to stand about 3 feet away.
- Remind them politely if they continue to talk while looking the other way, speak to you from another room or with their hands in front of their mouths.

Meetings and lectures:

- Get a good seat. (Arrive early, if necessary, so that you have more of a choice.)
- At a lecture or meeting, sit up front where you can best see and hear the main speaker.
- In smaller meetings or discussion groups, sit where you can see the most people clearly without moving your head.
- Around a table, sit at the head or the foot.
- In a living room, sit on a chair instead of a sofa.
- If possible, obtain a copy of the lecture notes or agenda beforehand. (It is easier to follow a discussion when you know what is scheduled.)
- Ask a friend to take notes for you and to let you know when the topic of discussion has changed.
- In small group discussions, ask participants to raise a finger and pause a moment before speaking to help you identify the speaker quickly.
- Ask speakers to use blackboards, overhead projectors, microphones and other audiovisual aids to enhance the presentation.
- Make sure the lighting in the room illuminates the speaker's face.
- Inquire in advance about the availability of special listening devices, such as induction loops, radio frequency hearing aids or infrared systems. (You may want to equip a meeting room with these devices; your audiologist should be able to provide you or your organization with information.)

At the movies, theatre or a concert:

- Inquire whether there are devices available to amplify sound.

Noisy places:

Since hearing aids amplify background noise as well as speech, it can be difficult to understand what is being said, especially in rooms without carpeting and drapes, where there may be reverberations.

- Remove the source of the noise or move to another room. If not possible:
- Suggest continuing the conversation at another time (continuing when you cannot adequately concentrate may lead to misunderstandings).
- If the noise is intermittent, talk during the lulls.

Table 17.3

portant role in the comfort and success of a hearing aid. This part should be custom fitted to the individual ear to hold the aid in place. An improper fit may lead to improper conduction of the sound into the ear canal, whistling or squealing sounds, irritation and even infection. (See Figure 17:4, Types of Hearing Aids.)

The most common hearing aid fits behind the ear and hooks over the top of the ear structure. This model can be worn by people with a wide range of hearing impairment, from mild to severe. A canal aid that is worn completely within the ear canal is the least visible of the hearing devices. It is suitable for mild hearing loss, but those with arthri-

Types of Hearing Aids

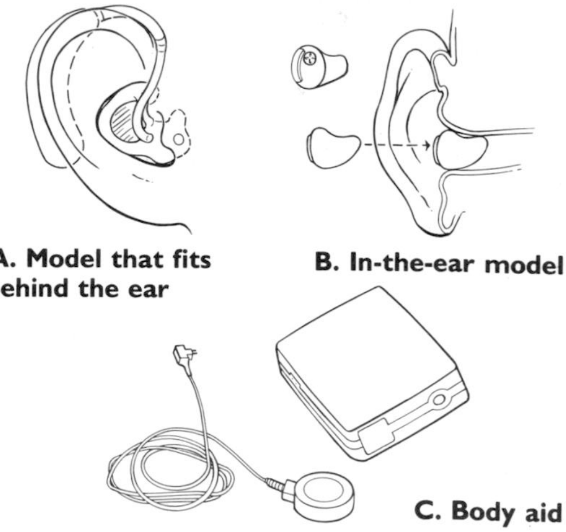

Figure 17:4

Before Buying a Hearing Aid

Some otolaryngologists and audiologists also sell hearing aids, eliminating the search for an independent dealer. Wherever you purchase your hearing aid you should:

1. Arrange for orientation with a professional in using and caring for the device so that you will receive maximum benefit from it.
2. Make certain you can return the device within thirty days for a full refund if it does not improve your hearing sufficiently.
3. Find out about service and warranty.
4. Make an appointment for a full hearing examination within the first month to determine if the hearing aid is functioning properly.

Table 17:4

Proper Care of Your Hearing Aid

A hearing aid should last approximately five years. With proper care you can increase the device's longevity and decrease maintenance and repair costs. Since exposure to extreme hot or cold can damage a hearing aid, do not:

- Wear it while under the hair dryer or for more than a few minutes in very cold weather.
- Store it near a source of heat, such as a radiator.

Keep the device dry:

- Avoid wearing it in the rain or when perspiring profusely.
- Store it in a plastic bag with silica gel overnight to help absorb moisture inside.
- Remove the aid before using hair spray.

When not in use:

- Turn the hearing aid off, remove it and take the battery out of the case. (If you do not turn off the aid before removing it, whistling may occur.)

Care of batteries:

- Keep spare batteries with you at all times and store others in a cool, dry place.
- Batteries should be dry and at room temperature when inserted into the aid.
- Do not buy more than a month's supply of batteries at a time.
- Clean the battery compartment and connections with a pencil eraser.

Cleaning:

- Keep ear mold clear of ear wax by cleaning periodically with soapy water.
- Never immerse the mechanical parts of the hearing aid in water.

Replace:

- Tubing on behind-the-ear hearing aids whenever it becomes dry or yellow.
- Broken or cracked wiring on body hearing aids immediately.

Table 17:5

tis or other trouble with their fingers may find making the necessary, frequent volume adjustments difficult with the tiny controls. Mild to moderate hearing loss can be improved by the in-the-ear model as well. This type is fitted into the ear canal and outer ear. It, too, has tiny controls that may present difficulties for those with arthritis.

People who have trouble with the miniaturized hearing aids may find a body aid easier to use. These larger models, carried in the pocket, are attached to the ear mold by a wire. Larger capacity batteries are used so it is not necessary to change batteries so often. This type of aid may also benefit people who have trouble with their eyes.

An alternative for patients who also wear eyeglasses is a hearing aid that fits into the eyeglass frame behind the ear and attaches to the ear mold similar to the behind-the-ear model. While this model is not conspicuous, it is suitable only for those who wear eyeglasses at least 80 percent of the time. It is advisable to have an alternative for both the glasses and the hearing aid, so if something happens to one, you will not be deprived of both corrected vision and hearing.

Two hearing aid features worth looking into are telecoil circuitry and tone control. By switching the microphone control to "T," telecoil circuitry improves the wearer's hearing over the telephone. For hearing-imparied people who hear some frequencies better than others (older people usually lose the ability to hear the higher frequencies first), tone control will amplify certain frequencies more than others. In the ear, behind the ear and body aids all can be fitted with tone control. (See Table 17:4.)

One or both ears may be fitted for a hearing aid. If one ear tests within the normal hearing range, the other ear will be set up with the aid. If hearing in both ears is impaired, the aid is usually fitted to the better ear. In either case, this is referred to as a monaural (one ear) fitting. In other cases, a binaural (two ears) fitting is recommended. The advantage of binaural fitting is the wearer can determine from which direction the sound is coming. (See Table 17:5.)

▪ *Other Age-Related Ear Problems*

VERTIGO AND DIZZINESS

Besides its primary role in hearing, the ear also plays a part, along with the eyes, muscles and brain, in maintaining balance (equilibrium). Within the inner ear is the labyrinth, containing, among other structures, the fluid-filled semicircular canals (see illustration) and two chambers, the utricle and the saccule, that have hair cells embedded in a jelly-like substance. Both the fluid in the canals and hair cells move as the head moves, sending impulses to the brain. The brain correlates this data with information from the eyes and other senses to determine the body's position and what kind of muscular reactions are needed to maintain balance.

Disorders of the labyrinth or inner ear therefore may lead to vertigo, or extreme dizziness accompanied by a feeling of movement or spinning and sometimes nausea and vomiting. This is caused by the contradictory information sent to the brain by the inner ear, eyes and skin.

Although dizziness and vertigo may occur at any age (indeed, most people have had at least one episode of dizzi ness), older adults seem prone to attacks. Benign positional vertigo, in which a person becomes severely dizzy upon moving the head in a certain way or changing position, may be a side effect of medications, such as some antihypertensive drugs. In most cases, the cause of vertigo is unknown and the attacks subside with time. Subsequent episodes may be prevented or curtailed by antivertigo medications or by simply avoiding the troublesome position.

However, vertigo may be a symptom of an underlying condition, such as ear wax accumulation, ear infection or certain viruses. In these cases, eradication of the underlying problem usually cures the vertigo. In still other cases, a more serious disorder such as hypertension, diabetes, heart disease, anemia and arteriosclerosis may be causing the symptoms of vertigo. Prolonged use of streptomycin may permanently destroy semicircular canal function and cause the disorder. Have any recurrent attacks of vertigo checked by a physician.

MÉNIÈRE'S DISEASE

Ménière's disease, which often appears at around age 50, is characterized by attacks of severe vertigo, accompanied by tinnitus (ringing in the ears), nausea and vomiting, and hearing loss. The duration of the attacks may vary from several minutes to several hours and frequency can be as often as once a week or as seldom as once a year, with each attack further impairing hearing.

The disease usually affects only one ear, but can affect both, and is caused by the accumulation of fluid (endolymph) within the labyrinth of the inner ear. Alternative terms for the disease more accurately describe the disorder: hydrops labyrinthi (hydrops means "accumulation of fluid") or endolymphatic hypertension. For reasons unknown, Ménière's disease affects slightly more women than men. The symptoms of vertigo, tinnitus and hearing loss may occur in any order. Tinnitus may precede a full-blown attack by as much as a year. Another accompanying symptom may be recruitment, in which the patient becomes hypersensitive to loud noises. Ironically, recruitment often occurs in patients suffering from hearing loss.

There are several different theories concerning the treatment of Ménière's disease. Restrictions on salt, caffeine and alcohol intake, as well as quitting smoking, do relieve symptoms in some cases. Another recommendation, a strict low-carbohydrate diet, is based on evidence that many Ménière's patients have high blood levels of insulin. Medications may offer symptomatic relief: antivertigo medications to alleviate feelings of spinning, antihistamines to drain the inner ear and sedatives to calm the patient suffering an attack. Stress seems to play some role in the disorder; attacks often coincide with times of emotional upheaval.

In more severe cases, large doses of antibiotics may be administered to destroy the labyrinth and thereby eliminate the root of the vertigo without affecting hearing. This treatment leaves the patient dependent on the eyes and muscle reflexes for balance and therefore unable to establish equilibrium in total darkness.

Surgical treatments include the implant of small tubes (shunts) in the inner ear to drain the endolymphatic fluid, cutting the vestibular nerve (which relieves vertigo but preserves hearing in most cases), and removal of the labyrinth (which relieves vertigo but also destroys hearing in that ear). This last operation is done only for patients with one ear affected and for whom hearing has already been severely impaired by the disease. All surgical treatment is considered only when other, less drastic measures have failed and attacks continue to be severe and frequent. Unfortunately, in come cases, tinnitus may persist even after surgery.

TINNITUS

Tinnitus, ringing in the ears, is an annoying symptom that may be due to any one of a number of underlying conditions. Excess ear wax, ear infections and overuse of aspirin or some antibiotics are some of the simpler treatable causes. Ménière's disease (see earlier), nerve damage from exposure to loud noise, and even neurological disorders may also cause the problem. In many cases, however, no underlying cause can be discerned.

An abnormally open Eustachian tube (which connects the middle ear to the mouth) can create a whistling noise in the ear. An aneurysm (an outpouching of a blood vessel) may cause a pulsating sound. In these cases, the tinnitus is called "objective" since the sound can be heard by the doctor as well. However, in most cases, the tinnitus is "subjective" and can be heard only by the patient, contributing to frustration.

There is no treatment for most cases of tinnitus, which may come and go or eventually disappear entirely. Surgery to remove the cochlea or sever the acoustic nerve sacrifices hearing and may not cure the tinnitus. Playing the radio softly may help block out the annoying ringing. Recently, tinnitus maskers have been used. These are worn like a hearing aid and continually transmit a more pleasant sound that "masks" the ringing. Biofeedback has also been used to teach tinnitus sufferers to relax despite the noise.

❑ THE TEETH

The outlook for teeth in the United States has improved tremendously in the past few decades. At the turn of the century, routine dental care was a "luxury" that only the rich could afford. Most people visited the dentist only when a tooth became so painful and decayed that extraction was the only alternative. Losing teeth was considered an inevitable part of life and excruciating pain an inevitable part of a visit to the dentist—two misconceptions that persist today despite advances that make both great pain and tooth loss avoidable.

Before age 35, dental caries, or cavities, are the primary cause of tooth loss. Fluoridated water supplies, toothpastes and mouthwashes have led to a significant decrease in the number of cavities, and experts predict that dental caries will soon be a disease of the past. But the outlook may not be as positive as this prediction sounds. Although fluoride reduces the incidence of adult caries, it is of most value for teeth when they are developing during childhood and adolescence, the so-called cavity-prone years. The number-one cause of tooth loss over age 40, periodontal disease, which is unaffected by fluoride, is still alarmingly prevalent. However, with cavities under control, the dental profession has now concentrated its efforts on the prevention of periodontal disease—the key to keeping your teeth for your lifetime.

▪ *Periodontal Disease*

Periodontal disease is a catchall phrase for several conditions affecting the periodontium, or the structures surrounding the teeth (*perio* means "around"; *donti* refers to the teeth). These structures include the gums (gingivae), the periodontal ligaments and alveolar bone around the teeth. (See Figure 17:5 for a diagram of tooth structure.)

Bacterial placque is the culprit in all forms of periodontal disease. The most common form is gingivitis, or inflammation of the gums. Three quarters of American adults suffer from gingivitis at some time. In the condition, bacterial plaque along the gumline infects the tissue. To fight the infection, blood flow to the area is increased, producing the characteristic red and swollen gums that bleed with the slightest pressure, such

Structures of the Teeth

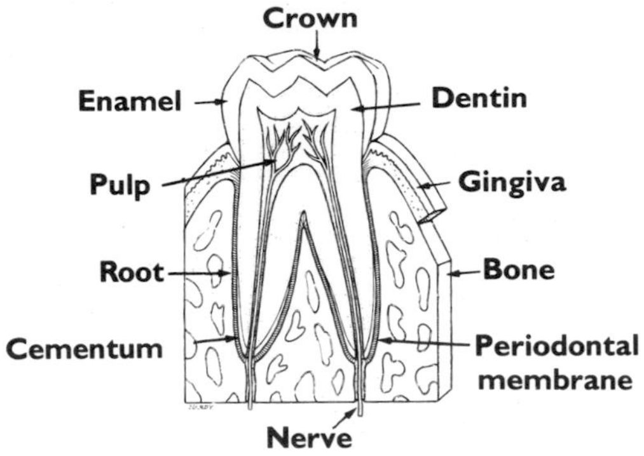

Fig. 17:5

as toothbrushing. Gingivitis, however, often does not cause pain and may be left untreated as a result, allowing it to progress to periodontitis.

In periodontitis, the plaque builds up in deposits just above and below the gumline, creating a "pocket" between the tooth and the gum. Inflammation of the gum in this area causes the pocket to expand, allowing it to accommodate an even greater amount of the harmful plaque. The inflammation also breaks down the periodontal ligaments and adjacent bone. Pus may collect in the pockets and ooze out (hence the former name for the condition, pyorrhea, which means flow of pus). Even at this destructive stage that often leads to tooth loss, periodontitis causes little, if any, pain.

It is estimated that 90 percent of American adults have some form of periodontal disease. Some systemic conditions, such as diabetes, parathyroid disorders and some blood diseases are associated with increased risk of periodontal disease. Smoking or chewing tobacco promotes gum disease. Certain medications, such as the anticonvulsant phenytoin (Dilantin) also adversely affects the gums. Deficiencies of vitamin C and perhaps folic acid may also lead to or exacerbate periodontal disease. There also seems to be a genetic predisposition to periodontal disease. But anyone, regardless of age or coexisting condition, who has his or her natural teeth is a candidate. However, the disease does increase significantly with age, both in frequency and severity. This is not due to the aging process itself, but rather to the cumulative effects of years of poor dental hygiene—improper brushing and flossing along with lack of professional cleaning. Fully 60 percent of people over age 45 suffer from the most severe form of periodontal disease, periodontitis, and 65 percent of those over age 65 will lose one or more teeth as a result of the disease.

Although these statistics suggest that the odds are against saving your teeth, periodontal disease and tooth loss are totally preventable with proper professional and personal dental care.

PREVENTION AND TREATMENT

Diligent home care and regular visits to the dentist can prevent, even reverse, periodontal disease and save your teeth. Dental care professionals differ on how often one should brush and floss, but a general recommendation would be to brush within one half hour of eating and to floss once or twice a day. Ask your dentist or hygienist for their advice based on your particular condition. Many dentists also recommend gum massage by means of an irrigating instrument (such as a WaterPik), specially designed toothpicks or the rubber tip on some toothbrushes. A new toothbrush that has electrical moving tufts is now on the market and recommended by some dentists for easier plaque removal. Although a new mouthwash and toothpaste have recently been tested and have received the approval of both the American Dental Association and the Food and Drug Administration as adjunctive aids in the prevention of plaque buildup, nothing can substitute for good routine care and flossing. At this particular time, there is no good long-term study to indicate the effectiveness of these new products.

Even with diligent home care, plaque will accumulate on the teeth. Some of this may calcify and adhere to the surface of the tooth at the gumline. The only way to remove such plaque (called tartar or calculus) is by professional cleaning. The dentist or hygienist may use a sharp, scraping instrument or an ultrasonic device to scale away the hardened material. (Toothpastes advertised as tartar-fighting have added abrasives that may prevent buildup of hardened plaque. Ask your dentist before switching and be sure the brand you choose has fluoride.)

In most cases of periodontal disease, personal home care has been inefficient and professional dental care neglected. People who put off a visit to the dentist's office to avoid expense and pain will find they have done neither. Treatment of advanced periodontitis is considerably more expensive and can be more painful than regular visits for preventive cleaning.

The early stages of periodontal disease are treated by removing plaque and infected tissue from around the teeth and within the "pockets." When this material is removed, the gum can begin to reattach itself to the tooth. Regular personal care and repeated visits to the dentist will keep the plaque from building up again and causing a recurrence.

More advanced cases may require a minor surgical procedure. Gingivectomy involves removing the gum tissue that has been separated from the tooth. Gingivoplasty gives the tissue a new shape that not only improves the appearance of the gums, but helps make them less receptive to subsequent buildup of plaque. If the bone has broken down and eroded, it may have to be reshaped in what is called a flap procedure. In this operation, the gumline is pulled back from the teeth and bone, deceased tissue and calculus (hardened plaque) removed, the bone reshaped, and the gum replaced in its proper position. In some cases, bone grafts are inserted to replace lost bone. All of these procedures are usually done under local anesthesia. After some periodontal surgery, the wound will be packed with a medicated dressing to promote healing for one to three weeks.

▪ *Dental Caries*

Being over 50 does not excuse you from the fight against cavities. While less likely to develop caries on the biting surfaces of teeth, older people, in whom the gums are likely to have receded, are more susceptible to root caries. The newly exposed tooth surface does not have the protective enamel coating but rather is covered by softer cementum, which is easily broken down by bacteria. Therefore regular brushing with fluoride toothpaste continues to be important throughout life. Rinsing with a fluoride mouthwash will also help preserve the strength of older teeth. But fluoride alone won't prevent cavities; diet can also help you save your teeth from decay.

Tooth decay is caused by the interaction of bacteria and sugar. Bacteria collect on the teeth in the form of plaque, the sticky, translucent substance that adheres to teeth. Dental work, such as crowns and fillings, indentations in tooth surfaces (pits and fissures), and the roots of teeth exposed by receding gums are particularly susceptible to plaque buildup. The source of energy for the bacteria is sugar. In the metabolization of the sugar, the bacteria release acids capable of breaking down the surface of teeth. Although any kind of sugar or starch can fuel these bacteria, sucrose (such as refined white sugar) causes by far the greatest damage in the least amount of time. (In fact, most of the damage is done within the first 20 minutes of eating.) Many times people are not aware they are consuming large amounts of sugar; for example, many cereals contain a percentage of sugar. (See Table 17:6.)

Limiting sugar intake is an important first step in preventing tooth decay. But the amount of sugar may not be as important as when and in what form the sugar is eaten. Sugar consumed as part of a complete meal or with a sufficient amount of liquid to wash out the mouth causes considerably less damage than in-between meal sweets. Sticky foods, such as caramels, dried fruits and honey, adhere to teeth and are particularly detrimental. Replacing these "cariogenic" foods with noncariogenic or anticavity snacks will discourage tooth decay. (See Tables 17:7 and 17:8.)

Certain vitamins and minerals may also help prevent tooth decay: Adequate vitamin C may help keep gums healthy and tightly fitted around the teeth; calcium may strengthen teeth; fibrous foods may help prevent caries by stimulating saliva that rinses the teeth. (Calling the apple "nature's toothbrush" is not so off the mark after all.)

The type of cavity that most often affects people over 50 can be considerably more painful than those affecting children. Pain and increased sensitivity to cold or to sweets are indications that you may have a root cavity and you should visit your dentist. In order to halt cavity development in its early stages, before pain occurs, see your dentist for a regular checkup.

In most cases, treatment of dental caries involves drilling to remove the decayed portion of the tooth, then filling the resultant indentation, usually with silver amalgam in back teeth. Front teeth are filled with gold foil, or sometimes a plastic composite material that can be matched to the tooth. Recently, a tooth-hued resin filling to be placed over to conceal the silver amalgam has been approved for use by the American Dental Association. This covering serves mostly a cosmetic function. Also, there is a new method of removing decay with a chemical that does not harm healthy tooth structures. It promises to replace a large percent of drilling with painless removal of decay.

Sugar Content of Cereals

Listed below are popular cereals and the percentage of dry weight that is sugar.

Cereal	% Sugar	Cereal	% Sugar	Cereal	% Sugar
Apple Jacks	54.6	Country Morning	30.5	Total	8.3
Froot Loops	48.0	Post Raisin Bran	30.4	Wheaties	8.2
Sugar Corn Pops	46.0	Nature Valley Granola	29.0	Rice Krispies	7.8
Frosted Rice Krinkles	44.0	Frosted Mini-Wheats	26.0	Grape-Nuts	7.0
Cap'n Crunch's Crunch Berries	43.3	Life (Cinnamon Flavor)	21.0	Special K	5.4
Lucky Charms	42.2	100% Bran	21.0	Corn Flakes	5.3
Sugar Frosted Flakes	41.0	All-Bran	19.0	Post Toasties	5.0
Alpha-Bits	38.0	Life	16.0	Corn Chex	4.0
Frosted Rice	37.0	Team	14.1	Cheerios	3.0
Trix	35.9	Grape-Nuts Flakes	13.3	Shredded Wheat	0.6
		Product 19	9.9	Puffed Rice	0.1

Source: U.S. Department of Agriculture.

Table 17:6

▪ *Root Canal Therapy*

If tooth decay has progressed to the point where the pulp has been infected, root canal therapy may save the tooth. The pulp of the tooth contains the nerves and blood vessels and is the only living portion of the tooth structure. However, removal of the pulp does not render the tooth useless, since it gains the bulk of its nourishment from the root covering. As long as the tooth remains firmly attached to the jawbone, it will remain viable and valuable, able to chew and even to support bridgework. The object of root canal therapy, then, is to remove the infected pulp and save the tooth. The alternative is generally extraction and replacement with a denture.

In root canal therapy (also called endodontia), a hole is drilled in the tooth through which the pulp is removed. With delicate instruments, the inside of the tooth is then reamed and filed to make certain that all infected material is extracted. This also makes the root canal easier to fill. X-rays are used to determine the size of the canal and whether it has been adequately cleaned. Then, over a series of office visits, the canal is irrigated, dried and sealed several times. When the tooth has been fully prepared, it is filled permanently with a sterilized material, such as gutta-percha cement. The tooth must be perfectly filled and sealed to prevent future infection.

Local anesthesia is usually adequate for all steps of the root canal therapy, but occasionally general anesthesia will be used. Advances have made root canal therapy easier, safer and more effective than ever before. New materials used for fillings will not cause the permanent discoloration earlier associated with the procedure. The tooth may darken slightly, but this is easily treatable by having the dentist bleach the tooth.

Comparing the Sweeteners

Sweetener	Sweetness Compared to Sugar	Uses in U.S.
Saccharin	300 times sweeter	Table sweetener, foods, beverages; often used with aspartame
Cyclamate	30 times sweeter	Banned for use
Aspartame	180–200 times sweeter	Table sweetener, foods, beverages
Honey	Varies; some are 40% more sweet than sugar; others are less sweet	No restrictions
Fructose	70% sweeter	No restrictions

Table 17:7

Snack Foods and Your Teeth

Snack foods we eat on the run, often without something to drink and without brushing afterward, generally do more damage to teeth than what we eat at the table. Following is a list of snacks to be avoided or encouraged between meals:

Cariogenic foods.
In general, sticky, sugary foods are most detrimental to your teeth and should be eaten only with meals. Promptly brush or rinse teeth afterward. Between-meal consumption of some fruits, especially oranges, pineapples and peaches, which are high in natural sugars, should be limited. Because acidic foods hasten the detrimental effects of sugar, avoid certain combinations, such as lemon and sugar. Examples of foods to avoid between meals are:

Candy bars
Caramels
Chewy granola bars
Dried fruits
Raisins

Noncariogenic foods.
These foods are not associated with increased cavities and are recommended as snack foods:

Bean dips
Eggs
Meats
Milk
Nuts
Popcorn
Raw vegetables
Sugarless products

Anticavity snacks.
Foods that help prevent cavities include:

Apples
Cheddar cheese (neutralizes acid)
Homemade bran muffins (fiber encourages the flow of saliva to rinse the mouth)
Sugarless soda (contains phosphates)

Table 17:8

▪ *Crowns (Caps or Jackets)*

In cases in which a tooth has been severely decayed or weakened by being filled too often for cavities, an artificial crown covering may be necessary. The tooth is prepared for the crown by removal of the enamel and some of the dentin. An impression is taken of the remaining structure and the surrounding teeth, and a cap is made to fit over it. For front teeth, a mixture of gold and porcelain or plastic may be used so that the cap will not be noticeable. In back teeth, the gold cap will provide a stronger biting surface.

Temporary caps are fitted onto the tooth (or teeth) while waiting for the permanent ones to be made. These do not fit as tightly but are comfortable and cosmetically acceptable for the short term. Medications may be incorporated into the temporary caps to help the teeth stay clean and healthy until the permanent jackets are ready to be cemented on. These temporary caps can come off, so care is needed not to eat hard or sticky foods, such as caramels.

▪ *Dentures*

Even though tooth loss is preventable in most cases, chances are good, according to current statistics, that one or more of your teeth will need to be replaced at some point. Over 50 percent of dental patients over age 50 have at least one replacement tooth.

A missing tooth, lost due to periodontal disease, accident or extensive decay, leaves a gap in your mouth, causing the surrounding teeth to gradually move into the gap. This may lead to bite problems, increased periodontal disease, dental caries and greater risk of losing more teeth. Therefore, it is imperative to have any missing tooth replaced, even if it is not noticeable to others.

A broken tooth in which the root is still intact may be replaced with a pivot crown. In this procedure, the broken crown is filed down and the pulp chamber is hollowed out using techniques common to root canal therapy. The chamber is then filled with a post that sticks above the gumline and provides the anchor for a gold crown. A pivot crown replacing a visible tooth may be covered with porcelain or plastic.

In cases in which the root cannot be preserved, a bridge, or partial denture, is constructed to replace the tooth (or teeth). A bridge can be either permanent (fixed) or removable. There are advantages and disadvantages to each type. Your dentist will discuss with you which is best suited to your teeth and your lifestyle.

Fixed Bridges. If a small space (only one or two teeth) must be filled, a fixed bridge may be recommended. In preparation for the bridge, surrounding teeth are shaved down in order to accommodate permanent artificial crowns. To these gold or stainless steel crowns, plastic or porcelain replacement teeth will be bonded and the complete structure is cemented to the teeth.

Fixed bridgework offers the advantage of convenience and a natural look and feel. The replacement teeth look and function just like your own, but there must be at least one healthy tooth on each side to support the stress on the replacement teeth. Because fitting a fixed bridge requires precision work, it is usually considerably more expensive than a removable bridge. Repair can also be extremely expensive. If an additional tooth must be replaced, it cannot be added to the existent bridge.

Removable Bridges. For this type of partial denture, replacement teeth are attached to a metal framework designed to snap into place by means of clasps around remaining teeth. The bridges can be designed so that the metalwork is barely visible, even when smiling or laughing.

Removable bridges are generally less expensive and involve less intricate procedures (such as the capping of teeth) than fixed ones, but may not be as comfortable and durable. Surrounding teeth may be loosened by the constant wear and tear of supporting the bridge, but any additional lost teeth may be added to the bridge. Repair and replacement are easier and less expensive than with the fixed bridge.

Both removable and fixed bridges require special care. Food can easily lodge in the dental work, so it is important to clean it carefully soon after eating. If it is not possible to brush after meals, then rinse thoroughly with plain water. Removable bridges should be taken out and thoroughly brushed at least once a day. Since food and plaque can collect under a fixed bridge as gums recede in the area, it may be necessary to floss underneath the bridge. Your dentist should inform you of any special cleaning methods your dental work requires.

FULL DENTURES

Saving the natural teeth, although sometimes more expensive, should be a dentist's first objective. However, if remaining teeth cannot be strengthened to support partial dentures, extraction and full dentures may be the only alternative.

Being fitted with full dentures takes emotional as well as physical adjustment. Recent developments in prosthodontics make the common associations of loss of attractiveness and inability to eat favorite foods with dentures obsolete. Dental implants in which artificial teeth are permanently implanted into the jaw may be an alternative for some people. It should be noted, however, that these implants are expensive and have not been used long enough to know how long they will last. Immediate dentures make a toothless waiting period between extraction and denture-fitting unnecessary in most cases. (See Table 17:9.)

Originally, teeth were extracted and dental impressions taken for the dentures. Then, while gums healed, the dentures were made, resulting in a period of weeks when the patient had no teeth, natural or artificial. Without the support structure of the teeth, the facial skin may sag, creating a sunken look. All this is avoided now that dental impressions may be routinely taken before extraction. The dentures are made and can be inserted immediately after the extractions. In cases where the patient is unable to tolerate the extraction of all teeth at one time, back teeth are taken out first. The gums are allowed to heal before the front teeth are extracted and immediate dentures worn.

Immediate dentures not only eliminate a toothless waiting period and all the inconveniences that go along with that, but also speed recovery of the gums and allow easier speech and eating. But since gums will recede after extraction, immediate dentures may need more adjustments before they fit perfectly.

Taking Care of Dentures

1. Clean dentures after each meal to prevent buildup of bacteria and food particles, which cause bad breath, gum irritation and permanent stains. If this is not possible, rinse your mouth with a warm saltwater solution after each meal, in the morning and before going to bed.
2. To avoid accidental breakage, clean dentures over a sink filled with water. Use a denture brush and denture paste or powder and scrub all surfaces thoroughly. People with partial dentures should clean their remaining teeth as described.
3. Remove your dentures for at least six to eight hours daily (usually overnight) to prevent mouth ulcers or other irritations. Place them in water (not hot) or a denture-cleaning solution.
4. See your dentist once a year to keep mouth and gums healthy and ensure well-fitting plates.

Table 17:9

Adjusting to Dentures

Because dentures play major roles in eating, talking and supporting facial structures, they must be comfortable. Only time wearing them and, if necessary, minor adjustments by the dentist can achieve that comfort, but there are some tips that may make the adjustment process easier:

1. Don't expect perfect comfort right away, but don't put up with unnecessary pain. Occasionally, projecting bone or tooth chips will cause tender spots, which your dentist can easily alleviate by shaving or removing.
2. New dentures should be worn 24 hours a day for 2 to 3 weeks, then removed, soaked and cleaned for at least 6 hours every day, usually overnight. Scrub thoroughly with a denture brush and denture powder or paste. (See Table 17:9, Taking Care of Dentures.)
3. Practice talking by reading aloud; your facial muscles need time to adjust to the new shape of your teeth and to holding your dentures in place. The upper denture has a greater area of contact (the roof of the mouth) for suction, but the lower denture may slip until your cheek and lip muscles learn how to keep it in place.
4. Eat soft foods until you get used to the way dentures feel and work. (You should eventually be able to eat most of your favorite foods.) To prevent slipping and rocking, divide food evenly on each side of your mouth. Chew slowly and evenly.
5. A poor fit can cause many problems, including mouth sores that have been associated with the development of cancer. Instead of using commercially available adhesives, see your dentist regularly for any minor adjustments necessary to maintain a comfortable, individual fit.

Table 17:10

The base of the denture is made of pink acrylic, and plastic or porcelain artificial teeth are placed on that base. The prosthodontist can shape and color the teeth any way you like—"perfect" or "imperfect," with built-in defects and discolorations. The first few weeks will require certain adjustments and allowances. (See Table 17:10.)

▪ *Dental Implants*

Recent developments in dental implants are offering a new alternative for denture wearers. Previously reserved for cases in which removable dentures were impossible or impractical, implants are now making permanent artificial teeth a reality for more patients.

There are two types of dental implants. In the first method, called endosteal, the new teeth are fastened by means of thin metal blades placed directly into the jawbone. The blades have small slits though which the bone grows, forming a firm and permanent anchor for the teeth. This method may be used to replace one or all teeth, but the jawbone must be strong and healthy to accept and support implants.

For those whose jawbones have atrophied or shrunk (a common occurrence in long-time removable denture wearers), another method, called subperiosteal, is used. A metal framework with posts is constructed from impressions of the jawbone or from images obtained through a computerized tomography (CT) scan. That framework is implanted within the patient's gums and the new teeth are snapped onto posts.

Both techniques of implanting permanent false teeth involve minor surgery under local anesthesia. Implants are not for everyone. They demand a greater initial investment of time and money and the patient must be in good health. But for some people, implants offer a whole host of advantages: Since they fit better and do not cause a change in jaw structure, they are likely to remain comfortable longer and may not need to be replaced as often. Also, because the teeth are fastened firmly to the jawbone, patients are able to eat a greater variety of foods.

Most of the above techniques have not been in use long enough to offer clear-cut evidence as to their effectiveness and how long they will last. They are also quite expensive. A set of good prosthodontic plates can be effective, attractive and very comfortable.

PART IV

HEALTH RESOURCES FOR OLDER PEOPLE

18

THE HEALTH-CARE SYSTEM AND HOW TO USE IT

Finding your way through the maze of health care in this country has become increasingly difficult in recent years. Should you choose a private doctor or a health maintenance organization? How does a recuperating patient manage at home? What happens in the event of illness while traveling? Despite federal health insurance the elderly are now spending a larger percentage of their income on health care than before the inception of Medicare. As people age, the increasing frequency of chronic illness and/or disability often coupled with a fixed or decreasing income make it vital to understand how to use this intricate system to meet basic as well as special needs.

❑ Choosing a Doctor

Many people do not have a regular physician, but seek care only when they are sick. This is unwise and causes a lack of continuity in care, the potential for missed diagnoses and development of conditions which would otherwise be avoided through regular screening. Everyone over 65—and people of any age suffering from chronic diseases such as diabetes and hypertension—should have periodic physical examinations, either every one or two years depending upon individual health. Those on medications requiring periodic blood tests to monitor drug levels may need more frequent visits. Health care of the elderly is often more complex than that of the young or middle-aged. Many body systems may be affected in a single individual. For example, a diabetic patient may have high blood pressure and cataracts. A woman may have recently become a widow, feel depressed and not be eating enough to ward off nutritional deficiencies and dehydration.

Symptoms of disease may be different

in the elderly—appendicitis without pain, pneumonia without fever or a heart attack without chest pain. The decreased efficiency of the liver and kidney, which break down and excrete most drugs, may dictate lower doses of medications for older individuals.

These specialized needs and the discovery that symptoms once considered to be a part of "growing old" are really symptoms of treatable disease make it important to choose a physician who will pay attention to significant quality-of-life complaints. He or she should help the individual function as independently as possible, given the frailty that often accompanies aging. Competence and interest in the comfort of the patient may even be more important than having a highly qualified specialist. To find a doctor, inquire at the nearest teaching hospital, your state's Department of Aging or check with your local county medical society. To find a family practitioner or internist for your general medical needs, contact these sources as well as departments of family medicine or internal medicine at a medical center. Word-of-mouth recommendations may be helpful in evaluating how a physician responds personally to the patient. (See Table 18:1.)

Guidelines for Selecting a Physician

The following guidelines can help you select a physician:

Accessibility. The physician should be conveniently located, have regular office hours and be available for brief telephone consultations. If you are homebound, pick a doctor who will make house calls.

Management of care. The physician should coordinate care given by any required specialists and be aware of medications prescribed by other doctors.

Advocacy. All reasonable complaints should be listened to and investigated—never tossed off with, "What do you expect? You're getting old." The physician should suggest surgery when appropriate and when it will improve the quality of life. Joint replacement for severe arthritis and cataract surgery may be appropriate even for patients in their seventies and eighties if their overall health is good.

Openness to non-drug interventions. Be wary of any physician whose automatic reaction to a complaint is to write a prescription. Weight loss, stress reduction and exercise may alleviate problems such as hypertension, either eliminating or reducing the need for medication. A physician should be willing to give these methods a fair trial.

Thoroughness. The physician should devote time to taking a complete medical history and performing a complete physical exam at regular intervals. The purpose, possible side effects and other important information regarding prescribed medications should be explained by either the physician or nurse. He or she should give you sufficient opportunity to ask questions regarding your treatment and be sensitive to your emotional as well as physical well-being. One researcher estimates that as many as 26 percent of the elderly suffer from treatable depression.

Second opinions. He or she should be quick to respond to requests for a second opinion and not take offense at this important patient right.

Contingency plans. The physician should have an associate to transfer care to during vacations, and in the event of retirement, illness or death.

Costs. You should have a clear understanding of all costs involved in your care before they are incurred. Ask your doctor what a recommended test is expected to reveal and whether the result would affect treatment. Sometimes less expensive, yet equally effective, alternatives are available—e.g., generic rather than brand-name medications. Ask your doctor what expenses are covered by your insurance.

Hospital affiliation. The physician should have admitting privileges at an accredited hospital, preferably one affiliated with a medical school. If you will need major surgery, the hospital staff should have sufficient experience in performing the particular kind of operation. (See text section, Choosing a Hospital.)

Concern with prevention. Does the physician talk about seat belts and driving tips? Do you get regular flu shots and other immunizations? Do you have time to talk about diet and drinking habits?

The above list is not all-inclusive. The most important thing to remember is that you are paying the physician and he or she is working for you. If the doctor doesn't meet these minimum requirements or is difficult to communicate with, you should change doctors. You have the right to have all your past records forwarded to the new physician. If you can do it comfortably, tell your physician why you are leaving.

Table 18:1

❑ Health Care Alternatives

Until recently, most people went to a primary doctor who handled basic medical problems, making referrals to a specialist as needed. Today, in response to pressures to cut medical costs, other options are available.

Physician partnerships and group practices offer lower costs to the health-care consumer while maintaining a fairly high degree of personal attention. These multi-doctor groups share office space and equipment and may practice single or diverse specialties.

Health maintenance organizations, or HMOs, offer a broad range of medical services to subscribers who prepay a set amount, whether or not they use the facilities. Part of the philosophy underlying the HMO concept is that people will make use of preventive services and avert costly treatment of illnesses which develop when periodic health screening is not available. HMOs offer lower costs in part due to outpatient rather than in-hospital testing and shorter periods of hospitalization. However, the structure of some HMOs makes it difficult for patients to be seen by their own doctors in a timely fashion. Therefore, anyone considering this form of health care should be able to make their needs assertively known; it may not be appropriate for people who are passive or reluctant to fight for their rights.

In selecting an HMO, keep in mind the two types of plans: prepaid group practices (PGPs), where patients may see a different doctor for nonscheduled visits; and individual, or independent, practice associations (IPAs), where subscribers see the same private physician in his or her own office. For more information, contact the Office of Health Maintenance Organizations, 5600 Fishers Lane, Rooms 9–11, Rockville, MD 20857, or call (301) 443-4106.

Another alternative available to those affiliated with a participating employer, union or insurance company is the preferred provider organization, or PPO. Private physicians belonging to a PPO agree to provide extremely low cost care—sometimes $5 to $10 per visit—to covered individuals. Your regular doctor may belong to a PPO or you may select one from a list of member physicians.

Nurse practitioners and physician's assistants working in association with supervising physicians can perform physical examinations, monitor chronic diseases such as diabetes and hypertension, administer routine treatments and provide health counseling—usually at a cost lower than what a physician charges. These specially trained nurses and assistants usually have master's degrees and advanced clinical training and work in hospitals, ambulatory care clinics and medically underserved areas.

An increasing amount of surgery is being done on an outpatient basis in ambulatory-care surgical centers. These facilities may be freestanding or part of a hospital and offer safe, low-cost care for selected patients. Outpatient procedures now include cataract removals, uncomplicated hernia repairs and some biopsies. Insurance coverage for ambulatory surgery varies with the procedure and type of facility. For a list of approved centers, contact the Accreditation Association for Ambulatory Heath Care, Inc., 9933 Lawler Avenue, Skokie, IL 60076; (312) 676-9610.

A growing category of medical groups is the freestanding emergency care center, which offers care to those living at a distance from a hospital, as well as to individuals accustomed to using a hospital emergency room for minor medical needs. These centers offer a range of care, from the treatment of upper respiratory infections and cuts requiring stitches, to stabilizing a patient with chest pain or other heart attack symp-

Avoiding Medical Quackery

The increase in chronic illnesses such as arthritis and certain forms of cancer for which there are no easy cures lead many older individuals to seek out practitioners who promise miracles. Following are some tips on how to spot medical quackery:

1. Watch out for phony "medical" degrees, such as Ms.D. (Doctor of Metaphysics) or D.N. (Doctor of Naturopathy). If you are in doubt as to an individual's credentials, check with your local county medical society or look up the name in the American Medical Association Directory or the Directory of Medical Specialists at a medical school library.
2. Beware of anyone who advocates one type of treatment for all types of cancer. Scientists now believe that cancer is as many as a hundred different diseases with different therapies effective for different forms.
3. If a practitioner recommends a new treatment, ask to see recent supporting evidence of its safety and effectiveness in medical literature. Some treatments that may have initially been promising are later disproved with additional research. Anecdotal accounts from persons who were "cured" of a disease are no substitute for hard scientific data.
4. Suspect anyone who ridicules the traditional medical establishment or says that he or she is being persecuted by other doctors.
5. Be suspicious of any treatment available only in a foreign country where policies on drugs and acceptable medical practice may not be as strict as in the United States.

Table 18:2

toms until he or she reaches the hospital. The centers usually have evening and weekend hours and are less expensive than an emergency room, but more costly than a typical doctor's office visit. It is advisable to check the credentials of a center's physicians and their hospital affiliations. (See Tables 18:2 and 18:3.)

❑ Choosing a Hospital

When choosing a doctor you should check his or her hospital affiliation, especially if your health status requires periodic hospitalization.

In this cost-conscious era, people facing hospitalization should keep in mind certain rights. For example, Medicare now reimburses hospitals a flat amount per patient, depending on the diagnosis. This often allows the hospital to save money by discharging patients earlier than in the past. If you think that you are being discharged too early, you have the right to complain to the administrator on call and to take legal recourse if necessary. You should not be frightened into accepting early discharge by the threat that you will have to pay. You do not have to pay unless discharge is truly medically indicated. Patients should volunteer information that will help the hospital staff in discharge planning. For example, if you are being admitted for a cardiac problem and will have to climb

Resources for Double-Checking

The following provide information on the legitimacy of treatments for arthritis and cancer. For other illnesses, contact the organization associated with the particular disease.

The Council of Better Business Bureaus
1515 Wilson Boulevard
Arlington, VA 22209
703-276-0100
Attn: Standards and Practices
For free brochures, "Tips on Medical Quackery" and "Arthritis: Quakery and Unproven Remedies," send a self-addressed stamped envelope.

The Food and Drug Administration
HFE-88
5600 Fishers Lane
Rockville, MD 20857
For questions regarding medications, medical devices, food supplements of questionable value or safety.

The Arthritis Foundation
3400 Peachtree Road N.E.
Atlanta, GA 30326
404-266-0795

The American Cancer Society, Inc.
90 Park Avenue
New York, NY 10016
212-736-3030

National Cancer Institute
Office of Cancer Communications
Building 31, Room 10A18
9000 Rockville Pike
Bethesda, MD 20205
301-496-4070 or 1-800-4CANCER

Table 18:3

three flights of stairs to your residence upon discharge, tell this to the appropriate staff person. A person may not be discharged from a hospital if a discharge plan has not been made and presented to the patient and/or a responsible family member.

People should always carry proof of health insurance. A hospital may refuse to admit any non-emergency patient who cannot show proof. Frail individuals who are hospitalized may benefit if an assertive relative or friend is available to see that basic care needs are being met. Many institutions are understaffed, making it difficult for personnel to spend sufficient time with those who need to be fed or need frequent assistance with elimination.

When choosing a hospital, consider the following:

Accreditation. The Joint Commission on Accreditation of Hospitals (JCAH) inspects hospitals every one to three years to be certain they meet standards for adequate staffing, that they monitor and control in-hospital infections and the quality of care, and have licensed physicians who are responsible for setting policies governing the professional staff.

The hospital should have a currently dated certificate displayed in a prominent place. To find out if a hospital is accredited, contact the JCAH at 875 North Michigan Avenue, Chicago, IL 60611 or call (312) 642-6061.

Nursing care. Good nursing care is a sign of a good hospital. Look for a facility that has a low nurse turnover rate, low nurse-patient ratio and a large percentage of registered rather than licensed practical, or vocational, nurses who are on the hospital staff and have not been hired by outside agencies. Check with your local state nurses' association for area hospital statistics.

Experienced staff. If you will require a highly specialized operation, choose a hospital that performs the surgery on a regular basis. The more frequently an operation is done, the more experienced is the medical team and the better chance there is for a successful outcome. Ask the physician how many of these operations were done in the past year. A hospital doing coronary bypass surgery should do at least a hundred a year to maintain competence.

Services. Pick a hospital with a 24-hour emergency room, intensive and coronary care units or other services to meet your specialized needs. For example, patients who may have a prolonged recuperation for a particular illness might look for a hospital with a cooperative care unit, emphasizing patient and family participation in recovery.

Costs. Large teaching hospitals with their sophisticated medical technology and wide variety of specialists will be more expensive than small community facilities. If you don't need the services of a large hospital, consider a smaller accredited one. (See Table 18:4, Types of Hospitals.)

❑ Home Care

With the development of sophisticated technology and pressures to reduce hospital costs, a vast array of home care services has come into existence. Providers include hospital-based organizations, agencies run by medical equipment supply companies, private for-profit and nonprofit companies and public health facilities.

Hospitals, faced with threats of federal funding (Medicare) cutoffs, are sending patients home earlier, and sicker, than they did ten years ago. Individuals recovering from hip surgery, receiving intravenous antibiotics or suffering from chronic respiratory disease are only a few examples of those who can now be treated at home, given the physician's approval and the willingness of the patient and/or family to learn any necessary procedures.

Home care services include visits by a registered nurse to monitor the patient's condition and instruct the patient or family in the use of medical equipment or procedures; occupational, physical or speech therapy, if needed; personal care by a home health aide and/or housekeeping by a homemaker. Depending on patient condition and the agency, social

Types of Hospitals

Community hospitals:
- Also known as general hospitals.
- Are the most common facilities in the United States.
- Handle the more common medical and surgical conditions.
- Operate on a profit or nonprofit basis.
- Vary in size, with the larger ones having a greater variety of specialists and medical technology.
- Offer personalized medical care.

Teaching hospitals:
- Are large, well-equipped institutions affiliated with medical schools.
- The majority of staff physicians hold teaching and/or research positions.
- Have highly qualified medical staff who treat unusual disorders as well as common problems.

Because they train medical students, patients may be frequently examined by groups of undergraduates, interns, residents and specialists, have to answer the same questions regarding their medical history and endure some discomfort caused by the relative lack of experience of new physicians.

Public hospitals:
- Are generally large facilities.
- May or may not be affiliated with medical schools.
- Are owned and operated by the city, state or federal government.
- May have a large percentage of low-income patients, leading to the often unjust assumption of mediocre care.
- Are often good medically, but sparse on the amenities.

Specialized hospitals:
- Treat a single family of diseases, such as cancer or pulmonary disease.
- Are limited to specific organizations or groups, such as Veterans Administration hospitals for former members of the armed services.

Table 18:4

Selecting a Home Care Agency

Because of the tremendous growth in home care in recent years, the National League for Nursing, which accredits home care agencies, has been able to assess only a minority of the 6000 providers in this country. Lack of accreditation does not necessarily mean substandard care. When selecting an agency, keep in mind the needs of the patient and the following guidelines:
- A registered, rather than a licensed practical, or vocational, nurse should monitor patient condition and instruct the patient/family in procedures and use of equipment. In large urban areas, the supervising nurse should carry a beeper.
- The nurse should maintain regular contact with the physician, apprise him or her of patient progress and relay instructions to appropriate personnel. For example, if the patient is receiving intravenous medication and the physician orders a dose change, the nurse should inform the pharmacist who prepares the medication.
- The agency should have a 24-hour phone number to call for emergencies or in case of equipment failure.
- Home health aides should be trained and supervised by a registered nurse. The agency should find a replacement if the aide or homemaker is not satisfactory or becomes ill.
- If the patient is homebound, check to see what arrangements can be made for lab technicians and other auxiliary services to come into the home.
- The agency should explain all charges and what will be covered by the patient's insurance. For example, dressing changes done by an R.N. may be covered, but those done by a home health aide may not be. Many agencies will work with the patient to phrase "gray areas" so that they are covered by the policy. If ongoing medical needs will put a strain on finances, services of a social worker would be helpful.

Table 18:5

work services, dental care and arrangements for collecting lab specimens may be available.

Home care services are covered to varying degrees by Medicare, Medicaid and private insurance companies, but rarely covered unless the patient has been hospitalized. Factors important in determining eligibility for coverage are whether the patient has an acute or chronic condition—pneumonia versus a stroke—and whether the services of a registered nurse or other skilled professional are needed. Coverage provisions are complex and subject to change, so it is wise to check with the home care agency and your insurer before being discharged from the hospital. (See Table 18:5, Selecting a Home Care Agency, and Table 18:6, Resources for Home Care.)

❑ Choosing a Nursing Home

The percentage of people over 65 who are confined to a nursing home is small, but as the population of the country ages, nursing home admissions are on the rise. If nursing home placement is a clear possibility for a family member, it is important to take a close advance look at available facilities to ensure the best affordable care for the individual. (See Table 18:7.)

Facilities range from those providing minimal medical monitoring in a sheltered living environment—suitable for a relatively healthy person who cannot manage shopping, cooking and housekeeping chores—to those with full-time staff physicians and nurses for a chronically ill patient who may be confined to a wheelchair and unable to feed him- or herself. Different states have different names for these levels of care, but the most intensive are usually known as skilled nursing facilities (SNFs).

The majority of nursing homes, about 75 percent, are proprietary or profitmaking; the remainder are run by nonprofit organizations or the government. Recently, hospitals have been buying or building homes or linking themselves to established facilities and functioning as a single unit. Whatever the affiliation, pick a home that is certified at least by the state and, if looking for a skilled nursing facility, by the Joint Commission on Accreditation of Hospitals. These agencies inspect periodically to make sure that minimum health, sanitation,

Resources for Home Care

Organizations:

The National League for Nursing
10 Columbus Circle
New York, NY 10019-1350
Hotline: 1-800-847-8480
1-800-442-4546 (New York residents)
Call for information on accreditation and to register complaints about an agency.

The National Home Caring Council, Inc.
235 Park Avenue South
New York, NY 10003
212-674-4990
For a copy of the brochure "All About Home Care: A Consumer's Guide on Choosing a Quality Agency," send $2 and a self-addressed, stamped business envelope.

Home Health Services and Staffing Association
815 Connecticut Avenue NW
Washington, DC 20006
202-331-4437
Provides a listing of proprietary home care services.

Books:

Friedman, Jo-Ann.
Home Health Care: A Guide for Patients and Their Families.
New York: W. W. Norton, 1986.

Nassif, Janet Z.
The Home Health Care Solution: A Complete Consumer Guide.
New York: Harper & Row, 1985.

Table 18:6

What to Look For in a Nursing Home

Because admission to a nursing home may represent a permanent move and a jolting change, it is important to visit each home prepared with a list of questions. In making your choice consider the following guidelines:

Convenient location:
- Should be close enough for regular visits, preferably located in the same community where the person has lived.

Physical appearance:
- Should be clean, brightly lit, with minimal odor.
- Rooms should have no more than four beds, with sufficient privacy and personal storage space.

Safety:
- General construction should be sound.
- There should be rails in corridors and bathrooms, and safety rails should be raised on beds of residents who are not fully ambulatory.
- Floors should be clean and dry to prevent falls.
- Be sure fire exits are clearly marked and sprinklers and fire extinguishers are in working order. Stop a nurse or aide and ask for the location of the nearest fire exit. Staff should be able to tell you the plan for evacuating residents in an emergency. Ask how often fire drills and fire department inspections are scheduled.

Residents' appearance:
- Residents should be clean, out of bed and dressed unless medical indications are otherwise.
- There should be regularly scheduled age-appropriate activities. If the home is large, there should be a recreation therapy department or other staff solely devoted to activity planning.

Medical and nursing staff:
- The house physician should perform a complete physical examination before or immediately after a resident moves in.
- At least one staff physician should be present or on 24-hour call. At a skilled nursing facility, a registered nurse should always be on duty.
- Each resident should have an up-to-date chart, noting medications, changes in medical status and other relevant information.
- Nursing staff should be sufficient so that resident calls are answered promptly. If there are staff shortages, the more demanding patients may be sedated beyond what is medically necessary to make the nurse's job easier.
- Staff should treat residents with kindness and respect.

Hospitalization:
- Find out which hospital will be used and how the resident will be transported during a medical emergency.
- Should there be an extended stay, find out how long the home will keep the bed open.

Other services:
- If the home is large, there should be physical, occupational and speech therapy departments to help in resident rehabilitation following stroke or hip fracture, for example. On-site clinics offering podiatry and dental services, among others, are also an advantage.

Financial:
- What services does the basic rate include?
- Does the home receive Medicaid reimbursement?
- There should be a full-time social worker to help obtain financial assitance, as well as facilitate resident adjustment and handle family concerns.

Nutrition:
- A full-time dietitian should plan tasteful, nutritionally balanced meals for all residents, as well as for those with special medical needs and religious preferences.
- Meals should be served (to those not confined to rooms) in a communal dining room to promote socializing, with enough staff to help those who cannot feed themselves.

For more information on how to choose a good nursing home, contact the National Citizen's Coalition for Nursing Home Reform, 1825 Connecticut Avenue NW, Suite 417-B, Washington, DC 20009; 202-797-0657.

Table 18:7

nutrition, safety and other standards are met.

❑ Hospice Care

As people age, they are prone to develop certain types of cancer and other inevitably terminal diseases. Although many forms of cancer have good prognoses—and this number will probably increase with new treatments and positive lifestyle changes—others do not. For terminally ill patients who cannot benefit from acute medical intervention, a hospice is an alternative which may help both the patient and family make the most of the last months of life.

Derived from the medieval word for

shelter, hospices provide emotional support to both patient and family, and treatment of symptoms without attempting to cure or prolong life. Pain prevention or control is one of their specialties, and many hospices tailor medications and dose schedules to make sure the patient remains pain-free and alert.

Programs vary from those consisting of home care to scattered beds in a hospital to separate, freestanding buildings. Patients are cared for at home with the assistance of the hospice team (a physician, nurse, social worker and home health aide) or in the facility, depending on changing needs. Whenever possible, there is an emphasis on providing a homelike atmosphere; some facilities even allow pets or serve gourmet meals.

For admission to a hospice, the patient's prognosis usually must be no longer than six months to one year. Private insurance companies are beginning to cover hospice services and Medicare already covers many facets of care. Check with your local social security office for Medicaid policies. (See Table 18:8 for a list of hospice referral services.)

Hospice Information and Referral Services

The National Hospice Organization
1901 North Fort Myer Drive, Suite 402
Arlington, VA 22209
703-243-5900

Cancer Care, Inc.
1180 Avenue of the Americas
New York, NY 10036
212-221-3300

The American Cancer Society
19 West 56th Street
New York, NY 10019
212-586-8700

Local Visiting Nurse Association
See the phone book.

Books:
Buckingham, Robert W.
The Complete Hospice Guide.
New York: Harper & Row, 1983.

Hamilton, Michael P., and Helen F. Reid.
A Hospice Handbook.
Grand Rapids, Mich.: Eerdmans, 1980.

The National Consumer's League
600 Maryland Avenue SW
Suite 202-West
Washington, DC 20024
A Consumer's Guide to Hospice Care

Table 18:8

❑ Health Insurance

▪ *Medicare*

Medicare is the federal government insurance program for those aged 65 and over, and for persons of any age with severe kidney disease and selected chronic disabilities. On reaching 65, every American citizen who has been covered by social security automatically receives a Medicare card from the local social security office. Offices also distribute a helpful free handbook explaining coverage, how to file a claim and other important information.

Medicare insurance is divided into two parts: Part A and Part B. (See Table 18:9.) Part A involves hospital stays and is provided without cost. It covers, to varying degrees, inpatient hospital care (excluding doctors' services), home health care and blood transfusions. Currently, there is a $500 deductible per admission. Part B is available at a monthly premium and covers doctors' services, physical therapy and rehabilitation, among other areas. If you do not take Part B when you become eligible for Medicare, it will be exorbitantly expensive if taken at a later date. People who are currently working, as well as those who have private insurance, should take advantage of Part B Medicare when it is first offered.

PART B

For many outpatient services, Medicare pays 80 percent of "reasonable charges" once an annual deductible of

Common Services and Medicare Coverage

Here are some examples of services covered and not covered. To receive reimbursement, you must obtain the service from a participating physician or institution and meet the conditions specified in your handbook. Regulations are subject to change, so be sure to check with your local social security office.

Covered	Not Covered
HOSPITAL INSURANCE (PART A)	
Semi-private room (2 or 4 beds)	Private room unless deemed medically necessary
Regular hospital nurses	Private duty nurses
Operating room fees	
Laboratory tests	
Part-time skilled nursing services, physical and speech therapy in the home	Full-time skilled nursing at home
Part-time home health workers, if you require any of the above services	Housekeeping services
MEDICAL INSURANCE (PART B) Doctors' services	
Diagnostic tests and procedures related to a specific treatment—e.g., urine specimen for a patient with a urinary tract infection	Routine physical examination and accompanying tests—e.g., routine urinalysis
Routine foot care for a patient with an illness affecting the legs and feet—e.g., diabetes	Routine foot care for healthy individual or one with illness not affecting legs and feet—e.g., hypertension
Outpatient hospital services	
Clinic or emergency room services	Routine physical exams and tests
Drugs that cannot be self-administered—e.g., intravenous chemotherapy	Oral medications such as antibiotics

Table 18:9

$75 has been met. Also known as approved charges, these are calculated partially by reviewing the customary fees for service in a particular part of the country. For example, if you live in Iowa and your doctor charges $80 for a procedure for which most Iowa physicians charge $60, Medicare may pay only 80 percent of the lower fee. If you live in New York and the customary charge is $80, Medicare will pay 80 percent of this. Approved charges are recalculated each year. If you disagree with the amount Medicare is willing to pay for a service, or if you think a service that isn't covered should be, you may request a formal hearing.

Medicare medical insurance pays bills by two methods: (a) on assignment (the provider of care is paid directly by Medicare and you receive a bill for the remaining 20 percent and any unmet deductible); or (b) you pay the entire bill and Medicare reimburses you for 80 percent of the approved charge. Supplementary insurance will only pay the remaining 20 percent that Medicare does not cover. Make sure to keep a copy of all medical bills to support your claims.

If your financial status doesn't allow large outlays for medical bills, be sure to pick a physician who accepts the assignment method. Except for HMO physicians, very few private doctors will accept assignment largely because Medicare fees have been "frozen" at a level far below the going rate for most physicians. The Physician/Supplier Assignment Rate List or the Medicare-Participating Physician/Supplier Directory at your local social security office lists doctors who accept Medicare assignment.

MEDICARE AND PRIVATE INSURANCE

If you do not already have private insurance, it is wise to purchase a policy. According to the Congressional Budget Office, during 1984 the average Medicare enrollee with Medicare Parts A and B still paid more than $1000 for medical expenses. To avoid duplicating coverage, contact your social security office for a copy of the pamphlet "Guide to Health Insurance for People with Medicare." Many organizations, such as the American Association of Retired Persons, have supplemental group policies.

As of this writing, Congress is considering adding coverage of catastrophic illnesses to Medicare, with the increased cost to be borne by higher individual premiums.

▪ *Medicaid*

During middle age many people cannot envision being poverty-stricken in their later years. However, loss of job income coupled with chronic illness or the need for nursing home care can deplete even a substantial "nest egg." For the newly poor elderly, as well as the chronically needy, state-sponsored Medicaid health insurance steps in.

Medicaid programs are administered by state social service departments and vary greatly as to income eligibility requirements and benefits provided. A low-income individual who is 65 or over can be covered by both Medicare and Medicaid. In general, Medicaid covers a broader range of services and for a longer period than Medicare. Depending on the state, long-term nursing home care, many prescription drugs and foot care may be covered. Medicaid has no deductible to be met and may pay the total amount for services rather than the 80 percent covered by Medicare.

Applying for Medicaid can be a grueling process and it is wise to take along a friend or relative when going for the interview. (Many communities have senior centers or religious organizations that help with the application process.) Your state may require you to bring many documents—rent receipts, bankbooks, utility bills—to prove financial need. Make sure you understand exactly what is required before you go to avoid a second trip. For example, you may have memorized your social security number years ago, but you may still need to bring your card for proof. Contact your state social service department for any guides to documentation or filling out the application.

If your income is somewhat above the cutoff point, and you have fairly substantial and ongoing medical expenses, you may be able to "spend down," or pay for a certain amount of services yourself and then qualify for Medicaid for the balance of your expenses. In any case, Medicaid must inform you within a specific time period whether you have been accepted. If you feel that you have been unjustly rejected, contact your state social service agency to arrange for a hearing.

Medicaid recipients may be sent a monthly card which they must present when going for medical services. The individual or facility providing care is reimbursed directly by the state and you will not receive a bill for any covered service. Certain expensive medical supplies or services, such as a wheelchair or private duty nursing, must have advance approval for reimbursement. Your physician should complete the required form and send it to Medicaid or the appropriate vendor for processing.

If your present doctor will not accept Medicaid, the social service department can supply a list of physicians who do. If your doctor is willing to make an exception and take you as a Medicaid patient, check to see how he or she can join the program.

Be sure to deal promptly with any Medicaid requests for recertification information so as not to let your eligibility lapse. In turn, if you have not received your monthly card by the usual date, notify the department so you do not forfeit benefits for the month. You must also let Medicaid know if your address, size of household or financial status changes.

Medicaid recipients should not cancel private insurance. The program can act as a supplement to pay an amount not

Getting the Most out of Your Insurance

- Calculate what your chief medical expenses are and look for a policy that will cover most of them. Since major expenses for older people are hospital-related, the consumer should look for a policy with a low inpatient deductible. Study each policy carefully. Most companies have a ten-day, "free-look" provision which allows for a full refund if the customer decides not to buy.
- Be honest in filling out your application. If you conceal a preexisting problem, you may not be entitled to later coverage. Many policies allow for coverage of a known preexisting problem once a specific time has elapsed.
- Deal only with a state-licensed insurance agent to protect yourself from fraud and substandard business practices.
- Arrange to pay premiums on an annual or quarterly basis. Monthly payments mean extra expense for the company, which they may pass on to you.
- Choose a policy that is guaranteed renewable; the company must insure you up to a certain age, and sometimes for life, as long as you continue to pay the premium. Guaranteed renewable also means that your premium cannot be raised unless all premiums for a particular category are increased. If this type of policy is not available, pick a conditionally renewable plan; the company must continue to insure you except for specific instances stated in the policy.
- Check your policy each year to see if benefits are keeping pace with medical costs. Basic coverage which has "inside limits" (only part of the hospital room or surgical costs are covered) may not be sufficient. Ask your agent if you can add coverage to prevent major outlays.
- Promptly and carefully complete claim forms to ensure speedy payments.
- Make sure your policies do not duplicate or overlap each other. Overinsurance is an unnecessary expense.

Table 18:10

covered by your policy. Depending on the state, your insurance premiums may be taken into consideration when determining eligibility.

▪ *Private Insurance*

Chances are, you may already have a policy which meets your needs. However, if your coverage is through your job and will end when you retire or if you are in the market for a better policy, there are some points to keep in mind.

Although costs and coverage differ from company to company, in general, group insurance offers the lowest cost protection. If you have a group policy at work, see if you can continue this after you retire. Group coverage may also be available through a union, fraternal organization or professional society. (See Table 18:10 for suggestions on how best to select and utilize insurance.)

TYPES OF COVERAGE

Basic hospitalization. This usually includes a semi-private room, meals, laboratory and diagnostic tests and operating room costs. Length of coverage depends on the policy, and you may have to wait a specified time period for coverage to begin in full. Outpatient coverage, when applicable, also falls into this category.

Basic medical/surgical. This pays for physician services related to hospitalization and surgery. It usually will not fully cover doctors' office visits and house calls.

Major medical. This covers long-term and major, "catastrophic" medical costs beyond those paid by basic hospitalization and medical/surgical insurance. Some policies will not cover any preexisting health problems until a certain time period has elapsed. Private duty nursing, home care and rehabilitation services may fall under this type of coverage.

A suggested minimum lifetime coverage figure is $250,000. Major medical policies cover between 75 and 80 percent of expenses. The deductible ranges between $1000 and $5000; in general, the higher the deductible, the lower the policy cost. Many plans feature a desirable "stop-loss" provision, which totally covers expenses incurred beyond a specified annual amount, up to the limit of your policy.

If you cannot afford both basic and supplementary major medical coverage, choose a comprehensive major medical policy which includes features of basic plans.

Long-term health care. Nearly seventy insurance companies now offer long-term health insurance which covers varying amounts of nursing home expenses for time periods of two to six years and sometimes home care expenses. Premiums are expensive—from $300 to over $1000 per year—but are usually guaranteed renewable and will not increase unless across-the-board increases are allowed in the particular state. Preexisting conditions are generally not covered on these policies.

The consumer should check to see if the policy covers the services of non-skilled employees (nurse's aides often give much of the direct patient care in a nursing home), as well as skilled professionals, such as doctors, nurses and physical therapists.

Insurance companies may not offer long-term policies in all states, but you may be able to purchase an out-of-state policy which will provide coverage. Some of the larger insurers offering these are:

Amex Life Assurance
1-800-321-9352
1-800-848-8179 (California residents)

AIG Life Insurance
1-206-454-8600

CNA Insurance
1-800-262-1919
1-800-325-1843 (Illinois residents)

Disability income. This coverage provides cash to an individual who is unable to work because of injury or illness. Policies vary as to definitions of disability, length of coverage and dates when benefits begin. The maximum benefit provided is two-thirds of the gross salary. You should choose a policy that provides income if you are unable to resume work in your regular occupation. For example, a mail carrier with a leg injury might not be able to deliver mail, but could work in a job that did not require a great deal of walking. With an own-occupation policy, he could collect income rather than have to look for a position for which he has no experience.

The best, and the most expensive, policies are noncancellable and guaranteed renewable. However, policy costs can be reduced if you can afford to wait awhile before coverage begins and if your pension plan covers disability after retirement, enabling you to discontinue the insurance.

❏ Traveling Healthy

One of the pleasures of retirement is having the time to travel. With this yen and a sufficient income, even those suffering from chronic illness or disability should feel free to travel, given some advance preparation. Here are some tips to help make your trip a happy and healthy one:

- If planning extensive travel, have a complete physical examination, including bloodwork, urinalysis and an update of routine immunizations. Allow plenty of time for special immunizations recommended for specific countries.
- Have a sufficient reserve of medications and supplies. Know the generic names for your drugs, as brand names may vary in different countries.
- Get a note from your doctor stating your diagnosis to avoid questioning by customs' authorities as to the legitimacy of medications or insulin syringes.
- If you are planning a cruise and have

a tendency toward motion sickness, ask your doctor to recommend an appropriate medication.

- Check with your insurance company to see if your policy covers illness abroad, and what forms you should bring on your trip. Some companies will reimburse you, but you must first pay for hospital, doctor and so forth. Medicare covers travel in United States territories such as Puerto Rico and the Virgin Islands but excludes other countries.

For more information, contact:

United States Government
Printing Office
Superintendent of Documents
Washington, DC 20402
202-783-3283

The above publishes a pamphlet "Health Information for International Travelers" (stock #017-023-00174-4), for $4.75, that covers vaccination recommendations, information on motion sickness and traveler's diarrhea, food and drink precautions, tips for the handicapped traveler and other facts. Also available at Government Printing Office bookstores in major cities. (See Table 18:11, Finding a Doctor Abroad; Table 18:12, Medical Insurance for Travelers; and Table 18:13, Resources for the Handicapped Traveler.)

Almost thirty states now have laws requiring medical personnel to ask survivors of a person who died in the hospital to permit donation of the deceased's organs, and it appears that more and more states will follow in this marvelous lifesaving trend. Some states include Uniform Donor Cards with driver's licenses. They are also available from the regional transplant program which is listed in the telephone directory or from organizations that deal with specific organs, such as the National Kidney Foundation. Other sources include:

American Medical Association
535 North Dearborn Street
Chicago, IL 60610

Medic Alert
P.O. Box 6725
Houston, TX 77005

National Kidney Foundation
116 East 27th Street
New York, NY 10016

The Uniform Anatomical Gift Act allows people to make a gift of their body or parts for medical purposes to hospitals, medical and dental schools, or institutions involved in medical research or storage of organs. Anatomical Gift Cards are available from any local medical school or research hospital.

Finding a Doctor Abroad

The International Association for
Medical Assistance to Travelers (IAMAT)
736 Center Street
Lewiston, NY 20402
716-754-4883
Publishes a list of English-speaking doctors in 120 foreign countries, available at no charge.

Intermedic
777 Third Avenue
New York, NY 10017
212-486-8900
Publishes a list of English-speaking doctors who have submitted their qualifications, including educational background, available to members. The annual membership fee is $6 for an individual, $10 for a family.

International SOS Assistance
P.O. Box 11568
Philadelphia, PA 19116
1-800-523-8930
215-244-1500 (Pennsylvania residents)
Offers a variety of services covering travel a hundred miles away from home as well as overseas. These include an international physician-referral network, free evacuation to adequate medical care if none exists in the country where you are vacationing, a cash advance against your credit card to cover hospitalization and medical supplies ordered by a physician except for first aid. Cost is $15 per week, $45 per month, or $195 per year.

Table 18:11

Medical Insurance for Travelers

Healthcare Abroad
Investment Building
1511 K Street NW, Suite 219
Washington, DC 20005
1-800-336-3310
1-703-255-9800 (Virginia residents)
Offers a comprehensive insurance plan for $3 per day which includes $100,000 accident and sickness coverage and medical evacuation.

BankAmerica
Offers travel insurance only to its credit card holders. For a $5 per 45-day fee, they will pay up to $1000 as a hospital deposit and refer the traveler to English-speaking physicians abroad.

American Express
Offers information and referral services and financial assistance to cardholders under the Global Assist program. Users may borrow up to $5000 for hospitalization at no interest if fully repaid within a month after receiving the bill.

AARP
Offers a supplemental policy to Medicare to cover overseas medical expenses up to a maximum of $25,000.

Table 18:12

Resources for the Handicapped Traveler

Society for the Advancement of Travel
for the Handicapped
26 Court Street
Brooklyn, NY 11242
718-858-5483
Free referral service to travel agency or tour operator, depending on the particular need.

Flying Wheels Travel
143 West Bridge
P.O. Box 382
Owatonna, MN 55060
1-800-533-0363
1-800-722-9351 (Minnesota residents)
Specializes in independent and group travel for those confined to a wheelchair.

Dialysis At Sea
65 East India Row
22G
Boston, MA 02110
1-800-343-0664, ext. 2000
1-800-322-1238 (Massachusetts residents)
Arranges for dialysis on board selected cruise ships.

Table 18:13

PART V

DEATH

19

COMING TO TERMS WITH MORTALITY

Dying is a natural part of living. It starts the moment we are born. Throughout the ages, the subject has inspired religious thinkers, philosophers and artists to many of their greatest achievements. It is an inevitable part of the miraculous life cycle of all creatures.

The attitude we have toward death—our own and those close to us—depends, to a great extent, on how we live. Those who remain active, are curious about the world around them, maintain close relationships with family and friends and continue to be challenged by new interests, are most apt to view death as the natural phenomenon it is.

With advances in medical science and in standards of living, life expectancy has increased. As people age, they are at greater risk for developing certain chronic conditions, making it more important than ever for them to pay attention to their diet, exercise and personal habits. But living longer and healthier lives also gives a person more opportunities to realize goals and accomplish tasks they once feared early death might preclude. By staying active and acquiring new interests and relationships, emotional and psychological health, which is as important as maintaining physical health, is preserved. In turn, these all contribute to a positive approach to death.

But a positive attitude should not be equated with pretending the event will not take place. Indeed, those who are able to accept death as a part of their life are most likely to continue cultivating activities that will sustain them when, for instance, a spouse dies. In addition, they will be able to make the practical plans for their family in the event of their own death. This is especially important, for many of the fears associated with dying involve not making adequate provisions for those we love and for whom we feel responsible.

Studies show that fear of death is greatest during a person's forties, when people typically have a lot of responsibilities, are involved in many activities and may have dependent children. But older people seem to have less fear of death. It is possible that life review, or reminiscing, helps older people come to terms with their past and prepare for what is to come. (For more on life review, see Chapter 9, Lifelong Learning.)

❑ Changing Norms

This century has witnessed a dramatic reduction in deaths in the young and middle-aged population from acute diseases and other environmental factors. According to statistics from the U.S. Bureau of the Census, three quarters of all deaths now occur in the 65-year and older population group. Death now often results from a chronic, perhaps prolonged illness in old age, rather than from an acute illness or accident.

It was not long ago that most people died at home surrounded by friends and family who, because they cared for the person and were often present at the death, did not view the event as mysterious or frightening. From early childhood onward, people came in contact with death. Today, with death occurring primarily in the elderly population, a person may not experience the death of someone close until late middle age or early old age when a parent dies—often in a hospital, which creates even more distance between the survivors and the loved ones. According to Martha Baum in her book *Growing Old* (New York: Prentice-Hall, 1980), as late as 1949, only 40 percent of deaths took place in a hospital. But by the 1970's the proportion had risen to 70 percent.

Unfortunately, this demographic change has affected many people's—and much of our society's—attitudes and approaches toward death. Dr. Elizabeth Kübler-Ross, a pioneer in working with the dying, attributes much of the difficulty modern society has in accepting death to our unfamiliarity with it. And because unfamiliarity often breeds fear, it is important to understand the psychological stages you—or those close to you—will go through when confronted with death. These stages of grief are discussed in full in the section that follows.

❑ Stages of Grief

Researchers have found that both those who are faced with their own death and those who are faced with the death of a loved one go through one or all of the same stages of grief, although not necessarily at the same time or in the same order. Here are the five stages of grief Dr. Kübler-Ross has identified.

Denial. Typically, this is a person's first reaction to being told of a terminal illness or the imminent death of a loved one, and may be expressed as shock or disbelief. Denial initially serves a valuable function by allowing the person to distance him- or herself temporarily from the reality of the issue, providing time to marshal the strength and resources to deal with illness and death. The person in the denial stage may insist on seeking several other medical opinions or investigating alternative therapies, or may refuse to make necessary changes in daily routine. A relative of the dying person may refuse to discuss any practical issues relating to the death or persist in discussing plans for the future. Denial can be a refusal to acknowledge the diagnosis. It is a natural and necessary reaction that cushions the blow at first, but if it is carried too far, it can be a barrier to honest communication and to real preparation for death.

Anger. Anger over the news of a terminal disease may be directed at health-care personnel, who are blamed for being incompetent or uncaring; at loved ones; at God or at oneself. Anger is a normal and justifiable reaction that should not be suppressed or disguised. Lingering in the anger stage, however, can keep a person from accepting the reality, can alienate those most important to have around at this time, and may even make hospital staff reluctant to deal with the patient. It is important for those who are around a dying person, like hospital staff and relatives, to recognize that expressions of anger fill an important need for the patient and that they are often a cry for help.

Bargaining. At first, a dying person may try to bargain—with God, with the medical establishment—for a cure. As the person moves closer to accepting death, his "bargaining" will become more realistic. He may hope to survive until a certain anniversary—a birthday, his grandson's commencement or even until the beginning of the next month.

Depression. This stage is characterized by a sense of helplessness and hopelessness. Death has been accepted as a reality but has not been adjusted to in a positive way. During this stage dying patients will often be uncommunicative and want to be left alone. For the grieving person who has lost a spouse or a close relative, temporary depression is a common reaction and should not be interpreted as a sign of mental illness. Basically, the grieving person should know that this stage will pass. Making conscious efforts to do something, to take care of small matters can help.

Acceptance. The dying person awaits death without anger—with peace and personal satisfaction with his or her life. He or she may begin a process of disengagement from most people, wanting only to be with close friends and family. For the person mourning a death, the stage of acceptance is characterized by the ability to remember the loved one without strong feelings of pain or sadness and to begin to make new emotional attachments.

It is also not unusual for someone to reach one stage and then "regress" to a previous stage. Although this is often a normal part of the person's grief, it can also be caused by medical personnel who insist on engaging in heroic measures to revive the patient after he or she has already accepted death, or by the family who may not be able to accept the person leaving them and as a result make the patient feel guilty or depressed. The dying person and his relatives will often be in different stages at different times.

❑ Practical Matters

It is as important to make preparations for death as it is for any other major life event—the birth of a child, college education, retirement, marriage, et al. Only by making prior arrangements can one be assured that his or her wishes will be carried out.

Ideally, all the necessary arrangements should be planned early in life or in a marriage, without haste or pressure. With the natural tendency to procrastinate, this is not usually the case and people often find themselves dealing with these issues only when they are forced to. In addition to making arrangements for a will, insurance policies, funeral plans and payment for burial, an individual or couple may want to investigate the alternate living arrangements of a continuing care community.

▪ *A Community Option*

"Continuing care" communities are among the range of options that have developed to meet the housing and health needs of the older population. These communities usually attract people in what is considered the second stage of retirement—the 75-year-old and up group. They offer living arrangements that include a studio or apartment, community and health centers, a nursing home on the grounds and a wide variety of elective services. Usually one meal a day is eaten in the communal dining room, although residents may arrange for more if they wish. These communities operate in a number of ways but they usually charge a one-time entrance fee, which may or may not be partially refundable, and a monthly maintenance fee. Entrance fees range anywhere from $25,000 to $150,000. At some, the entrance and monthly fees cover all costs, others operate on a "fee-for-service" arrangement, while still others charge extra only for certain items, such as nursing home care. For the most part, these communities are designed for people who have already experienced health problems, who may not be as independent as they once were or who simply want to give up some of their responsibilities, such as the care of a large home.

Before making a commitment, one should spend a few days there. In addition, ask for the community's financial history, including details such as whether monthly fees have been raised frequently and what sort of reserve fund there is. The American Association of Homes for the Aging will begin accrediting these communities in the near future according to quality of facilities, care and reserve fund. State officials in the Department of Aging may be able to provide information on local communities. (For where to obtain more information, see Table 19:1, Continuing Care Communities.)

Continuing Care Communities

Typical services:
- Linen service
- Housekeeping
- Utilities
- Building maintenance
- Garbage pickup
- Shuttle buses to town or events
- Parking
- Aids or other assistance at extra fee
- Social activities

Where to Go for Information:
The American Association of Homes for the Aging is a nonprofit organization whose membership consists of various types of residential houses for older people, including nursing homes and retirement communities, as well as life-care communities. For information on continuing care communities write:

The American Association of Homes for the Aging
1129 20th Street
Suite 400
Washington, DC 20036

In addition, the American Association of Retired Persons is updating its directory on continuing care communities. The directory is available from the American Association of Homes for the Aging or from the local chapter of the AARP.

Table 19:1

▪ *The Living Will*

A Living Will is a statement by which the signer expresses his or her refusal to undergo invasive measures or to be subjected to artificial life-support systems in the case of a terminal illness or natural death after an accident. The legality of a Living Will varies from state to state and is currently subject to frequent reinterpretations. (See Table 19:2 for a sample Living Will.) Although the Living Will may not be accepted as legally valid, it can often be used in court as proof of the signer's intent and wishes. A Living Will should be treated as any other legal document: It should be witnessed and filed with other important papers. Family members should be aware of the existence of the will so that they will know of the signer's wishes if a relevant situation arises. If the family knows what the person wants, the difficult decision to stop life-support systems will be much easier to make. Information on and forms for a Living Will are available from Concern for Dying, 250 West 57th Street, New York, NY 10107, 212-246-6962.

Sample Living Will
(The following sample is distributed by Concern for Dying)

My Living Will
To My Family, My Physician, My Lawyer and All Others Whom It May Concern

Death is as much a reality as birth, growth, maturity and old age—it is the one certainty of life. If the time comes when I can no longer take part in decisions for my own future, let this statement stand as an expression of my wishes and directions, while I am still of sound mind.

If at such a time the situation should arise in which there is no reasonable expectation of my recovery from extreme physical or mental disability, I direct that I be allowed to die and not be kept alive by medications, artificial means or "heroic measures." I do, however, ask that medication be mercifully administered to me to alleviate suffering even though this may shorten my remaining life.

This statement is made after careful consideration and is in accordance with my strong convictions and beliefs. I want the wishes and directions here expressed carried out to the extent permitted by law. Insofar as they are not legally enforceable, I hope that those to whom this Will is addressed will regard themselves as morally bound by these provisions.

(Optional specific provisions to be made in this space)

DURABLE POWER OF ATTORNEY (optional)

I hereby designate ______________________________ to serve as my attorney-in-fact for the purpose of making medical treatment decisions. This power of attorney shall remain effective in the event that I become incompetent or otherwise unable to make such decisions for myself.

Optional Notarization:

"Sworn and subscribed to

before me this __________ day

of __________, 19 _____."

____
Notary Public
(seal)

Signed ______________________________

Date ______________________________

Witness ______________________________

____
Address

Witness ______________________________

____
Address

Copies of this request have been given to ______________________________

______________________________ ______________________________

(Optional) My Living Will is registered with Concern for Dying (No. __________)

Reprinted with permission of Concern for Dying, 250 West 57th Street, New York, NY 10107.

Table 19:2

▪ *Organ Donation*

For many people, a way of ensuring that a part of them will continue into the future is by donating their body or organs for medical research or therapy. As medical skill in the area of transplantation has become more sophisticated, it has become possible to transplant more organs, and the success rates of transplantation operations have increased substantially. Organ donation is indeed a gift of life at no cost to the giver. Nevertheless, health-care personnel have often been hesitant to ask survivors to allow such a gift to be made at the time of a loved one's death. Family members may be hesitant to allow donation because they are afraid the body will be too mutilated for a proper funeral. This fear is unfounded: Doctors can remove the organs and repair a body so that it is suitable for whatever type of funeral service is desired. After an individual has signed a Uniform Donor Card, he or she should inform family members to be assured the wishes are carried out.

▪ *Preparing for Your Own Death*

Having a written description of the type of funeral or memorial service a person wants can eliminate disagreement among family members who have different opinions after the death. These instructions should be kept with other important papers. A file should also be kept, including a record of all insurance policies held, social security card, marriage certificate, and a list including names of the attorney, insurance agent, stockbroker, union official and anyone else involved in financial matters. (See Table 19:3, Essential Papers.)

If the will is joint, both spouses should examine it, to be sure it is up-to-date and the provisions are as they wish. Insurance policies should also be checked to make certain that the beneficiaries are correct, including any company- or union-held policies. When a person knows that he or she is going to die, it is often a good idea to transfer property held only in one name into the spouse's name. (See Table 19:4, Making Arrangements.)

Essential Papers

The following information should be kept in a file at home or at your lawyer's office and *not* in a bank safety deposit box. It should be updated periodically. Family members, an attorney or a friend should know where this file is kept:

- Written description of desired type of funeral or memorial service
- Copies of all insurance policies
- Social security card
- Marriage certificate
- Deeds and mortgages
- Safe deposit box number
- Veteran's discharge papers
- Birth certificates of family members
- W-2 form
- Names of:
  attorney
  insurance agent
  stockbroker
  union official
- Living Will
- Indication of Uniform Donor Card

Table 19:3

Making Arrangements

A number of concerns must be addressed in making plans for death:

- Living Will
- Organ donation
- Disposition of estate
- Type of medical insurance

If you become seriously ill, what kind of care do you want?

- Hospital
- Nursing Home
- Hospice

What kind of death arrangements?

- Burial
- Cremation
- Religious service
- Memorial service
- Donation of body

Table 19:4

▪ *The Funeral*

The funeral may hold several meanings for the survivors: It can be seen as the last opportunity to say goodbye, as a means of showing respect for the deceased and as a way of affirming his or her place in the family and community.

Ideally, a funeral director should be sympathetic and able to accommodate the degree of involvement the bereaved wishes and help him or her in the initial acceptance of the death. However, some feel the funeral industry in the United States takes advantage of survivors during this time, encouraging them to plan extravagant funerals and perhaps making them feel guilty if they want to keep things simple. The best way to prevent this is for an individual to put his or her wishes in writing, preferably years before it is needed. By doing this, survivors need not feel pressured into having anything other than what they know the deceased wanted. They should also not hesitate to ask the mortician for prices and explanations of other options.

In addition to outlining in advance what kind of funeral one would like, an individual should also try to make financial arrangements for it. According to the Continental Association of Funeral and Memorial Societies, the average cost of a funeral in the United States, not including cemetery costs, runs $3500 today. Providing for the costs of a funeral ahead of time helps the surviving spouse not only financially, but psychologically, by relieving him or her of making decisions under stress. Insurance may be purchased to pay for a funeral and/or a burial plot, a savings account earmarked for that purpose may be opened, or provisions can be made in the will.

MEMORIAL SOCIETIES

One way to get accurate information about costs and options for funerals, and perhaps to be eligible for a discount, is to join a memorial society. Memorial societies grew out of the consumer movement that arose to protest the high cost of funerals. They are nonprofit organizations that keep up-to-date information on low-cost funerals, cremation, organ and body donations and other details. Many are affiliated with churches or civic organizations, although it is not usually necessary to be a member of these organizations to join the memorial society.

There is a one-time fee to become a member. Funeral costs are not paid to the memorial society but directly to the funeral director. Some memorial societies have formal contracts with one or more local funeral directors who agree to provide set types of funeral services to members at a discount rate. Others simply provide information about available services and costs. A local memorial society can be found by looking in the yellow pages of the telephone directory under associations or in the white pages, usually under "Memorial Society of . . ."

The Continental Association of Funeral and Memorial Societies is an umbrella organization that acts as a clearinghouse for information about memorial societies and works with government agencies on matters that affect funeral arrangements. For information write:

The Continental Association of
Funeral and Memorial Societies
2001 S Street NW
Suite 530
Washington, DC 20036

Information about funeral arrangements is also available from the state board of undertakers and embalmers or the office of the state attorney general.

❑ Dying—the Modern Way

To a person who has suffered through a long illness or to someone who knows that he or she is going to die, death may not necessarily be unwelcome. To one who has accepted death, it can mean an end to pain, to the limitations of illness and a peaceful end to a full life. (For factors affecting a person's ability to cope with death, see Table 19:5.)

Hospitals are cure-oriented, not care-oriented. Because physicians and other health-care professionals are trained to cure their patients, they are often uneasy when nothing can be done to prevent death.

But because the dying are not in need of the interventions of modern medicine does not mean that they do not need care; he or she needs a certain type of care. A dying person and his or her loved ones need a holistic sort of care that attends to their emotional, psychological and physical needs. The dying person and spouse or relatives need to know that the patient will be kept as pain-free as possible and will not be subjected to any unnecessary procedures. But aside from that, the dying patient needs the time and opportunity to discuss his or her feelings. Studies have shown that the majority of people with a terminal illness want to know it—and that once they know, they eventually want to be able to discuss their death in an open and honest manner. Being in an environment that is designed to combat death rather than accept it is counterproductive for them.

The Ability to Cope with Death

Some of the factors that positively affect a person's ability to cope with death include:

- Past ability to cope with stressful situations
- Supportive relationship with spouse
- View of life as meaningful and fulfilled
- Ability to communicate openly about his or her illness and death
- Strength of belief system, whether that system is based on a traditional religion or a belief in something or in oneself
- The opportunity for close contact in the past with someone going through a terminal illness who accepted death peacefully
- Ability to accept reality

Table 19:5

▪ *Alternatives to Hospitals*

The hospice movement grew out of the desire to provide dying patients with both the physical and psychological care that they need in a humane setting capable of integrating family and friends. Although still not the standard practice in this country, the availability of hospice care is increasing.

The hospice philosophy is to keep the patient free of pain while providing him or her and the family with as much emotional support as possible and the opportunity to talk about their concerns with someone who has experience with dying patients. Hospice workers generally will not perform the dramatic resuscitation attempts that medical personnel might in a hospital setting, although they will make every effort to see that the patient is comfortable and attend to nutritional and other needs. The hospice is meant to be a place where a person can die with dignity. There is no pretense of "cure." In fact, in many cases, the hospice may insist that the patients acknowledge that they are dying before they will be accepted.

The forms of hospice care include a separate institution, a separate wing or beds in a hospital, beds in a nursing home and care in the patient's home, but most of it takes place in the patient's home with the help of visiting nurses, social workers and other hospice staff. The spouse or other close relative or person is the primary care-giver. Even in a hospice in a separate setting, the spouse may be responsible for much of the care. Hospice staff are available to help, but they do not attempt to intrude on the relationship between the dying person and the loved one. Hospices offer care and counseling to the care-giver as well as to the dying person. The "patient" is considered to consist of all parties involved. Many hospices offer counseling and support to the spouse after the death of the patient.

RESOURCES AVAILABLE

Home nursing care is available through most hospices or through the Visiting Nurse Association. Caring for a dying person can be exhausting, both physically and emotionally, and this assistance can relieve some of the burden. An invaluable service is respite care—someone to come in periodically and take over all the care so that the care-giver can get away—whether for a few hours or a couple of days. If several days off are needed, readmission to the hospital is usually an option. The hospice can also be helpful in providing or locating equipment that may be needed for the care of the dying person, such as oxygen, feeding tubes, etc. For information on respite care, contact the local chapter of the American Cancer Society, the local Visiting Nurse Association or the Older Women's League.

FINANCING CARE

Some private insurers will cover hospice costs, to some degree, but it is not standard coverage so each policy must be looked at carefully. According to the article "Hospices" in *Consumer Reports* (January, 1986), Medicare's payments to hospices are not very generous and therefore only a small number of them have applied for certification.

Medicare coverage is available under these certain conditions:

- The patient is eligible for Medicare coverage
- The patient's doctor and hospice medical director certify that the patient has a life expectancy of six months or less (which can be revised or renewed by a physician)
- The patient signs a statement choosing hospice care
- The hospice is Medicare-certified

The publication, "Hospice Benefits under Medicare" (Pub. No. HCFA 02154) is available from the local social security office of the Health Care Financing Administration, 6325 Security Boulevard, Baltimore, MD 21207. (For information on where to find a hospice, see Table 18:8.)

▪ *Does Hospice Care Work?*

Surveys have shown that the main concerns of a patient with a terminal illness are being a burden to others, separation from loved ones and concern about their welfare, and painful death. Although hospice care does place a great responsibility on the care-giver, there are resources available to help alleviate the burden. An honest discussion of this concern can help the dying person and the spouse decide whether hospital care or hospice care is best. The options of home nursing, respite care or even occasional readmission to the hospital may help allay the dying person's fears about being a burden. However, some couples may find that they are fully insured for hospital care but not for hospice care, and this may influence the decision.

Since the focus of hospice care is on making the patient as comfortable as possible, pain relief is a priority. Hospice staff are less likely than hospital staff to insist on a set schedule of pain medication and instead will administer medication to prevent pain from surfacing instead of waiting until the patient is already suffering. Of course, attitudes and procedures in hospitals regarding dying patients are slowly changing and the final decision may depend on what is available in the specific community.

▪ *Coping with the Death of a Spouse*

The loss of a spouse in old age can sometimes mean a complete restructuring of life, and there is no way to assign a timetable or a set of rules to that process. The bereaved go through the same stages of grief as the dying do. It's helpful to remember that grief is not a disease but a process, a period of transition that involves a gradual letting go of the old and a creation of new networks, identities and roles.

It is not unusual to have mixed feelings at first when a spouse dies after a long illness, especially if there has been prolonged suffering or severe deterioration. The surviving spouse has probably gone through some anticipatory grieving, although opinions vary on whether this speeds up the grieving process or creates additional stress.

Sudden or unexpected deaths do not seem to be accompanied by longer or more intense grieving, although the survivor may be stuck longer in the initial stage of shock or denial. Viewing the body is important because it helps establish the reality of the death. The survivor may have to cope with the need for an autopsy in many cases and later, if no planning was done, with the practical and financial affairs.

THREAT TO IDENTITY

The death of a spouse may constitute a serious threat to a person's sense of self, especially if his or her role was largely defined by the spouse. In the elderly population, when the family is often reduced to a couple, the spouse may be the only significant other. Widows, whose roles were defined by the marriage, will often feel a serious loss of self. Although more men may have jobs which provide them with a sense of identity, women tend to establish stronger and broader networks of friends who can help during this period.

Helping the Bereaved

- Initially, friends and neighbors can help with practical details and responsibilities.
- Later they should encourage him or her to take on responsibility.
- Visits after the funeral period will help make the widow/widower feel less alone.
- Visitors should accept emotional outbursts as normal and not show surprise or uneasiness.
- Friends and relatives should not avoid discussing the deceased or the facts of the survivor's situation. They should be willing to listen to what the bereaved has to say and not insist on talking about trivial matters.
- Conversation is not always necessary. Sometimes, just the presence of someone who cares will be genuinely appreciated.
- Written expressions of sympathy are helpful.
- After making initial contact with the bereaved after the death, friends should make the effort to stay in touch. Later, they should include the widow/widower in activities and treat him or her as a normal person.

Table 19:6

Grief is often referred to in physical terms—as a blow, for instance. In time, the impact of the "blow" or "injury" will lessen, but many people going through this difficult period may fear that they are not "normal" or that they will never recover. Immediately after the death the survivor is usually surrounded by relatives and friends, but afterward he or she may be left to deal with the unfamiliar and often frightening effects of grief. (For how friends and family can help, see Table 19:6.)

▪ *Common Symptoms of Grieving*

Being aware of what is normal in a state of grief will not relieve mourning, but it may reduce anxiety in the person experiencing changes in behavior and emotions.

In the early stages of grief, emotions may be intense and difficult to control. Outbursts of crying and even anger are common. The newly bereaved may find that he or she cries unexpectedly in public. Preoccupation or even obsession with the deceased is also common, and it is not unusual to see visions of the deceased and to search in crowds or familiar places for the loved one. These are natural reactions to loss and will gradually lessen in intensity.

In many cases, the bereaved will idealize the spouse or the marital relationship. This, too, is a natural reaction. But, if it goes on too long it can inhibit the grieving process because it makes it difficult for the survivor to remember the spouse realistically and put their relationship and the death into perspective. Also, idealization can increase the survivor's guilt and make it difficult to form new relationships. The survivor may feel disloyal to the spouse or may feel that no one can measure up to the "perfect spouse."

Many grieving people increase their use of alcohol, drugs or cigarettes at first to deaden their intense anxiety or sadness, but they should gradually return to the normal level of use as they begin to learn to cope. (For other common symptoms of grief after death of a spouse, see Table 19:7.)

Gradually the symptoms of grief will subside: There may still be bursts of crying, but they will not come on unexpectedly in public. Depression will be less intense, and as the habits that were previously connected with the deceased are altered, the daily routines of life will not automatically remind the survivor of the bereaved. Health will improve and energy will begin to return to normal as the survivor passes from intense griev-

Common Symptoms of Grief After Death of a Spouse

- Outbursts of crying
- Idealization of deceased
- Hallucinations
- Searching for deceased in crowds
- Memory lapses
- Insomnia
- A succession of illnesses, such as colds or flu
- Ulcers and gastritis
- Nervousness
- Use of drugs and alcohol
- Depression
- Feelings of panic
- Nightmares
- Loss of appetite
- Fatigue
- Inability to concentrate

Table 19:7

Strategies for Coping After the Death of a Spouse

There are some steps the survivor can take to better cope during this time:

- At first, concentrate on handling practical matters that demand attention. Do not make any major decisions about changes.
- Ask for help when you need it—from family, friends, clergy or counselors—whether it's someone to come over and stay with you or to help fix your car. Don't expect people to guess what you need and don't ignore your own needs.
- Look for community programs or groups of people who are going or have been through what you are experiencing. Sharing similar experiences with others helps you work through your feelings and reassures you of the normalcy of your emotions. If you do not seem to be able to cope or to move on at all, seek professional help from a grief counselor.
- When you feel ready, go through the deceased's belongings yourself or ask a friend to help you. Do not let someone else dispose of the spouse's things without consulting you.
- Don't sell the house or move to a new city right away. Not only is this a way of avoiding the situation, but it will add even more stress at this difficult time.
- Look for new avenues of interest and new sources of friends. It may not be possible—or best—to involve yourself in an outside activity at first, but it is a good idea to gradually explore potential new activities.

Table 19:8

Sources of Support

Widowed Persons Service
1909 K Street NW
Washington, DC 20006

Parents Without Partners
7910 Woodmont Avenue
Bethesda, MD 20049

Table 19:9

ing into the stage where he or she starts to put together the pieces of a new life. (For strategies for coping, see Table 19:8; for sources of support, see Table 19:9.)

Eventually, life will take on a new look. The memories of the deceased will be an important part of your life, but they will not rule your actions. Allowing yourself to feel and express your grief is the first step toward coping with loss. Dr. Kübler-Ross, in her book *Death, The Final Stage of Growth* (Englewood Cliffs, N.J.: Prentice-Hall, 1975), writes: "Learning to invest yourself in living when you have lost someone you love is very difficult, but only through doing so can you give some meaning to that person's death."

APPENDIX

❑ Medical Prefixes and Suffixes

a-, an-: no, not, without. For example, anoxia (lack or deficiency of oxygen).

-algesia, algia: pain. For example, neuralgia (pain along a nerve pathway).

bi-: two.

brachy-: short. For example, brachycephalic (abnormally short head).

brady-: slow. For example, bradycardia (slow heart rate).

cat-, cata-: against, down. For example, catabolism (breakdown of complex parts into simpler ones—protein into amino acids).

-cele: herniation, swelling. For example, rectocele (protrusion of the rectum into the vagina).

-cide: killing. For example, bacteriocide (bacteria-killing agent).

co-, con-: together. For example, constriction (narrowing, often used to describe conditions affecting blood vessels).

contra-: against, opposite. For example, contraindication (any condition that prevents the use of a medicine or particular treatment).

cyan-, cyano-: dark blue. For example, cyanotic (describing bluish gray skin tone).

cyt-, cyto-: cell. For example, cytotoxic (pertaining to substance that kills cells).

de-: from, down. For example, decalcification (removal of calcium from bones).

dia-: through, across. For example, diathermy (therapeutic application of heat to warm tissues).

dipla-, diplo-: double. For example, diplopia (double vision).

dys-: bad, difficult. For example, dysphagia (difficulty swallowing).

ect-, ecto-: out, outside. For example, ectropion (turning out of the eyelid).

-ectomy: surgical excision. For example, nephrectomy (removal of a kidney).

-emesis: vomiting. For example, hematemesis (vomiting up blood).

-emia: blood. For example, bacteremia (bacteria in the blood).

en-, endo-: into, within, inner. For example, endometrium (membrane lining the inside of the uterus).

epi-: upon, over. For example, epigastric (over the stomach).

erythro-: red. For example, erythrocyte (a red blood corpuscle).

-esthesia: sensation. For example, paresthesia (abnormal sensation with no obvious cause—often tingling or pricking).

eu-: normal, well. For example, euthyroid (pertaining to normal thyroid function).

ex-, exo-, extra: out, outside of. For example, exophthalmia (protrusion of the eyeball, often associated with thyroid disorders).

hemi-: half. For example, hemianopia (blindness in half of the field of vision).

hetero-: different.

homo-: same, alike.

hyper-: excess, over, above. For example, hyperlipidemia (excess fats in the blood).

hypo-: under, insufficient, below. For example, hypoglycemia (low blood sugar).

-ia, -iasis: diseased or abnormal state. For example, mydriasis (abnormal pupil dilation).

infra-: beneath.

-itis: inflammation. For example, endocarditis (inflammation of the heart lining).

kera-, kerat-, kerato-: horny layer, also relating to cornea. For example, keratosis (horny growths on the skin) and keratitis (inflammation of the cornea).

lact-, lacto-: milk.

laparo-: loin, flank. For example, laparoscopy (viewing of the abdominal organs through a lighted tube).

leuk-, leuko-: white. For example, leukocytosis (abnormal increase in white blood cells).

lipo-: fat. For example, lipoprotein (molecule containing a fat and a protein).

-lysis: disintegration, breakdown. For example, hemolysis (destruction of red blood cells).

macro-, mega-, -megaly: large.

melan-, melano-: black, darkened. For example, malignant melanoma (invasive skin cancer often appearing as darkened—brown, blue or black—growth).

micro-: small.

mono-: one.

myc-, myco-: fungus, fungal. For example, mycosis (a disease caused by a fungus).

neo-: new. For example, neocortex (later-developing section of the cerebral cortex).

-oid: resembling, of the same form as. For example, uterine fibroid (fiber-like growth in the uterus).

olig-, oligo-: few, little. For example, oliguria (reduced urine production).

-oma: tumor (either benign or malignant).

ortho-: straight, normal. For example, orthopnea (difficulty breathing in any position other than sitting erect or standing).

-osis: condition, disease, increase. For example, nephrosis (degenerative change in the kidneys).

-ostomy: surgery to create an opening or outlet. For example, colostomy (opening of a section of the colon out onto the abdomen).

-otomy: incision. For example, cystotomy (incision into the bladder).

pan-: all, whole. For example, pancytopenia (reduction in all types of blood cells).

-penia: deficiency, lack. For example, leukopenia (decrease in white blood cells).

peri-: surrounding, around. For example, periodontal (surrounding the tooth).

-plasia, -plasm, -plastic: growth, formation, mold. For example, hyperplasia (excessive cell growth).

-plegia: paralysis. For example, hemiplegia (paralysis of one half of the body).

-pnea: breath. For example, dyspnea (difficulty breathing).
poly-: many, much.
presby-: old, aging. For example, presbycusis (decrease in hearing accompanying aging).
py-, pyo-: pus. For example, pyogenic (pus-producing).
retro-: backward.
-rhage, -rhagia: flow, discharge. For example, menorrhagia (excessive bleeding during the menstrual period).
sclero-, -sclerosis: hard, hardening, dryness. For example, arteriosclerosis (decreased elasticity resulting in stiffening of the artery walls).
-scopy: viewing an internal structure with a lighted tube.
sub-: under.
super-, supra-: above, over.
syn-: with, together.
tachy-: abnormally rapid. For example, tachypnea (abnormally fast breathing).
trans-: across.
tri-: three.
-uria: pertaining to urine. For example, polyuria (oversecretion of urine).
xanth-: yellow. For example, xanthoderma (yellowed appearance of the skin).
xero-: dryness. For example, xerophthalmia (dryness of the conjunctiva of the eye).

❑ Prefixes Denoting Organs or Body Systems

aden-, adeno-: gland.
angio-: blood or lymph vessel.
arth-, arthro-: joint.
bleph-: eyelid.
bronch-, broncho-: bronchi, bronchioles, trachea (windpipe).
cardio-: heart.
cephal-: head.
cerebr-: brain.
chol-, chole-: bile, gallbladder.
cyst-: bladder.
dent-: teeth.
derm-, derma-: skin.
entero-: intestine.
gaster-, gastro-: stomach.
glosso-: tongue.
gyn-, gyne-: related to women.
hem-, hemato-: blood.
hepa-, hepar-, hepato-: liver.
hyster-: uterus.
mamma-, mast-: breast.
my-, myo-: muscle.
myelo-: bone marrow.
neph-, nephro-: kidney.
neuro-: nerve.
oculo-: eye.
odont-, odonto-: teeth.
orchi-, orchid-: testicles.
osteo-: bone.
ped-: foot.
phleb-: vein.
pneumo-: lungs.
procto-: anus, rectum.
pyelo-: pelvis.
rhino-: nose.
sarco-: flesh.
somat-, somato-: body.
stom-, stomato-: mouth.
thoraco-: chest, chest wall.
trichi-, tricho-: hair.
vaso-: vessel.

Metric Conversions

Current Measurement	Multiply By	Desired Measurement	Current Measurement	Multiply By	Desired Measurement
Length			**Volume**		
inches	2.54	centimeters	teaspoons	5	milliliters
yards	0.9	meters	tablespoons	15	milliliters
miles	1.6	kilometers	fluid ounces	30	milliliters
centimeters	0.4	inches	pints	.47	liters
meters	3.3	feet	quarts	.95	liters
meters	1.1	yards	gallons	3.8	liters
kilometers	0.6	miles	liters	2.1	pints
Weight			liters	1.06	quarts
ounces	28	grams	liters	.26	gallons
pounds	.45	kilograms	**Temperature**		
grams	.035	ounces	Fahrenheit	(F − 32) × .555	Centigrade
kilograms	2.2	pounds	Centigrade	(C × 1.8) + 32	Fahrenheit

❑ Recommended Adult Immunizations

Influenza. Recommended for all persons over 65; adults of any age who have diabetes, chronic heart or lung disease, kidney failure or other chronic diseases; nursing home residents; certain health-care workers. Should be avoided by people who are hypersensitive to eggs. Should be given annually.

Pneumococcal Pneumonia. Recommended for all persons over 65 and for people at risk of complications of pneumonia—for example, people with diabetes or chronic heart or lung diseases. People who have had any type of pneumococcal polysaccharides vaccine should not receive a second immunization against pneumonia.

Rubella (German Measles). Recommended for all adults who lack documentation of having received rubella live-virus vaccine or whose blood tests fail to show immunity against the disease. Not recommended for people with immune-system deficiency or history of hypersensitivity to neomycin.

Tetanus/Diphtheria. Recommended for all adults who have not been immunized previously. Two doses of the combined vaccine should be given four weeks apart, with the third dose six to twelve months after the second. A booster should be given every ten years. In addition, tetanus immune globulin should be given to people with large cuts, punctures or other wounds that may be contaminated by dirt, to people who are uncertain whether they have received their full tetanus/diphtheria immunization or who have not received a booster in the last ten years. Tetanus/diptheria vaccine should be avoided by people who have had a hypersensitive reaction to a previous dose.

Hepatitis B. Recommended for all adults at risk of developing the disease. This includes health-care workers, hemophiliacs or others who receive large amounts of transfusions and other blood products, family members or sexual partners of people with hepatitis B infection or male homosexuals at high risk of hepatitis exposure.

❑ Other Possible Vaccines

Mumps. Most adults are probably immune, but anyone thought to be susceptible to the disease can be immunized. Not recommended for people with immune-system deficiency or history of hypersensitivity to eggs or neomycin.

Polio. Recommended for adults who have not previously received a complete series of either killed- or live-virus vaccines. Especially important for people traveling to areas where polio is endemic and for incompletely immunized adults in households where children are to be immunized. The live-virus (oral vaccine) should be avoided by people with immune-system deficiency.

Rabies. Recommended for veterinarians, animal handlers, certain laboratory workers or travelers to countries where rabies is common.

Miscellaneous. Vaccines against cholera, meningitis, plague and yellow fever are recommended for travelers to areas where the diseases are common and for people who are at special risk of exposure.

INDEX

F

I

O